Equality, Inequalities and Diversity

MANAGEMENT, WORK AND ORGANISATIONS

Series editors: **Gibson Burrell**, The Management Centre, University of Leicester
Mick Marchington, Manchester Business School
Paul Thompson, Department of Human Resource Management, University of Strathclyde

This series of new textbooks covers the areas of human resource management, employee relations, organisational behaviour and related business and management fields. Each text has been specially commissioned to be written by leading experts in a clear and accessible way. The books contain serious and challenging material, take an analytical rather than prescriptive approach and are particularly suitable for use by students with no prior specialist knowledge.

The series is relevant for many business and management courses, including MBA and post-experience courses, specialist masters and postgraduate diplomas, professional courses and final-year undergraduate courses. These texts have become essential reading at business and management schools worldwide.

Published

Emma Bell **Reading Management and Organization in Film**
Paul Blyton and Peter Turnbull **The Dynamics of Employee Relations** (3rd edn)
Sharon C. Bolton **Emotion Management in the Workplace**
Sharon C. Bolton and Maeve Houlihan (eds) **Searching for the Human in Human Resource Management**
Peter Boxall and John Purcell **Strategy and Human Resource Management** (2nd edn)
J. Martin Corbett **Critical Cases in Organisational Behaviour**
Susan Corby, Steve Palmer and Esmond Lindop **Rethinking Reward**
Ian Greener **Public Management**
Keith Grint **Leadership**
Irena Grugulis **Skills, Training and Human Resource Development**
Geraldine Healy, Gill Kirton and Mike Noon (eds) **Equality, Inequalities and Diversity**
Damian Hodgson and Svetlana Cicmil (eds) **Making Projects Critical**
Marek Korczynski **Human Resource Management in Service Work**
Karen Legge **Human Resource Management:** anniversary edition
Patricia Lewis and Ruth Simpson (eds) **Gendering Emotions in Organizations**
Patricia Lewis and Ruth Simpson (eds) **Voice, Visibility and the Gendering of Organizations**
Stephen Proctor and Frank Mueller (eds) **Teamworking**
Pullen et al (eds) **Exploring Identity**
Helen Rainbird (ed.) **Training in the Workplace**
Jill Rubery and Damian Grimshaw **The Organisation of Employment**
Harry Scarbrough (ed.) **The Management of Expertise**
Hugh Scullion and Margaret Linehan (eds) **International Human Resource Management**
Adrian Wilkinson, Mick Marchington, Tom Redman and Ed Snape **Managing with Total Quality Management**
Colin C. Williams **Rethinking the Future of Work**
Diana Winstanley and Jean Woodall (eds) **Ethical Issues in Contemporary Human Resource Management**

For more information on titles in the Series please go to www.palgrave.com/business/mwo

Series Standing Order
If you would like to receive future titles in this series as they are published, you can make use of our standing order facility. To place a standing order please contact your bookseller or, in case of difficulty, write to us at the address below with your name and address and the name of the series. Please state with which title you wish to begin your standing order.

Customer Services Department, Macmillan Distribution Ltd
Houndmills, Basingstoke, Hampshire RG21 6XS, England

Equality, Inequalities and Diversity
Contemporary Challenges and Strategies

Edited by

Geraldine Healy
Professor of Employment Relations at Queen Mary,
University of London, UK

Gill Kirton
Professor of Employment Relations and Human Resource Management,
Queen Mary, University of London, UK

Mike Noon
Professor of Human Resource Management,
Queen Mary, University of London, UK

First published 2011 by
PALGRAVE MACMILLAN

Palgrave Macmillan in the UK is an imprint of Macmillan Publishers Limited,
registered in England, company number 785998, of Houndmills, Basingstoke,
Hampshire RG21 6XS.

Palgrave Macmillan in the US is a division of St Martin's Press LLC,
175 Fifth Avenue, New York, NY 10010.

Palgrave Macmillan is the global academic imprint of the above companies
and has companies and representatives throughout the world.

Palgrave® and Macmillan® are registered trademarks in the United States,
the United Kingdom, Europe and other countries.

ISBN: 978–0–230–23107–8

This book is printed on paper suitable for recycling and made from fully
managed and sustained forest sources. Logging, pulping and manufacturing
processes are expected to conform to the environmental regulations of the
country of origin.

A catalogue record for this book is available from the British Library.

A catalog record for this book is available from the Library of Congress.

10 9 8 7 6 5 4 3 2 1
20 19 18 17 16 15 14 13 12 11

Printed and bound in Great Britain by
CPI Antony Rowe, Chippenham and Eastbourne

Contents

Figures

Tables

Preface

This collection of articles emerged through initial discussions with Ursula Gavin of Palgrave Macmillan. Ursula was aware of the Centre for Equality and Diversity Research (CRED) at Queen Mary, University of London and encouraged us to put together a collection for Palgrave Macmillan's series on *Management, Work and Organisations*. We were delighted to do this given the breadth of experience of research on equality, inequalities and diversity in CRED. Our contributors are current and associate members of CRED including colleagues in the Queen Mary Department of Law and current and past PhD students. This brings together a unique blend of scholars which has led to a book that genuinely provides new insights, delves into unintended consequences of legislative initiatives; challenges the taken for granted and provokes important questions on the contemporary nature of inequalities and diversity.

Abbreviations

BAME	Black, Asian and Minority Ethnic
BFBM	Bundesverband der Frau in Business und Management
BME	Black and Minority Ethnic
BNP	British National Party
BPW UK	Business and Professional Women United Kingdom
CRE	Commission for Race Equality
CSICH	Convention for the Safeguard of Intangible Cultural Heritage
DCLG	Department for Communities and Local Government
ECHR	European Convention on Human Rights
ECJ	European Court of Justice
EEOC	The Equal Employment Opportunity Commission
EHRA	Equality and Human Rights Act
EHRC	Equality and Human Rights Commission
ELFS	European Labour Force Survey
EOC	Equal Opportunities Commission
ESOL	English for Speakers of Other Languages
EU	European Union
HR	Human Resources
ILO	International Labour Organization
ISCRE	Ipswich and Suffolk Council for Racial Equality
LEA	Local Education Authority
LFS	Labour Force Survey
LGBT	Lesbian, Gay, Bisexual and Transgender
NCCRI	National Consultative Committee on Racism and Interculturalism
N.I.	Northern Ireland
OECD	Organisation for Economic Cooperation and Development
RRA	Race Relations Act
SSCI	Social Science Citation Index
SDA	Sex Discrimination Act

TUC	Trades Union Congress
UK	United Kingdom
UNESCO	United Nations Education, Scientific and Cultural Organization
WINs	Women's independent networks
WLB	Work Life Balance

Contributors

Sanchia Alasia holds a BSc in Politics and Sociology from Brunel University and an MSc in Politics, Policy and Government from Birkbeck College, University of London. She currently works as a diversity manager for Newham University Hospital Trust. She is actively engaged with the equalities agenda and has held a variety of diversity roles including a former race equality officer for the University of London union, an Independent Advisory network member on diversity issues, the Former Joint Chair for the Black and Asian staff network group of The British Transport Police – Transport for London and a member of Newham Independent advisory group on race to the Police in Newham.

Peter Alldridge is Drapers' Professor of Law and Head of the Department of Laws at Queen Mary University of London. He has written widely in the areas of criminal law, law of evidence, information technology and law, disability law and jurisprudence. He is the author of *Relocating Criminal Law* (2000) and *Money Laundering Law* (2003). He served as Specialist Advisor to the Joint Parliamentary Select Committee on the Bribery Bill 2009.

Lizzie Barmes is Professor of Labour Law in the School of Law, Queen Mary University of London. She is a specialist in Employment and Equality Law, with a background in legal practice and in law reform work for the Law Commission of England and Wales. Her current research interests include the legal regulation of behavioural standards at work, the translation of legal rules into organizations, the law on positive action and on workplace bullying, the common law of the contract of employment and the case for, and the capacity of regulation to bring about greater judicial representativeness.

Harriet Bradley is Professor of Sociology at the University of Bristol. Her research interests include social inequalities, young people and gendered work. Her recent publications include *Gender, Ethnicity and Gender at Work* (with G. Healy) and *Business in Society* (with M. Erickson, C. Stephenson and S. Williams and her current research explores the impact of class on the student experience. Among her previous books are *Gender and Power, Fractured Identities* and *Ethnicity and Gender at Work.*

Hazel Conley is a senior lecturer in HRM in the School of Business and Management and a member of the Centre for Research in Equality and Diversity (CRED) at Queen Mary University of London. Her research interests include labour market 'flexibility', its impact on equality and diversity and the role of the State and trade unions. Her research has been published in leading journals and Hazel is the co-editor, with Tessa Wright, of *A Hand-book of Discrimination at Work* (Gower forthcoming).

Nicole Avdelidou-Fischer recently completed her PhD in the Centre for Research in Equality and Diversity at Queen Mary, University of London. Nicole has worked for a decade in German and British corporations, where she observed, as well as experienced, how women get neglected or intentionally excluded from men's networking activities. Inspired by gaps in the academic literature and personal curiosity on the topic of networking as a working woman and social science researcher, her research sets out to investigate independent networks for business and professional women at the crossroads of feminist and social movement theories.

Cynthia Forson is Associate Head of Department of Management, Leadership and Organisation at the Business School, University of Hertfordshire. Her PhD was a study of black women entrepreneurs and their access to capital, which she completed at Queen Mary's Centre for Research in Equality and Diversity. She has also worked on an EOC project on Workplace Culture and Ethnic Minority Women with Geraldine Healy and Harriet Bradley. Her publications centre on gender, ethnicity and entrepreneurship.

Geraldine Healy is Professor of Employment Relations and director of the Centre for Research in Equality and Diversity in the School of Business and Management at Queen Mary, University of London. She has published widely in academic journals on gender and ethnicity in organizations including trade unions and public bodies. She is joint author with Harriet Bradley of *Ethnicity and Gender at Work: Inequalities), Careers and Employment Relations* (Palgrave 2008) and co-editor of *The Future of Worker Representation* (Palgrave 2004) and joint author with Franklin Oikelome of *Diversity, Ethnicity, Migration and Work* (Palgrave, forthcoming). She is on the editorial board of *Industrial Relations Journal, Work Employment and Society and Equal Opportunities International.*

Gill Kirton is Professor of Employment Relations and Human Resource Management at the Centre for Research in Equality and Diversity, School of Business and Management, Queen Mary, University of London. Her current research focuses on organizational equality and diversity in a variety of different contexts. She is particularly interested in employee experiences, especially those of marginalized groups. She has published articles on gender and trade unionism, workplace equality and diversity management in a range of refereed journals. She has also published four books – a diversity management textbook, *The Dynamics of Managing Diversity* (Elsevier 2010, 3rd edition) co-authored with Anne-Marie Greene; a critical review of women's employment *Women, Employment and Organizations* (Routledge 2006) co-authored with Judith Glover; a research monograph *The Making of Women Trade Unionists* (Ashgate 2006); and a research based book *Diversity Management in the UK: Organizational and Stakeholder Experiences,* co-authored with Anne-marie Greene (Routledge 2009).

Luke McDonagh is currently a Ph.D. candidate at Queen Mary, University of London. During the past three years he has given tutorials in European Union and Administrative Law as a Graduate Student Advisor at Queen Mary. His current PhD research explores the potential conflicts between Copyright Law and Irish Traditional Music. He holds a B.C.L from the National University of Ireland, Galway and an LL.M from the London School of Economics.

Ann Mumford is a senior lecturer in the department of laws at Queen Mary University of London. Her principal, recent publications have addressed a number of different aspects of socio-legal perspectives on taxation. She is the author of *Taxing Culture* (Ashgate 2002), and *Tax Policy, Women and the Law* (Cambridge University Press, forthcoming).

Mike Noon is Professor of Human Resource Management in the School of Business and Management at Queen Mary, University of London. His research explores the effects of contemporary management practices on the work of employees. One of his main areas of research covers equality, diversity and discrimination. He has published widely in academic journals. His recent books are: *The Realities of Work* (co-authored with Paul Blyton, third edition, Palgrave 2007); *Equality, Diversity and Disadvantage in Employment* (co-edited with Emmanuel Ogbonna, Palgrave 2001); *A Dictionary of Human Resource Management* (co-authored with Ed Heery, Second Edition, Oxford University Press 2008). He is associate editor of *Human Relations.*

Franklin Oikelome is a lecturer In Human resources and organizational behaviour at the University of Hull. His research interest is in the interconnecting field of equality and employment relations. He is a member of the Editorial Advisory Board of Equal Opportunities International and an Associate Member of the Centre for Research in Equality and Diversity at Queen Mary University of London. He holds a PhD in Industrial Relations from the London School of Economics.

Cliff Oswick is Professor in Organization Theory at the School of Business and Management, Queen Mary, University of London. In addition to his academic role, he is also Dean for the Faculty of Law & Social Sciences. His research interests focus on the application of aspects of discourse, dramaturgy, tropes, narrative and rhetoric to the study of management, organizations, organizing processes, and organizational change. He has published over 100 academic articles and contributions to edited volumes, including contributions to *Academy of Management*

Review, Human Relations, Journal of Management Studies, Organization, and *Organization Studies.* He is also the European Editor of *Journal of Organizational Change Management* and co-director of the International Centre for Research on Organizational Discourse, Strategy and Change.

Cathrine Seierstad is a PhD student in the Centre for Research in Equality and Diversity in the School of Business and Management, Queen Mary, University of London. Her main research interests are women, leadership and the use of affirmative action strategies. In particular, her research has mainly focused on the Scandinavian countries, Norway, Sweden and Denmark in relation to the share of women and the use of affirmative action strategies in areas such as politics, academia and company board of directors.

Prakash Shah is a Senior Lecturer in Law at Queen Mary University of London, specializing in the legal aspects of ethnic diversity, religion, and immigration. His recent edited books include: Ralph Grillo et al. (eds): *Legal Practice and Cultural Diversity.* Aldershot: Ashgate 2009; *Law and Ethnic Plurality: Socio-Legal Perspectives.* Leiden and Boston: Martinus Nijhoff 2007; *Migration, Diasporas and Legal Systems in Europe.* London: RoutledgeCavendish 2006 (with Werner F. Menski); and *The Challenge of Asylum to Legal Systems.* London: Cavendish 2005. He is author of *Legal Pluralism in Conflict: Coping with Cultural Diversity in Law.* London: Glass House 2005.

Ahu Tatli is a Lecturer in the School of Business and Management at Queen Mary, University of London, where she has completed her PhD. Her research interests are in the field of equality and diversity in organizations with a particular focus on multilevel exploration of agentic power and strategies of the key actors in the field. Ahu has widely published in academic journals and books as well as in practitioner journals in the areas of diversity management in public and private sector organisations in different industries, agency and change in organizations, inequality and discrimination in recruitment and employment.

Tessa Wright has many years experience of research on equality and discrimination at work, and in particular on trade union action in this field. She worked for the trade union movement at the Labour Research Department as a researcher and editor for several years, followed by a position as Senior Researcher at the Working Lives Research Institute, London Metropolitan University, where she has also undertaken research on migration. Tessa is currently completing a PhD on the experiences of women in traditionally male work at the Centre for Research in Equality and Diversity in the School of Business and Management, Queen Mary, University of London.

1

Inequalities, intersectionality and equality and diversity initiatives

The conundrums and challenges of researching equality, inequalities and diversity

Geraldine Healy, Gill Kirton and Mike Noon

Equality and diversity issues and concerns have come in from the cold margins of academic and business life. Diversity in particular is now part of the discourse of modern business and public organizations. The normalizing of work related to equality, diversity and inclusion has resulted in benefits and greater awareness. It has also provided career opportunities for diversity managers, consultants and academics alike. Nevertheless, the shifting trend to diversity management has arguably removed the campaigning edge from much work on equality and diversity and replaced it with an individualization that may work to disguise what motivated many equality and diversity activists and scholars in the first place; challenging oppression in the workplace and society. Walsh has noted that the bureaucratic and portfolio careers emerging from the growth of the field of equality and diversity has led to greater incidence and enhancement of equality policies (Walsh 2007). However, she also noted poor employer response to fairly mainstream expectations with respect to monitoring and reviewing of procedures associated with discrimination, recruitment and selection, promotion and relative pay rates (Walsh 2007). We know there is a considerable amount of 'talking the talk' of diversity which tends not to challenge the factors that reproduce inequalities in the workplace and society. Moreover, we find formal apparently transparent systems within organizations and societies which are accompanied by powerful and opaque informal systems that really determine the decisions and outcomes, and thereby sustain a system of inequalities.

Wherever equality, inequalities and diversity are investigated, discrimination, disadvantage even violence is a regular experience of women, minority ethnic groups, people with disabilities and lesbian, gay, bisexual and transgender people. We find that people are further discriminated against because of their nationality, because they are married, and because they are considered to be too old or too young. Moreover, others will find that their discrimination is the outcome of their complex and mutually constituted identities, as for example may be the case for a woman, who is black and Muslim. The form and nature of discrimination is context specific and may be constrained by legislation. In this volume, we cast light on the nature of inequalities and experiences of discrimination, and we reveal some of the flaws and contradictions in legal systems and also the opportunities that legal initiatives offer. Not covered by legislation, but increasingly of concern is the importance of class in understanding the nature of inequality and the way class forms a constant intersectional backcloth to our understanding of inequalities.

This book is the work of a group of scholars who remain committed to challenging inequalities. It seeks to expose the realities of contemporary inequalities and diversity. It doing so it reveals not only the predictable resilience of inequalities, but also the unanticipated and unintended impact of legislation and unforeseen and surprising findings in both the national and international context.

We have chosen to focus on key issues that are of significance for the European and North American agenda. These boundaries enable an in-depth analysis of key contemporary areas of investigation and bring under-researched issues to the fore. Inevitably, there are limitations. Outside the scope of this volume is the issue of equality and diversity in developing countries. On the contrary we have contributed to this literature particularly by explorations of diversity policies in developing countries (e.g. Healy and Oikelome 2007 forthcoming), the gendered nature of trade unions in a post-colonial country (Kirton and Healy forthcoming), the processes of migration (Oikelome and Healy 2007) and vertical segregation in a developing country (Healy et al. 2005). There is a need for more work on equality and diversity strategies in developing and emerging economies; but this will not form the subject of study in this volume.

In this volume we have focused on four themes: intersectionality, the shift from equality policies to diversity management, the limits and possibilities of legislation and transformative action. This opening chapter explains these key themes that contextualize the contributions in the volume and importantly which shape contemporary debates in equality and diversity in a globalized world. We begin with the increasing recognition of 'difference' in academic debate, public policy and among practitioners, and discuss social difference in the context of intersectional discrimination and inequalities. We then move on to discuss the shift from equality policy to diversity management. The limits and possibilities of the law are then considered including the consequences of radical positive action initiatives followed by alternative means of transformative action.

The increasing recognition of difference

If we were to stop 100 people in the street at random and ask them how to ensure equality at work, the vast majority are likely to say 'Treat everyone the same', because this is a 'common sense' understanding of what equality is about. But if we were to push them a little and ask whether this means they would not consider taking into account someone's disability, childcare responsibilities or religious beliefs then many would probably acknowledge the need for special provision for some employees. The issue is one of the central dilemmas in policy making: is equality achieved through treating people the same or by recognizing their differences and treating them according to their distinctive needs. The answer is that both same treatment and different treatment are required in order to deal with disadvantage that occurs due to differing circumstances – an observation that is eloquently summed up in relation to gender by Liff and Wajcman (1996: 86):

> ...it is possible to see that sometimes women are disadvantaged by being treated differently when in fact they are the same (e.g. denied a job for which they are perfectly well qualified) and at other times be being treated the same when their difference needs to be taken into account (e.g. having their absence to look after a sick child treated the same way as a man who is absent with a hangover).

There has been increasing recognition of the differences between people as a result of globalization because the exchange of goods, information and labour between countries highlights the racial, ethnic, cultural and religious differences. At the national level this recognition translates into policies that range from multiculturalism to integration and assimilation, while at the local level they might find expression in the active hiring or exclusion of minority ethnic groups because of stereotypes about work values and attitudes. Supranational politics have also impacted on the recognition of differences; for example, European Union directives have required Member States to legislate to protect citizens against unfair discrimination on the basis of age, disability, sex, sexual orientation, race/ethnicity and religion. More generally there is the increasing emphasis on human rights and the toleration of differences between people.

Although it is a truism that because people differ they have different needs – and in this sense this is not a contentious statement – the problematic issue is *how* people should be treated differently. Should their needs be evaluated in terms of their membership of a social group (sex, race/ethnicity, disability, religion, sexuality and so on) or should the assessment be of their specific, individual needs? The distinction is significant because it brings into question whether social group classification is relevant for analytical and policy-making purposes.

The challenges of intersectionality:
policy, methodological and theoretic perspectives

The analysis of inequality has often concentrated on one social group (e.g. women, minority ethnic groups, young people). This approach has the strength of focusing on a particular form of discrimination based on say race or sex or age. However, often it is not sufficient. Increasingly the focal point is the intersection of different social groups or categories so that attention is shifted from for example, 'woman' as a homogenous social group, to the multiple, overlapping categories that make up the heterogeneous category of 'woman' (e.g. black women, white women, older women). In different ways, this collection engages with the concept of intersectionality, either directly or indirectly. This is not a new concept, yet in the last decade it has been increasingly used in both the academic literature and policy-oriented documents and debates.

The use of the term intersectionality is not unproblematic. It often implies fixity of meaning yet the manner of use, its purpose and its underlying philosophy indicates that the term is used in multiple ways. Davis (2008) argues that key theoretical and methodological differences arise between theorists of race/gender/class and post-structuralist feminist theorists. They have different motivations: the latter are inspired by the post-modern project of deconstructing modernist philosophical traditions, while race, class and gender theorists are motivated by contemporary gender politics (Davis 2008: 73) – and we would add anti-racist politics too. While post-structuralist feminists are concerned with deconstructing gender thereby avoiding essentialism and categories, feminist and anti-racist commentators critique post-structural thinking for its lack of attention to the material consequences of these categories of difference and the danger of political relativism. Moreover, they noted the importance of identity politics in specific historical contexts when, according to Crenshaw, which has been a more effective strategy of resistance for combating the effects of racism and sexism than the deconstruction of categories (Crenshaw 1991). Key differences emerge between those who seek to use intersectionality as part of an emancipatory politics, whether at the macro or meso level (e.g. Acker 2006a, 2006b; Collins 2004; Crenshaw 1991; hooks 2000) and those concerned with the insights from deconstruction itself. We would argue that while the study of intersectionality may draw on insights and emphases from post-modern approaches, the material and emancipatory aspects should remain at the fore.

Some reflection on the multiple uses of intersectionality may be necessary in an era where the demand for intersectional analysis is called for by academics (Acker 2006a; 2006b; Adib and Guerrier 2003; Baines 2009; Bradley and Healy 2008; Brah and Phoenix 2004; Crenshaw 1991; Essers et al. 2008; Holgate et al. 2006) and by policy makers (United Nations 2001). While philosophically, the argument for intersectionality seems uncontested, 'doing intersectionality' is complicated and fraught with dangers.

In the field of equality and diversity, intersectionality normally relates to the intersections of the key strands (although not exclusively) of gender, ethnicity/race/ nationality, age, disability, sexuality religion and class. Indeed, the 'doing of inter-sectionality' may be reduced to mere description related to two or more strands.

Whenever one intersection is deployed, another is lost. Therefore the quest for intersectional analysis has multiple boundaries and may perhaps always be partial. Moreover, intersectionality of what and for what are key questions. This raises the question of the 'value-free' nature of the concept. We recognize that what we choose to study is imbued with values and subjectivities. The chapters in this volume in many ways are the outcome of the positionality of the authors. We would argue that the social justice basis of intersectional research is key in avoiding a version of inter-sectionality that is an ahistorical and acontextual concept that could relate to mere descriptions of multiple forms of intersectionality. Instead for us, intersectionality relates specifically to intersectional forms of oppression and it is in this sense that we would argue that intersectionality is best viewed.

In many ways this approach is picked up by those international agencies that high-light intersectional discrimination or intersectional subordination, for example, United Nations Division for the Advancement of Women (DAW), the Office of the High Commissioner for Human Rights (OHCHR), the United Nations Development Fund for Women (UNIFEM) and the EU Fundamental Agency of Human Rights. Implicit then is the embedding of social justice in the concept of intersectionality.

Our concern is the world of work and we come from sociological and industrial relations backgrounds. Yet the development of work on intersectionality lies not only in sociology (and certainly not in industrial relations), but also in political the-ory, law, philosophy and feminist theory, and in particular to the work of black femi-nists (e.g. Collins 2004; Crenshaw 1991; hooks 2000; Young 1990, 1997). Moreover, its roots are emancipatory and its principles of social justice seek to enlighten and critique academic debate and public policy.

bell hooks' pertinent title of her first book expressed outrage at the way white feminists excluded black women from their feminist theorizing. *Ain't I a woman too?* captured the exclusion of black women from white feminist thinking and theorizing (hooks 1981). hooks drew these powerful words from Sojourner Truth (1797–1883), who was born Isabella Baumfree, a slave, in New York State. After gaining her freedom in 1827, Truth became a well-known anti-slavery speaker, and delivered a speech which became known as Ain't I a Woman? at the Akron, Ohio Women's Convention in 1851. Truth argued that the gendered privileges accorded to white women were not extended to black women. Thus her story of oppression and emancipation demonstrates that 'woman' was never sufficient as a category to explain the conditions of different women, of black women, of working-class women and of middle-class women. Similarly, in Britain, the stories of working-class women in the nineteenth century bore no relationship to the lives of their middle-class counterparts of the time. The women who combined together for better conditions and better pay at, for example, the Bryant and May factory in East London had little in common with the women who at the same historical moment were struggling to win rights to enter universities and the professions. While both groups of women were simultaneously engaged in struggle, their material circumstances ensured that a wide social and political gulf remained between them. Their gender, class and age were inextricably linked with their experiences of life, work and their disadvantage.

These early struggles signified intersectional oppression. Black feminists developed important academic treatises on the nature of interlocking oppression, which began with the exclusion of black women from 'white women's' feminism and has now broadened out to take account of different oppressed categories (Collins 2004; Crenshaw 1991; hooks 2000; Young 1990, 1997). Crenshaw points to structural intersectionality where the location of women of colour at the intersection of race and gender make their experiences qualitatively different from those of white women and argues that an intersectional sensibility should be a central theoretical and political objective of anti-racism and feminism (Crenshaw 1991: 1243). Collins, points to the groundbreaking work of Angela Davis, the Combahee River Collective and Audre Lorde in exploring systems of intersections of oppression (2000: 21). For Collins, intersectionality referred to particular forms of intersecting oppressions, for example, intersections of race and gender, or of sexuality and nation (ibid. 2000: 21). She goes on to remind us that intersectional paradigms cannot be reduced to one fundamental type, and that oppressions work together in producing injustice (ibid.: 21). In contrast she uses the term matrix of domination which refers to how these intersectional oppressions are actually organized. Moreover, regardless of the particular intersections involved, structural, disciplinary, hegemonic and interpersonal domains of power reappear across quite different forms of oppression (Collins 2000: 21). For Brah and Phoenix, intersectionality signifies the complex, irreducible, varied and variable effects that ensue when multiple axes of differentiation intersect in historically specific contexts (2004: 76). To the historical context, we must add the related politics of the historical moment and of course its geography; therefore context in all its forms is fundamental to intersectional analysis. In this volume, the backdrop of the geographical and historical context informs implicitly or explicitly its chapters.

Black feminist thought is also about activism and it is interesting to see the philosophical links with the more recent work of policy makers. There is an increasing transnational awareness of intersectionality. The United Nations for example defined intersectionality as,

> an integrated approach that addresses forms of multiple discrimination on the basis of racism, racial discrimination, xenophobia and related intolerance as they intersect with gender, age, sexual orientation, disability, migrant, socio-economic or other status. Intersectional discrimination is a form of racism and racial discrimination which is not the sum of race PLUS another form of discrimination to be dealt with separately but is

a distinct and particular experience of discrimination unified in one person or group. (United Nations 2001 quoted in Bradley and Healy 2008: 44)

To state differently, as Anthias and Yuval Davis (1983: 62–3) state 'race gender, and class cannot be tagged onto each other mechanically for, as concrete social relations, they are enmeshed in each other and the particular intersections involved produce specific effects'. Therefore it is not an additive concept; rather race and gender for example are mutually constituted. Therein lie some of the challenges for those undertaking research on intersectionality. The rationale for such research is not hard to find, but the 'doing' is more problematic.

Policy makers' attempts to deal with some of the problems involved in operationalizing intersectionality are reflected in current legal developments in Britain. It is well recognized that existing equality legislation in its enactment is unduly slow, complex and, as we see in this volume, has unforeseen consequences. The introduction of a single equality body (Equality and Human Rights Commission [EHRC]) in Britain raises important questions about intersectionality. The EHRC is charged with:

> responsibility to protect, enforce and promote equality across the seven 'protected' grounds – age, disability, gender, race, religion and belief, sexual orientation and gender reassignment...
>
> But the heart of the Commission's mission, our integrated mandate, means that we will act across all the areas for which we are responsible, promoting fairness through structural change that benefits the 60 million people in Britain.
>
> We will always be ready to tackle the specific issues of discrimination, inequality and human rights failings that matter to each of the protected groups we are concerned with. There can be no fair society if age, disability, gender, race, religion and belief, sexual orientation and transgender status remain as markers of disadvantage; and there can be no lasting or deep-rooted progress for disadvantaged groups unless we make a robust case for fairness which involves everyone. (http://www.equalityhumanrights.com/)

These are strong and robust statements, with which few committed to challenging inequalities, would quibble. However, the practice of the EHRC may be fraught with challenges and difficult decisions. While there is little doubt that intersectional claims are potentially more feasible under the Equality Bill, in practice there are strict limitations on intersectional claims. Moreover, there is also concern that the replacement of the separate equality bodies (i.e. the former Equal Opportunities Commission, Commission for Racial Equality, Disability Rights Commission) by a single equality body will dilute the focus of the Commission's work and lead to political decision-making as to which strand needs the greatest attention and therefore resources. Already we see the tip of the iceberg with respect to legislation on intersectionality.

The concept of intersectionality therefore raises particular challenges for legislators and has led to distinctions in different kinds of discrimination involving one or more oppressed category. The term *multiple discrimination* is frequently used which is more additive than intersectional. In the UK, legal redress will be allowable on two grounds in the form of *dual discrimination* (see the Equality Act 2009). The confining to two grounds has predictably been criticized with critics referring to the US and Canadian experiences. Cloisters and the Discrimination Law Association explain that multiple discrimination may be additive (a disabled woman whose employer discriminates on the grounds of sex and disability will be doubly disadvantaged by her combined disability and sex), or it may be intersectional (a disabled woman whose employer discriminates only against disabled women, but not against non-disabled women or disabled men will be uniquely disadvantaged by her combined disability and sex)' (www.parliament.co 2010). This gives some idea of the complexity of legal challenges to intersectional oppression.

Methodological analysis of intersectional discrimination carries its own difficulties. The methodological challenges of intersectionality have been laid out by McCall (2005) who argues that there has been little discussion of methodology in studies of intersectionality. She summarizes her concerns by stating that 'research practice mirrors the complexity of social life, calling up unique methodological demands' (ibid.: 1772). She describes three approaches that are defined in terms of their stance towards categories, that is how they understand and use analytical categories to explore the complexity of intersectionality in social life (ibid.: 1773). These are:

> *Anti-categorical complexity*: based on a methodology that deconstructs analytical categories. Social life is considered too irreducibly complex –overflowing with multiple and fluid determinations of both subjects and structures – to make fixed categories anything but simplifying social fictions that produce inequalities in the process of producing differences. (ibid.: 1773)
>
> *Intracategorical complexity*: this approach falls conceptually in the middle of the continuum between the first approach, which reflects categories and the third approach which uses them strategically. McCall states that this approach is so called because authors working in this vein tend to focus on particular social groups at neglected points of intersection in order to reveal the complexity of lived experiences of particular groups.
>
> *Intercategorical complexity*: requires scholars to adopt existing analytical categories to document relationships of inequality among social groups and changing configurations of inequality along multiple and conflicting dimensions (ibid.: 1773–4).

While it is the case that analysis of social life is always complex and perhaps always partial, this is not a reason to react to this complexity by an anti-categorical approach. Rather in this volume, we find contributions that recognize intracategorical and intercategorical complexity in their approaches to understanding social groups in particular contexts.

The clustering of people in social groups for analytical and policy-making purposes helps simplify the complexity of the social world, but increasingly the question being asked by equality researchers is whether this is an over-simplification. For example, the category of 'ethnic minority' covers a range of people for whom employment experiences differ widely, so increasingly specific ethnic groups are studied, and then further differences within these groups, such as along the lines of religion, gender or age are being explored. Geraldine Healy and Harriet Bradley (Chapter 16) adopt such an approach when they evaluate career ambitions and experiences of ethnic minorities. They argue that a full understanding of opportunities and disadvantages can be gleaned only by recognizing the relationship between ethnicity, gender and class.

Similarly, in a study of the extent to which work-life balance concerns are important for graduates, Gill Kirton (Chapter 15) demonstrates that an intersection of identities (gender, race/ethnicity and age) informs the attitudes of her interviewees. So, for both men and women ethnic, cultural and religious values were invoked to explain their views, yet these differed according to gender; for example, women were more likely to see work-life balance policies as essential for the practicalities of family life, while men see them as improving the quality of family life.

Tessa Wright's (Chapter 14) intersectional analysis incorporates sexuality. Her research explores the challenges for women in male-dominated environments and she argues that, depending on context, the added dimension of being a lesbian does not simply add another layer of discrimination, but rather provides different ways of coping and sometimes can be associated with fewer gendered constraints. Thus the intersection of sexuality with other strands requires more subtle analysis than simply considering it as having a multiplying effect.

This analytical point about not simply adding strands of discrimination, but considering their unique intersections is a theme from all four authors noted above, and surfaces in some of the other chapters in this volume. The case for focusing on the intersections of the strands is based on the view that this offers greater explanatory power and might provide a better guide to policy formation.

Although an intersectional approach helps to deal with the problem of over-simplification resulting from dividing people into social groups according to one primary characteristic, there is a counter-concern that reducing categories to ever smaller sub-groups might lead researchers to overlook some common patterns in discrimination and disadvantage. For example, in Chapter 12, Franklin Oikelome's comparison of racism in the US and UK makes a poignant observation that despite fundamentally different historical contexts and political conditions, all minority ethnic people in the two countries have in common the systematic exclusion from opportunities that has meant on average (compared with the ethnic majority) lower economic prosperity and less upward mobility. Similarly Hazel Conley (Chapter 9) identifies the common experience for women across Europe of exposure to non-standard work and the systemic failure of 'flexicurity' to deliver on the 'security' part of the bargain. Both chapters illustrate the continuing value of broad classification as an analytical starting point and as a valuable tool for policy making.

The three positions noted above share the view that social group classification has some relevance. However, an extreme version of the anti-categorical approach is that group classification has no value either for analysis or policy making. Commentators from this perspective (e.g. Ross and Schneider 1992; Wheatley and Griffiths 1997) argue that a much broader range of differences need to be taken into account, and that the relevant focal point is not the group but the individual. Extended to its logical conclusion, this line of reasoning reduces difference to the smallest unit of analysis (the employee) and in the process negates the validity of decision making and policy formation based on any collective interest or group similarity. Although rarely propounded at this extremity, the emphasis on individual difference informs the approach that has come to be known as the management of diversity.

A shift from equality policy to diversity management?

The proposition that there is a distinction between equal opportunities and diversity management and that there has been a shift towards the latter is now familiar to equality researchers and policy makers. Diversity management has been heralded enthusiastically as a new paradigm, particularly by American business school scholars (e.g. Gilbert et al. 1999) and by many UK and North American employing organizations. This so-called new paradigm can have multiple meanings and be subject to different interpretations (Kirton 2008). Greene and Kirton (2009: 26–8) trace the historical roots of the diversity management concept to the 1980s political and popular backlash against 'affirmative action' hiring policies in the US that were seen to give minority ethnic workers preferential treatment and unfair advantage. Around the same time, American academics Johnston and Packer sparked what proved to be an explosive debate with publication of their report *Workforce 2000* (1987). The report made various predictions about the changing demographics of the American workforce. The prediction that caused the greatest stir was the claim that by 2000 white males would no longer be the dominant demographic group entering the US labour market. Suddenly it seemed that there was a strong business case for being interested in diversity and that developing equality and diversity policies was a rational response to a competitive labour market. Diversity became a hot management topic in the UK around the mid-1990s following a period of disillusionment by equality activists concerned that organizations seemed to be paying no more than 'lip service' to equality. Even though by the 1980s many large organizations had developed 'equal opportunity' policies (following the introduction of the sex and race equality legislation in the mid-1970s), change was too slow in coming to satisfy equality activists and the policies did not seem to be leading to significant transformation of the structures of inequality and disadvantage (Cockburn 1989). The election in 1997 provided a more equality friendly political context than Britain had witnessed for many years (under the Conservative administration 1979–97). For example, the Labour Party Manifesto of 1997 promised that a future Labour government would 'eliminate unjustifiable discrimination wherever it exists' (Johnson and Johnstone 2010). However, the Labour government was also keen not to alienate the business community and has strenuously promoted the business case for diversity. Greene and Kirton (2009) argue that the changing social and economic context and changing political and public discourses of equality paved the way for the emergence in the UK of diversity management, just as had occurred earlier in the US. The diversity discourse is now spreading through Europe. Recent evidence from corporate websites shows that around 40 per cent of companies in seven selected European countries (other than the UK) use the term diversity (compared with over 80 per cent of UK companies [Point and Singh 2003]).

In Chapter 2, Cliff Oswick puts forward new evidence that the discourse of diversity has made a significant impact. His bibliometric analysis shows the demise of the term 'equality' and a growth in the use of the term 'diversity' in academic discourse, and more recently the sign of a replacement of 'diversity' with 'inclusion'. A similar substitution of terms was found in a sample of web-based, public forums. This shift in language use, however, does not necessarily constitute a paradigm shift in the approach taken by organizations to issues of equality. Commentators have argued that some initiatives that are now associated with diversity management are not particularly distinctive from their equal opportunity predecessors (e.g. Kaler 2001; Kirton and Greene 2010). It seems that those responsible for implementing diversity initiatives (e.g. line-managers) struggle to understand exactly what is expected of them (Foster and Harris 2005; Greene and Kirton 2009). However, differences between the *principles* of traditional equal opportunities and diversity management policies have been identified (Greene and Kirton 2009). Nevertheless, the move from equal opportunities to diversity management is perhaps better viewed as a change in *emphasis* rather than a paradigm shift. In particular, diversity management tends to emphasize an economic rationale for equality (the business case), in contrast to the social justice focus of traditional equal opportunity approaches. However, the impact of the change in emphasis should not be understated. For instance, in Chapter 8, Sanchia Alasia and Ahu Tatli theorize the resources (in the form of cultural, symbolic and social capital) available to diversity officers for convincing other managers and enacting change, and then illustrate these through a practitioner account. The symbolic change to diversity, the arguments for an economic rationale to diversity and the legal backdrop provide diversity practitioners with influence compared with what is claimed to be the former moral imperative of equality officers. Nevertheless, we should avoid concluding that equality officers claimed that *only* morality underpinned their efforts and that they were not concerned with the 'business case'. Bradley and Healy looked back some 30 years and found that the economic, social and demographic factors (i.e. the business case) all played a part in legitimating equal opportunities at a time when diversity did not figure in the discourse (2008: 88–9).

Diversity practitioners are among a wider group of stakeholders who had (and have) an interest in accepting the distinctiveness of a 'diversity' approach (Greene and Kirton 2009). Thus the change in emphasis to diversity has served a useful purpose for diversity consultants who wanted to repackage equality; equality officers in organizations who wished to persuade sceptical line managers of the value of equality; trade unionists who needed a means of bringing equality into the bargaining arena and equality researchers and academics who were keen to deploy and write about new conceptual tools.

As commentators have pointed out (Dickens 1994; Noon 2007) there are limitations to relying on an approach underpinned by a business case rationale (whether or not this is described as diversity management) because sometimes the cost-benefit analysis that is required comes out against acting in the interests of equality. An alternative is a multi-pronged approach (for instance, Booth and Bennett 2002; Dickens 1999) whereby equality is embedded through deploying a range of rationales and policies, not least of which is the legislative provision.

The limits and possibilities of the law

The importance of the regulatory context for redressing inequality is indisputable. The law has always shaped equal opportunities and set limitations to the actions of managers in organizations. The scope of British equality legislation has been widened enormously since the introduction of the anti-sex and anti-race discrimination acts in the mid-1970s. However, although much of the legislation has been driven by an underlying perceived need for social change, it creates rights for individuals in the form of legal protection against discrimination and the right to make a claim for financial compensation. The individual complaints-based nature of the system is the source of one of the main criticisms of British equality law (Dickens 2000). As important as it is for individuals to have a channel for redress and compensation, this approach does very little to *promote* equality and diversity. Even with the recent introduction in the public sector of the so-called equality duties on race, disability and gender, the glaring gap in legal duties imposed on the private sector remains. The legally focused chapters in this collection explore some of the foundational and operational weaknesses of the law, but also how it might be used creatively to effect social change.

Two chapters in particular show the power of the law in influencing equality, and at the same time its lack of efficacy in delivering equality in a uniform and predictable manner. In Chapter 4 Lizzie Barmes argues that the EU legal framework with respect to positive action has in one sense brought legislative order to the range of permissible action across Member States by obliging them to develop protective legislation, but in another sense opened up confusion and inconsistency due to the legal ambiguity and varied interpretation of the legislation.[1] Similarly, Prakash Shah (Chapter 5) points to the limits of legislation and in particular examines how the increasing complexity of defining race, ethnicity and religion means that legal professionals seem ill-equipped (or unwilling) to adopt ethnic pluralist approaches and recognize greater diversity. This is perhaps not surprising given that the judiciary may not be well informed on the complexity of diversity issues. Healy et al. (2010) in their work on judicial selection found that the substantive value-based rationalities of some judicial assessors often took precedence over the formal rule making. This was partly because their understanding of diversity was interlinked with their focus on the daily demands of judicial work. Moreover it was evident from this study that many judicial candidates and assessors had only a partial understanding of diversity (see also Kirton and Healy 2009).

While the legislative context can lead to confusion and intransigence in relation to equality initiatives, it can also provide the foundation for organizations to build new approaches. Three of the chapters in this volume illustrate this in different ways and provide insight into different forms of radical initiatives. Peter Alldridge's discussion of disability hate crime in Chapter 7 illustrates how the UK's law imposing a duty on public authorities to promote equality and put in place a disability equality scheme has had a substantial impact both on the police and the Crown Prosecution Service, since both are obliged to report on how they handle disability as service providers – including how they protect victims of crime who are disabled. In Chapter 11, Cathrine Seierstad's evaluation of approaches taken in Scandinavian countries (often assumed to be models of equality), demonstrates the persistence of vertical and horizontal sex segregation. She argues that where more radical policy initiatives (such as quotas) are in place, gender representation has risen significantly, while in areas where equality policies are based on encouragement and suggestion, gender representation has seen only minor improvements. Seierstad also exposes some unanticipated consequences of the rise in women's representation. Ann Mumford (Chapter 6) extends the idea of radical intervention through an exploration of the actuality and possibility of tax laws. She shows that tax incentives can have impact, such as encouraging employers to act in the interests of equality or moving women away from unpaid labour in the home to paid employment, but could be more radically extended, such as allowing family members explicitly to pay for the unpaid domestic activities of relatives (typically women undertaking childcare, household work and eldercare).

The radical requirement to translate public documents in minority languages has recently been the subject of some debate, with some arguing that this practice is holding back the social inclusion of non-English speaking people. Equally without such translations, some minority groups may be denied the rights available to the English speaking community. Luke McDonagh in Chapter 3 engages with these issues, but he goes further by exposing the possible human rights contradictions between providing translation in languages that are minority languages in Britain but not endangered, with translations into endangered languages (particularly Celtic languages), where the populations are mostly bi-lingual. McDonagh picks through the complex arguments and offers a solution to a conundrum that again was not foreseeable.

All six chapters reveal that the law plays an important role but is not enough. Its limitations are both structural and institutional, and radical change is unlikely to occur if left purely to legal intervention; transformation to greater equality requires more than government intervention, and organizational equality and diversity policies and regulation.

A transformative agenda

A long-standing concern from equality commentators (e.g. Cockburn 1991) (Liff 1997; Richards 2001; Rees 1998; Webb 1997) has been the problem of embedding equality in ostensibly hostile organizations. Policy and legislation play a role but they can only have marginal impact on the white, male-dominated structures and processes that control access and limit opportunities for those on the outside. Typified by Cockburn's (1989) call for a long (transformative) agenda whereby the organizational norms, practices and hierarchies are overturned, the argument is for a radical challenge to the structural conditions of exclusion. A transformative agenda can be organizationally focused and build on the foundations laid down by short-term strategies such as those found in traditional liberal equal opportunity policies, but confront the limitations of such policies in terms of their capacity to achieve radical change (Rees 1998). Cockburn's (1989) 'long agenda' is an ambitious and progressive strategy for transforming organizations. Part of the project is to understand the processes by which power is created and maintained, so that the barriers that prevent under-represented groups from gaining positions of power and influence can be gradually dismantled. Rather than focusing on the internal structures of large organizations, two chapters in this volume provide insight into the means through which disadvantage is overcome by developing *shadow-structures* that lie outside of white, male-dominated control. Disadvantaged groups may turn to these shadow-structures out of disappointment, disillusionment, feelings of exclusion and so forth in order to find new and creative ways of empowering themselves. Such strategies, while external to large employing organizations, can have an impact on opportunities for social transformation in the wider context.

In Chapter 13, Nicole Avdelidou-Fischer explores the experiences of professional women in Germany and the UK. The quotations from her interviewees illustrate how the male-dominated organizational environment is hostile and structured and culturally imbued in such a way as to hold down women's advancement or close off opportunity. Outside of the formal organization, through the networks constructed by women themselves, women find support and empowerment. Through the networking process, the women 'become increasingly aware and confident of their ability to negotiate new structures [which] makes them more vocal and visible within them'.

In Chapter 10, Cynthia Forson explores the issue of self-employment. Her analysis reveals that 'black women might seek to gain control over their labour market participation through self-employment, but find that the all-pervasive gendered, ethnocentric and class-based structures they encounter in employment rear up in self-employment as well'. To make their businesses successful they must mobilize specific forms of social and cultural capital.

Common to these two chapters is the finding that the women take control and develop networks that are different from the male-dominated norm but within a capitalist, neo-liberal value framework. The mobilization of resources is part of a shadow-structure, but crucially not a counter-structure. The location is outside of male-dominated organizations and the developments have transformative potential, although not transformative power unless transposed into those white, male-dominated organizations. Importantly, in these and the other chapters in this volume, the complex and multifaceted nature of discrimination emerges, which increasingly pushes researchers towards approaches that require them to take into account 'intersectionality' and directs managers and organizations towards expanded concepts of equality that engage with workforce diversity without objectifying and commodifying it.

Conclusion

This chapter has introduced the four themes that permeate the book: the importance of intersectionality, the shift from equality policy to diversity management, the limits and possibilities of the law and the need for a transformative agenda. These themes interrelate and overlap in this volume which embraces a common recognition of the complexities, contradictions, unpredictability in the analysis of inequalities, equality and diversity. Thus the chapters that follow explore one or more of these themes by presenting original empirical data. It is a particular feature of research within the field of equality and diversity that the analysis must be underpinned by a credible and persuasive argument because those who need convincing (policy makers and managers) often have a very sceptical outlook, while those who are already convinced of the arguments (equality/diversity officers and activists) frequently require plausible evidence. We believe that the chapters in this volume offer new insight, fresh evidence and thoughtful reflection on some key contemporary equality issues.

Note

1. The Joint Committee on Human Rights cited a draft of Barmes' chapter (Chapter 4) in their 2009 October report on the Bill where they analyse the positive action provisions.

References

Acker, J. (2006a) 'Inequality regimes: gender, class, and race in organizations', *Gender and Society*, 20(4): 441–64.

—— (2006b) *Class Questions: Feminist Answers*. Lanham, MD: Rowman & Littlefield Publishers Inc.

Adib, A. and Y. Guerrier (2003) 'The interlocking of gender with nationality, race, ethnicity and class: the narratives of women in hotel work', *Gender Work and Organization*, 10(4): 413–32.

Anthias, F. and N. Yuval-Davis (1983) 'Contextualizing feminism – gender, ethnic and class divisions', *Feminist Review*, 15: 62–75.

Baines, D. (2009) 'Gender mainstreaming in a development project: intersectionality in a post-colonial un-doing?' *Gender, Work and Organization*, 17(2): 119–49.

Booth C. and C. Bennett (2002) 'Gender mainstreaming in the European Union towards a new conception and practice of equal opportunities?', *The European Journal of Women's Studies*, 9(4): 430–46.

Bradley, H. and G. Healy (2008) *Ethnicity and gender at work: inequalities, careers and employment relations*. London and New York: Palgrave and Macmillan.

Brah, A. and A. Phoenix (2004) 'Ain't I a woman? Revisiting intersectionality', *Journal of International Women's Studies*, 5(3): 75–86.

Cockburn, C. (1989) 'Equal opportunities: the short and the long agenda', *Industrial Relations Journal*, 20(3): 213–25.

—— (1991) *In the way of women*. Basingstoke: Macmillan.

Collins, P. H. (2000) *Black feminist thought*. New York: Routledge.

—— (2004) 'Learning from the outsider within: the sociological significance of black feminist thought', In S. Harding (eds), *The feminist standpoint theory reader – intellectual and political controversies*. New York and London: Routledge.

Crenshaw, K. (1991) 'Mapping the margins: intersectionality, identity politics and violence agains women of color', *Stanford Law Review*, 43(6): 1241–99.

Davis, K. (2008) 'Intersectionality as buzzword: a sociology of science perspective on what makes a feminist theory successful', *Feminist Theory*, 9(1): 67–85.

Dickens, L. (1994) 'The business case for equal opportunities: is the carrot better than the stick?', *Employee Relations*, 16(8): 5–18.

—— (1999) 'Beyond the business case: a three-pronged approach to equality action', *Human Resource Management Journal*, 9(1): 9–19.

Dickens, L. (2000). 'Collective bargaining and the promotion of gender equality at work: opportunities and challenges for trade unions', *Transfer: European Review of Labour and Research*, 6: 193–208.

Essers, C., Y. Benschop and H. Doorewaard. (2008) 'Female ethnicity: understanding muslim immigrant businesswomen in The Netherlands', *Gender, Work & Organization*, 17: 320–39.

Foster, C. and L. Harris (2005) 'Easy to say, difficult to do: diversity management in retail', *Human Resource Management Journal*, 15(3): 4–17.

Gilbert, J., B. A. Stead and J. M. Evencevich (1999) 'Diversity management: a new organizational paradigm', *Journal of Business Ethics*, 21: 61–76.

Greene, A. M. and G. Kirton (2009) *Diversity management in the UK. Organizational and stakeholder experiences*. London: Routledge.

Healy, G. and F. Oikelome (2007) 'A global link between national diversity policies? The case of the migration of Nigerian physicians to the UK and USA', *The International Journal of Human Resource Management*, 18(11): 1917–33.

—— (forthcoming) *Diversity, equality migration and work: an international perspective*. Basingstoke: Palgrave Macmillan.

Healy, G., G. Kirton, M. Özbilgin and F. Oiklelome (2010) 'Competing rationalities in the diversity project of the UK judiciary: the politics of assessment centres', *Human Relations*, 63(4): 807–34.

Healy, G., M. Özbilgin and H. Aliefendioğlu (2005) 'Academic employment and gender: a Turkish challenge to vertical sex segregation', *European Journal of Industrial Relations*, 11(2): 247–64.

Healy, G., G. Kirton, M. Özbilgin and F. Oikelome (2010) 'Competing rationalities in the diversity project of the UK judiciary: The politics of assessment centres', *Human Relations*, 63: 807–34.

Holgate, J., G. Hebson and A. McBride (2006) 'Why gender and "difference" matters: a critical appraisal of industrial relations research', *Industrial Relations Journal*, 37(4): 310–28.

hooks, b. (2000) *Feminist theory: from margin to center.* Cambridge: South End Press Classics.

Johnson, L. and S. Johnstone (2010) 'Equality, Diversity and the Law' in G. Kirton and A. M. Greene (eds), *The Dynamics of Managing Diversity*, Elsevier.

Kaler, J. (2001) 'Diversity, equality, morality', In M. Noon and E. Ogbonna (eds), *Equality, diversity and disadvantage in employment.* Basingstoke: Palgrave, pp. 51–64.

Kirton, G. (2008) 'Managing multi-culturally in organizations in a diverse society', In S. Clegg and C. Cooper (eds), *Handbook of macro organizational behaviour.* London: Sage, pp. 309–22.

Kirton, G. and G. Healy (2009) 'Using competency-based assessment centres to select judges – implications for equality and diversity', *Human Resource Management Journal*, 19(3): 302–18.

Kirton, G. and A. M. Greene (2010) *The dynamics of managing diversity.* Oxford: Elsevier (3rd edition).

Liff, S. (1997) 'Two routes to managing diversity: individual differences or social group characterstics', *Employee Relations*, 19(1): 11–26.

Liff, S. and J. Wajcman, (1996) ' "Sameness" and "difference" revisited: which way forward for equal opportunity initiatives?', *Journal of Management Studies*, 33(1): 79–94.

McCall, L. (2005) 'The complexity of intersectionality', *Signs: Journal of Women in Culture and Society*, 30(3): 1771–800.

Noon, M. (2007) 'The fatal flaws of diversity and the business case for ethnic minorities', *Work, Employment and Society*, 21(4): 373–84.

Oikelome, F. and G. Healy (2007) 'Second-class doctors? The impact of a professional career structure on the employment conditions of overseas- and UK-qualified doctors', *Human Resource Management Journal*, 17(2): 134–54.

Point, S. and V. Singh (2003) 'Defining and dimensionalising diversity: evidence from corporate websites across Europe', *European Management Journal*, 21(6): 750–61.

Rees, T. (1998) *Mainstreaming equality in the European Union.* London: Routledge.

Richards, W. (2001) Evaluating equal opportunities initiatives: the case for a "transformative" agenda', In M. A. Noon and E. Ogbonna (eds), *Equality, diversity and disadvantage in employment.* Basingstoke: Palgrave.

Ross, R. and R. Schneider (1992) *From equality to diversity.* London: Pitman.

United Nations (2001) 'Background briefing on intersectionality', *Working group on women and human rights, 45th session of the UN CSW.* Available at: http://www.cwgl.rutgers.edu/csw0`1/background.htm.

Walsh, J. (2007) 'Equality and diversity in British workplaces: the 2004 Workplace Employment Relations Survey.' *Industrial Relations Journal*, 38(4): 303–19.

Webb, J. (1997) 'The politics of equal opportunity', *Gender, Work and Organisation*, 4(3): 159–69.

Wheatley, R. and A. Griffiths (1997) *The management of diversity.* Corby: Institute of Management Foundation.

Young, I. M. (1990) *Justice and the politics of difference.* Princeton: Princeton University Press.

—— (1997) *Intersecting voices – dilemmas of gender, political philosophy and policy.* Princeton: Princeton University Press.

The social construction of diversity, equality and inclusion

An exploration of academic and public discourses

Cliff Oswick

Introduction

Diversity and diversity management have become increasingly popular concepts among practitioners and academics in recent years (Harrison and Klein 2007). There has been a proliferation of articles which have largely originated in the US which extol the virtues of diversity management (Edelman et al. 2001; Page 2007) and make the business case for diversity (Cox and Blake 1991; Richard 2000; Watson et al. 1993). By contrast, a more critical literature on diversity management has developed among European scholars (see e.g.: Kirton and Greene 2000; Lorbiecki 2001; Perriton 2009; Zanoni and Janssens 2007). Whether the focus is on endorsement or critique, it is clear that issues of diversity have somewhat overshadowed the consideration of aspects of equality in recent years (Noon 2007). Indeed, in many instances where equal opportunities approaches have been discussed it has often been as an inferior or less effective alternative to diversity-based initiatives (e.g. Kandola et al. 1995). In terms of general trends in the field, there is some tentative evidence of the emergence of a discourse concerned with inclusion (Hyter and Turnock 2006; Miller and Katz 2002).

We know something about the etymological characterization of the concepts of 'diversity', 'equality' and 'inclusion' (see e.g.: Jewson and Mason 1986; Liff 1997, 1999). However, macro-level empirical evidence regarding the momentum and relative popularity of these differing constructs is rather limited (Edelman et al. 2001).

Moreover, from a discursive perspective we know relatively little about the inter-penetration, mutual implication and correspondence between diversity, equality and inclusion in the everyday language of academics, practitioners and the general public.

This chapter seeks to consider the trajectory of, and interplay between, the discourses of diversity, equality and inclusion through an engagement with two very different sources of data, namely: an academic database and an online video-sharing website. The two sources used have been chosen because they facilitate different discursive level of analysis (i.e. macro-level patterns and micro-level interaction). This is important insofar as it enables connections to be made, and inferences to be drawn, between the everyday, situated use of language (written or spoken) and the more generalized, abstract meta-discursive perspectives which are informed and reinforced through these localized interactions and texts (Alvesson and Karreman 2000; Boje et al. 2004; Oswick and Richards 2004). A further reason for selecting the chosen sources is that it also presents the opportunity to gather data from two different groups of stakeholders (i.e. via the published work of academics and public discourse of practitioners).

The breadth of coverage of the analysis undertaken here lends itself to identifying overall themes, contrasting trends and overarching patterns of insight across the field of inquiry. However, it does not permit detailed and robust inferences to be drawn. In this regard, this contribution should be seen primarily as using two contrasting pockets of data as part of an exploratory investigation rather than an exhaustive and rigorous empirical study. Given the scope of this work, a blended approach based upon 'critical discourse analysis' (Fairclough 1992, 1995, 2003) and 'thematic narrative analysis' (Boje 2001) is employed to examine the various layers of discourse and explore the emerging meanings that arise from the narrative themes uncovered.

There are three main sections to this chapter. First, a macro-level analysis of the academic discourse is provided by considering patterns and trends within a large sample of published work on diversity, equality and inclusion found in the Social Science Citation Index (SSCI). Second, a more micro-oriented analysis of the public discourse of practitioners is offered via the scrutiny of a focused sample of corporate videos contained on the 'YouTube' website. Finally, the significant points of similarity and difference between the two areas of inquiry are highlighted and the resultant implications discussed.

Diversity, equality and inclusion: academic trends

A systematic interrogation of the SSCI was undertaken to identify a pattern of usage of the concepts of equality, diversity and inclusion within the extant literature. This involved an extensive bibliometric analysis of almost four decades of publications (i.e. between 1970 and 2008).[1]

Bibliometric analysis has a content analytic emphasis and encompasses a process of longitudinal aggregation. The primary benefit of this approach is that it enables general trends and patterns of academic interest in relation to a particular phenomenon (or phenomena) to be identified. Bibliometric analyses of social science and management-related constructs have become more prevalent in recent years (e.g. Oswick 2009; Oswick et al. 2009).

A search of the SSCI enabled instances where either equality, diversity or inclusion was cited – either in the title, abstract or highlighted as a keyword – to be identified. For the purposes of this chapter, the analysis was restricted to instances where any of the three concepts were contained in the title of publications. In effect, those privileged articles where equality, diversity or inclusion was the core concept and enabled instances where any of the terms were mentioned in passing (e.g. in an abstract) or listed as an ancillary theme (e.g. in a cluster of keywords)' are to be ruled out.

The analysis of the SSCI produced a number of interesting results. With regards to the insights that could be derived from aggregated data, it is clear that equality, diversity and inclusion have proved to be popular areas of research over the past four decades. In the period between 1970 and 2008 a combined total of 12,986 publications on these topics appeared in the SSCI. This represents an average of 332.9 articles per year. The most popular of the three areas of inquiry is diversity which comprised 53 per cent ($n = 6887$) of the aggregated total. By comparison, equality and inclusion accounted for 34 per cent ($n = 4448$) and 13 per cent ($n = 1651$), respectively.

Moving beyond aspects of collective aggregation, the general trajectory of diversity is also significant insofar as it has exhibited a sustained pattern of growth in the number of articles published on a year-by-year basis (see Figure 2.1). In 1970 there were only 35 articles published on diversity (representing 0.04 per cent of the total SSCI articles for the year). By 2008, the proportion of annual SSCI publications on diversity had risen to 491 which constituted quarter per cent (i.e. 0.247 per cent) of all recorded SSCI output work for the year.[2]

Overall, academic interest in diversity appears to have considerably exceeded that shown towards equality and inclusion. However, beyond this general observation, it is informative to look at the respective trends of the three constructs (see Figure 2.1). Figure 2.2 shows the work published as a percentage of the total SSCI publications for each year.[3] It is worth noting that while diversity has received extensive academic attention in recent years, equality was a more popular area of inquiry during the first half of the period of analysis (i.e. from 1970 through to 1989). Since 1990, the gap between research on diversity and equality appears to have widened. In effect, interest in diversity has blossomed since about 1984–85, while interest in equality has remained fairly constant over the whole period of analysis (i.e. from 1970 to

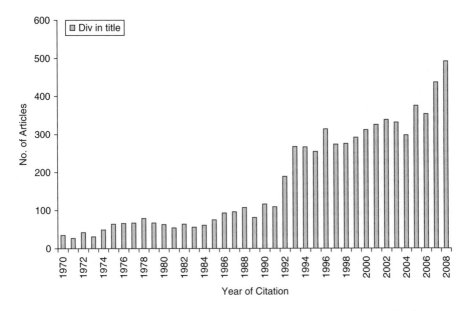

Figure 2.1 Articles on diversity appearing in the Social Science citation index (between 1970 and 2008)

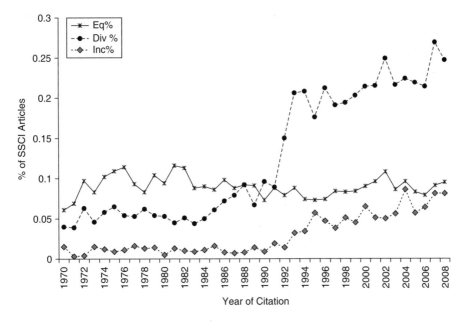

Figure 2.2 Comparison of the proportion of articles on equality, diversity and inclusion (between 1970 and 2008)

2008). The general trend for inclusion appears to more closely resemble the publication pattern exhibited by diversity than equality albeit on a more modest scale.

Publications on inclusion have remained lower than those for diversity and equality throughout the period of analysis. Interest in inclusion appears relatively constant and 'flat' up to the early 1990s and from this point onwards output appreciably increases on a yearly basis. Indeed, by the final year for which complete data are available (i.e. 2008), inclusion is almost on a par with equality in terms of publication levels.

In summary, it would seem that interest in equality has remained stable while interest in inclusion has grown moderately and interest in diversity has grown significantly. Extrapolating from the data presented in Figure 2.2, we might expect two things to occur in the future. First, based upon their respective trajectories and a continuation of the existing trends, inclusion is likely to continue to grow as an area of academic inquiry. Second, interest in diversity looks set to remain the dominant area of the three for some time, but following a steep rise in the early to mid-1990s levels of publication have consolidated and may now be beginning to 'flatten out'. The implications of these respective trends will be discussed later and in relation to the findings from the data collected from practitioners.

Diversity, equality and inclusion: patterns of public discourse

Having considered the broad longitudinal development of equality, diversity and inclusion, this part of the analysis has a narrower and more current flavour. More specifically, and in contrast to the SSCI analysis, it focuses on a restricted sample of recently produced video footage rather than an extensive sample of academic texts. YouTube, the popular video-sharing website, was selected as a suitable source of rich data on the basis that it contains a large amount of audio-visual material from which a targeted and representative sample of videos could be drawn. The other reason for using YouTube is the contemporary nature of the content (i.e. continually updated postings and, at the point of data collection, all the content had been added within the preceding four years).

YouTube was founded in 2005 by Steve Chen, Chad Hurley and Jawed Karim. In 2006, YouTube was bought by Google Inc. for $1.65 billion. According to newspaper reports in *USA Today*, by 2006 a staggering 65,000 new videos were being uploaded everyday and, in terms of audience, there were more than 100 million viewings per day. In a company press release in 2009, YouTube reported that 20 hours of videos are posted on the site every minute and, although based in California, it is estimated that three-quarters of the material uploaded on to the site emanates from outside the United States. Arguably, the sheer volume of data, the contemporaneous nature of the content and the degree of international representation make YouTube an excellent site from which to select a sample of pertinent videos.

A preliminary search on YouTube, using the terms equality, diversity and inclusion, identified a total of 56,090 videos. Of these, inclusion threw up 6390 videos, equality produced 19,900 videos and the most popular area was diversity with almost 30,000 videos (the actual number was 29,800). Unlike the SSCI, where contamination via the spurious and extraneous usage of key search words was limited, YouTube contained an overwhelming amount of unrelated content. That said, it is an interesting aside that although the content is extremely broad, the general distribution of videos mirrors the aggregated results for the SSCI with 'diversity' accounting for just over half the total content in both cases (i.e. 53.03 per cent in the SSCI and 53.13 per cent on YouTube).

In order to screen out irrelevant material and to meaningfully refine the analysis, the key search words were used in combination (e.g. diversity and inclusion, equality and diversity and so on).[4] This meant that erroneous videos were removed (e.g. inclusion in isolation would include a video clip on the *inclusion* of a particular footballer in a national squad, but inclusion and diversity would exclude the same video).

The pairing of terms reduced the total sample to manageable proportions (i.e. 893 videos). The distribution among the combinations being: equality and inclusion = 39 videos (posted since October 2007); diversity and inclusion = 325 videos (posted since July 2006); and, equality and diversity = 529 videos (posted since August 2006). In line with the SSCI and the unrefined YouTube results reported above, it would appear that diversity is dominant (i.e. inclusion and equality as a combination only account for just over 4 per cent of the total videos).

Clearly, an analysis of 893 videos is still somewhat impractical. Therefore, the sample was further narrowed in two ways. First, only videos uploaded on the site within the past year (i.e. 12 months preceding the point of data collection [September 2009] were considered. Second, given the original point of interest was practitioners, only videos with an identifiable individual speaking on behalf of an organization were included. These criteria ruled out a significant number of videos. In particular, it excluded non-corporate content, such as: short rants by members of the general public, consultants advertising their services, conference presentations and training videos, and artistic performances and dramatizations. Table 2.1 summarizes the

Table 2.1 Summary of equality, diversity and inclusion video combinations appearing on YouTube

Categories of video search undertaken	Total no. of videos	Videos posted in the past year (i.e. since August 2008)	Videos with an individual representing an organization
Equality & Inclusion	39	31	1
Inclusion & Diversity	325	133	15
Diversity & Equality	529	121	2

videos produced in total, during the period between September 2008 and September 2009, and the final sample composition.

Equality and inclusion videos

Of the 31 videos on equality and inclusion appearing in YouTube during the period between September 2008 and September 2009, there is only one containing an individual representing an organization. The video in question is of Boris Johnson, The Mayor of London, introducing an initiative titled 'The New Life Equality Framework for London' in August 2009 (see www.youtube.com/watch?v=ZTWw8GBQJDs). The main emphasis is on equality of opportunity and it presents London as an exciting, vibrant, fair and inclusive place to live and work. Hence, equality and inclusion are presented in a proactive and upbeat way.

A brief review of the 30 'non-corporate' videos on equality and inclusion appearing between September 2008 and September 2009 revealed that the majority involved short video clips from individuals expressing personal opinions and sharing anecdotes about issues of equality and equity. In contrast to the Boris Johnson recording, it is noticeable that much of the content of these videos is negatively framed in terms of individuals' experiences of unfair treatment and broader observations of the inequality in society. On the limited occasions when inclusion is mentioned it is positioned as an absence of involvement or a lack of opportunities (i.e. it foregrounds exclusion rather than inclusion).

There are perhaps four inferences that can be drawn in relation to this category. First, equality and inclusion is by some way the least popular pairing with regard to the total videos produced in the three categories (i.e. 31 videos out of the 285 posted during the past year). Second, with only one corporate-oriented video produced in the past year, it would seem that organizations are not seeking to primarily position themselves by championing a combination of equality and inclusion issues. Third, in the sample of videos produced over the past year ($n = 31$), equality is foregrounded and inclusion is consistently incorporated as a secondary construct. Finally, the overwhelming emphasis among non-affiliated individuals in videos (i.e. those expressing opinions outside of an organizational setting) is about equality, and to a lesser extent inclusion, as a 'problem' (i.e. a negative framing) while the single corporate video presents equality and inclusion as an 'opportunity' (i.e. a positive framing).

Diversity and equality videos

There are only two videos, out of the 121 produced in the last year on diversity and equality, which have individuals explicitly representing their organizations. Rather surprisingly both examples are from the UK and in both instances the organizations represented are local authorities. The first video is titled 'Diving into

Diversity'. It features the Director of Ipswich and Suffolk Council for Racial Equality (ISCRE) and is sponsored by Forest Heath District Council (see www.youtube.com/watch?v=4n5TO-Yk-4). The emphasis is on the challenges of equality (especially racial equality) and raising awareness of issues of diversity. The message is positive and the arguments emphasize the moral and ethical case for diversity and there are no references to the business case.

The second video, produced by Leicestershire County Council, is titled 'Equality and Diversity: It's Everybody's Business' (see www.youtube.com/watch?v=dFEuOU83jUY). It opens with a discussion of the diverse constitution of Leicester as a community and goes on to promote the authority as an equal opportunities employer. The video then focuses on a Project Manager of an initiative called 'Care Online' which aims to provide computers and technological support for older people and people with disabilities who have limited mobility. The Project Manager talks about 'engaging with the community' and that older people and those with disabilities 'should not feel excluded'. As with the other video in this category, the message is concerned with good practice, serving the community and the business case is not directly evoked at any point.

Of the non-corporate videos in this category uploaded in the last year ($n = 119$), many involved individual monologues similar to those found for equality and inclusion (see section 'Equality and Inclusion Videos'). One significant difference was the preponderance of videos by individuals and interest groups concerning 'marriage equality' for the gay, lesbian, bisexual and transsexual (LGBT) community.

Overall, the two corporate videos gave equal weight to aspects of equality and diversity and offered practical insights into what could and should be done. The business case, which is often equated with the benefits of diversity, was not discernible in either video. The other 'non-corporate' videos on equality and diversity tended to slightly privilege facets of equality over diversity and, in common with the corporate videos, the 'good business sense' case for diversity was also absent in this cluster of videos.

Inclusion and diversity videos

This was the most popular coupling both in terms of the total number of videos uploaded in the past year and the number of videos with individuals representing their organizations (see Table 2.1). In all 15 corporate-oriented videos were identified. Summative details of the video sample are presented in Table 2.2.

There are a number of interesting facets to the videos presented in Table 2.2. First, although three-quarters of the content of YouTube originate from outside of the US, all of the 15 videos that formed the 'inclusion and diversity' sample were of US-based contributions. This means that there was a marked contrast between categories insofar as all three corporate videos with an equality emphasis were

Table 2.2 Summary of corporate-oriented 'inclusion and diversity' videos

Person and job title	Organization (and sector)	Title of video and web link	Date of upload	Emphasis and message
Mr A, *Senior Vice President of Community Impact*	United Way of America (non-profit, specializing in community partnering)	'Mr A on Diversity and Inclusion' www.youtube.com/watch?v=WoreTAw0LfQ	May 2009	Almost entirely about inc. (div. not mentioned at all). Promotes the organizational benefits of inc.
Mr B, *Diversity Director and Mr C, HR Manager*	Best Buy (online supplier of electrical goods)	'Best Buy Memphis Immersion' www.youtube.com/watch?v=dH2XC4qbdd8	Oct. 2008	Focus on div. (inc. not mentioned). about personal and company devt.
Mr D, *President (for Atlanta, Georgia)*	United Way of America (non-profit, specializing in community partnering)	'Mr D on Diversity and Inclusion' www.youtube.com/watch?v=ZcDxrsOAtO8	May 2009	Inc. is primary – div. is secondary. Talks about individual and societal benefits.
Ms E, *Exec VP – Strategic Alliances and Inclusion*	United Way of America (non-profit, specializing in community partnering)	'Ms E on Diversity and Inclusion' www.youtube.com/watch?v=Se218-YKFs4	June 2008	Inc. is primary – div. is secondary. Inc. as being about 'the common good'.
Mr F, *Chairman and CEO and Ms G, VP – Inclusion and Talent*	Burger King (multinational fast food chain)	'Burger King – Diversity and Inclusion' www.youtube.com/watch?v=Cnj8etaswxU	April 2009	Inc. and div. given equal weighting. Exclusively focuses on the business benefits.
Mr H, *President and CEO (for Columbia)*	United Way of America (non-profit, specializing in community partnering)	'Mr H on Diversity and Inclusion' www.youtube.com/watch?v=ua8Nju8Rs98	May 2009	Inc. and div. equally covered. Business and community needs seen as aligned.
Ms I, *Exec Director for Diversity, Equity and Inclusion*	Johnson County Community College (educational institution)	'Many Voices, One Community' www.youtube.com/watch?v=MDC2e5jE9qM	July 2009	Inc. is primary – div. is secondary. Inc. as a means of serving and engaging with the local community.
Ms J, *President and CEO (North Arizona)*	United Way of America (non-profit, specializing in community partnering)	'Ms J on Diversity and Inclusion' www.youtube.com/watch?v=WxEZzmnDNuw	May 2009	Inc. is primary – div. is secondary. Inc. key to bringing about social change.

Name	Organization	Video title / URL	Date	Comments
Mr K, *President and CEO*	United Way of America (non-profit, specializing in community partnering)	'Mr K on Diversity and Inclusion' www.youtube.com/watch?v=o5aI-y-_XPE	June 2009	Inc. primary (div. mentioned only twice). All about the business case for inc.
Ms L, *Director of Global Inclusion and Diversity*	Cisco Systems (internet and network equipment and support)	'Ms L on Diversity and Inclusion at Cisco' www.youtube.com/watch?v=B8nrY7AEB70	Nov. 2008	Inc. is given slightly more emphasis. Focus is on the business case.
Mr M, *Snr Manager – Office of Inclusion and Diversity*	Honda Corporation (car and motorcycle manufacturer)	'RiverCity Examiner at Honda' www.youtube.com/watch?v=lqwjqxYaacU	Jan. 2009	Inc. and div. given limited, but equal weight. Emphasis is on community support and community engagement.
Mr N, *President and CEO (Metropolitan Nashville)*	United Way of America (non-profit, specializing in community partnering)	'Mr N on Diversity and Inclusion' www.youtube.com/watch?v=v-UU4jBcjdU	May 2009	Inc. is primary – div. is secondary. Focus is on the business case.
Mr O, *President and CEO*	Rockwell Collins (communication and aviation electronics)	'Rockwell Collins Diversity and Inclusion' www.youtube.com/watch?v=se9ZEEESYHU	Jan. 2009	Inc. and div. equally covered. Offers firm a source of competitive advantage.
Ms P, *Exec VP, Chief Strategist and Administrative Officer*	Safeway (food retailer)	'Safeway's Commitment to Diversity and Employee Inclusion' www.youtube.com/watch?v=s-B_cgVSeRw	Aug. 2009	All about inc. (in relation to disability). Strong emphasis on the resultant business benefits.
Mr Q, *Executive Director (Lincoln and Lancaster County)*	United Way of America (non-profit, specializing in community partnering)	'Mr Q on Diversity and Inclusion' www.youtube.com/watch?v=EZMkOl5I-IA	May 2009	Inc. primary (div. not mentioned). Both the moral case and the business case are presented.

UK-based while 15 out of the 16 videos which included an inclusion orientation were produced in the US.

Second, given the core subject matter of the videos and the sheer volume of video-taped material, it is significant that the phrases equality and equal opportunities were not evident. Indeed, careful scrutiny of all 15 inclusion and diversity videos revealed that these wordings were not even uttered in passing in any of the videos. This perhaps is symptomatic of the relative status of equality in relation to diversity and inclusion. This latter issue will be discussed further in the subsequent main section, titled 'Discussion', of this chapter.

Third, on the basis of the pervasiveness of diversity in the academic literature ($n = 6887$ articles) and as a general category in YouTube (i.e. 29,800 videos), one might expect diversity to overpower inclusion as the dominant partner within the sample of corporate-oriented videos. This was not the case. Inclusion was the primary focus in 10 of the 15 videos. Moreover, in 4 videos (i.e. Mr A, Mr K, Ms P and Mr Q in Table 2.2) the issue of diversity was either only mentioned very briefly or not mentioned at all. Of the 5 instances where inclusion was not the primary focus, it was perceived to enjoy more or less equivalent coverage to diversity on four occasions (i.e. Mr F/Ms G, Mr H, Mr M and Mr O). Hence, in only 1 of the 15 videos (i.e. Mr B) was diversity the predominant theme.

Beyond the centrality of inclusion within the actual content of the videos, it is also informative to look at the composition of the company representatives with regard to job title. Of the 17 organizational representatives, appearing in the 15 videos, we have 8 who occupy generalist roles (e.g. Executive Director, President and CEO). The 9 remaining specialist roles being:

Senior Vice President of Community Impact (Mr A)
Diversity Director (Mr B)
HR Manager (Mr C)
Executive Vice President – Strategic Alliances and Inclusion (Ms E)
Vice President – Inclusion and Talent (Ms G)
Executive Director for Diversity, Equity and Inclusion (Ms I)
Director of Global Inclusion and Diversity (Ms L)
Senior Manager – Office of Inclusion and Diversity (Mr M)
Executive Vice President, Chief Strategist and Administrative Officer (Ms P)

Inclusion is explicitly stated in five of the nine roles compared with diversity appearing four times. This, along with the foregrounding of inclusion in the content of the videos, indicates that it is starting to become more conspicuous and pronounced within the general field of equality and diversity and among practitioners and corporations.

While an inclusion discourse was obviously popular among the practitioners in the sample of videos, the underlying rationales offered for embracing it varied. In seven videos the argument centred directly and overtly on the business case (see

Mr A, Mr F/Ms G, Mr K, Ms L, Mr N, Mr O and Mr P). For these organizational representatives, the concept of enhancing the potential for innovation and generating innovative ideas featured as a benefit along with the notion of increased effectiveness and productivity through improved workforce harmony, morale and commitment. In a further four videos, a two-pronged justification for inclusion was offered by simultaneously espousing the business case and the moral case (see Mr B, Ms E, Mr H and Mr Q). Here arguments were articulated around 'the common good' (i.e. inclusion is in everyone's interests) and synergies between individual benefits and business interests and/or synergies between community needs and organizational goals. In the remaining four cases (i.e. Mr D, Ms I, Mr J and Mr M), a morally embedded argument was privileged where inclusion was framed as producing societal benefits and being crucial to desired processes of social change.

Finally, if we directly turn our attention to the corporate representatives' articulation of the relationship between inclusion and diversity a pattern is discernible. In the statements of the majority of practitioners inclusion was presented as the process by which we engage with diversity. This is apparent in Mr H's assertions: 'Inclusion is important because it is really about how we as local [company name] reflect the diversity of our community. It's about our ability to be able to bring people to our mutual table.'

Similar sentiments about using inclusion to access diverse communities are expressed by Mr A:

> To think 'we need to be inclusive' – to me is the same thing as saying we need to think about the future. ... I think that as we look to the future, whether that is five years from now or ten years from now, this country is going to look a lot different and if you don't have the right folks at the table, representing different ethnic groups and different demographic groups, you are going to miss out on an awful lot.

The nature of the relationship between inclusion and diversity is reinforced, and further extended, in the comments of Ms L (the Director of Global Inclusion and Diversity at Cisco Systems). She observes:

> Diversity is what you see when you get a group of people together. Whenever there is a different person in the room from you, you got a diverse group going on. But what do we do with it? So, its how we leverage the fact we bring different perspectives, that we bring different cultures and backgrounds together and what we do when we get those folks together, how that promotes innovation and helps us work as a better multicultural global organization. ... I think that's the inclusion part of the equation.

Ms L's observations render explicit something which is perhaps implicit in the earlier quotes and throughout the sample of videos. The message is that diversity is inevitable and unavoidable – communities and organizations are, to a greater or lesser extent, always diverse and, as such, constituted through diverse groups. This is apparent in Ms L's suggestion above that: 'Whenever there is a different person in the room from you, you got a diverse group going on.' In this sense, diversity is a given. Inclusion, however is not an ever-present phenomenon. It is a process and it involves a choice. In effect, it is the means by which the latent potential of diversity can be operationalized and utilized (or as Ms L frames it in corporate-speak: 'Leveraged'). Hence, the leverage offered via a deliberate and strategically chosen process of inclusion facilitates the achievement of corporate goals and socially desirable outcomes albeit that, as in the case of Ms L, it is the business case which it tends to take precedent.

Discussion

Certain similarities and consistencies are apparent when the SSCI results for academics and the YouTube results for practitioners are compared. In order to fully explore the substantive points of interest, it may be helpful to consider equality, diversity and inclusion in turn before drawing some overarching conclusions.

The equality discourse

The results of the bibliometric analysis indicate that there was a slight increase in interest in equality between 1974 and 1983, and after this there was a 'settling down' and 'levelling out' of interest which has since persisted (see Figure 2.2). Arguably, there is a residual, but enduring, level of academic interest in equality. In particular, a closer inspection of the underlying disciplinary roots within the extant literature suggests that one of the core realms of abiding interest is Law. This prevailing interest is international in scope with work being produced in the US, Europe and throughout the rest of the world (for recent examples see: Bodensteiner 2009; Hertogh 2009; Knight 2009; Kochenov 2009; Smith and McPherson 2009; Vakulenko 2009). Scholarship around aspects of equality also remains relatively buoyant in the fields of Sociology (e.g. Achin 2009; Dolney 2009; Doucet 2009; Dworkin 2008; Hardin and Whiteside 2009) and Women's Studies (e.g. Desrues and Nieto 2009; Floro 2009; Horne and Biss 2009; Lee 2009; Woodward 2009).

Of the 448 articles published on equality over the past three years i.e. in 2007, 2008 and 2009), 14.5 per cent were in law journals ($n = 65$), 13 per cent in sociology journals ($n = 58$) and 10 per cent in women's studies ($n = 44$). By contrast, only 11 articles (i.e. 2.5 per cent) appeared in management journals over the same period. This difference is compounded when the management sample is further interrogated: six of the eleven articles (namely: Fudge 2008; Jeanes 2007; Jemielniak 2008; McKay 2007; Moreau et al. 2008; Powell et al. 2009) appeared in two non-mainstream journals – *Gender, Work and Organization* and *Work, Employment and Society* – which were also respectively listed in the women's studies and sociology databases. Hence, it would seem that interest in equality persists in academic circles, but it does so largely outside of the Business School.

The limited interest in equality among management scholars is reflected in a concomitant decline of interest among practitioners. Most notably, the YouTube sample of videos registered a discernible shift away from equality. Although equality was addressed in the three UK-based public sector videos, the remaining 15 US-based videos did not mention the words equality or equal opportunities at any stage in their discourse. Given that novel approaches and good practice regarding issues of discrimination in the workplace tend to evolve in the US and then diffuse to the UK and mainland Europe, it is probable that the disappearance of equality from the US corporate discourse is likely to be replicated in the UK in due course.

In conclusion, the prospects for equality are not good. It may continue to enjoy a 'technical interest' in Law and a 'phenomenological interest' more generally in the Social Sciences (especially in Sociology, Women's Studies and Politics), but the more transitory, pragmatic and practical interests of management scholars and managers no longer seem to be adequately served by continuing to embrace an 'equality discourse'. The evidence would suggest that mainstream interest in equality has become somewhat overshadowed and marginalized by other more seductive discourses which are more malleable and attuned to the business case.

The diversity discourse

As an academic discourse, diversity remains an extremely popular area of inquiry. There is also a burgeoning level of practitioner interest. The domination of the discourse of diversity is apparent if we consider the aggregated data. To summarize the earlier findings, diversity accounts for: 53 per cent of the total SSCI output on equality, diversity and inclusion (i.e. 6887 out of 12,986 articles); 53 per cent of all YouTube postings for equality, diversity and inclusion (i.e. 29,800 out of 56,090 videos); and, of the sample of YouTube videos, refined according to paired relevance, diversity coupled with equality and coupled with inclusion constituted 96 per cent of the total sample of 893 videos (i.e. diversity with equality = 59.5 per cent and diversity with inclusion = 36.5 per cent compared to 4 per cent for equality and inclusion).

The academic and practitioner legitimization for the deployment of a diversity discourse continues to be based on an overt linkage to the business case. For example, in 2007 a special issue of the US-based *Academy of Management Perspectives* – a practitioner-oriented journal – on diversity explored the etymology, application and status of the concept, but the contributions (e.g. Bell and Berry 2007; Klein and Harrison 2007; Kravitz 2007; Page 2007) did not seek to question the core premise of justifying diversity on the basis of the business case. More recently, there have been rigorous empirical studies which posit a relationship between diversity and boardroom innovation (Miller and Triana 2009) and between diversity and high-quality decision-making in top management teams (Boone and Hendriks 2009). Arguably, it is the link with business objectives which makes a diversity discourse far more palatable for management scholars than formulations based around equality.

Although the diversity discourse is the most prevalent in terms of aggregated interest over time, if we focus on trends there are nevertheless a couple of indications of an imminent shift of discursive emphasis. First, the volume of work in the SSCI appears to be levelling out having previously accelerated at a significant rate (see Figure 2.2). Second, of the 18 corporate-oriented videos appearing on YouTube during the past year, it is apparent that diversity was a secondary focus when juxtaposed with a noticeable preference for espousing a discourse which centred on inclusion.

The inclusion discourse

The bibliometric analysis highlighted a significant increase in the number of articles being written about inclusion in recent years. Indeed, to the point that it is now almost on a par with equality and, based on the current trajectory, work on inclusion looks set to surpass that produced on equality in the next few years. An upsurge of academic interest has coincided with an expanding interest among practitioners.

On the basis of corporate-oriented videos produced during the past year, the inclusion is gaining momentum. In particular, it has started to permeate through into the job titles of practitioners and a shift in the respective positioning of a discourse of inclusion and the 'diversity discourse' is discernible in two ways. First, diversity is presented as a given (i.e. all communities and organizations are diverse to a lesser or greater extent) and, as such, the challenge becomes harnessing and leveraging it via processes of inclusion. Second, and related to the first point, practitioners present inclusion as the means by which companies ensure competitive advantage, enhance their creative potential, improve their operational effectiveness and so on. In this regard, the practitioner claims which used to be made about the benefits of diversity and diversity management have been relocated and superimposed on to inclusion. In short, it would seem that inclusion is in vogue and is, in effect, becoming the new diversity.

Conclusions

The inferences that can be drawn from an exploration of academic texts and the public discourse of practitioners are relatively consistent. Equality has become a somewhat marginalized discourse over time while the discourse of diversity has become dominant. This is perhaps not an entirely novel finding and it is something that most academics interested in aspects of workplace discrimination would expect, albeit it intuitively, to be the case. That said, hopefully this chapter contributes to understanding the pattern and magnitude of this discursive transition.

What is more surprising, and less obvious, are the signs that a discourse of inclusion has started to gain real momentum. Although at an early stage of its development, it is important to acknowledge that the source of the 'inclusion discourse' is primarily the US and it is embedded in practice rather than in academic circles. As with other strategies and approaches to tackling discrimination, we might expect the emerging trend in the US to start to take hold in the UK. Equally, there is also often a lag in the carryover from practitioners to academics. Hence, we might also expect the growing interest in inclusion in organizations to attract further attention from academics and this recursive cycle of interest will further promote the concept of inclusion.

On a slightly cynical and speculative note, the longitudinal formation of anti-discrimination discourses exhibits a strikingly similar pattern to the literature on management fads and fashions. In their analysis of employee-management techniques, Abrahamson and Eisenman (2008) observed five waves of discursive activity (i.e. from management by objectives to job enrichment to quality circles to total quality management to business process engineering). In the case of anti-discrimination initiatives the pattern arguably involves a movement from equal opportunities to equality and diversity to diversity management to diversity and inclusion and perhaps in the future a move to inclusion management. Abrahamson and Eisenman assert that 'Lexical shifts over time serve to differentiate a fashion from its predecessor, creating a sense of novelty and progress from the earlier to the later fashions' (2008: 719). It is perhaps the sense of progress, newness and leverage offered by successive discursive transitions from equality to diversity to inclusion that makes them so attractive to both management academics and practitioners.

Finally, we might hope that the formation of a new inclusion discourse is more than just a rhetorical re-branding of the diversity discourse (i.e. it offers scope to engage with issues beyond the business case). In particular, a discourse of inclusion, through an emphasis of engagement with local communities, has the potential to integrate aspects of class, especially in relation to the consideration of intersectionality, in a way which diversity has failed to do. That said, the prospects for inclusion, based upon the insights presented in this chapter, are not encouraging.

Notes

1. SSCI records began in 1970 and reliable data are unavailable before this date. Also, there is a considerable lag in published work appearing on the SSCI and at the time of producing this chapter records for 2009 were incomplete and could not therefore be incorporated into the analysis.
2. The samples of articles on diversity, equality and inclusion were cross-checked for instance where the terms were used in instances not related to issues of organization and social aspects of discrimination-related activity (e.g. 'bio-diversity' or the use of inclusion in relation to statistical processes). Extraneous usage of the terms was found to be greatest in relation to diversity, but it was still a relatively small proportion of the annual samples (i.e. it was less than 12 per cent of the 491 articles appearing in the SSCI in 2008).
3. In the interests of being representative, the proportion of articles as a percentage of total SSCI output is presented rather than just the number of articles per year because this avoids an inappropriate level of distortion resulting from the significant variance of total

SCCI output each year (e.g. 87,163 articles in 1970 compared with 199,109 articles in 2008).

4. The search engine on YouTube assigns equal weight to the two search terms. Hence, for example, a search on inclusion and diversity generates exactly the same results as a search on diversity and inclusion.

References

Abrahamson, E. and M. Eisenman (2008) 'Employee management techniques: transient fads or trending fashions?', *Administrative Science Quarterly*, 53(4): 719–44.

Achin, C. (2009) 'Lost equality, parity, feminists and the Republic', *Sociologie du Travail*, 50(4): 556–8.

Alvesson, M. and D. Karreman (2000) 'Varieties of discourse: on the study of organizations through discourse analysis', *Human Relations*, 53(9): 1124–49.

Bell, M. P. and D. P. Berry (2007) 'Viewing diversity through different lenses: avoiding a few blind spots', *Academy of Management Perspectives*, 21(4): 21–5.

Bodensteiner, I. E. (2009) 'The Supreme Court as a major barrier to racial equality', *Rutgers Law Review*, 61(2): 199–230.

Boje, D. (2001) *Narrative methods for organizational and communication research*. London: Sage.

Boje, D. M., C. Oswick and J. Ford (2004) 'Language and organization: the doing of discourse', *Academy of Management Review*, 29(4): 571–7.

Boone, C. and W. Hendriks (2009) 'Top management team diversity and firm performance: moderators of functional-background and locus-of-control diversity', *Management Science*, 55(2): 165–80.

Cox, T. and S. Blake (1991) 'Managing cultural diversity: implications for organizational competitiveness', *Academy of Management Executive*, 59(3): 45–56.

Desrues, T. and J. M. Nieto (2009) 'The development of gender equality for Moroccan women – illusion or reality?', *Journal of Gender Studies*, 18(1): 25–34.

Dolney, B. (2009) 'The logic of democracy: reconciling equality, deliberation and minority protection', *Sociologia*, 41(2): 173–80.

Doucet, A. (2009) 'Gender equality and gender differences: parenting, habitus, and embodiment', *Canadian Review of Sociology*, 46(2): 103–21.

Dworkin, A. G. (2008) 'Education, equality and social cohesion: a comparative analysis', *International Sociology*, 23(5): 749–52.

Edelman, L. B., S. R. Fuller and I. Mara-Drita (2001) 'Diversity rhetoric and the managerialization of law', *American Journal of Sociology*, 106(6): 1589–641.

Fairclough, N. (1992) *Discourse and social change*. Cambridge: Polity Press.

— (1995) *Critical discourse analysis: papers in the critical study of language*. London: Longman.

— (2003) *Analysing discourse: textual analysis for social research*. London: Routledge.

Floro, M. S. (2009) 'Global perspectives on gender equality, reversing the gaze', *Feminist Economics*, 15(2): 125–30.

Fudge, J. (2008) 'Women, gender and work: what is equality and how do we get there?', *Gender, Work and Organization*, 15(2): 228–30.

Hardin, M. and E. E. Whiteside (2009) 'The power of "small stories": narratives and notions of gender equality in conversations about sport', *Sociology of Sport Journal*, 26(2): 255–76.

Harrison, D. A. and K. J. Klein (2007) 'What's the difference? Diversity constructs as separation, variety, or disparity in organizations', *Academy of Management Review*, 32(4): 1199–228.

Hertogh, M. (2009) 'What's in a handshake? Legal equality and legal consciousness in the Netherlands', *Social and Legal Studies*, 18(2): 221–39.

Horne, S. G. and W. J. Biss (2009) 'Equality discrepancy between women in same-sex relationships: the mediating role of attachment in relationship satisfaction', *Sex Roles*, 60(9/10): 721–30.

Hyter, M. C. and J. L. Turnock (2006) *The power of inclusion: unlock the potential and productivity of your workforce*. New York: John Wiley & Sons.

Jeanes, E. (2007) 'Gender injustice: an international comparative analysis of equality in employment', *Gender, Work and Organization*, 14(3): 302–4.

Jemielniak, D. (2008) 'Elusive equality: gender, citizenship, and the limits of democracy in Czechoslovakia 1918–1959', *Gender, Work and Organization*, 15(6): 675–7.

Jewson, N. and D. Mason (1986) 'The theory and practice of equal opportunity policies: liberal and radical approaches', *Sociological Review*, 34(2): 307–34.

Kandola, R., J. Fullerton and Y. Ahmed (1995) 'Managing diversity: succeeding where equal opportunities has failed', *Equal Opportunities Review*, 59(1): 31–6.

Kirton, G. and A. M. Greene (2000) *The dynamics of managing diversity: a critical approach*. Oxford: Elsevier Butterworth-Heinemann.

Klein, K. J. and D. A. Harrison (2007) 'On the diversity of diversity: tidy logic, messier realities', *Academy of Management Perspectives*, 21(4): 26–33.

Knight, C. (2009) 'Describing equality', *Law and Philosophy*, 28(4): 327–65.

Kochenov, D. (2009) 'Equality law in an enlarged European Union: understanding the Article 13 directives', *European Journal of International Law*, 20(2): 483–5.

Kravitz, D. A. (2007) 'Can we take the guesswork out of diversity practice selection', *Academy of Management Perspectives*, 21(4): 80–1.

Lee, E. K. (2009) 'Boundary agenda between gender equality and human resource: the establishment of policy for women in science and technology in Korea', *Asian Women*, 25(2): 29–47.

Liff, S. (1997) 'Two routes to managing diversity: individual differences or social group characteristics', *Employee Relations*, 19(1): 11–26.

— (1999) 'Diversity and equal opportunities: room for a constructive compromise?', *Human Resource Management Journal*, 9(1): 65–75.

Lorbiecki, A. (2001), 'Changing views on diversity management: the rise of the learning perspective and a need to recognise social and political problems', *Management Learning*, 32(3): 354–63.

McKay, A. (2007) 'Why a citizen's basic income? A question of gender equality or gender bias', *Work, Employment and Society*, 21(2): 337–48.

Miller, F. A. and J. H. Katz (2002) *The inclusion breakthrough: unleashing the real power of diversity*. San Francisco: Berrett-Koehler Publishers.

Miller, T. and M. D. Triana (2009) 'Demographic diversity in the boardroom: mediators of the board diversity-firm performance relationship', *Journal of Management Studies*, 46(5): 755–86.

Moreau, M. P., J. Osgood and A. Halsall (2008) 'Equal opportunities policies in English schools: towards greater gender equality in the teaching workforce?', *Gender, Work and Organization*, 15(6): 553–78.

Noon, M. (2007) 'The fatal flaws of diversity and the business case for ethnic minorities', *Work, Employment and Society*, 21(4): 773–84.

Oswick, C. (2009) 'Burgeoning spirituality: a textual analysis of momentum and directions', *Journal of Management, Spirituality and Religion*, 6(1): 15–26.

Oswick, C., P. Jones, and G. Lockwood (2009) 'A bibliometric and tropological analysis of globalization', *Journal of International Business Disciplines*, 3(2): 60–73.

Oswick, C. and D. Richards (2004) 'Talk in organizations: local conversations, wider perspectives', *Culture and Organization*, 10(2): 107–24.

Page, S. E. (2007) 'Making the difference: applying a logic of diversity', *Academy of Management Perspectives*, 21(4): 6–20.

Perriton, L. (2009) ' "We don't want complaining women!" A critical analysis of the business case for diversity', *Management Communication Quarterly*, 23(2): 218–43.

Powell, A., B. Bagilhole and A. Dainty (2009) 'How women engineers do and undo gender: consequences for gender equality', *Gender, Work and Organization*, 16(4): 411–28.

Richard, O. C. (2000) 'Racial diversity, business strategy, and firm performance: a resource-based view', *Academy of Management Journal*, 43(2): 164–78.

Smith, M. A. and M. S. McPherson (2009) 'Nudging for equality: values in libertarian paternalism', *Administrative Law Review*, 61(2): 323–42.

Vakulenko, A. (2009) 'European Union non-discrimination law: comparative perspectives on multidimensional equality law', *European Law Journal*, 15(5): 672–4.

Watson, W. E., K. Kumar and L. K. Michaelson (1993) 'Cultural diversity's impact on interaction process and performance: comparing homogeneous and diverse task groups', *Academy of Management Journal*, 36(3): 590–603.

Woodward, A. E. (2009) 'The price of gender equality: member states and governance in the European Union', *Journal of Women, Politics and Policy*, 30(1): 89–91.

Zanoni, P. and M. Janssens (2007) 'Minority employees engaging with (diversity) management: an analysis of control, agency and micro-emancipation', *Journal of Management Studies*, 44(8): 1371–97.

3

Linguistic diversity in the UK and Ireland

Does the meaning of equality get lost in translation?

Luke McDonagh

Introduction

This chapter examines the law in the area of linguistic diversity in the UK and the Republic of Ireland,[1] with particular focus on the provision of language services such as interpretation and translation.[2] While English remains the dominant language, there are a vast number of minority languages spoken within both states (Barbour 2000: 43). However, as noted over the course of this chapter, while there is a diverse range of minority languages, the legal status of each language is not equal in either the UK or the Republic of Ireland (Dunbar 2006: 198; McCleod 1998: 1; Sutherland 2000: 200). In fact, there are two distinct legal frameworks. The legal framework to be used depends upon the category the language falls into. One model covers the category of 'indigenous' or 'regional' minority languages,[3] such as the Celtic languages of Welsh, Scots-Gaelic and Irish.[4] The other framework generally covers the languages of immigrants, and for the purpose of this chapter these languages are described as 'immigrant' languages. However, to some extent it is arguable that the terms indigenous and immigrant are unsatisfactory. For instance, Barbour has noted that it is unclear how long a language must be present in a territory before it is described as indigenous (2000: 21). Hence, the terms indigenous and immigrant are used with some trepidation and these terms are used purely for the purposes of offering a critique on whether such a distinction is necessary and justifiable.

This chapter also assesses the relevant European and international jurisprudence on language rights, which includes issues of minority rights as well as cultural heritage measures. For instance, the significance of minority language rights in Europe is examined, with particular reference to the provisions of the Charter for Regional and Minority Languages, which was enacted by the Council of Europe in 1992. It has been argued that the distinction between categories of language, as identified above, is mirrored to some extent at the European level (Hogan-Brun and Wolff 2003: 14). However, it is further arguable that from a minority rights perspective, the provision of two distinct models, dependent on whether a language is classed as indigenous or immigrant, is not desirable (Rodriguez 2006: 687–9). This chapter argues that a single, general right to linguistic diversity may be preferable. In addition, recent European jurisprudence appears to point in this direction (Burch 2009: 140–8).

Regarding the issue of linguistic heritage, it is possible that certain provisions for the promotion of particular languages are objectively justifiable, when framed within an internationalist and universal cultural heritage model. Measures that are enacted for 'mere' nationalistic grounds or measures that do not have the specific aim of promoting or safeguarding an endangered language may not be acceptable within a universal cultural heritage framework (Dunbar 2006: 196–8). Furthermore, it is possible that an international cultural heritage perspective, considered in the light of the UNESCO Convention for the Safeguarding of the Intangible Heritage, 2003, has the potential to provide a framework for a heritage-based language policy.

This chapter concludes with an assessment of the current legislation of the UK and the Republic of Ireland in light of this internationalist perspective. Ultimately, this chapter argues that it may be justifiable to treat some languages unequally, but only in limited circumstances, and only so far as any 'dissenting voices' are properly taken into account (Howard 2003: 30).

Linguistic diversity in the UK and Republic of Ireland – exploring two distinct legal frameworks

This section outlines the law in relation to the indigenous Celtic languages in the UK and Republic of Ireland, as well as the law in relation the immigrant languages spoken in both states. It is clear that there are two distinct legal frameworks. Regarding the Celtic languages, it is necessary to add that there is also a distinction between the status of Welsh in Wales and Irish in the Republic of Ireland, in contrast to the status of Scots-Gaelic in Scotland and Irish in Northern Ireland. This is discussed further below.

In Wales, the *Welsh Language Act 1967* made provision for rights to use *Cymraeg/*Welsh in courts and helped to galvanize the Welsh language movement. The *Welsh Language Act 1993* went further and provided that the Welsh language had equal status with English regarding the functions of public bodies. In terms of language promotion, the Welsh Language Board was set up in accordance with the 1993 Act to promote and facilitate the use of the Welsh language. In Wales, around 20 per cent of the population describe themselves as Welsh speakers according to the 2001 census, and the highest proportion of speakers is in the north-west.

In Scotland, the *Gaelic Language (Scotland) Act 2005* became the first piece of legislation to give official recognition of *Gàidhlig*/Scots-Gaelic, commanding equal respect to English. The legislation also included a national Gaelic language plan. An estimated 1.2 per cent of the Scottish population describe themselves as Scots-Gaelic speakers according to the 2001 census, which is a decline from the previous census. One of the reasons for the enactment of the 2005 Act was to make provision for the reversal of this decline. *Bòrd na Gàidhlig* was set up, pursuant to the Act, to promote, develop and encourage the use of Scots-Gaelic in Scotland.

Following the enactment of The Agreement Reached in Multi-party Negotiations of 1998 (sometimes referred to as 'the Belfast "Good Friday" Agreement'), *An Gaeilge*/Irish received official recognition for the first time in Northern Ireland, although not all official documents require translation and translation is primarily directed towards areas of particular importance or relevance to Irish language speakers.[5] Furthermore in 1998, *Foras na Gaeilge* was established as a cross-border organization for the promotion of the Irish language in Northern Ireland and the Republic of Ireland. Around 10 per cent of the population of Northern Ireland has 'some knowledge' of the Irish language according to the 2001 Census.

In the Republic of Ireland, *An Gaeilge*/Irish is the first official language, as enumerated by Article 8.1 of *Bunreacht na hÉireann*/the Constitution of Ireland. The *Official Languages Act, 2003* set up the office of the Irish Language Commissioner and the act provided that all official forms and documents created by public bodies must be translated into Irish. According to the 2006 Census, 40.9 per cent of the Irish people describe themselves as 'competent' in Irish and the main *Gaeltachtai* (Irish speaking areas) are located in the counties of Donegal, Galway, Mayo, Kerry and Cork, with smaller areas in the counties of Waterford and Meath. However, according to the 2006 Census, outside of the education system only around 7 per cent of the Irish people speak Irish on a daily basis.

In contrast to the situation regarding the indigenous Celtic languages above, the majority of legislative measures covering immigrant languages are not specific to a particular language or even to the issue of provision of language services. In the UK, the *Race Relations Act 1976* (as amended by the *Race Relations Amendment Act 2000*) remains the primary framework for the provision of language services by government, as detailed below. In addition, the *Human Rights Act 1998*, through the enactment of Article 6 of the European Convention on Human Rights (ECHR) on the right to a fair trial, requires translation and/or the provision of an interpreter where necessary when someone is arrested or charged with a criminal offence. The primary aims of the *Race Relations Act* (RRA) are to prevent discrimination and to promote equality and good relations between different racial groups. For instance, section 71 requires local authorities to make appropriate arrangements so that their functions are carried out in line with these aims. Therefore, government policy in the area of language services for immigrants has been largely delegated to the local authorities. The principal reason for this is the fact that there are a diverse range of immigrant languages spoken within each particular area and no two local authorities will have identical language responsibilities. Hence, each local authority provides translation services based on the practical needs of the immigrant communities in its area.[6]

The *Race Relations Act 1976* did not extend to Northern Ireland. Instead the *Race Relations Order (N.I.) Order 1997* (as amended by the *Race Relations Order [Amendment] Regulations [N.I.]* of 2003) has similar provisions to the RRA. The *Human Rights Act 1998* applies to Northern Ireland therefore Article 6 ECHR is applicable. In addition, section 75 of the *Northern Ireland Act 1998* makes similar provisions regarding equality of opportunity and interpretation services as in the RRA.

In the Republic of Ireland, the *Refugee Act 1996* states that interpretation services are to be provided during asylum interviews. The *Equal Status Act 2000* and the *Equality Act 2004* (known together as *Equal Status Acts 2000–2004*) prohibit discrimination on the basis of nine possible grounds including race, religion and family status. It is thought that failure to provide an interpreter could violate the *Equal Status Acts*, but so far no case has been taken on this issue (National Consultative Committee on Racism and Interculturalism Report 2008: 7). The *European Convention on Human Rights Act 2003* incorporates Article 6 into Irish law in a similar fashion to the Human Rights Act in the UK, to the extent that interpretation services would be required in criminal proceedings.

It is arguable that the two models, as outlined above, reflect a level of inequality in relation to the perceived value and status of indigenous and immigrant languages in the UK and the Republic of Ireland. However, this distinction is by no means an obvious one and it is questionable whether it is justifiable (McCleod 1998: 1). Gupta has noted that the decision to prioritize one language as indigenous and another as immigrant is potentially problematic from a human rights perspective (2002: 295–7). In line with this, Robert Dunbar has stated 'while the United Kingdom has taken positive steps with regard to Scots-Gaelic and Welsh, there is a clear argument for a much more comprehensive approach to minority-language communities more generally' (2006: 198). In a diverse society with limited resources, where dozens of minority languages are relatively widely spoken, questions arise with regard to which ones should be safeguarded and promoted and which ones should not.

For instance, in recent years the UK has, through the Welsh Assembly government, consistently provided a large amount of funding, around £13 million, to the Welsh Language Board each year.[7] In addition, the relevant Scots-Gaelic organization, *Bòrd na Gàidhlig* received £4.4 million in government funds during 2007–08.[8] Furthermore the UK government, in conjunction with the Irish government, has continued to fund the development of *Foras na Gaeilge*. However, although it has continued to fund Celtic language services at a consistently high level, the UK government has recently changed its policy towards provision of translation services for immigrants. In recent decades, the level of immigration into the UK has continued to increase and different language communities have become ever more widely dispersed. Therefore, it is no surprise that more attention has been paid in the media to the amount of money spent by local authorities on basic translation services. In late 2006, the BBC reported that over £100 million of public money is spent on translation services in the UK, each year.[9] As a result, it was reported that the government intended to change its policy on translation services.[10] In the face of some criticism,[11] the government pressed ahead with its new policy and the Department for Communities and Local Government published the report entitled 'Guidance for Local Authorities on Translation of Publications' in 2007. The report noted that provision of services for immigrants to learn English are a priority. However, there are long waiting lists for services for learning English such as ESOL.[12] Thus, the report recognized that some translation services are necessary, particularly with regard to legal, medical or financial issues. The report provided a checklist to help local authorities decide when translation services are required.

In spite of the policy change, there is still some media criticism in relation to provision of translation services in the UK. For instance, in London, Haringey Council was recently criticized in the news media for producing translated documents that were in the case of a number of languages, not viewed by a single person.[13] It is true that there may be genuine public interest cost concerns in the case of documents that are translated, yet remain unread. However, these criticisms could also be made in relation to translation of documents into Welsh, Irish and Scots-Gaelic.[14] The issue of translation in relation to immigrant languages is often discussed on a 'need' basis, but the issue of 'need' is arguably not as prevalent in discussions over the translation of documents into the indigenous Celtic languages.[15]

For example, in the Republic of Ireland, the *Official Languages Act 2003* provides for the translation of official documents into Irish, many of which are never used by citizens.[16] In contrast, there is a lack of governmental policy and guidelines concerning language services for immigrants in the Republic of Ireland (NCCRI Report 2008: 7). In fact, there is an acute shortage of interpretation and translation services for immigrants in other crucial areas and this has been described as a 'barrier' to integration (NCCRI Report 2008: 18). Hence it is arguable that the distinction between categories of language is even clearer in the Republic of Ireland than in the UK. Therefore it appears that due to the requirements of the constitution and national legislation, translation services for the indigenous, national language of Irish are prioritized over translation services for other languages.

In fact, due to the various constitutional and legislative provisions outlined above, Irish, in the Republic of Ireland, and Welsh, in Wales, are embedded in the Irish and Welsh legal frameworks in a way that goes beyond the position of many minority languages, including Scots-Gaelic, in Scotland, and Irish in Northern Ireland.

Moreover, while the Welsh language revival has been a partial success, it does not necessarily follow that the provision of a formal right to translation services, or the right to conduct legal affairs through Welsh, are the most vital aspects of the revival. It is important to also note the presence of cultural innovations such as the provision of radio and television services through Welsh, as well as the thriving 'Welsh-speaking youth culture' that exists in Wales (Barbour: 42). Indeed, it has been noted that in the case of Irish, considering the amount of Government resources that are spent on the formal requirements of Irish as an official language, the Government's policy in this area over recent decades has led to 'depressingly poor results' – only a small minority of people speak the 'national' language on a daily basis (Barbour: 38). As is discussed later in the chapter, with regard to Irish in Northern Ireland and Scots-Gaelic in Scotland, the provision of translation services is arguably more proportionate to the actual needs of the particular language speakers than it is in the Republic of Ireland or Wales.

Therefore, the question remains – is the distinction between categories of language justifiable? Clearly, the person who has just arrived from India or Pakistan or Malaysia, who cannot speak English would have a far greater practical need for language translation and other services than any Celtic language native speaker, because today, although there are substantial minorities in areas of Wales and the Republic of Ireland where Welsh and Irish are the native languages, it would be highly unusual today to find somebody who would not be bilingual i.e. be able to speak Welsh or Irish but not English (Sutherland 2000: 201). Nevertheless, the provision of translation and interpretation services to native speakers in their native language may well be important, from a minority rights perspective (McCleod 1998: 1). However, while the UK and Irish governments are supporting speakers of the indigenous Celtic languages through the provision of translation and other language services, translation services for immigrant languages are under threat in some parts of the UK and remain scarce in the Republic of Ireland.

Exploring international perspectives on language rights

In light of the distinction between categories of language, as identified above, it may be useful to assess European jurisprudence on minority language rights and international cultural heritage law. With regard to the law of the European Union, it has been said that traditionally the EU has not focused much attention on the issues surrounding minority languages (Nic Shuibhne 2002: 107–10). Indeed, the European Court of Justice has primarily ruled on this issue in relation to free movement of people under EU law principles.[17] However the Charter of Fundamental Rights of the European Union is potentially relevant to language rights. This Charter provides for group-oriented language rights in Article 22. Interestingly, Article 22 of the Charter of Fundamental Freedoms is not expressly limited to indigenous languages of Europe, and as Burch has noted (2009: 120) it is not clear from the text of the document that language 'preservation' is a key principle. Nonetheless, it is clear that a number of national and regional minority groups within the EU have taken Article 22 to mean that such rights are implicit in the document[18] (Burch 2009: 120).

The most relevant[19] Council of Europe measures in the area of language rights are the Charter for Regional and Minority Languages of 1992 and the Framework Convention for the Protection of National Minorities of 1995. These treaty documents have framed the last decade of discussion of the rights of linguistic minorities in Europe. However, these documents primarily apply to the minority languages usually described as indigenous or 'of regional significance' to Europe. For instance, the text of the Charter explicitly excludes immigrant languages. In addition, the language rights in these documents are group-oriented, rather than individual rights.[20] The UK has ratified the European Charter for Regional and Minority Languages in relation to Welsh in Wales, Scots-Gaelic in Scotland and Irish in Northern Ireland. In relation to Ireland, under the definition in Article 1(a) (2) of the European Charter for Regional and Minority Languages, Irish cannot be recognized as a minority language of Ireland as it is an official language of the State. However, as stated above it does have minority language status in Northern Ireland (as part of the UK). It is arguable that with regard to Welsh in Wales, the UK has even gone beyond its obligations under the European Charter for Regional and Minority Languages, due to the extent that Welsh is embedded in the Welsh legal framework, as noted above.

Hence it can be said that the two distinct frameworks, identified above, are mirrored to some extent at the European level. For instance, Stephen May (2001: 65–80) has argued that the position within the EU of speakers of regional or indigenous languages in comparison with speakers of immigrant languages cannot be described as equal. As Burch has recently argued, it is clear European language rights 'were originally understood to be preservationist, group-oriented, and available to territorially-defined national minority groups' (2009: 120). Indeed as is the case in the UK and the Republic of Ireland, in Europe, until recently, the rights of indigenous language speakers and the rights of immigrant language speakers have been categorized separately (Hogan-Brun and Wolff 2003: 14). Indeed, speakers of indigenous minority languages have been accorded rights which generally have not been extended to speakers of immigrant languages. For instance, it has been noted that speakers of European minority indigenous languages are more able to avail of the cultural aspects of their language (Burch 2009: 106). Additionally, members of indigenous minority language communities generally have the right to communicate with their regional, national and in some cases even their EU governments in their minority language, something which is generally only available to immigrant communities on an ad hoc basis dependent on the law of the individual member state.[21]

Despite this, Burch has recently argued that although EU language policy has historically made a firm distinction between the rights of speakers of regional languages and immigrant languages, there is some evidence that at an EU level, the two distinct frameworks are beginning to converge (2009: 147–8). She has noted that it is clear from the recent case law of the ECJ and the actions of treaty bodies, that instruments designed to give rights to speakers of European regional or indigenous languages can in certain circumstances be invoked to give rights to speakers of minority immigrant languages. Burch has stated that what began as a right to 'preservation' may eventually become a fully fledged 'right to linguistic diversity' leading to comparable rights for speakers from both groups (2009: 106–9). Arguably, it is logical to envisage this happening, particularly with regard to 'minority rights' issues, such as the right to communicate with local or national government, which may include related translation rights.

For instance, it has been noted that originally protection was given on the basis of 'group-inhering, territorially-defined, preservationist' rights (Burch 2009: 108–9). However, Burch has argued that a reformulation began with the recognition of the rights of Yiddish and Romani speakers who are scattered across Europe (2009: 108). These languages are recognized as 'non-territorial' languages in the European Charter for Regional and Minority Languages. Following this development, the ECJ and the Council of Europe were instrumental in pushing for the 'right to recognition of the languages of all European migrants throughout the European Union' (Burch 2009: 108). Burch has noted that even though treaties such as the European Charter for Regional and Minority Languages and the Framework Convention on the Rights of National Minorities explicitly excluded immigrant languages, treaty bodies often now consider these rights. For instance, in 2007 the Advisory Committee on the Framework Convention for the Protection of National Minorities considered the language needs of children and adults from immigrant communities in the United Kingdom.[22] Furthermore, in relation to EU law, in *Haim* the ECJ stated that provisions should be made, in relation to the state healthcare system, for individuals to speak in their native language with dentists, even if the language is not the national language[23] (Case C-424/97, 2000: 60). Hence, it is arguable that immigrant linguistic minorities are beginning to gain 'recognition similar to that accorded European migrants' (Burch 2009: 109). Ultimately, it is possible that the original formulation of European protectionist linguistic rights may eventually lead to the formulation of a 'right to linguistic diversity' for all minority language speakers in Europe, including immigrants. In the near future this general right could prove to be the most progressive way of dealing with issues of minority rights, including the provision of translation and interpretation services.

Nonetheless, it is true that issues of cultural and linguistic heritage are also important in this area. Furthermore, the Celtic languages are genuinely endangered. In fact, many of the world's languages are in a similar position. A UNESCO press release of 2002 noted:

> About half of the 6,000 or so languages spoken in the world are under threat. Over the
> past three centuries, languages have died out and disappeared at a dramatic and steadily

increasing pace, especially in the Americas and Australia. Today at least 3,000 tongues are endangered, seriously endangered or dying in many parts of the world. (UNESCO 2002: 1)

This point is important because, as noted below, language is potentially the 'vehicle' by which culture is passed on. For example, it is arguable that the Celtic languages, and the traditional music and literature associated with the languages, are cultural resources that can and have been used to inspire individual creativity.[24] With this in mind, it is arguable that the Convention for the Safeguarding of the Intangible Cultural Heritage (CSICH), adopted by UNESCO in 2003, is potentially relevant to the Celtic languages. The CSICH defines intangible cultural heritage in Article 2(1). Rieks Smeets (2004: 157) has noted that there were some experts in favour of including language under the definition of intangible cultural heritage in Article 2(1) during the drafting stages of the CSICH. However, it was not eventually included. Nonetheless, language was included in Article 2(2) which specifically states that intangible cultural heritage covers language as 'a vehicle of the intangible cultural heritage'. Smeets (2004: 161) remarked that language is the medium 'par excellence' of communication between performers of traditional cultures. One of the important points that Smeets referred to was that the language planning, preservation and re-invigoration envisaged under the CSICH, would only go as far as these measures are necessary for safeguarding the intangible cultural heritage of the selected community or group (2004: 162). This is arguably a positive development. Potentially, the CSICH provides a universal cultural heritage framework to safeguard and promote endangered languages, as discussed further below.

For instance, at a national level, contracting parties draw up inventories regarding the 'intangible cultural heritage' within their territories, and at the international level Article 5 establishes an Intergovernmental Committee to make 'representative lists' of intangible heritage. Once the CSICH is ratified by a State, applications can be made to the fund established by the CSICH in Article 25. The Committee administers the funds on the basis of guidelines laid down by the General Assembly. UNESCO had previously issued the 'Proclamation of Masterpieces of the Oral and Intangible Heritage of Humanity' in 2001. Once a State had signed the Proclamation, its 'masterpieces' could be considered. Since neither Ireland nor the UK was a signatory, no Celtic masterpieces of intangible heritage have been considered. The CSICH representative lists encompass and replace the earlier masterpieces proclamations. Without doubt there are many examples of Welsh, Scots-Gaelic and Irish heritage that could potentially be recognized under the CSICH, once ratified by the UK and Irish governments.[25] However, neither the UK nor Ireland has ratified the agreement as yet. As noted above, it appears that legal measures aimed at safeguarding and promoting the Celtic languages in the UK and Republic of Ireland currently work within a nationalist framework, rather than an internationalist one.

Furthermore, despite the enactment of legislative measures outlined above as well as the continued support of the UK and Irish governments, the Celtic languages remain endangered. It may be possible that a cultural internationalist approach, as outlined by the CSICH, could provide more opportunities for recognition of each language as a 'cultural resource'. This may be preferable to placing emphasis on a State's responsibilities towards a language as based upon a rather formalistic part of the constitutional or legislative character of the 'nation', as it arguably is in the Republic of Ireland and Wales. Indeed, as noted below, it is arguable that the legislation covering Scots-Gaelic and Irish in Northern Ireland strikes a more rational balance between legal formalism and language promotion.

Some thoughts on recent legislation in the UK and the Republic of Ireland

As noted above, the constitutional and legislative provisions which cover the Welsh language in Wales, and the Irish language in the Republic of Ireland, appear to be based upon the premise that each language is a fundamental part of the 'national' character. However, scholars such as Hobsbawm (1990: 9–11) and Gellner (1983: 1–4) have noted that the concepts of 'nation' and 'nationality' are not immutable, and are in fact 'constructed'. Therefore, it is arguably necessary to question whether such nationalistic policies are rationally justifiable. For instance, it is questionable whether a language which is spoken by only a minority of people within a national territory, can truly be described as a national language in a practical sense. This does not mean that the language cannot have a particular national or regional cultural significance. Nonetheless, such analysis may lead to the question of whether legal formalism is in fact the most appropriate way to recognize the significance of the language. As noted above, it may well be the case that there is a strong argument, based on universal cultural heritage grounds, that the Celtic languages should be safeguarded as a cultural resource. However, whether this means that scare resources should be allocated for translation services that are at a basic level, unnecessary, is another question, especially where resources for immigrant language translation, where there is much less competence in English are under threat.

This issue was brought into sharp focus during the debate over the *Gaelic Language (Scotland) Act 2005*. Dunbar noted that in 2002 the Commission for Racial Equality, regarding the then proposed Gaelic Language (Scotland) Bill, argued that resources for Gaelic interpretation and interpretation should not be prioritized over other minority needs (2006: 196–8). The CRE also stated that since Gaelic speakers are generally bilingual, language resources should be allocated to immigrant groups with little or no English (Education, Culture and Sport Committee 2003). The CRE further argued that the then-proposed Bill could be potentially harmful to race relations in Scotland, if it was seen as prioritizing one culture over others (Education, Culture and Sport Committee 2003).

However as Dunbar remarked (2006: 196), 'There may be both "objective" and "reasonable" grounds which justify the special support for Gaelic and Welsh provided by the Gaelic and Welsh Acts respectively.' Dunbar argued that there was little or no evidence that other ethnic or linguistic groups themselves had objections to the provisions of the Bill (2006: 196–9). In addition, when the law was enacted, it explicitly stated that Gaelic required unique legislation and resources because, as Dunbar stated (2006: 197):

> Unlike most other languages spoken in Scotland, and, indeed, in the United Kingdom, Gaelic is a seriously threatened language, is unique to Scotland, and given its long history here, often characterized by marginalization and even persecution, it has a special claim to support.

This point is important. Many of the non-indigenous minority languages such as Chinese, Bengali and Hindi are spoken worldwide by far greater numbers than any of the Celtic languages, and as such they are not in a 'fragile' state of existence (Sutherland 2000: 200–01). Hence, it is arguable that the 2005 Act was ultimately justifiable only from a perspective which comes close to an international cultural heritage position, similar to the one outlined above in the CSICH. However, it is arguable that there are certain measures, and in particular some of the formal measures covering the Irish language in the Republic of Ireland and the Welsh language in Wales, that are not justifiable from an internationalist perspective, as outlined below.

A prescient example regarding translation services is evident in the Republic of Ireland, where under the *Official Languages Act* every official document must be produced in the Irish language as well as in English. Arguably this is unnecessary and a waste of resources, in relation to the actual value of the translation services. For instance, the *Gaeltacht* populations do require translation of documents, and there are genuine concerns for people who have Irish as a first language, who wish to use that language when dealing with government. However, the value of translating official documents, for no practical purpose, and no purpose other than an official, national and constitutional one, must be questioned. A similar criticism could be made of the legal requirements of the *Welsh Language Act,* which required that Welsh be held at an equal level with English in the public sector, despite the fact that only a minority of the population is Welsh-speaking. A policy that sought to provide translation and other language services to speakers where it is appropriate, perhaps in line with the provisions of European Charter on Regional or Minority Languages, such as is the case with Irish in Northern Ireland and Scots-Gaelic in Scotland, might strike a more rational balance between the aims of language promotion and minority rights, while accepting the reality that Irish and Welsh are minority languages, even within the 'nations' of 'Ireland' and 'Wales'. Indeed, as noted above, it is possible that a general 'right to linguistic diversity' could provide a guide for the provision of translation services for the minority of people in predominantly Welsh, Scots-Gaelic or Irish-speaking areas who need to communicate with government in their language, as well as providing comparable rights for the speakers of immigrant languages.

It is true that Will Kymlicka has argued in favour of the position that certain claims made by 'indigenous' communities may carry greater weight than claims of immigrant communities (1995: 33). However, this chapter argues that any heritage policy should take account of the diversity of all languages in the UK and the Republic of Ireland. A policy enacted to promote one category of language, indigenous, rather than another category, immigrant, must also be 'concerned for the dissenting voice' (Howard 2003: 30). In line with this, Martti Koskenniemi has referred to international law as the 'gentle civilizer of nations' (2001). Hence, for the purposes of this chapter it is argued that international cultural heritage law has the potential to 'civilize' aspects of national policy in relation to the Celtic languages in the UK and the Republic of Ireland. This point is related to the argument of Cristina Rodriguez that drawing a large distinction between two sets of minority language speakers is problematic, especially if the distinction is drawn on the basis of the national verses immigrant dichotomy (2006: 687–99). Furthermore, Bryan has argued that it is 'not enough to simply arrange national identities in a way which satisfies the maximum number of people' (2007: 6). Hence a more open and discursive approach would require the government, whether at a local, national or supra-national level, to address the concerns of minority 'dissenting' voices when enacting measures aimed at safeguarding or promoting an endangered language. While some measures for the promotion of an endangered language may be appropriate and objectively justifiable, the same cannot be said of allocation of translation services where these services are not actually required or necessary from a practical point of view. At a time when resources for language are scarce in some areas, the CSICH framework may provide a better framework for the provision of language services. The CSICH provides a universal framework for the safeguard of endangered languages, with language viewed as the 'vehicle' of 'intangible cultural heritage'. In the UK and the Republic of Ireland, the CSICH framework could provide a bulwark against what is arguably often a nationalist-based distinction between two sets of minority language speakers. Furthermore, an 'internationalist' perspective, based on cultural heritage concerns, could provide a rational framework for enacting measures aimed at ensuring that the language is respected, promoted and safeguarded as a cultural resource.

However, it must be noted that in the Republic of Ireland, due to the constitutional recognition of Irish, as well as its recognition as an official language of the EU, any change in legislative policy towards the language would require a constitutional amendment as well as a change to EU law. Similarly in Wales, at present it may not be politically tenable to change the status of Welsh due to the current, popular view of the language as an emblem of nationalist revival (Barbour: 42). This does present a substantial practical barrier to policy change, but it is submitted that it does not negate the underlying principles discussed in this chapter. Ultimately, this chapter argues that if there are justifiable, universal arguments for specific measures aimed at safeguarding and promoting intangible cultural and linguistic heritage then there is arguably no reason to resort to nationalist arguments. If there are no justifiable, rational, universal grounds for specific measures designed to safeguard an endangered language, then to resort to mere nationalist arguments may be unacceptable.

Conclusion

First, it is probably fair to say that language is equally important to members of indigenous and immigrant groups. Furthermore these groups tend to face similar difficulties in dealing with national and local authorities, as recent European jurisprudence has shown. Thus, it is arguable that the rights of indigenous language speakers and the rights of immigrant language speakers should not be distinct, from a minority rights perspective (Gupta 2002: 295–7). Hence, issues of minority rights protection are probably better observed through a general right to linguistic diversity, rather than through separate models. This is particularly important since these two separate models are sometimes based on a questionable value judgment on the comparative worth of indigenous and immigrant languages, and are often tied to complex questions of nationalism, multiculturalism and integration.

From a political perspective, this chapter is of the view that cultural internationalism is preferable to cultural nationalism. For instance, this chapter has argued that language has a value as a cultural resource. Furthermore, unlike many immigrant languages prevalent in the UK and the Republic of Ireland, the Celtic languages are genuinely endangered. Therefore, when a universal cultural heritage perspective is considered, some particular measures do appear to be objectively justifiable. However, these measures are more likely to be justifiable if they are genuinely aimed at the promotion and safeguard of the languages as a cultural resource. Whether it is justifiable to provide translation services for indigenous languages, even where they are not genuinely required, and yet fail to provide them for immigrant languages, where they are genuinely required, is a question that is perhaps best answered by examining all of the issues through an 'internationalist' prism.

Hence, from an equality perspective, the framework of a 'right to linguistic diversity' appears to be the best way to resolve minority rights issues fairly. However, the remaining cultural issues, such as the value of endangered languages as cultural resources, are probably best resolved by using a framework of universal cultural heritage law. In pursuing this heritage policy, it may be necessary to prioritize some languages because they are genuinely under threat of extinction – in other words some inequality between languages may be objectively justifiable. This is not to say that any language is intrinsically more valuable than any other – it is merely a question of practical implication. For instance, it might be necessary to allocate greater resources to the promotion of, for example, Scots-Gaelic as an endangered cultural resource, but not Polish, Chinese, Hindi, Bengali or English, since although these languages could also be seen as 'cultural resources', they are not endangered. However, such measures will, in all likelihood, only be objectively justifiable if they are enacted from a universal heritage perspective, with any dissenting voices, such as those which may come from members of immigrant communities, are taken into account. In other words, to preserve linguistic diversity in the UK and the Republic of Ireland, some inequality is arguably necessary and objectively justifiable. However measures aimed at protecting linguistic diversity must be enacted very carefully so that any potential inequality is minimized.

Notes

1. Over the course of this chapter 'Republic of Ireland' is used as the legal description for the State (*Republic of Ireland Act 1948*, Section 2) in relation to its government and laws, while the term 'Ireland' (known as *Éire* in Irish) is used as it is the official name of the State (*Constitution of Ireland*, Article 4) and is used when the State signs or ratifies international agreements such as the European Charter for Regional or Minority Languages or the UNESCO Convention for the Safeguarding of the Intangible Cultural Heritage.
2. The area of language is also important in the area of education, as many commentators have noted. However, the law in relation to language and education in the UK and Ireland is generally outside the scope of this article, which has a particular focus on translation and interpretation services.
3. For the purposes of this chapter, Welsh in Wales, Scots-Gaelic in Scotland, Irish in Northern Ireland and Irish in Ireland are grouped together. What these languages have in common, apart from their shared Celtic linguistic history, is that these languages are of regional and/or national significance and have a special legal status within each regional or national legal framework, despite the fact they are spoken by a minority of people within that territory or region, as outlined over the course of this chapter. However, the legal status of these languages is not necessarily the same. As noted over the course of this chapter, within this grouping there is a divergence that can be identified between the status of Welsh in Wales and Irish in Ireland, in comparison with the status of Scots-Gaelic in Scotland and Irish in Northern Ireland.
4. For the purposes of this chapter, the relevant languages covered are Welsh, Scots-Gaelic and Irish. However, both Manx and Cornish are also Celtic languages of the UK and Ireland. These languages are omitted from the discussion in this chapter. Nonetheless the general thrust of the chapter is arguably relevant to all the Celtic languages, including Manx and Cornish.
5. The requirement to translate documents into Irish does not apply to all documents because it is framed around the European Charter for Regional or Minority Languages, as noted by the policy document accessible at; http://www.dcalni.gov.uk/guidance_for_public_servants.doc.doc. It is important to note that the status of the Ulster-Scots dialect was also recognized as a result of the Agreement. Since this is not one of the Celtic languages, it is not dealt with by this chapter. For more information on the status of Ulster-Scots, see http://www.ulsterscotsagency.com/
6. For instance, based on the needs for the immigrant population in its area, Peterborough Council recently translated a guide to life the locality into Czech, Lithuanian, Polish, Portuguese, Slovak, Ukrainian, Latvian, Kurdish-Sorani, Punjabi and Urdu. For further details refer to the report accessible at; http://www.peterborough.gov.uk/page-7297
7. The 'National Action Plan for a Bi-lingual Wales' was published in 2003 and the report has the aim of providing people in Wales with the option of living through a choice of Welsh or English. Funds are managed in light of this report. The fact that there is a larger amount of funding available for Welsh than for Scots-Gaelic is largely due to the fact that the 'National Action Plan' in Wales is a more expansive plan than the comparative Scots-Gaelic plan. As noted over the course of this chapter, there are a far greater proportion

of Welsh speakers in Wales in comparison with Scots-Gaelic speakers in Scotland. Furthermore, the number of Welsh speakers has increased in recent years, while the number of Scots-Gaelic speakers has been in decline. Hence, the Welsh 'National Action Plan' aims to increase the number of Welsh speakers in Wales. In contrast, the principle aim of the 'National Plan for Gaelic' is to arrest the decline in the number of speakers of Scots-Gaelic and keep the numbers at a sustainable level.

The 'National Action Plan for a Bi-lingual Wales'. Available at: http://cymru.gov.uk/about/cabinet/cabinetstatements/2003/17.01.2003Iaithpawb;jsessionid=hrJZKV4L2S1cSnjh41gLDYT3Jpg9P0g13BHGYtb1pCBjNQMLShSr!-845036832?lang=en

The 'National Plan for Gaelic'. Available at: http://www.bord-na-gaidhlig.org.uk/national-plan-for-gaelic.html

Further details of the level of funding in Wales. Available at: http://wales.gov.uk/funding/fundgrantareas/welshfund/?lang=en

8. The funding comes through the Scottish Government grant system. Further details, Available at: http://www.bord-na-gaidhlig.org.uk/funding.html

9. The BBC referred to this statistic in a news report which is Available at: http://news.bbc.co.uk/1/hi/uk/6174303.stm

10. In July 2007, Ruth Kelly stated that the amount of money spent on translation of official documents by councils should be cut to encourage immigrants to learn English, in a report Available at: http://www.guardian.co.uk/society/2007/jun/11/communities

11. Community groups and Trevor Phillips countered Ruth Kelly's statements, and argued that translation services are necessary for the transition from one country and language to another, and this was reported at: http://news.bbc.co.uk/1/hi/uk_politics/6738603.stm

12. ESOL is an English language learning services. For further details refer to page 6 of the Home Office document which notes that there are a shortage of classes and long waiting lists for ESOL services, available at: http://www.homeoffice.gov.uk/rds/pdfs2/rdsolr1403.pdf

13. The Telegraph newspaper recently reported this story which is available at: http://www.telegraph.co.uk/news/newstopics/politics/5523716/Councils-spend-50m-a-year-translating-documents-no-one-reads.html

14. The cost of Welsh translation services have come under fire in the UK media recently. See for example: http://www.dailymail.co.uk/news/article-1134310/Private-firms-utility-companies-forced-offer-services-Welsh-new-equality-law.html. Furthermore, there has been debate over whether the Welsh translation services are value for money: http://www.guardian.co.uk/uk/2009/aug/15/wales-language-diverse-literature or even worth-while: http://www.guardian.co.uk/theguardian/2008/nov/01/5

15. It was recently reported that one Welsh council even decided to opt-out of Welsh translation services: http://news.bbc.co.uk/1/hi/wales/7717042.stm

16. There has been some recent criticism in the Irish media of the amount spent on translation services, particularly when these services are not accessed. See for example: http://www.irishtimes.com/newspaper/ireland/2009/0202/1232923381440.html
http://archives.tcm.ie/irishexaminer/2007/11/05/story47087.asp

17. Cases involving language rights in ECJ include *Groener*, Case C-378/87 and *Angonese*, Case C-281/98

18. Burch noted in footnote 98, p.120 that groups in France as well as Italy have taken Article 22, to give rights to speakers of 'indigenous' languages.

19. The ECHR is also relevant, but only in the limited sphere covered in section 3.1, regarding Article 6 on the right to a fair trial, which is incorporated into UK law under the

Human Rights Act 1998 and in Ireland under the European Convention on Human Rights Act 2003.

20. It is beyond the scope of this chapter to examine the positives and negatives of group vs. individual rights. However, it is clear that there is some 'tension between individual rights and minority group rights' within the EU (Weber 2007: 411–3). Weber has argued in favour of sui generis group rights, rather than individual-based rights, which would inhere in national and regional minority language groups.

21. However, as is stated in sub-section three of section two, it is possible that Europe is already moving in an individualist direction in terms of language rights, and the possibility remains that a single right of linguistic diversity will apply to all individuals who speak a minority language (Burch, 2009).

22. The Advisory Committee is a committee of independent experts which periodically assesses a state's obligations under the Framework Convention and reports to the Committee of Ministers at the Council of Europe – http://www.coe.int/t/dghl/monitoring/minorities/2_Monitoring/ACFC_Intro_en.asp. In the report below, the Advisory Committee considered the rights of immigrant communities including the African-Caribbean, Pakistani and Bangladeshi communities. See report p.92–3 for further details – http://www.coe.int/t/dghl/monitoring/minorities/3_fcnmdocs/PDF_2nd_OP_UK_en.pdf

23. In this case the language was Turkish and the case involved a Turkish dental patient in Germany.

24. For instance *Sean nós* music is a popular traditional style of singing and many traditional songs in the Irish language are performed in this style. It is very much associated with the *Gaeltacht* areas in Ireland. This style of singing is usually unaccompanied, which allows the singer to add his own unique ornamentation to a piece. The Scots-Gaelic musical tradition of *puirt á beul* is comparable in terms of its uniqueness and its link with the language. The Welsh language also has unique cultural forms and a rich literary history including the popular and influential *Eisteddfod*, an annual cultural festival. It is possible that recognition of these traditions as 'intangible cultural heritage', as envisaged by the CSICH, could foster more interest and respect in the languages, especially in areas where English is the dominant language. For more information on Celtic cultural traditions refer to Sawyer, 2001.

25. See 16.

References

Legislation, policies

Advisory Committee on the Framework Convention for the Protection of National Minorities (October, 2007) *Second Opinion on the United Kingdom*, accessible at: http://www.coe.int/t/dghl/monitoring/minorities/3_fcnmdocs/PDF_2nd_OP_UK_en.pdf

Barbour, S. (2000) 'Britain and Ireland: the varying significance of language for nationalism', In S. Barbour and C. Carmichael (eds), *Language and Nationalism in Europe*. Oxford: Oxford University Press.

Bòrd na Gàidhlig (2006) *National Plan for Gaelic*. Available at: http://www.bord-na-gaidhlig.org.uk/national-plan-for-gaelic.html

Bunreacht na hÉireann/Constitution of Ireland (1937) Available at: http://www.taoiseach.gov.ie/upload/publications/297.pdf

Charter of Fundamental Rights of the European Union (2000) Available at: http://www.europarl.europa.eu/charter/pdf/text_en.pdf

Department for Communities and Local Government (2007) *Guidance for Local Authorities on Translation of Publications*. Available at: http://www.communities.gov.uk/documents/communities/pdf/580274.pdf

Department of Justice, Equality and Law Reform (2005) *Planning for Diversity: The National Action Plan against Racism 2005–2008*. Available at: http://www.nccri.ie/pdf/ActionPlan.pdf

Education (Northern Ireland) Order (1998) Available at: http://www.opsi.gov.uk/si/si1998/19981759.htm

Education, Culture and Sport Committee (2003) *4th Report, Stage 1 Report on the Gaelic Language (Scotland) Bill*, 2, Evidence, SP Paper 785, Session 1

Equality Act (2004) Available at: http://www.oireachtas.ie/documents/bills28/acts/2004/A2404.pdf

Education, Culture and Sport Committee (2003) *4th Report, Stage 1 Report on the Gaelic Language (Scotland) Bill*, 2, Evidence, SP Paper 785, Session 1; accessible at http://www.scottish.parliament.uk/business/committees/historic/education/reports-03/edr03-04-vol02-02.htm

Equal Status Act (2000) Available at: http://www.irishstatutebook.ie/2000/en/act/pub/0008/index.html

European Convention on Human Rights (1950) Available at: *http://www.echr.coe.int/nr/rdonlyres/d5cc24a7-dc13-4318-b457-5c9014916d7a/0/englishanglais.pdf*

European Convention on Human Rights Act (2003) Available at: http://www.dail.ie/viewdoc.asp?DocID=1321&CatID=87&StartDate=01%20January%202003&OrderAscending=0

FrameworkConventionfortheProtectionofNationalMinorities(1995)ETS157,http://www.coe.int/t/dghl/monitoring/minorities/1_AtGlance/PDF_H(1995)010_FCNM_ExplanReport_en.pdf

Gaelic Language (Scotland) Act (2005) Available at: http://www.opsi.gov.uk/legislation/scotland/acts2005/asp_20050007_en_1

Human Rights Act (1998) Available at: http://www.opsi.gov.uk/acts/acts1998/ukpga_19980042_en_1

The Agreement Reached in Multi-party Negotiations (1998) Available at: http://www.nio.gov.uk/agreement.pdf

National Consultative Committee on Racism and Interculturalism (2008) *Developing Quality Cost Effective Interpreting and Translating Services For Government Service Providers in Ireland*. Available at: http://www.nccri.ie/pdf/Interpreting%20and%20Translating%20Services.pdf

Northern Ireland Act (1998) Available at: http://www.opsi.gov.uk/acts/acts1998/ukpga_19980047_en_1

Official Languages Act (2003) Available at: http://www.dail.ie/viewdoc.asp?fn=/documents/bills28/acts/2003/a3203.pdf

Race Relations Act (1976) Available at: http://www.england-legislation.hmso.gov.uk/RevisedStatutes/Acts/ukpga/1976/cukpga_19760074_en_5

Race Relations Amendment Act (2000) Available at: http://www.opsi.gov.uk/acts/acts2000/ukpga_20000034_en_1

Race Relations Order (Amendment) Regulations (N.I.) (2003) Available at: http://www.opsi.gov.uk/si/si2003/20031626.htm

Race Relations Order (N.I.) Order (1997) Available at: http://www.opsi.gov.uk/sr/sr1997/Nisr_19970273_en_1.htm

Refugee Act (1996) Available at: http://www.irishstatutebook.ie/1996/en/act/pub/0017/index.html

Republic of Ireland Act (1948) Available at: http://www.irishstatutebook.ie/1948/en/act/pub/0022/index.html

UNESCO Convention for the Safeguarding of the Intangible Cultural Heritage (2003) Available at: http://unesdoc.unesco.org/images/0013/001325/132540e.pdf

UNESCO Proclamation of Masterpieces of the Oral and Intangible Heritage of Humanity (2001) Available at: http://www.unesco.org/bpi/intangible_heritage/

UNESCO (2002) 'Linguistic Diversity: 3000 Languages in Danger' *UNESCO Press Release 2002–2007.* Available at: http://www.unesco.org/education/imld_2002/press.shtml

Welsh Assembly Government (2003) *National Action Plan for a Bi-lingual Wales.* Available at: http://cymru.gov.uk/about/cabinet/cabinetstatements/2003/17.01.2003Iaithpawb; jsessionid=hrJZKV4L2S1cSnjh41gLDYT3Jpg9P0g13BHGYtb1pCBjNQMLShSr!-845036832?lang=en

Welsh Language Act (1967) Available at: http://www.uk-legislation.hmso.gov.uk/Revised Statutes/Acts/ukpga/1967/cukpga_19670066_en_1

Welsh Language Act (1993) Available at: http://www.opsi.gov.uk/ACTS/acts1993/ukpga_19930038_en_1

Cases

Angonese (2000) Case C-281/98. E.C.R. I-7637.

Groener (1989) Case C-378/87. E.C.R. I-3967.

Haim (2000) Case C-424/97. E.C.R. I-5123.

Burch, S. J. (2009) 'Regional minorities, immigrants, and migrants: the reframing of minority language rights in Europe', pp.101–48, draft paper. Available at: http://ssrn.com/abstract=1332151

Bryan, C. (2007) *The possibilities of nationalism.* M.Litt., NUI Galway.

Dunbar, R. (2006) 'Is there a duty to legislate for linguistic minorities?', *Journal of Law and Society,* 33(1): 181–98.

Gellner, E. (1983) *Nations and nationalism.* Oxford: Blackwell.

Gupta, A. F. (2002) 'Privileging indigeneity', In J. M. Kirk and D.O. Ó Baoil (eds), *Language planning and education: linguistic issues in Northern Ireland, the Republic of Ireland, and Scotland.* Belfast: Cló Ollscoil na Banríona.

Hobsbawm, E. J. (1990) *Nations and nationalism since 1780: program, myth, reality.* Cambridge: Cambridge University Press.

Hogan-Brun, G. and S. Wolff (2003) 'Minority languages in Europe: an introduction to the current debate', In G. Hogan-Brun and S. Wolff (eds), *Minority languages in Europe: frameworks, status, prospects.* Basingstoke: Palgrave Macmillan.

Howard, P. (2003) *Heritage management, interpretation, identity.* New York: Continuum.

Koskenniemi, M. (2001) *The gentle civilizer of nations: the rise and fall of international law 1870–1960.* Cambridge: Cambridge University Press.

Kymlicka, W. (1995) *Multicultural citizenship: a liberal theory of minority rights.* Oxford: Oxford University Press.

May, S. (2001) *Language and minority rights: ethnicity, nationalism and the politics of language.* Harlow: Pearson Education.

McCleod, W. (1998) 'Autochthonous language communities and the Race Relations Act', *Journal of Current Legal Issues, 1.* Available at: http://webjcli.ncl.ac.uk/1998/issue1/mcleod1.html#contents

Nic Shuibhne, N. (2002) *EC law and minority language policy: culture, citizenship and fundamental rights.* The Hague: Kluwer International.

Rodriguez, C. M. (2006) 'Language and participation', *California Law Review*, 94: 687–769.

Sawyers, S. J. (2001) *Celtic music: a complete guide*. New York: Da Capo Press.

Smeets, R. (2004) 'Language as a vehicle of the intangible cultural heritage', *Museum International*, 221–2(56):156–65.

Sutherland, M. B. (2000) 'Problems of diversity in policy and practice: Celtic languages in the United Kingdom', *Comparative Education*, 36(2): 199–209.

Weber, R. (2007) 'Individual rights and group rights in the European Community approach to minority languages', *Duke Journal of Comparative and International Law*, 17: 361–413.

Online statistical resources

The Bòrd na Gàidhlig Scots-Gaelic Language statistics. Available at: http://www.bord-na-gaidhlig.org.uk/gaelic-education.html

The Department of Culture, Arts and Leisure. Available at: http://www.dcalni.gov.uk/guidance_for_public_servants.doc.doc.

The Home Office ESOL statistics. Available at: http://www.homeoffice.gov.uk/rds/pdfs2/rdsolr1403.pdf

The Irish 2006 Census results. Available at: http://www.cso.ie/census

The UK 2001 Census, carried out by the General Register Office for Scotland. Available at: http://www.scrol.gov.uk/scrol/common/home.jsp.

The UK 2001 Census statistics for England and Wales. Available at: http://www.statistics.gov.uk/census2001/census2001.asp

The UK 2001 Census statistics for Northern Ireland. Available at: http://www.statistics.gov.uk/STATBASE/Source.asp?vlnk=84&More=Y

The Welsh Language Board statistics. Available at: http://www.byig-wlb.org.uk/English/welshlanguage/Pages/WhoaretheWelshspeakersWheredotheylive.aspx
http://wales.gov.uk/funding/fundgrantareas/welshfund/?lang=en

Peterborough Council. Available at: http://www.peterborough.gov.uk/page-7297

BBC. Available at: http://news.bbc.co.uk/1/hi/uk/6174303.stm
http://news.bbc.co.uk/1/hi/uk_politics/6738603.stm
http://news.bbc.co.uk/1/hi/wales/7717042.stm

Council of Europe. Available at: http://www.coe.int/t/dghl/monitoring/minorities/2_Monitoring/ACFC_Intro_en.asp

The Daily Mail. Available at: http://www.dailymail.co.uk/news/article-1134310/Private-firms-utility-companies-forced-offer-services-Welsh-new-equality-law.html

The Examiner. Available at: http://archives.tcm.ie/irishexaminer/2007/11/05/story47087.asp

The Guardian. Available at: http://www.guardian.co.uk/society/2007/jun/11/communities
http://www.guardian.co.uk/uk/2009/aug/15/wales-language-diverse-literature
http://www.guardian.co.uk/theguardian/2008/nov/01/5

The Irish Times. Available at: http://www.irishtimes.com/newspaper/ireland/2009/0202/1232923381440.html

The Telegraph. Available at: http://www.telegraph.co.uk/news/newstopics/politics/5523716/Councils-spend-50m-a-year-translating-documents-no-one-reads.html

4

Navigating multi-layered uncertainty
EU member state and organizational perspectives on positive action

Lizzie Barmes

Introduction

The scope in EU Member States for lawfully taking many kinds of positive action is significantly determined by European Union (EU) equality legislation and constitutional principles as interpreted and developed by the European Court of Justice (ECJ). The activities affected include the conduct of employment relations and the provision of goods and services. There are two mechanisms through which relevant EU law polices the positive action that may be taken within and by Member States. First, domestic legislation (or other law) is liable to be scrutinized by the ECJ for compliance with EU law, either at the behest of the EU Commission or in the course of judicial review proceedings in the Member State. If the domestic legislation is found to be in breach, the EU position will prevail even to the extent of requiring domestic legislation to be disapplied. There would then very often be direct legal liability for organizations for the breaches of EU law in question. Secondly, it may be contended in domestic litigation that a specific instance of positive action, even if apparently lawful in the Member State, breaches EU law. In certain situations this question will be referred for determination by the ECJ, or at least for exposition of how the national court must analyse the issue.

It is important in relation to this possibility that, while organizations (especially public ones) are frequently directly liable for breaches of EU law, the legality under domestic law of what was done may anyway be affected. The point is that domestic legislation may survive EU law scrutiny subject to being interpreted in line with an ECJ determination, with the consequence that any organization that took specific positive action based on the ultimately discredited legal view would be liable under domestic law for unlawful discrimination. Moreover this would be true irrespective of how reasonable or defensible the organization's original legal understanding had been and, indeed, of how far it accorded with the Member State's own view of what it had legislated to permit. A significant effect of this state of affairs is that in areas of uncertainty and contestation, of which positive action is a paradigm example, organizations are ill advised to take domestic law at face value. Rather they need to look behind the facade to see if EU law has an impact. This in itself demonstrates the complexity in the EU legal order either of Member States legislating to extend the scope of permitted positive action, or of organizations actively, let alone innovatively, taking advantage of the opportunities provided.

In this chapter I investigate the operation of this multi-layered, interlocking power to regulate positive action. First I analyse EU law on positive action to tease out its uncertainties. Secondly, I use recent experience in the United Kingdom as a case study to show the impact that the resultant uncertainty can have on Member States wanting to relax the legal constraints on positive action, and, by extension, on organizations wishing to take advantage of such latitude. My conclusion is that the existing EU legal framework needs much more clearly to articulate its vision about the limits of permissible positive action. Until such clarification occurs, I contend, the regulatory system will impair the potential in the EU for positive action optimally to be deployed to promote equality or social justice.

The EU dimension: boundary-setting in conditions of complexity

Sketching the normative starting points of EU equality law helps to make sense of the developing rules on positive action. This must be only a sketch because it is in the nature of law, and undoubtedly equality law, that its normative underpinnings are elusive and alterable. Law's premises are rarely fully articulated at the start. The accretions of legislation and case law over time complicate the picture, and the translation of law into 'real life' settings produces other unpredicted meanings. This makes it all the more striking, however, when it is possible to discern enduring normative threads or stories.

An important such thread is the symmetrical, individual, equal treatment requirement at the heart of EU equality law. Observing that this exists, however, does not entail denying that other, sometimes difficultly reconcilable, threads are increasingly present (Fredman 2005, 2008). But it matters that the equality guarantee translated into the EU legal order, as in many other legal (Western and non-Western) systems, at its heart vindicates individually held rights for various aspects of identity not to affect decision-making. It is therefore embedded in EU law that treating others as equals requires consideration of their beliefs, their race, their religion, their sex and their sexual orientation, to be erased from a broad range of decisions affecting them. (The Council of the EC, 1979 and 1986; The Council of the EU, 2000a, 2000b, 2004; European Parliament and the Council of the EU, 2006) This conception also influences EU law on age and disability despite its different structure (e.g. The Council of the EU, 2000b, Article 2(a)) and ECJ, 2009, Advocate General's opinion, 634 at [68]–[71]). From this point of view positive action has the character of paradox, since it claims in the name of equality to breach the foundational precept of that ideal.

It follows that law on this model constructs positive action as permissible only exceptionally and within tightly circumscribed limits. While the survey of legislation and case law below demonstrates that views shift and alter over time about the contours of the allowable exceptions and the nature of the requisite limits, it remains structural to EU equality law as currently framed to view positive action with scepticism and suspicion. This tendency was in fact recently referred to by Advocate General Mazák commenting in the Heyday case on the 2000 employment directive on age, disability, religion or belief and sexual orientation (The Council of the EU 200b), as follows:

> [O]ver time, some classifications have been recognised by the [EU] legal order as being unacceptable and contrary to the values underlying it. .... Classifications or differences in treatment based, directly or indirectly, on ... [religion or belief, disability, age or sexual orientation] are accordingly in principle 'suspect', and may constitute unlawful discrimination, although it follows from the possibilities of justification provided for by art 2 of the directive that that need not be so. (ECJ 2009, Advocate General's opinion, 634 at [70]–[71])

The bottom line legal risk that ensues for a Member State in legislating about, and for an organization in taking, positive action (other than in relation to disability), is that steps will, respectively, be permitted and taken, that unlawfully either directly or indirectly discriminate against members of identity groups who have symmetrical EU anti-discrimination rights. The risk is of lesser magnitude in respect of positive action targeted at an age group, but even then, and undoubtedly in respect of other identity groups (e.g. women) positive action in their favour is liable to be direct discrimination against individuals from groups with symmetrically protected identities (e.g. men). This risk exists whenever positive action within the scope of EU law, formally or informally, wholly or partially, confers a benefit, or protects from a disbenefit, on the basis of a protected identity. Even if there is no direct reliance on the relevant protected identity in individual decision-making, positive action is liable to be indirect discrimination if there is a systematic negative impact on holders of symmetrical anti-discrimination rights and the practice with this impact cannot be objectively justified. It is an important legal conundrum, discussed further below, that EU law is unclear as to whether and when, prima facie indirectly discriminatory measures may be objectively justified as positive action.

Whether positive action in Member States can avoid these pitfalls depends on whether it falls within the exceptions that have been carved out of EU law's equal treatment requirements. It is important, however, that EU legislation has evolved in recent years so that it appears now more hospitable to positive action.

EU legislation and positive action

A series of EU legislative provisions in effect permit positive action.[1] Specific instances of this include several regarding pregnancy and maternity. So the symmetrical, work-related, equal treatment obligations in the gender directive of 1976, and its 2002 and 2006 successors, were all stated to be 'without prejudice to provisions concerning the protection of women, particularly as regards pregnancy and maternity' (The Council of the EU 1976, 2002, Articles 2(3) and 2(7) respectively; European Parliament and the Council of the EU 2006, Article 28).

In addition, the 2000 directive on age and so on made distinctive provision for positive action regarding disability. Aside from protection being asymmetrical such that only people affected by disability (including because of caring responsibilities) may claim, an obligation to make reasonable accommodations was imposed (The Council of the EU 2000b, Articles 2(2)(b)(ii) and 5). The same directive took an unusual stance on age, making distinctive provision for the justification of measures that would otherwise be unlawful as either direct or indirect age discrimination. Indeed the Directive included the following as an example of differential treatment on grounds of age that would, if proportionate, be justifiable:

> (a) the setting of special conditions on access to employment and vocational training, employment and occupation, including dismissal and remuneration conditions, for young people, older workers and persons with caring responsibilities in order to promote their vocational integration or to ensure their protection. (The Council of the EU 2000b, Article 6(1)(a))

Turning to general provisions on positive action, EU gender equality law has of course the longest history because of inclusion from the start of a Treaty requirement of equal pay between men and women (Signatory Member States, 1957, Article 119). Until the late 1990s, however, this made no reference to positive action. Legislative provision for such conduct was first made in Article 2(4) of the gender directive of 1976, as follows:

> This Directive shall be without prejudice to measures to promote equal opportunity for men and women, in particular by removing existing inequalities which affect women's opportunities [as regards access to employment, including promotion, and to vocational training and as regards working conditions...]

The following sub-section was finally added to the equal pay treaty article (now Article 141) by the 1997 Treaty of Amsterdam:

> With a view to ensuring full equality in practice between men and women in working life, the principle of equal treatment shall not prevent any Member State from maintaining or adopting measures providing for specific advantages in order to make it easier for the under-represented sex to pursue a vocational activity or to prevent or compensate for disadvantages in professional careers.

This was inserted into the Treaty Establishing the European Community that came into force on 1 May 1999. But the new Article 141(4) had a precursor in the Agreement on Social Policy (Signatory Member States 1992, Article 6(3)) from which the UK opted out. Now that the 2007 Treaty of Lisbon has finally come into force, the equal pay article has again been re-numbered as Article 157 and forms part of the re-named Treaty on the Functioning of the European Union.

The 2002 gender directive more recently amended the work-related positive action provision to dovetail with Article 141(4). The phrasing then used has been retained in Article 3 of the 2006 consolidating gender directive: 'Member States may maintain or adopt measures within the meaning of Article 141(4) of the Treaty with a view to ensuring full equality in practice between men and women in working life.' Finally on gender, Article 6 of the 2004 directive on gender equality in the provision of goods and services said the following: 'With a view to ensuring full equality in practice between men and women, the principle of equal treatment shall not prevent any Member State from maintaining or adopting specific measures to prevent or compensate for disadvantages linked to sex.'[2] This different formulation echoed the wording which had been used in the two 2000 directives, respectively, on race, age and so on. So the widely applicable race directive provided that, 'With a view to ensuring full equality in practice, the principle of equal treatment shall not prevent any Member State from maintaining or adopting specific measures to prevent or compensate for disadvantages linked to racial or ethnic origin' (The Council of the EU 2000a, Article 5). The work-oriented directive on age and so on was in similar terms:

> With a view to ensuring full equality in practice, the principle of equal treatment shall not prevent any Member State from maintaining or adopting specific measures to prevent or compensate for disadvantages linked to [religion or belief, disability, age or sexual orientation] ... (The Council of the EU 2000b, Article 7(1)).[3]

The variations in language are interesting in themselves but their major importance lies in the differences in interpretation that they could give rise to.

ECJ case law and positive action

The meaning in practice of the various EU provisions on positive action depends on how the ECJ understands them over time. It therefore follows from the amount of recent legislative activity and that most of it is yet to be construed by the Court, that there are gaps in EU law on this topic.

Unknowns I: justification dilemmas

The first important unknown is whether, and in relation to which identities, organizations may be permitted objectively to justify a prima facie indirectly discriminatory practice on the basis that it constituted lawful positive action. An example might be working time arrangements being altered for everyone with a view to reversing structural disadvantage to women because of labour in the home continuing, systematically, to be unequally divided between the sexes. If the new work system had a systematic negative impact on men, the question would be whether an indirect discrimination claim by a man could be defeated by an argument that the change consisted in objectively justified positive action. The reason it may not be permissible even to make the argument is that the early EU legislative formulation of the wrong of indirect sex discrimination (based on earlier ECJ decisions) specified that any objective justification must be unrelated to sex (The Council of the EU 1997, Article 2(2)).

The requirement that any objective justification of prima facie indirect discrimination must be irrespective of the protected identity in issue was not, however, explicitly included in later EU definitions (The Council of the EU 2000a, 2000b, 2002 and 2004, Articles 2(2)(b), 2(2)(b)(ii), 2(2) and 2(a) respectively, and the European Parliament and the Council of the EU 2006, Article 2(1)(b)). Moreover, as we have seen, recent legislation took a distinct approach to disability and also suggested that positive action may potentially justify conduct that would otherwise be direct or indirect age discrimination, with the evolving case law regarding justification for age differentials tending, at least to some extent, to confirm this (Connolly 2009; ECJ 2009; Kilpatrick 2009: 186–8). There are also references in some ECJ decisions on gender to selection criteria which, while gender neutral, have been designed with women in mind (e.g. positively to recognize relevant experience outside the workplace, or negatively to downgrade the importance of criteria related to years in the paid workforce) (ECJ 2001: 112–3 at [31]–[32] and 2002: 952 at [47]–[49]). These suggest that 'neutral' acts of this kind are potentially permissible positive action under EU law, provided they are transparent and amenable to review for arbitrariness. It would seem logically to follow that an employer would have a potential objective justification 'defence' at EU level to an indirect sex discrimination challenge to such practices by a man (De Vos 2007: 15), and, by extension that there would be analogous potential 'defences' available regarding other types of prima facie indirect discrimination.

Nonetheless the view is widely held that outside the age and disability field, a prima facie indirect discriminatory practice can only be justified by factors unrelated to the protected identity in question (e.g. Schiek et al. 2007: 460, 474–5). There will consequently be doubt on this issue until the point is directly addressed by the ECJ (Barnard 2006: 332, 402; McColgan 2005: 142).

Unknowns II: gender case law debates

Further mapping of the terrain depends on analysis of the major line of ECJ positive action cases which interpreted Article 2(4) of the 1976 gender directive, and have made some comment more recently about the difference the new wording in Article 141(4) might make. Owing to the scope of the 1976 directive the decisions relate to work only. Still, they point to how the Court is likely to approach the more recent legislative provisions on positive action and the non-work context.

It is helpful analytically to distinguish between cases about substantial benefits (or detriments), like jobs or promotions, and those about other, lesser, benefits. I shall however present the cases chronologically because this reveals the recurrent debates and oscillations in the Court's decision-making. The first case, EC Commission v France in 1988, concerned collectively bargained benefits for women. The French legislation implementing the 1976 Directive was challenged by the (then) EC Commission as defective because it left in being practices, and terms in either contracts of employment or collective agreements, granting entitlements to women only. Employers, organizations of employers and organizations of employees were only required by the new French law progressively to equalize such terms through collective negotiation. The rights included extended maternity leave, reductions in working hours for women nearing retirement age, retirement age being brought forward, time off to look after sick children, extra holidays per child, a day off on the first day of school, time off on Mothers' Day, daily breaks for women working on computer equipment, as typists and as switchboard operators, pension bonuses after a second child and allowances to pay for nursery or child minders (ECJ 1988; 417 at [8]). The catalogue of preserved rights was found to be too expansive to enable the legislation to come within either the 'pregnancy or maternity' or the Article 2(4) exceptions to the equal treatment requirement. Rejecting the French Government's argument that preserving collectively agreed rights for women should be permitted because these had the object of compensating for the de facto situation in most French households, the ECJ said that Article 2(4) 'has the precise, limited object of authorising measures which, although discriminatory in appearance, actually aim to eliminate or reduce de facto inequalities which may exist in actual working life' The Court found nothing in the facts to indicate that France's general retention of such rights for women came within what Article 2(4) had envisaged (ECJ 1988, 418 at [14]–[15]).

The first jobs case was in the mid-1990s and entailed scrutiny of various German 'tie-break' schemes designed to redress the under-representation of women in certain occupational categories. Such a scheme was found to breach EU law in Kalanke v Freie Hansestadt Bremen. Partially echoing EC Commission v France, Article 2(4) was acknowledged to be 'specifically and exclusively designed to allow measures which, although discriminatory in appearance, were in fact intended to eliminate or reduce actual instances of inequality which may exist in the reality of social life' (ECJ 1995: 331–2 at [18]). Accordingly it permitted measures related to access to employment, including promotion, giving a specific advantage to women with a view to improving their ability to compete on the labour market and to pursue a career on an equal footing with men. But Article 2(4) should be interpreted restrictively as derogating from an individual right, with the ultimate effect that:

> National rules which guarantee women absolute and unconditional priority for appointment or promotion go beyond promoting equal opportunities and overstep the limits of the exception in Article 2(4) of the Directive 76/207/EEC. (ECJ 1995: 332 at [22])

This decision gave rise to something of an outcry (ECJ 1997: 49, 58–60, Advocate General Jacob's opinion at [11], [46]–[50]) and soon after a rather similar 'tie-break' scheme was found in Marschall v Land Nordrhein-Westfalen to be acceptable. In reaching this result the ECJ went against the strongly worded opinion of Advocate General Jacobs. The Court notably contradicted the idea that equally qualified candidates self-evidently had, and continue to have, equal opportunities. Instead it observed that:

> [I]t appears that, even where male and female candidates are equally qualified, male candidates tend to be promoted in preference to female candidates particularly because of prejudices and stereotypes concerning the role and capacities of women in working life and the fear, for example, that women will interrupt their careers more frequently, that owing to household and family duties they will be less flexible in their working hours, or that they will be absent from work more frequently because of pregnancy, childbirth and breastfeeding... (ECJ 1997: 65 at [29])[4]

The Court went on to distinguish Kalanke, admittedly rather artificially, on the basis that the present scheme contained a particular kind of savings clause. This guaranteed to equally qualified male candidates that their applications would be objectively assessed taking account of all criteria specific to individual candidates, such that the priority to female candidates would be overridden if one or more of these tilted the balance, always provided the criteria in question did not discriminate against female candidates (ECJ 1997: 65–6 at [33]). Accordingly this case established that it is sometimes permissible in EU law to address gender under-representation at work through certain kinds of 'tie-break' mechanisms.

Subsequent cases have reiterated, and sought to apply, the delicate balance struck by Marschall. Proceedings for A Review of Legality by Georg Badeck is perhaps the most difficult to interpret, including factually. On the surface the ECJ adhered to the Marschall account of the law, but it seemed also to signal approval of a range of quite far-reaching positive action measures. Most clearly and strikingly, a distinction was made between places in employment and in training 'with a view to obtaining qualifications with the prospect of subsequent access to trained occupations in the public service' (ECJ 2000: 116 at [52]). It was said by the Court that Article 2 of the 1976 Directive would not preclude a Member State allocating, subject to there being sufficient numbers of female applicants, at least half its training places to women for occupations in which women are under-represented and for which the State does not have a monopoly of training (ECJ 2000: 117 at [55]). Notably also, there were signs here of a more permissive approach to benefits short of jobs or promotions, particularly through approval being indicated for a system of automatic interviews for equally qualified women in sectors in which they were under-represented (ECJ 2000: 117–8 at [59]–[63]).

This case is also noteworthy because Advocate General Saggio's opinion canvassed the radical argument that EU equality law should not be seen to construct positive action as exceptional:

> [I]f substantive equality can be achieved by measures that are, by their very nature, discriminatory, then such measures are in fact pursuing the same objective as the [principle of non-discrimination or of formal equality]..., but with the additional twist that the legislature finds itself obliged to remedy a situation where some sections of the population face a real difficulty which cannot be addressed by applying the general principle of non-discrimination. If we follow this line of reasoning, we may come to doubt whether substantive equality is the exception to the rule of formal equality or, in other words, whether the provisions on which positive action is based – in this case Article 119(4) of the EC Treaty and Article 2(4) of the Directive – are in the nature of exceptions and must therefore be interpreted strictly. (ECJ 2000: 92–3, [A26])

This passage evidenced the lurking possibility, mentioned at the start, of long-standing elements in the underlying normative structure of law being recast. The argument made was, effectively, for the ECJ to reconfigure the conceptual relationship between EU legal requirements not to discriminate (enshrined in various equal treatment obligations) and EU legislative commitments to ensuring equal opportunities (evidenced in the provisions permitting positive action).

Further decisions have, however, more straightforwardly stuck to the Marschall formula. Abrahamsson v Fogelqvist concerned a Swedish positive discrimination measure in respect of certain higher education posts. Where it operated, a sufficiently qualified candidate from an under-represented sex could be chosen in preference to a better qualified candidate of the opposite sex, subject to a proviso that the appointment must not breach the requirement of objectivity. In the particular case this had resulted in appointment of a woman ranked third by the selectors. The ECJ found this practice to be contrary to Article 2(4). Not only did the scheme allow for a less well-qualified person to be appointed, the nature of the proviso was unclear and did not allow for objective assessment taking account of the specific personal characteristics of all candidates. Interestingly, a cursory analysis led to the same conclusion in respect of Article 141(4) (ECJ 2000: 653 at [54]–[55]).

Griesmar v Ministre de l'Economie, Des Finances et de l'Industrie in 2001 was about one year service credits per child granted to French female civil servants for pension purposes. The Court analysed the case under (the then) Article 119. Having found that this practice prima facie breached the Treaty requirement of equal pay between men and women, the question was whether it was rescued by the positive action exception. This was decided under Article 6(3) of the 1993 Agreement on Social Policy, the similarly worded predecessor to Article 141(4). The answer was a resounding no, on the basis that the payments did not remedy problems female civil servants might encounter during their careers, as opposed to granting such workers who were mothers a benefit at the date of their retirement (ECJ 2001: 130 at [65]). Importantly, the ECJ adopted a somewhat narrow reading of Article 6(3), very close to existing interpretations of Article 2(4), as follows:

> Article 6(3) of the Agreement on Social Policy authorises national measures intended to eliminate or reduce actual instances of inequality which result from the reality of social life and affect women in their professional life. It follows that national measures covered by that provision must, in any event, contribute to helping women conduct their professional life on an equal footing with men. (ECJ 2001: 130 at [64])

This seemed to echo the interpretation of Article 6(3) in the opinion of Advocate General Tesauro in Kalanke. In his view the only specific pay advantages that might be allowable consisted:

> at most in allowances for mothers who have to pay nursery charges and relate to other similar contingencies, and certainly [do] not consist of discriminatory measures based on sex which are not designed to remove any obstacle [adversely affecting womens' opportunities]. (ECJ 1995: 326 at [21])

Given the change of direction after Kalanke, this similarity arguably indicated that the Court's reasoning in Griesmar was out of keeping with the more recent evolution in the case law. Still, it illustrated that the new wording in Article 141(4), and by extension in other more recent legislation, could perfectly well be interpreted so as to change little. Indeed in reaching this conclusion the ECJ went against the recommendation of Advocate General Alber who had contended that a quite different, more expansive approach should be followed. In his view

> The principle of equal pay ... does not preclude a rule restricting the grant of service credits to mothers where the purpose of the restriction is to compensate for the career handicaps entailed by motherhood, provided that there is sociological and statistical evidence that in terms of their career profiles mothers and fathers are not in the same position. (ECJ 2001: 117 at [AG84])

As such, he analogized the case with Abdoulaye v Regie Nationale de Usines Renault SA in which a father brought an equal pay challenge to lump sum payments to female workers on maternity leave. These were found not to breach Article 119 where the payment was designed to offset occupational disadvantages arising from absence on maternity leave. The Court reasoned that male and female workers were not in comparable situations for the purposes of the payment. But the ECJ in Griesmar preferred a more restrictive general approach to lawful positive action in EU gender equality law.

Evidencing further the ongoing contestation, the ECJ reverted to a more liberal stance, echoing aspects of the Badeck decision, in Lommers v Minister van Landbouw, Natuurbeheer en Visserij. This was about the compliance with Article 2(4) of a scheme at the Dutch Ministry of Agriculture under which a limited number of subsidised nursery places were normally available only to female officials. Male officials had access to the scheme solely in cases of emergency.

The Court treated it as important that the scheme did not reserve places of employment for women, but only 'enjoyment of certain working conditions designed to facilitate their pursuit of, and progression in, their career...' (ECJ 2002: 1171 at [38]). The scheme could in principle come within Article 2(4) as a measure 'designed to eliminate the causes of women's reduced opportunities for access to employment and careers, and...intended to improve their ability to compete on the labour market and to pursue a career on an equal footing with men' (ECJ 2002: 1171 at [38]). The Court went on to apply familiar EU proportionality analysis, requiring the scheme to be an appropriate and necessary means of achieving its (legitimate) aim. The ECJ concluded that the scheme was proportionate, but only on condition that the exception in favour of male officials was construed 'as allowing those of them who take care of their children by themselves to have access to th[e] nursery places scheme on the same conditions as female officials' (ECJ 2002: 1173 at [50]).

Returning again to jobs, a case before the EFTA Court, EFTA Surveillance Authority v Norway, dealt with academic positions that had been earmarked for women by the Norwegian Government or the University of Oslo in order to address the under-representation of women in certain fields. Arguably in tension with Badeck, the EFTA Court found that 'even for training positions, the law requires a system that is not totally inflexible' (EFTA Court 2003: 738–9 at [50]).[5] It found a clear breach of Article 2(4), noting that the Norwegian measure went even further than that in Abrahamsson, which had at least involved an assessment of all candidates (EFTA Court 2003: [51]–[54]).

The most recent of the positive action decisions, Briheche v Ministre de l'Interieur, was again about jobs. It dealt with French legislation that exempted widows who had not remarried, but not widowers in the same situation, from the age limit for obtaining access to certain posts in the public sector. Predictably, this was found to go beyond what was permitted by Article 2(4) and Article 141(4). Again the ECJ's analysis of Article 141(4) was perfunctory, but it did explicitly leave open that this may be more permissive that Article 2(4) (ECJ 2005: 8990 at [27]–[32]).

It is of interest, however, that possibilities for significant change were carefully dissected by Advocate General Poiares Maduro (ECJ 2005: 84–5 at [AG48] –[AG51]), arguably taking up similar challenges to Advocate General Saggio in Badeck. He put it to the Court that the reference to compensatory purposes in Article 141(4) may have been intended to provide Member States with broader discretion positively to discriminate. It was true that it remained necessary to reconcile these with the EU's general principle of equality and non-discrimination. But the Advocate General contended that the ECJ's understanding of the equal treatment principle might be compatible with reading Article 141(4) as meaning 'that the adoption of [positive discrimination] measures of a compensatory type is necessary in view of the fact that the non-discriminatory application of the current societal rules is structurally biased in favour of the members of the over-represented groups' (ECJ 2005: 84–5 at [AG49]–[AG50]). He explained the thinking behind this approach as follows:

> Measures favouring the members of certain groups are therefore not conceived as a means to achieve equality among groups or equality of results but, instead, as an instrument to bring about effective equality of opportunities. The purpose of compensatory measures of this type becomes that of re-establishing equality of opportunities by removing the effects of discrimination and promoting long-term maximisation of equality of opportunities. Compensation refers in this case to reinstating a balance between the opportunities given by society to the members of the different groups. (ECJ 2005: 85 at [AG50])

On this conception, while the possibilities for lawful positive action should be extended, limits and conditions on what was allowed would flow from the continuing pre-eminence in EU law of equality among individuals. Hence, for example, it was argued that permissible positive discrimination should be of a transitional nature only and should be subject to restrictions regarding, first, the burden on individuals in the over-represented group and, secondly, the likelihood that real equality of opportunities would result. Under-representation should also be shown not only generally but in the specific sector or institution concerned.

To re-cap, the gender case law on positive action under Article 2(4) of the 1976 Directive has established that, subject to important conditions being satisfied, it is lawful to have a tie-break scheme for the allocation of jobs and promotions, whereby women (on indeed men) are preferred between two equally qualified candidates. The pre-requisites for such a scheme to be lawful are, first, that there is sufficient under-representation of women (or men) to justify positive action of this kind and, secondly, that the scheme ensures that no absolute, unconditional priority is afforded to any candidate, but instead that objective assessment is undertaken of everyone taking their specific personal characteristics into account (ECJ 1997: 2000a, 2000b, 2004 and the EFTA Court 2003). The cases also establish that targeted benefits of other kinds are permissible, provided they are proportionate, in the EU sense of pursuing an aim provided for by the relevant positive action provision and by means that are appropriate and necessary.

What, then, are the remaining legal issues in the gender field? First, we have seen that there are indications of a more liberal approach still to training posts. But the position is not sufficiently unambiguous for it to be safe to place entire reliance on these. Secondly, there is no clear guidance on what would constitute sufficient under-representation of one sex to justify a modified tie-break scheme, nor any discussion of whether other factors might be relevant to justifying such a scheme like, perhaps, known attrition rates further up a hierarchy. Thirdly, the nature of the modified tie-break requirement that each candidate be objectively assessed is under-specified. In particular, when would it be inappropriate for the tie-break to operate given the premise that both candidates are equally qualified? The only coherent reason not to operate the tie-break in such circumstances is that it would be unfair to a competitor from a systematically 'advantaged' group where they had suffered disadvantage analogous to that the positive action scheme was meant to redress. This flows logically from the fact that, by definition, neither candidate is better suited professionally to the post than the other. The point was explicitly made by Advocate General Saggio in Badeck (ECJ 2001b: 97). But it has not been clarified by the ECJ.

Fourthly, the cases evidence considerable dissension, especially apparent from the opinions of different Advocates General, about when positive action is justified in principle. This makes it impossible to foretell the evolution of the law when Article 141(4), and the provisions on goods and services, come directly to be interpreted. It seems likely that what has already been permitted will remain lawful and that equivalents will be transposed to the goods and services context. But even this is not definite. And what will happen beyond this is importantly contingent, including potentially on the facts in the context of which the Court determines how EU law is to develop. Simply put, if the cases that happen to come before the Court bear out or amplify anxieties about positive action causing individual unfairness, this could push the ECJ towards a restrictive reading of what is permitted. Equally, if they decide to liberalize the law, it is hard to know how far they will go or on what rationale.

Unknowns III: lost in translation?

Finally, it is not known how the ECJ will translate its decision-making to date to other forms of positive action. We have seen that case law is beginning to emerge on the justification of age differentials. While this is both quite inscrutable and not straightforwardly transferable to other situations, it may be that this evolving jurisprudence, as well as experience with the distinctive design of the law on disability, will affect ECJ thinking about positive action more generally. Putting this more speculative possibility to one side, who knows whether, or how far, the ECJ will analogize from the gender context in considering the defensibility of positive action that is argued to pursue racial equality, equality between people of different beliefs and religions or equality between people of different sexual orientations? Whether it does or doesn't, what difference might the varied legislative wordings make?

The point within this complex of questions that I regard as most important and unclear, is how far the ECJ will go in signalling some aims as illegitimate for Member States, and in turn organizations, to pursue by means of appropriate and necessary positive action. The ECJ's treatment of the analogous issues in the Heyday case, of which goals might age differentials legitimately pursue, evidenced the Court being prepared to set some limits, although somewhat vaguely and ambiguously (ECJ 2009: 645 at [46]). The particular question in this context is which goals will be encompassed by the legislative formula that applies outside the gender employment field, according to which Member States are permitted to resile from the principle of equal treatment by 'maintaining or adopting specific measures to prevent or compensate for disadvantages' linked to age, disability, race, religion or belief and sexual orientation, where this is done with 'a view to ensuring full equality in practice'.

I extrapolate two major alternatives from the recurrent case law debates and oscillations, both of which are reconcilable with the written law. The first would, outside the disability – and possibly the age – fields, retain the underlying normative structure evidenced in the more restrictive decisions, recently Griesmar, such that positive action is seen as legitimate only as a means to include those 'others' who can or will conform to existing ways of doing things. The implication is that positive action, first, is only appropriate to redress group-based disadvantages that are identifiable from comparison with dominant group experience and secondly, that it should be aimed at enabling members of the disadvantaged group to conform to current practices. It would follow that organizations should not use positive action to redress group-based disadvantages in respect of which no equivalent 'in-group' benefit or advantage is evident, for example where systematic group-based disadvantage or exclusion derives from religious or cultural practices whose accommodation requires arrangements, whether at work or in the provision of goods and services, not currently available to anyone. In any event, even if this model were altered to recognize this kind of exclusion as properly the subject of positive action, measures premised on facilitating conformity to existing systems would plainly not help.

The alternative model, to some extent inspired by the law on disability (and perhaps learning from the developing law on age), would accept that it is sometimes legitimate also for organizations to reconstruct what they do, either differentially or not, in order to advantage the systematically disadvantaged or to include the systematically excluded. On this view the permissible zone of positive action in respect of race, gender, religion or belief and sexual orientation should incorporate, first, neutral practices that are objectively justified as positive action measures and, secondly, differential treatment in pursuit of defensible equality aims that is proportionate, subject to individual fairness safeguards of the kind enumerated by Advocate General Poiares Maduro in Briheche.

Such an evolution might involve the law developing by analogy particularly with the law and practice in respect of reasonable accommodations in the disability sphere. This would, unlike the model above, be well suited to dealing with situations where group membership systematically precludes people from conforming to dominant, established ways of being. At the same time, it would be textually valid, because it would only sometimes give conditional permission for differentiations to be made between people of different races, genders, religions, beliefs and sexual orientations through the mechanism of constituting positive action as a potential defence to a direct or indirect discrimination claim. It is especially in that respect that there might be insight to be gained from the age context. Crucially, however, to this being a valid interpretation in technical legal terms, the structure would differ from the disability context where reasonable accommodations are a legal obligation.

The member state dimension: UK case study

Navigating uncertainty I: legislative innovation de-railed

An EU funded study, Positive Action Measures in the European Union, Canada, United States and South Africa, has just been published (Archibong et al. 2009). It is a rich source of contemporary information about positive action in various EU countries, to add to other recent studies of this kind (de Vos 2007; Singh Dhami et al. 2006). My concentration here, however, is the UK. This is because it is in the closing stages of a long reform process, one aspect of which is intended to result in UK law permitting positive action to the limits of what the EU allows. The fact that the goal of the UK's positive action law reform was expressed in this way in itself demonstrated the significant impact of EU law. What is more striking, however, is the highly contestable way that the UK proposal for legislation introduced to Parliament in April 2009 implicitly interpreted the EU position. In my contention the end result was draft legislation that coped very poorly with the gaps and uncertainties in the relevant EU law, being weirdly both less and more permissive than at EU level.

My focus is the general provisions on positive action in the Equality Bill as it was introduced to the UK House of Commons (Harman 2009). Note that these were unaltered (aside from re-numbering) in the 8 July 2009 print of the bill following completion of the committee stage in the House of Commons. Accordingly I do not consider, for example, the long-standing pregnancy and maternity exception to the equal treatment principle, nor the specific provision regarding political parties.

It is notable that the two general provisions were drafted to apply across the range of protected identities. My first worry relates to clause 152 (clause 154 in the July print) on 'non jobs and promotions' situations. This would mandate positive action where it was reasonably thought that: either 'persons who share a protected characteristic suffer a disadvantage connected to the characteristic', or 'persons who share a protected characteristic have needs that are different from the needs of persons who do not share it', or 'participation in an activity by persons who share a protected characteristic is disproportionately low'. Sharing a protected characteristic would be defined for the various different grounds by clauses 4–12. So persons would share a protected characteristic where they were, respectively, of the same age group (as defined) (Harman 2009: cl 5), had the same disability, also separately defined (Harman 2009: cl 6(3)(b)), were transsexuals (as defined)

(Harman 2009: cl 7), were married or a civil partner (Harman 2009: cl 8), and also, again respectively, had the same racial group (as defined) (Harman 2009: cl 9), belief or religion (as defined (Harman 2009: cl 10), sex (Harman 2009: cl 11) or sexual orientation (as defined) (Harman 2009: cl 12).

It was made clear that the action potentially permitted under clause 152 would not include 'treating a person (A) more favourably in connection with recruitment or promotion than another person (B) because A has the protected characteristic but B does not', this being the subject of the 'jobs and promotions' clause 153 (clause 155 in the July print). The action permitted under this draft of clause 152, therefore, would be anything else (provided it was not otherwise unlawful) that was a proportionate means of achieving the aims, deriving from the reasonable beliefs above, first of enabling or encouraging persons with the relevant shared characteristic to overcome or minimize the disadvantage from which they were reasonably thought to suffer, secondly, to meet the different needs the relevant group were reasonably thought to have, or, thirdly, to enable or encourage the group members in question to participate in the activity in which their participation was reasonably thought to be disproportionately low.

I hope it is already striking readers that there could be no certainty that these various aims would be seen as legitimate by the ECJ, nor that this would be the case across all the grounds. Undoubtedly the draft took a maximalist approach to what the ECJ would permit in this regard, in the nature of the second model described above. The draft was also both expansive and vague about when group-based disadvantages, needs or disproportions would justify proportionate positive action, on the face of it giving wide discretion to organizations, constrained only by an undefined reasonableness standard, to determine this for themselves. It follows that legislation following this approach would be at clear risk of being read down, possibly differentially between grounds, under the influence of EU law. In effect, for such legislation to be found by the courts to mean what it said would depend, ultimately, on the ECJ throwing its customary caution to the wind; indeed being prepared to go beyond even what Advocate General Poiares Maduro suggested in Briheche. Not only does this seem an ill-advised assumption, the latitude apparently given to organizations would heighten the risk of the rational evolution of the law being impaired by an ill-judged positive action scheme being the occasion for further ECJ deliberation on the topic.

Turning to clause 153, the April 2009 draft seemed to propose allowing both more and less than the ECJ has sanctioned in the gender decisions on jobs and promotions. An individual tie-break to decide the award of jobs or promotions would be permitted where it was reasonably thought that either 'persons who share a protected characteristic suffer a disadvantage connected to the characteristic' or 'participation in an activity by persons who share a protected characteristic is disproportionately low'. In that case it would be allowable to treat someone more favourably in connection with recruitment or promotion because they had the relevant protected characteristic, if the aim was to enable or encourage persons with that identity either to overcome or minimize the disadvantage they were reasonably thought to suffer from or to participate in the activity in question. There would be provisos, however, first, that the people being chosen between were equally qualified for the job or promotion and, secondly, that the organization did not have 'a policy' of favouring people with the relevant identity in recruitment or promotion.

This wording was, with respect, disappointingly muddling. Assuming, however, that I have unraveled its meaning, first, again, it is not clear that all the aims described would be capable of being goals in pursuit of which it would be legitimate for identity sometimes to influence the award of jobs and promotions. Secondly, even if the specified aims were found to be potentially legitimate, law on this model would especially contentiously leave it to organizations to work out what degree of disadvantage or under-representation was sufficient to render this kind of positive action justifiable. For example, unlike under clause 152, organizations would not even be steered towards EU proportionality analysis to work out whether what they were proposing was justifiable. Thirdly, the condition that the final decision must not be based on a policy of favouring, say, women, is, with respect, bizarre. On the one hand this seems a recipe for disconnecting individual decisions from the equality goal in relation to which they would have to be justified. It would seem instead to envisage organizations basing individual decisions on identity in some rather ad hoc way, albeit that the organization had previously identified systematic disadvantage or under-representation of certain kinds. On the other hand, as drafted the clause would not ensure the kind of individualized, objective consideration of all candidates that the EU case law proviso requires. The logical point of that proviso, as I have argued above, is to avoid unfairness to equally qualified candidates who have suffered equivalent, analogous disadvantage to that the positive action is meant to redress. Yet this draft does not insist on that kind of individualized scrutiny once candidates have been found to be equally qualified.

Finally, this time seeming to allow less than the EU gender cases suggest is likely to be permissible, clause 153 was limited to jobs and promotions. This is a curious move from a legal point of view because the most likely extrapolations from the existing gender decisions is for the ECJ to approve modified Marschall-type tie-breaks, first in relation to other protected identities (as clause 153 presumably intended to achieve) and, secondly, in the provision of other substantial benefits either in the work context or in the provision of goods and services. In other words there is a much stronger legal argument for this expansive interpretation of what EU law permits than that implicitly relied on to justify the rest of clause 153 and the whole of clause 152. Yet suddenly, perplexingly, we find caution and wariness in this aspect of the draft.

The fate of these positive action clauses is not yet known. But whatever happens, their existence illustrates what a minefield legislators enter when they undertake reform in this area. It is true that the multi-layered technicality of the law is echoed in the conceptual and philosophical difficulty of determining when and under what

conditions positive action is justified. Moreover the topic is highly politically contentious, with the issues liable to distortion in political and public debate. Perhaps,
then, it is unsurprising that the legislative draft introduced to the UK Parliament
should have done so badly at steering a course through the EU legal dilemmas. Still,
as a case study of an attempt by a Member State innovatively to re-design the law to
enable positive action more optimally to be used to enhance equality, it could hardly
be more discouraging. Most worrying is that there should be such flaws from the
point of view of EU law despite the UK having undertaken a long, detailed, wide-
ranging reform process involving extensive policy work, detailed legal analysis and
widespread consultation (Department for Communities and Local Government
2007; Phillips et al. 2007; Government Equalities Office 2008).

Navigating uncertainty II: dilemmas for UK organizations

Having built up the EU and UK pictures, it is possible shortly to draw out the implications for organizations. Quite simply organizations operating in the UK would be
well advised to approach this legislation, if enacted,[6] with immense caution. They
should read it, in particular, acknowledging the risks, as described above, either of
aspects of the legislation being set aside (with consequent organizational liability in
some instances for unlawful discrimination directly under EU law) or of the legislation being read down by the UK courts to permit less than it purports to (with
consequent organizational liability for unlawful discrimination under UK law as re-
interpreted). It follows from the existence of these legal risks that law reform on this
model would be in danger either of discouraging organizations contemplating positive action from making use of their apparent new freedom or, if they did go ahead,
of exposing them to legal entanglements that were liable to put them off forever.

This would be an unfortunate fate for any law reform. It would be all the more
so where the difficulty and importance of the underlying practical and principled
issues calls for open, collaborative efforts across organizations, sectors and Member
States. The urgent need in this situation is for law to facilitate and inform organizations to assist them in making justifiable, effective decisions about the use of positive action. The last thing law should be doing is adding to the risk of organizational
energy and effort being dissipated and frustrated.

Conclusion

A solution proposed by Caruso is that, much as 'the enforcement of non-
discrimination provisions at a supranational, as well as national, level remains a
major tool for the social inclusion of marginalised groups in Europe', the ECJ
should refuse to hear complaints from 'traditionally non-discriminated majorities,
determined to offset positive action policies that a national system, through the

complexity of its own politics and through its own constitutional filter, has come to approve' (Caruso 2003: 275–376). Yet it is inescapable for the ECJ to rule on such claims because it would be constitutionally improper (aside from being a recipe for doctrinal chaos) for it selectively to shirk its duty to give effect to generally worded EU anti-discrimination obligations. In any event there are principled objections to the ECJ refusing jurisdiction in claims by 'traditionally non-discriminated majorities', since this would give licence to Member States to ignore what may be justified complaints by individuals in respect of whom positive action was not taken.

Rather, the urgent need is for the EU to articulate a clear, precise account of the limits within which Member States must operate in legislating to permit positive action, ideally informed by thoroughgoing, collaborative analysis of what is justified in principle and in practice to enhance equality and social justice. The aim should be an EU framework within which Member States have the space to develop positive action regimes that help to build organizational capacity to confront the complex, variable dynamics of inequality, exclusion and disadvantage.

Experience in Member States might well then helpfully feed back into the evolution of EU law. Recent UK experience, however, highlights that until there is greater clarity about the EU constraints on positive action, Member States (and organizations) wishing to make greater use of this mechanism to enhance equality need to guard their initiatives from becoming hostages to litigation fortunes.

Notes

1. There are, of course, other EU provisions mandating differential treatment like those on occupational requirements, but these should be separately analysed.
2. See also Article 4(5) to the effect that: 'This Directive shall not preclude differences in treatment, if the provision of the goods and services exclusively or primarily to members of one sex is justified by a legitimate aim and the means of achieving that aim are appropriate and necessary.' These are another EU equivalent of single sex provisions in domestic law.
3. Article 7(2) states: 'With regard to disabled persons, the principle of equal treatment shall be without prejudice to the right of Member States to maintain or adopt provisions on the protection of health and safety at work or to measures aimed at creating or maintaining provisions or facilities for safeguarding or promoting their integration into the working environment.'
4. Cf Advocate General Tesauro in *Kalanke* (ECJ 1996: 322 at [13]).
5. Also cf *Lommers* on *Badeck* (ECJ 2004: 1170 at [33]).
6. The Equality Bill became the Equality Act 2010 on 8 April 2010. The clauses in the Bill analysed above were enacted as sections 158 and 159 with the addition of a proportionality requirement to the 'tie-break' provision regarding jobs and promotions (s. 159). This amendment addressed one of the technical legal flaws identified above. But the others remain. Further there is doubt about whether or not the Conservative/Liberal Democrat Government that came to power in the UK in May 2010 will implement these provisions.

References

Archibong, U. et al. (2009) 'Positive Action Measures in the European Union, Canada, United States & South Africa', *European Commission & University of Bradford*, Vols 1, 2, 3.

Barnard, C. (2006) *EC employment law*. 3rd edition, Oxford University Press, Oxford.

Caruso, D. (2003) 'Limits of the classic method: positive action in the European Union after the new equality directives', *Harvard International Law Journal*, 44(2): 332.

Connolly, M. (2009) 'Forced retirement, age discrimination and the Heyday Case', *Industrial Law Journal*, 38(2): 233.

Department of Communities and Local Government (2007) Discrimination Law Review, A Framework for Fairness: Proposals for a Single Equality Bill for Great Britain.

De Vos, M. (2007) Beyond formal equality, positive action under directives 2000/43/EC and 2000/78/EC (European Commission).

Government Equalities Office (2008) The Equality Bill – Government Response to the Consultation.

Fredman, S. (2005) 'Changing the norm: positive duties in equal treatment legislation', *Maastricht Journal of European Law*, 12(4): 369.

—— (2008) *Human rights transformed, positive rights and positive duties.* Oxford University Press: Oxford.

Harman, H. (2009) Equality Bill (ordered by the House of Commons to be printed on 24 April 2009).

Kilpatrick, C. (2009) 'The ECJ and Labour Law: A 2008 retrospective', *Industrial Law Journal*, 38(2): 180.

McColgan, A. (2005) *Discrimination law, text, cases and materials.* 2nd edition. Oxford: Hart.

Phillips, T., R. Kerslake and J. Mayhew Jonas (2007) Fairness and Freedom: The Final Report of the Equalities Review.

Schiek, D., L. Waddington and M. Bell (eds) (2007) *Cases, materials and text on national, supranational and international non-discrimination law.* Oxford: Hart.

Singh Dhami, R., J. Squires and T. Modood (2006) Developing positive action policies: learning from the experiences of Europe and North America. DWP Research Report No 406.

Legislation and Treaties

The Council of the EC (1976) Directive 76/207/EEC of 9 February 1976 on the implementation of the principle of equal treatment for men and women as regards access to employment, vocational training and promotion, and working conditions.

—— (1979) Council Directive 79/7/EEC of 19 December 1978 on the progressive implementation of the principle of equal treatment for men and women in matters of social security.

—— (1986) Directive 86/613/EEC of 11 December 1986 on the application of the principle of equal treatment between men and women engaged in an activity, including agriculture, in a self-employed capacity, and on the protection of self-employed women during pregnancy and motherhood.

—— (1997) Directive 97/80/EC of 15 December 1997 on the burden of proof in cases of discrimination based on sex.

—— (2000a) Directive 2000/43/EC of 29 June 2000 implementing the principle of equal treatment between persons irrespective of racial or ethnic origin.

—— (2000b) Directive 2000/78/EC of 27 November 2000 establishing a general framework for equal treatment in employment and occupation.

The Council of the EC (2004) Directive 2004/113/EC of 13 December 2004 implementing the principle of equal treatment between men and women in the access to and supply of goods and services.

The European Parliament and the Council of the EU (2002) Directive 2002/73/EC of 23 September 2002 amending Council Directive 76/207/EEC on the implementation of the principle of equal treatment for men and women as regards access to employment, vocational training and promotion, and working conditions.

—— (2006) Directive 2006/54/EC of 5 July 2006 on the implementation of the principle of equal opportunities and equal treatment of men and women in matters of employment and occupation (recast).

Signatory Member States (1957) Treaty of Rome establishing the EEC, in force from 1 January 1958.

—— (1992) Treaty on European Union, signed in Maastricht, in force from 1 November 1993.

Cases

ECJ (1988) EC Commission v France [1989] 1 C.M.L.R. 408.

—— (1995) Kalanke v Freie Hansestadt Bremen Case C-450/93, [1996] I.C.R. 314.

—— (1997) Marschall v Land Nordrhein-Westfalen Case C-409/95 [2001] I.C.R. 45.

—— (1999) Abdoulaye v Regie Nationale de Usines Renault SA Case C-218/98, [2001] I.C.R. 527.

—— (2000a) Proceedings for A Review of Legality by Georg Badeck Case C-158/97 [2001] 2 C.M.L.R.79.

—— (2000b) Abrahamsson v Fogelqvist Case C-407/98 [2002] I.C.R. 932.

—— (2001) Griesmar v Ministre de l'Economie, Des Finances et de l'Industrie Case C-366/99 [2003] 3 C.M.L.R. 95.

—— (2002) Lommers v Minister van Landbouw, Natuurbeheer en Visserij Case C-476/99 [2004] 2 C.M.L.R. 1141.

—— (2004) Briheche v Ministre de l'Interieur Case C-319/03 [2005] 1 C.M.L.R. 73.

—— (2009) R (on the application of the Incorporated Trustees of the National Council on Ageing (Age Concern England) v Ss for Business, Enterprise and Regulatory Reform [2009] All E.R. (EC) 619.

EFTA Court (2003) EFTA Surveillance Authority v Norway Case E-1/02 [2003] 1 C.M.L.R. 725.

5

Ethnic and religious diversity in Britain
Where are we going?

Prakash Shah

Introduction

When the early British Race Relations legislation was being crafted, it is doubtful whether anyone really envisaged the extent to which the goalposts would be shifted so dramatically against the liberal model of equality which was encoded in them. In fact, that model is increasingly coming into question as the claims of ethnically and religiously diverse individuals and groups present themselves within and outside official legal systems. There is, however, no agreement, if there ever was, about what sort of response legal systems should be making to the fact of ethno-religious plurality, and it appears that British legal systems have become the sites of contestation about which vision of the future should be pursued. In this scenario, the anti-discrimination laws appear to be just one tool with which such battles are being waged, albeit with dissatisfaction on all sides.

It may also be necessary to excavate what we think anti-discrimination law is there for. Here we waver between speaking of 'equality' and 'diversity' in the same breath. While equality is a cherished value in the treasure trove of Western jurisprudence we ought to recall that its basis lies in the Protestant notion of the priesthood of all believers, and is not a value necessarily subscribed to universally (Benthall 2005). I therefore prefer to pin my analysis on the facts of diversity and to examine the possibilities of how we can develop a 'plurality-conscious' jurisprudence (Menski 2006) with that in mind.[1]

Meanwhile, there seems to be deep unease among legal personnel, at all levels, including academics, about plurality and the legal requirements and demands of the 'other', and being told that we are 'institutionally racist' does not go down terribly well, particularly when we are never quite sure what that is or what to do about it. While one can certainly point to examples of cases in which judges and statutory laws have tried to accommodate claims of the 'other', there is simply too much evidence of ineptitude or fussiness in handling such claims, and perhaps even resentment about how much 'we' are giving in to 'them', positions which do not make for a strong foundation if we want to move towards a deeper constitutional commitment to plurality.

Implicit in this chapter is a search for an alternative approach to legal and, in particular, judicial activism that might be better suited to the post-modern condition of ethnic plurality, however much that condition is being brought into a dialectic relationship with a post-imperial nationalism under the umbrella of which it is sought to consolidate a socially cohesive notion of 'Britishness'. These are all large questions which can only be dealt with in a much more detailed work, so I can claim at best to be inching towards such an alternative framework. Steeped as we contemporarily are in human-rights-ism, it has become tempting to argue that human rights constitute the best anchor for any movement towards an activist 'jurisprudence of difference' (Cotterrell 2003). Certainly, Sebastian Poulter (1998), the pioneer British writer in the field of ethnic diversity in law, argued that a human rights methodology might be the best way in which claims of ethnic minorities should be assessed. I am not so convinced that this is the only way to look at things, although that may well turn out to be an important hook upon which plurality-conscious lawyers and judges will wish to hang their activism.[2] Rather, my suggestion is for an activist jurisprudence concerning issues of ethnic plurality to be based firmly in an awareness of socio-legal realities, notwithstanding their ex-post juristic grounding in the semantics of human rights.

The converse of my argument is that our legal personnel, being rather conceptually ill equipped, have generally failed to harness relevant facts in litigation and other law-making processes in a plurality-conscious manner. In effect, this is a plea for legal decisions to reflect the social reality of inter-ethnic relations and how they lead to emerging conflicts and tensions requiring responses (although not necessarily resolution). This entails difficult choices, but those choices ought to be based on a wider and more explicit appreciation of social patterns about which, it appears, judges and others are not especially well informed. This may be a systemic problem of litigation generally, with legal personnel not being responsive enough to a wider range of evidentiary material. It may, in the context of general ignorance about plural Britain, also be to do with the under-use of expert evidence in pluri-ethnic contexts (Ballard 2006, 2007). This is also a plea for judicial decisions to be more explicit about the policy goals they wish to promote through the choices they have made.

Conceptual versatility

Once I was teaching courses on ethnic minorities and the law from the early 1990s, it was obvious that the dominant framework of the Race Relations Act 1976 had to be a critical component of the curriculum. In particular, the material under examination could provide an index of how inter-ethnic encounters that led to social problems were surfacing and were being handled by the official law. The early debates on the race relations legislation revealed the lack of consensus on how far minorities should be protected by law. Among the framers and promoters of the legislation was the Home Secretary, Roy Jenkins, who presented its objectives as being 'the promotion of equal opportunity, accompanied by cultural diversity in an atmosphere of mutual tolerance' (cited by Loveland 1993: 342).[3] Jenkins' vision was in stark contrast to Enoch Powell's who spoke out earlier against the Race Relations Bill of 1968:

> Here is the means of showing that the immigrant communities can organize to consolidate their members, to agitate and campaign against their fellow citizens, and to overawe and dominate the rest with the legal weapons which the ignorant and the ill-informed have provided.

Far from being a 'weapon of the weak', in Powell's view the race relations legislation carried the seeds of a mechanism to oppress Britain's native population. It is difficult to see how the legislation would have worked to promote an atmosphere of mutual tolerance if Powell and his many silent supporters had come to view it as an act of antagonism. Further, as Britain was pluralizing, it seemed evident from the framework of the legislation and, indeed, many of the judgments given under it, that the legal system was unable or unwilling to respond positively either to the country's general condition of plurality or to the web of tensions that it would be called to rule upon in individual cases.

The shadow of slavery and the history of black–white relations in the US dominated the thinking of the framers of the British race relations legislation, and legal developments in the US were to provide the model for anti-discrimination law here too. As Gregory notes (1987: 5), 'the British legislation was quite explicitly drafted on the basis of developments in American case law'. Meanwhile, as Füredi (1998) shows, British legal developments were not without a wider global context. The global challenge to colonialism, and its basis in white supremacy, had led to a concerted Western-sponsored international law-making on racial discrimination, notably in the International Convention on the Elimination of All Forms of Racial Discrimination (1965). It remains open to debate whether in Western Europe the lessons of events leading up to and during World War II have been more influential in establishing different legal approaches to questions of ethnic plurality. Thus, in 2007, when the German Presidency of the EU attempted a ban on Nazi symbols, Hindus across Europe registered a protest against the resulting outlawing of the swastika.[4] In the East Bloc meanwhile, the old questions about minority protection persisting since the League of Nations days appear to have been blanked over by the prevailing socialist emphasis on equality, but have resurfaced since the end of the Cold War. These different histories will make the job of establishing a broader EU-wide normative agreement on ethnic diversity extremely difficult. Although discrimination on grounds of race, ethnicity, national origin and religion is now covered in the so-called Race and Employment Directives, it remains to be seen how the European Court of Justice (ECJ) will interpret them.[5]

The US and the UK have meanwhile increasingly diversified in ethnic and religious terms as a result of continued large-scale immigration from a far wider set of source countries (as have virtually all current EU member states). As a result, the race-and-class structuralism that pervaded British race-relations thinking has significantly come into question (Ballard 1992), although the class factor still remains fairly influential in informing explanations of discriminatory practices. Conceiving of inter-ethnic relations is no longer constricted by the opposition of 'whites' and 'blacks', a term which once included *all* non-white ethnic minorities.[6] The earlier term 'coloured' has interestingly persisted as a feature in some judgments as a euphemism for 'non-white' people, although it does not seem to be in use more widely any longer.[7] Questioning of the term 'black' initially led to the bifurcation between African-Caribbeans and South Asians ('Asians') upon which public policy responses tended to be based, but this framework is itself now questioned and we are now not sure quite what we should make of 'super-diversity' (Shah 2008; Vertovec 2006). Meanwhile the excruciating persistence in public policy usage of the abbreviation BME (black and minority ethnic), once broken down, reveals its own conceptual confusions; Black people are separated from 'minority ethnic' people as if the former do not engage in processes of ethnic boundary making and self-consciousness as everybody else. The term might nevertheless belie the widespread assumption that indeed black people are only different in colour and otherwise (should) assimilate to the majority's value system. So, for example, a nursery for two to five year olds with largely African-Caribbean children which sought to replace an African-Caribbean employee of the same background on the basis that she would have knowledge of various aspects of African-Caribbean culture, has to jump through hoops before establishing the lawfulness of such a preference.[8] Similar assimilationist assumptions would appear to lie behind the virulent opposition to black-only schools in Britain although they seem to have proved a success in the United States.

The legal community is hardly well placed to respond to such questions. Legal academics appear to have largely kept a distance from developments in other social sciences while, with some exceptions, other social scientists have tended to keep away from addressing problems underlying legal issues. Although ethnic and religious plurality has moved to a level now extremely difficult to monitor and assess, the anti-discrimination law is itself increasingly being used in ways and by people that the framers may well not have anticipated, while its conceptual apparatus is arguably ill adapted to cope with the multi-stranded claims now being made upon it. Thus terms like religion, ethnicity and culture, assimilation, hybridity and pluralism remain under-utilized within an impoverished legal discourse. The assimilationist claims of Western 'legal technicalism' (Ehrlich 1917) and its methodological nationalism (Cotterrell 2008) are thereby allowed to undernourish the acceptance of cultural diversity that Jenkins foresaw. In fact, implied within such assimilationism, now repackaged under the label of 'cohesion', is a reading of ethnicity and religion as matters of choice underpinned by the majoritarian presupposition that one's best strategy is to minimize one's difference and not 'rock the boat'.

It remains a fact that the definition of ethnic group for the Race Relations Act 1976 continues to be applied asymmetrically. Thus while some Sikhs had been able to mount a successful campaign to have their status as an ethnic group established by the House of Lords in *Mandla*,[9] members of other communities have fared less well. Rastas in particular were unsuccessful in having their status recognized as an ethnic group in the *Dawkins* case.[10] While it is arguable that, had the legislation spelt out that religion may be part and parcel of an evaluation of ethnicity, and perhaps even a central component of it, then those seeking recognition would not have been subject to judicial nitpicking as to whether a religious group qualifies as an ethnic group also. Or perhaps our judges just don't like Rastas, and prefer loyal Sikhs? But then we get recent cases like *Watkins-Singh*[11] some 25 years after *Mandla*, with a schoolgirl having to establish her right to wear a Sikh *kara*. Was this a case of faulty legal advice or simply official bloody-mindedness?

Although religious group membership can now found a basis for discrimination claims under the Human Rights Act 1998, the EU Employment Directive, and the domestic Equality Act 2006, recent decisions reflect judicial opposition to allowing Muslim girls and women to wear distinctive clothing.[12] Each of these recent cases is accompanied by a judicial statement that the decisions do not reflect general policy. For example, Silber J's statement in the *X* case concerning a schoolgirl is illustrative:

> This judgment is fact-sensitive and it does not concern or resolve the issue of whether the wearing of the niqab should be permitted in the schools of this country. That is not a question that a court could or should be asked to resolve. Nothing that appears in this judgment seeks to resolve or to throw any light on this problem or the circumstances in which a veil should be permitted to be worn in schools or any other arena in this country. Indeed it follows that nothing in this judgment is intended to be any comment on the traditions or the requirements of the religion of Islam.[13]

However, the trend of recent case law shows that there is some kind of consistency of approach being followed by judges. This undeclared judicial policy sits uncomfortably with the findings of a recent report which shows widespread nature of discriminatory barriers faced by Muslim women, particularly if they wear distinctive clothing (Bunglawala 2008).

Early commentaries on the race relations legislation of the 1960s concentrated on the lack of effective remedies, the extent of coverage and the definition of discrimination (Lester and Bindman 1972). While the Race Relations Act 1965 legislated against discrimination in public places, the Race Relations Act 1968 extended it to include employment and housing. The Race Relations Act 1976 then extended the definition of discrimination so that acts of unlawful discrimination may be concluded not just when one has, for example, been flatly denied a job or a tenancy 'on racial grounds' (direct discrimination), but also when a lower proportion of a particular racial group is able to comply with the requirement or condition used (indirect discrimination). This latter form of discrimination was aimed at tackling institutionalized forms of exclusion that could not necessarily be put down to individual actions but, at the same time, the rules do not allow for group or class actions. Remedies were restructured to allow access to industrial tribunals (now employment tribunals) in employment cases and the county court in non-employment cases. The government-appointed Commission for Racial Equality (CRE) was placed in a supervisory role, with powers to make investigations, and allowed to either fund claims it thought were worth backing or to take legal action on its own initiative. While these developments allowed an extension of the types of claims which could be made upon service providers, employers and state agencies, the very mechanics of legal practice tended to be trusted to deliver just outcomes. Very little thought was therefore devoted to just how, when faced with factual scenarios giving rise to certain claims, the legal system might arrive at a plurality-conscious appreciation of the context.

Later incisive and critical comment on the legislation focused on its 'internal' and 'external' limits. On the one hand, the limits within legal practice were revealed by writers such as Lustgarten (1980) who wrote that the 'alien standards of the statute' would cause problems for decision-makers, particularly in employment cases, where judicial thinking had been confined within the narrow framework of contract law doctrine. Lustgarten's was effectively a pessimistic evaluation of how the legislation would work in practice given the assumptions upon which judges based their role. This evaluation identified potential problems with their ability to grasp new concepts such as indirect discrimination which implied a shift in the line drawn between privately and publicly acceptable behaviour. Ultimately, with Lustgarten, it was not a case of statute frustrating judicial activism, but a case of judicial conservatism not sitting easily with a statute imposing new duties on judges to be more active. This view of judicial inertia was borne out by others (Gregory 1987; Griffith 1997) who reflected on the developing case law under the 1976 Act.

Allott (1980), on the other hand, wrote critically about the wider effects of this sort of reformist legislation which would merely result, he felt, in discriminatory practices going 'underground' as people would cease to reveal the real reasons for their decisions. Attitudes, he feared, would remain unchanged as a result. Some British judges too have been imbued with this sort of scepticism about statutory reformism essentially drawing a limit to law's capacity to police and alter public attitudes. In an early case Lord Diplock had said:

> The arrival in this country within recent years of many immigrants from disparate and distant lands has brought a new dimension to the problem of the legal right to

discriminate against the stranger. If everyone were rational and humane – or, for that matter, Christian – no legal sanction would be needed to prevent one man being treated by his fellow men less favourably than another simply upon the ground of his colour, race or ethnic or national origins. But in the field of domestic or social intercourse differentiation in treatment of individuals is unavoidable. No one has room to invite everyone to dinner. The law cannot dictate one's choice of friends...

Thus, in discouraging the intrusion of coercion by legal process in the fields of domestic or social intercourse, the principle of effectiveness joins force with the broader principle of freedom to order one's private life as one chooses.[14]

Allott's and Diplock's may be legitimate critiques of ambitious positivism, and may also be salutary correctives to Jenkins' arguably exaggerated vision of the role of state agency. Gregory (1987: 4) for instance cited evidence of ongoing discrimination, segregation and glass ceilings in the workplace some ten years after the 1976 Act. The reproduction of such patterns of discrimination has more recently been described by Ballard and Parveen (2008) as a kind of 'low-intensity conflict' against minorities in Britain. However, such critiques should not necessarily be taken as legitimating judges' passivity in questions of considerable public importance. While advocacy of an activist judicial stance must be alive to the limits of how far state law can alter perceptions or behaviour, does it necessarily mean that judicial pronouncements ought to bear no educative role? We go on to examine what role judges have taken in such conflicts by a closer reading of some key judgments.

The lessons of litigation

There were series of early cases in which judges effectively crippled the CRE's attempts to investigate suspected discriminatory practices, deflated the 'activist' strain within that organization on the basis that it was trying to promote its own brand of political correctness, and forced it to stick closely to demanding 'fairness' criteria during investigations (Gregory 1987: 118–25; Griffith 1997: 178–9).[15] The organization had become a kind of piggy-in-the-middle and bound to be accused of failing in its statutory function to promote good relations between persons of different racial groups. Gregory (1987: 6), writing of both the CRE and the EOC, argued that after some ten years their impact had been minimal and they had 'become convenient whipping posts; frequently ignored by government, undermined by the courts and criticized by disillusioned civil rights campaigners'. Some local authorities, which had taken up the cudgels on the basis of their duty to promote good relations between persons of different racial groups against firms and sports bodies seen as breaching their commitment to the anti-apartheid movement, were also told to 'cool it'.[16] Legal activism by these public bodies, which had interpreted their statutory duties robustly, was therefore effectively limited and much of the onus of litigating under the Race Relations Act was therefore down to individuals.

While the legislation does not seek to ascribe a notion of guilt to discriminatory behaviour that is the way in which it appears to be interpreted in practice by judges. The concept of direct discrimination requires only less favourable treatment on racial grounds to be shown, and motive or intention is irrelevant. But it seems that in practice the motives or intentions of the alleged discriminator often become the central issue (Gregory 1987: 35). In indirect discrimination actions, while intention or motive is also not relevant to establishing that a requirement or condition is unlawful, for damages to be awarded an intention to discriminate must additionally be shown. While, this can act as an obvious disincentive to any claimant, it is interestingly hidden away in a latter part of the 1976 Act (s. 57(3)). Implicit here is the notion of the guilty mind, deriving from the Christian notion of culpability, and, tied to this, the fear that a defendant is being potentially branded as 'racist'.

Now we can turn to examining some cases which have arisen in education contexts. Here issues about respect for familial values, diversity and culture, ensuring non-exposure to institutional discrimination and, perhaps most centrally, the welfare of children, are evidently (though not necessarily explicitly) interspersed with all sorts of other public policy considerations and the interest positions of a variety of public and private actors. These problems are not of course unique to the education field. A recent study on Hindu law adoptions in British immigration law (Shah 2009), reveals the intense ethno-centrism and state-centrism of the British adoption model being applied to transnational adoption decisions among Hindu and Sikh families. In this plural field, consideration of how best to ensure the interests of children appears to take a back seat despite the ostensible claim of decision-makers that they are concerned to ensure that those interests are taken account of.

Much of the formative case law in the 1970s and 1980s was concerned with employment issues, and often involved the first generation of migrants experiencing problems in the workplace. While such cases of migrant generations do and will forseeably continue to come up, the education cases constitute a 'second generation' of cases, particularly from the 1990s, in which parents of children being schooled in Britain seek through their lawyers to argue for their interests.[17] These cases also demonstrate that legal arguments are often not well chosen to properly inform courts of the multi-ethnic context of the cases and that, perhaps as a result, judges are not willing to go much beyond the arguments placed before them, and are more prone to stick to the letter of the law than being interested in considering wider policy issues particularly as they affect ethnic minorities.

In *Cleveland*[18] one parent had asked to have her daughter, then five years of age, removed from a school in which the majority of the children were Asian to one where the majority were white. She wrote to the county education officer:

> My reason for this is I do not think its fair for Katrice to go through school with about four white friends and the rest Pakistan, which she does not associate with. I think the school is a very good school, but I do not think its right when she comes home singing in

Pakistan. I know they only learn three Pakistan songs but I just do not want her to learn this language.

In a later affidavit presented for judicial review proceedings, brought by the CRE against the decision of the local authority acceding to her request, she wrote:

I was simply concerned about what Katrice was being taught and the foreign language she was being taught to speak at a time in her schooling when in my view she had to learn to read, write and speak her own language first. I was also concerned that because the Asian girls did not speak good English and did not mix with the white children that Katrice was not making enough friends and that this would also be bad for her development.

The parent's concerns were informed by several considerations especially regarding exposure to different languages in a child's early education. However, this aspect of the case is not addressed at all in the ensuing litigation. The case does however illustrate the point made above about the ways in which judges have attempted to absolve defendants when, as they see it, a charge of moral guilt is implied by legal proceedings taken against their actions. Macpherson J (later to chair the Stephen Lawrence inquiry) stated in the High Court that, 'I have no reason at all to doubt that Mrs Carney has in fact no objection whatsoever to Asian people. She has lived amongst them and has always got on well with them.' Parker LJ, giving the only reasoned speech in the Court of Appeal, said that, 'Mrs Carney can leave this court as she left the court below with no racist stain upon her.' Interestingly, in absolving Katrice's mother of any blameworthy intention, Macpherson J also found it relevant that 'Katrice's father is partly African and is obviously coloured and that Katrice herself is thus of mixed race'.[19]

This case is also important for role of the CRE, which had been increasingly concerned about the effects of the Education Act 1980 and the right given therein to parents to opt for a school, which the CRE thought was leading to segregationist tendencies as a consequence of school choices. The CRE came in for intense questioning in the High Court and Court of Appeal about what was to be achieved by highlighting the express reasons given by a parent when local education authorities were obliged to act upon choices made by parents even where no reasons or false reasons were given for those choices. Consequently, both courts found that the duty to act on parental preference under the Education Act 1980 overrode any duties under the Race Relations Act.

Poulter (1990: 84) later commented on the tendency towards segregation being furthered by the Education Reform Act 1988, stating:

The 1988 Act may further encourage white parents to attempt to move their children from excellent multiracial schools...for no good educational reason at all. However, there is no reason why Asian parents should not apply to the same schools as those specially favoured by white parents if they wish to do so. In this way segregation of children by colour or culture may be avoided.

Poulter's advice was that if white parents choose to opt for white-dominated schools, there was no reason why Asian parents should not follow suit. In *Sikander Ali*[20] a parent who tried to do precisely that for his son found that he was not allocated a place at any of his three chosen schools. It was discovered that the Local Education Authority (LEA) had defined the admissions policy according to 'traditional links' which gave priority to siblings of those who were already at the schools and, in the second place, according to catchment areas which varied in size according to the extent of oversubscription. The catchment area for the preferred school tended not to cover the area of Manningham in Bradford where the family lived, a city in which a high level of segregation along ethnic lines in schools amidst profound inter-ethnic tensions has been noted.[21] It also appears that this case was being seen as a sort of test case, as some 30 Asian parents were interested in the outcome of the legal proceedings.

One of several grounds of challenge was that the policy was indirectly discriminatory in that there was a higher proportion of Asian families living in Manningham and their chances of securing a place at a preferred school were significantly lower than that of a white family living inside a school catchment area. Jowitt J held on this point that there was no indirect discrimination because even though non-Asian parents outside Manningham were far more likely to have their preference upheld than Asians living in Manningham, this was an inappropriate basis of comparison. Rather the correct approach was to compare the rate at which the preferences of Asian and non-Asian parents living in Manningham were met and, when this comparison was made, Asians in Manningham were no worse off than non-Asian residents of that area. The basis of the claim thus brought into play what the appropriate comparator should be. There is of course a great deal of lawyerly and judicial leeway as to how an argument like this can be put. It does not appear to have been considered, given that Manningham was known to be an area of heavy Asian immigrant concentration, that to effectively limit the number of school places obtainable as a matter of preference for those resident there could in itself have amounted to discrimination because it would have affected a greater number of Asian families in the overall area of the LEA's jurisdiction. Rather, the comparators chosen by counsel for the applicant and by Jowitt J effectively defeated the cogency of the indirect discrimination claim.

It was also argued on behalf of the applicant that the traditional catchment areas policy was an improper consideration and therefore unreasonable if the respondents already knew there was an immigrant community only sparsely represented in those areas. Arguably that ought to have been an additional basis of the claim for discrimination, rather than founding a claim of unreasonableness. Perhaps therefore there are also grounds for thinking that the arguments for the applicant were not as carefully crafted as they could have been. Interestingly, in deciding to reject the claim of discrimination the choice of terminology by Jowitt J is telling: 'there is no case made out here of indirect racial prejudice'. The issue of course was not whether there was 'prejudice' but indirect discrimination because a member of a particular racial group could not comply with the requirements set. Jowitt's J's use of the term 'prejudice' again shows the extent to which judges have persisted in interpreting discrimination as a matter of subjective intent or motive, and then somehow seeking to limit the moral opprobrium entailed.

Other cases also demonstrate that especially for Asian parents the issue of school places and admission continued to be problematic. In *Parveen Malik*[22] the challenge was against the decision of the Secretary of State to turn down the governors' application for grant-maintained status for an all-girls school and to approve its closure. The challenge rested on the Sex Discrimination Act (insofar as authorities were obliged not to discriminate on grounds of sex in performing their education duties). However, one of the arguments made was that it was unlawful to have approved closure in light of the fact that there was rising demand for single-sex places for girls, especially as a result of an increase in the Asian population in the area. The judgment by Rose J was largely based on the limited amount of information available to the Secretary of State at the time the decisions were made, while the existence of another all-girls school in the LEA's jurisdiction loomed large in the reasoning. The judgment devotes no space to whether the situation of Asian parents should have been specifically considered and, again, it is arguable that an additional ground of challenge based on the Race Relations Act ought to have been considered by the lawyers.[23] Could it have been a tactical decision to keep 'race' out of the equation altogether since there might be more points in alleging sex rather than racial discrimination?

Recent developments

In the last few years, there has been a spurt of legislative activity which is particularly pertinent to the issues of ethnic and religious diversity. At the same time the field has become intensely polemicized, with the many contradictions keeping tensions high. The Human Rights Act 1998 has of course been a key factor and many discrimination challenges tend to tack on, or are based squarely upon, human rights grounds. EU legislation in the form of two Directives of 2000 has also given a further fillip to Europe-wide discussions of anti-discrimination law as it affects questions of ethnic and religious diversity.[24] While the employment Directive covers discrimination on grounds of religion and belief in workplace only (perhaps reflecting European reservations about how far religion should be a protected characteristic), the UK's Equality Act 2006 now takes matters further and reflects almost the same level of statutory coverage for religion or belief as under the Race Relations Act 1976. Although it looks as though the grievances of members of religious groups, particularly Muslims, who had argued that the Race Relations Act favoured Jews and Sikhs, have now been finally mitigated, the cases cited above leave some doubt.

The Race Relations (Amendment) Act 2000 further develops the 1976 Act by closing the gap for much of the public sector, given that the 1976 Act was interpreted by judges as not applicable to public authorities generally unless specifically stated. The 2000 amendment came in the background of some hard questioning of public authorities which had been identified as failing to live up to non-discrimination standards. This was particularly raised by the Macpherson Inquiry Report (1999) which had recommended that the police and other authorities should be covered by the race relations law, a recommendation immediately accepted by the government. Crucial to the report was the Inquiry's own definition of 'institutional racism':

> The collective failure of an organisation to provide an appropriate and professional service to people because of their colour, culture or ethnic origin. It can be seen or detected in processes, attitudes and behaviour which amount to discrimination through unwitting prejudice, ignorance, thoughtlessness, and racist stereotyping which disadvantage minority ethnic people.

Indeed, the then Home Secretary, Jack Straw, was almost self-flagellistic when he stated in the House of Commons:

> In my view, any long-established, white-dominated organisation is liable to have procedures, practices and a culture that tend to exclude or to disadvantage non-white people. The police service, in that respect, is little different from other parts of the criminal justice system – or from Government Departments, including the Home Office – and many other institutions.[25]

So while the 2000 amending Act extended the 1976 Act's coverage to public authorities (partially excepting immigration and some other governmental functions), it also imposed on all such authorities the old section 71 duty to eliminate unlawful racial discrimination, to promote equality of opportunity and good relations between persons of different racial groups, and supplemented it with duties to undertake monitoring. The concepts contained within section 71 are broad, and can be linked to the formula of tolerance and diversity which Jenkins had earlier spoken of. But on their face, they do not appear to reflect the Macpherson definition of institutional racism nor its acceptance by the Home Secretary on the publication of the Inquiry's report. Thus public authorities may be none the wiser about how precisely to address the problem of inequitable, culture-blind service provision and can continue to go about their 'unwitting' ways unless challenged by coherent and plurality-conscious litigation strategists.[26] In light of the criticisms made in this chapter about the lack of a plurality-conscious perspective informing litigation tacticians and judges, it would be interesting to now study the role of the assessors who are meant to sit with county (or sheriff) court judges.[27]

Except for the Equality Act of 2006 much energy appears to have been expended legislating prior to 9/11 and 7/7. Particularly since 9/11 the atmosphere has changed dramatically and it would be difficult for a Home Secretary today to publicly make the kinds of statements which Jack Straw had made in the lead up to the 2000 amending Act. Since 9/11 'multiculturalism' has acquired many critics and national cohesion is now the order of the day. Alterity is now to be scrutinized in light of the resurgent values of the Enlightenment, even though some figures like Dr. Rowan Williams have refused to cow down to such contemporary McCarthyism. The Equality Act 2006 itself appears to perpetuate ambivalence about whether the aim of anti-discrimination laws should be to encourage respect for our differences or the kind of assimilationism which is implied in the concept of equality. It is perhaps no coincidence that the new supervisory body for anti-discrimination law is named the Commission for Equality and Human Rights. The Equality Bill introduced in April 2009 mirrors this semantic approach although its important provisions cannot be analysed here. Its potential and actual impact will need to be monitored carefully in light of the picture drawn in this chapter of the experiences so far regarding the role of law and also in light of current 'neo-assimilationist' (Castles 2008) fashions.

Notes

1. Menski (2006: 19) states: 'Since law is itself an internally plural phenomenon, a globally-focused legal theory cannot avoid taking a realistic plurality-conscious approach that respects and highlights different perspectives, never totally ignoring consideration of "the other".' Plaut (2002) found among students in the United States that those who engaged primarily in European American cultural contexts held the view that diversity among people is relatively superficial, while those who engaged in non-European American cultural contexts, or who occupied a lower social position in a mainstream context, are more likely to be aware of significant differences between themselves and others. White students supported assimilationist models of diversity, while minority students were more supportive of a model whereby the majority culture should change to accommodate minority perspectives. I am not aware of any British research of a similar nature but it would not be surprising to find parallels.

2. For judicial attempts to combine human rights with plurality conscious decision-making, see for example Munby J in *Singh v Entry Clearance Officer New Delhi* [2004] EWCA Civ 1075, esp. paras. 61–9 and Arden LJ in *Khan v Khan* [2007] EWCA Civ 399, para. 46.

3. In fact this was a slight reworking of a definition of 'integration' which Jenkins had publicized in the 1960s and, although it has subsequently become a classic definition for that term, it is debateable how much it is subscribed to in practice.

4. See 'Hindus opposing EU swastika ban', http://news.bbc.co.uk/1/hi/6269627.stm, last accessed 14 October 2009.

5. Council Directives 2000/43/EC and 2000/78/EC respectively.

6. Gregory (1987), for instance, reflecting the dominant usage in the 1980s, often employs the term 'black' in this way.

7. See Lord Templeman in *Savjani v IRC* [1981] 1 QB 458, at 468A; Macpherson J as cited in *R v Cleveland County Council and Others ex parte Commission for Racial Equality* [1993] 1 FCR 597; Latham LJ in *R v Anthony Stock* [2008] EWCA Crim 1862, para. 55.

8. *Tottenham Green Under Fives' Centre v Marshall* [1989] IRLR 147, [1989] ICR 214, EAT and (No. 2) [1991] IRLR 162, [1991] ICR 320, EAT. The relevant aspects of African-Caribbean

culture were stated to be: '(1) maintaining the cultural background link for the children of the African-Caribbean background; (2) dealing with the parents and discussing these matters with them; (3) reading and talking where necessary in dialect; (4) generally looking to their skin and health and including the plaiting of their hair.'

9. *Mandla v Dowell Lee* [1983] 1 All ER 1062 [HL], [1983] IRLR 209.
10. *Dawkins v Department of the Environment* [1993] IRLR 284. On the case law on ethnicity see, in detail, Jones and Welhengama 2000: 27–57.
11. *R (on the application of Watkins-Singh) v Governing Body of Aberdare Girls' High School* [2008] EWHC 1865 (Admin).
12. *R (on the application of Begum) v Headteacher and Governors of Denbigh High School* [2006] UKHL 15 (school girl); *R (on the application of X) v The Headteacher of Y School* [2007] EWHC 298 (Admin) (school girl); *Azmi v Kirklees Metropolitan Borough Council* [2007] IRLR 484, EAT (teacher).
13. *R (on the application of X) v The Headteacher of Y School* [2007] EWHC 298 (Admin), para. 1.
14. *Dockers' Labour Club and Institute Ltd. Appellants v Race Relations Board Respondents* [1976] A.C. 285 at 296.
15. See *CRE v Amari Plastics* [1982] 2 All ER 499, *R v CRE, ex parte Hillingdon LBC* [1982] AC 779, *CRE v Prestige Group plc* [1984] 1 WLR 335.
16. *Wheeler v Leicester CC* [1985] 2 All E.R. 151; *R. v Lewisham LBC Ex p. Shell UK* [1988] 1 All ER 938.
17. The rise in such cases may also be a function of the tendency for educational matters to become legalized and a consequent increase in litigation more generally in the field, as well as the continuing development of administrative law.
18. *R v Cleveland CC and Others ex parte CRE* [1993] 1 FCR 597.
19. Whether this is a case of 'aversive racism' can be debated. Plaut (2002: 36) describes 'aversive racism' as

    a form of prejudice that surfaces in subtle ways – not as hostility or hate but rather as discomfort, uneasiness, or fear that motivates avoidance of race rather than intentionally destructive behaviours. This form of bias can lead to a failure in acknowledging one's negative racial sentiment, and it can be rationalized by principles such as fairness and equality.

20. *R v Bradford, ex p Sikander Ali, The Times,* 21 October 1993, [1994] ELR 299, [1994] Admin. LR 589, [1995] L.G. Rev. 81.
21. For a vivid account of the Asian presence in Bradford and responses to it through writings see McLoughlin (2006), and specifically on segregation in education in Bradford see Johnston et al. (2006).
22. *R v Sect. of State for Ed., ex parte Parveen Malik* [1994] ELR 121.
23. Many parents concerned to secure single-sex education, particularly for their daughters, are often choosing denominational schools, although the schools' right to select to give preference to religious background has been, perhaps rightly, upheld by the House of Lords: *Choudhury v Bishop Challoner RC School* [1992] 3 All ER 277, [1992] 3 WLR 99, and see also Education Act 1996, s. 411(3)(b).
24. Council Directives 2000/43/EC and 2000/78/EC respectively.
25. Hansard HC, 24 February 1999, col. 391. See, further, Hill (2001: 5–6).
26. This lack of clarity has not prevented litigants from charging defendants with 'institutional racism'. See e.g. *Henry v Newham London Borough Council* [2004] All ER (D) 124 (Mar), *Commissioners of Inland Revenue and Cleave v Morgan* [2002] IRLR 776, *Rihal v London Borough of Ealing* [2004] IRLR 642 EWCA.

27. The relevant provision is section 67(4) and reads:

> In any proceedings under this Act in a designated county court or a sheriff court the judge or sheriff shall, unless with the consent of the parties he sits without assessors, be assisted by two assessors appointed from a list of persons prepared and maintained by the Secretary of State, being persons appearing to the Secretary of State to have special knowledge and experience of problems connected with relations between persons of different racial groups.

It is not clear why the role of assessors is not extended to employment tribunals. The leading case on the proper approach a court must adopt when considering the views of the assessors is *Ahmed v. University of Oxford* [2002] EWCA Civ 1907.

References

Allott, A. (1980) *The limits of law*. London: Butterworths.

Ballard, R. (1992) 'New clothes for the emperor? The conceptual nakedness of the race relations industry in Britain', *New Community*, 18(3): 481–92.

—— (2006) 'Ethnic diversity and the delivery of justice: the challenge of plurality', In P. Shah and W. F. Menski (eds), *Migration, diasporas and legal systems in Europe*. London: Routledge-Cavendish, pp. 29–56.

—— (2007) 'Common law and common sense: juries, justice and the challenge of ethnic plurality', In P. Shah (ed.), *Law and ethnic plurality: socio-legal perspectives*. Leiden: Martinus Nijhoff, pp. 69–105.

Ballard, R. and T. Parveen (2008) 'Minority professionals' experience of marginalisation and exclusion: the rules of ethnic engagement', In J. Eade, M. Barrett, C. F. and R. Race (eds), *Advancing multiculturalism, post 7/7*. Cambridge: Cambridge Scholars Press, pp. 73–96.

Benthall, J. (2005) 'Confessional cousins and the rest: the structure of Islamic toleration', *Anthropology Today*, 21(1): 16–20.

Bunglawala, Z. (2008) *Valuing family, valuing work: British Muslim women and the labour market*. London: The Young Foundation.

Castles, S. (2008) 'Migration and social transformation'. Migration Studies Unit, London School of Economics, Working Paper, No. 2008/01.

Cotterrell, R. (2003) *The politics of jurisprudence*. London: LexisNexis.

—— (2008) 'Transnational communities and the concept of law', *Ratio Juris*, 21(1): 1–18.

Ehrlich, E. (1917) 'Judicial freedom of decision: its principles and objects', In *Science of legal method*. Modern Legal Philosophy Series, Vol. 9, Boston: Boston Book Company, pp. 47–84.

Füredi, F. (1998) *The silent war: imperialism and the changing perception of race*. London: Pluto.

Gregory, J. (1987) *Sex, race and the law: legislating for equality*. London et al: Sage Publications.

Griffith, J. A. G. (1997) *The politics of the judiciary*. 5th edition. London: Fontana.

Hill, H. (2001) *Blackstone's guide to the Race Relations (Amendment) Act 2000*. Oxford: Oxford University Press.

Johnston, R., D. Wilson and S. Burgess (2006) 'Ethnic segregation and educational performance at secondary school in Bradford and Leicester.' Working Paper No. 06/142, Centre for Market and Public Organisation, University of Bristol.

Jones, R. and G. Welhengama (2000) *Ethnic minorities in English law*. Group for Ethnic Minority Studies, School of Oriental and African Studies and Stoke-on-Trent: Trentham Books.

Lester, A. and G. Bindman (1972) *Race and law*. Harmondsworth: Penguin.

Loveland, I. (1993) 'Racial segregation in state schools: the parent's right to choose?' *Journal of Law and Society*, 20(3): 341–55.

Lustgarten, L. (1980) *Legal control of racial discrimination*. London: Macmillan.

Macpherson, Sir William et al. (1999) *The Stephen Lawrence inquiry*. 4262-I. The Stationery Office.

McLoughlin, S. (2006) 'Writing a BrAsian city: 'Race', culture and religion in accounts of postcolonial Bradford', In N. Ali, V. S. Kalra and S. Sayyid (eds.), *A postcolonial people: South Asians in Britain*. London: Hurst and Co., pp. 110–40.

Menski, W. F. (2006) *Comparative law in a global context: the legal systems of Asia and Africa*. 2nd edition. Cambridge: Cambridge University Press.

Plaut, V. C. (2002) 'Cultural models of diversity in America: the pathology of difference and inclusion', In R. Shweder, M. Minow and H. R. Markus (eds), *Engaging cultural differences: the multicultural challenge in liberal democracies*. New York: Russell Sage Foundation, pp. 365–95.

Poulter, S. (1990) *Asian traditions and English law*. Stoke-on-Trent: Runnymede Trust and Trentham Books.

—— (1998) *Ethnicity, law and human rights. The English experience*. Oxford: Clarendon.

Shah, P. (2008) 'Religion in a super-diverse legal environment: thoughts on the British scene', In R. Mehdi, G. R. Woodman, E. R. Sand and H. Petersen (eds), *Religion and law in multicultural societies*. Copenhagen: DJØF Publishing, pp. 63–81.

—— (2009) 'Transnational Hindu law adoptions: recognition and treatment in Britain', *International Journal of Law in Context*, 5(2): 107–30.

Vertovec, S. (2006) 'The emergence of super-diversity in Britain', Centre on Migration, Policy and Society, Working Paper No. 25, University of Oxford: Oxford. http://www.compas.ox.ac.uk/publications/

6

Tax law as an instrument of workplace diversity

Ann Mumford

Introduction

The title of this chapter has the potential to cause concern to any scholar who cares about tax law. The tax system has some pretty important aims, and is threatened in its course by serious obstacles, not least of which is tax law itself. The legislation underpinning tax systems is lengthy and obscure. The simple and important goal of funding government can falter under the weight of political machinations. In this context, the last, additional burden that tax law needs is the promotion of diversity and protection of equality in the workplace. The acceptable role of tax, if any, in the cause of workplace diversity should be to collect a proportion of money earned by taxpayers within the paid marketplace (as distinguished from the unpaid labour which women, predominantly, perform), and these funds should then be deployed to fund programmes which train and support potential employees from different backgrounds to enter paid employment. Tax, this line of argument would conclude, strictly should not be used to change the economics of hiring employees from diverse backgrounds, or to make it either more or less profitable to promote and progress employees from historically disadvantaged groups.

Why not? The fear is that moving the employer's – indeed, the marketplace's – virtual eye from anything other than the goal to make a profit will damage the economy. Such arguments in many ways engage classic arguments against corporate social responsibility, which fear anything other than pursuit of profit and the interest of the shareholder, as ultimately damaging to the corporation itself (and by extension the wider economy). Interestingly, it is not uncommon to describe corporate social responsibility as a 'tax' against corporations in this literature (Campbell 2006), although it is important to distinguish that scholars who argue for the protection of the tax system against well-intentioned but, ultimately, potentially damaging instrumentalist objectives also may be strong advocates of a corporate social responsibility agenda for businesses. In any case, the wide and rich corporate social responsibility literature addresses the claims to advantages for shareholder (as opposed to stakeholder) primacy more than effectively, and in a way which engages tax issues, so it is not necessary to re-engage these arguments in this chapter. Additionally, this chapter does not propose to recommend tax advantages for businesses which ensure diversity within the workplace. Rather, it proposes that tax law should be viewed as an actor within the culture of the workplace diversity, and will consider the arguments for, and against, attempting to redefine its role.

This chapter will consider the various arguments for using tax law to promote diversity, and in so doing will engage literature which would appear to have particular potential for understanding the instrumentalist potential of tax law. This will include consideration of whether fiscal legislation is capable of bearing the burdens of principle, including the principle or ideal that tax law directly should support workplace diversity (Burawoy 2007, 2003). The chapter will argue that this question has particular relevance to the emergence of the 'sandwich generation', and a generation of women balancing elder care in both their own family, and perhaps in-laws as well, alongside child care, and paid labour in the workplace.

The chapter also will consider the critical tax theory movement in the US, as indicative of some of the difficulties in achieving consensus on questions of equality. Although critical race theorists who have written about tax, as well as gay and lesbian legal theorists, have been included within the category of 'critical tax theory', this chapter will confine its analysis to questions of gender. The chapter will explain that what traditionally 'liberal' tax scholars, and critical tax scholars, often may have in common is support for feminist goals. Yet the search for consensus on the role of tax in equality is less than simple. Perhaps the reason for this strong reaction to the deployment of tax in diversity and wider equality projects is, as will be suggested, that tax law in some sense has been isolated from the challenges posed to other disciplines. This need not be the case. Thus, this chapter ultimately will advance the thesis that tax serves as a useful filter for acknowledging the contributions of individuals to the workplace, and presents a forum for consideration of the value that is accorded to these contributions.

Ways of thinking about workplace diversity and tax

By suggesting that tax is an actor within the workplace, and one of many factors that may impact upon the success of diversity initiatives, this chapter is moving slightly away from the rights discourse literature, which is rich, and has contributed much to this subject. Menkel-Meadow's work, for example, emphasizes the responsibilities of the employer in achieving workplace equality (Menkel-Meadow 1989). This approach is filled with potential, not least because it declines to problematize the presence of women in the workplace. The question is not the 'problem' caused by women's difference; or, the line of enquiry that it is important not to 'penalize' women for their difference from men – but, rather the obligations of employers to their employees.

Other approaches to gender equality in the workplace have integrated diversity with the corporate social responsibility platform, specifically through the gender mainstreaming movement in EU law (Grosser and Moon 2005). Indeed, there is a growing literature acknowledging the importance of tax law to influencing corporate behavior, and the significance of this to the corporate social responsibility movement (McBarnet 2006). A theme of literature pre-dating the more modern research into corporate social responsibility is division of labour, and the importance of considering how potentially progressive initiatives may have unanticipated results. For example, do maternity leave laws address historical, gendered workplace injustice, or do they further the belief that pregnancy is exclusively women's responsibility (Williams 1984)? Additionally, what are the difficulties caused by the fact that, for single mothers in particular, it may only be financially worthwhile for them to take on jobs that are relatively well paid (Van Drenth et al. 1999)?

Some tax laws have been constructed to deal with the latter problem – in particular, earned income tax credits – in efforts that appear, in some cases, to be part of global movements. Indeed, the development of tax credits in the 1990s, in both the US and the UK, seemed to involve a strong element of transatlantic exchange. The tax initiatives were similar, but by definition their effects upon diversity were culturally specific. Thus, the 'American Dream' is predicated upon the possibility of socio-economic mobility. Is the 'UK Dream' founded upon a similar assumption? This is a complicated question, but it is clear that the importation of, for example, the estate tax debate into the UK has been accompanied by claims to rights founded in American Dream discourse – and, this has had the effect of muddling the debate (Mumford 2007).

Questions surrounding the intervention of the state into the workplace must be constructed along lines that are culturally specific. The power of the individual in relation to the state will vary between countries and jurisdictions. The power of the individual in relation to the marketplace also will vary, but the ability of individual states to control the forces of an increasingly internationalized market will be questionable, and the case for international tax cooperation – indeed, international tax instrumentalism – may be stronger. The issues are also more difficult than regulation of issues that may be described as, in a straightforward way, 'domestic'. For example, critical trust law scholarship suggests that trusts are founded on the egalitarian idea that the individual has some power in relation to the state. A manifestation of this is the fact that the individual is allowed to own property. The law of trusts allows for the intricacies of multiple ownership – indeed, of invisible ownership. A person may have an interest in the property in which his parents' reside, but this interest may not be apparent in an obvious sense. In this context, as Cotterrell argued 20 years ago, trusts law allows the individual's power to own property to become 'disembodied' (Cotterrell 1987). It is separate from the person, and – importantly, for this chapter – in addition to all of the forms it may assume and analyses to which it may be subjected, it may survive the person.

The intricacies of 'disembodied' power will not be universal; rather, they will depend upon the state in question. They will depend, for example, upon tax laws, certainly, but also upon the power which individuals possess in relation to the state. As Cotterrell argued, '[i]f the concept of property allows an ideological separation of the human actor from those characteristics or attributes which give such an actor power, the device of the trust can be seen as further distancing' (Cotterrell 1987: 83). In an examination of the link between the concept of property and trust law, Cotterrell explains that the power to own property is linked to an individual's autonomy, and the law's recognition of (to some extent) each person's right of self-determination (ibid.). The power to own property, thus, is about personal power, disembodied. This is significant because 'private power' becomes 'all but invisible' as the legal discourse focuses on things, that is, property, and not the people who own them (i.e. 83). The law of trusts is like this, Cotterrell explains, but only more so. It allows ownership by a collective – for example, by a testator's children – and thus recognizes their 'property power' while permitting them to remain 'invisible' as 'property owners' (id.).

To what extent can tax law act to empower employees in the workforce, so as to achieve more diversity and greater opportunities for equality? Typically, the idea (certainly of tax credits) is to use tax to encourage people from all background into the marketplace, and then to rely on the market to achieve a form of meritocracy, which is inherently egalitarian. Yet the reliance upon the marketplace to cure all ills, under the premise that, as long as a profit is pursued, then other prejudices will be ignored, has been less important in recent years. The rise of managerialism in the 1980s and 1990s meant that 'Adam Smith's "invisible hand" of the market was replaced by the managerial "visible hand", unconstrained by shareholders' (Dignam and Galanis 2008). The managerial visible hand might choose to pursue a diverse workforce, or other objectives within the realm of corporate social responsibility, or it might not. If the manager did choose to pursue corporate social responsibility, the fact that few tools would be available to help achieve this would become evident. In this US, affirmative action appeared to be one of the only tools available. As Thomas argued, the '...fact remains that first you must have a work force that is diverse at every level, and if you don't, you're going to need affirmative action to get from here to there' (Thomas 1990: 117).

Affirmative action in some cases proved to have something in common with tax instrumentalism; or, using tax advantages to influence economic choices of business – put simply, using tax to make it profitable for a business manager to 'do the right thing'. The element of commonality is an occasionally imprecise aim.

Diversity may be identified as an important goal for the workforce by affirmative action, and this may achieve important results, but not everyone may benefit from the sometimes blunt methods used to achieve it. (Brooks and Purdie-Vaughns 2007, 386: 'Although developing practices to increase demographic diversity is important, it is worth considering whether some groups may inadvertently benefit more than others.') Similarly, on the question of tax, business managers are accustomed to pursuing profit, and not necessarily to distinguishing between a 'real' profit, and a tax-motivated profit. If the businesses only pursue tax advantages – for example, investing in certain equipment because of the potential to write off capital allowances – then businesses will end up with a lot of disused equipment, but nobody actually will make anything with the equipment. Thus, the economy will not grow. The parallels in anti-affirmative action rhetoric, which focuses upon the damage to businesses if the 'wrong' employees are hired, are evident.

Sociological perspectives on understanding the pragmatic potential of tax

Sociology has its roots in a search beyond the limits of law, or beyond the understanding of social interaction that law offers (with its emphases on rules/limitations and actions/reactions). Thus, '... sociology was born in a sense of hostility to the law in the lawyer's sense of that term' (Pound 1943: 1). Turning to sociological literature, such as institutional sociology, offers the possibility of understanding law as an actor within a greater pattern. Law is not a dictator of action or behaviour, but an interactive element. Thus, tax law need not be relied upon to dictate, produce or cause workplace diversity. Rather, given the importance of tax law to the paid marketplace, it is a factor – whether there is fiscal legislation addressing workplace diversity, or not – in the achievement, or the absence, of a diverse workplace with equality of opportunity for employees from a wide range of backgrounds.

The institutional, sociological approach has been used to study a variety of issues within law, including, in particular, the judging process. This theoretical construct has been relied upon to determine whether it is possible to for judges to decide cases according to a set of agreed principles – or, must the process be dismissed as endlessly interactive and reactive, with little predictability (King 2008: 409). This literature would appear to have particular potential for understanding the instrumentalist potential of tax law, and whether fiscal legislation is capable of bearing the burdens of principle: for example, the principle that tax law directly should support workplace diversity. Are legislators capable of agreeing as to what workplace diversity means? If so, would legislators then be able to agree as to how these principles should be brought into the taxing process? These are difficult questions, which would have to be addressed even before the issue of whether taxing to achieve diversity would ever be effective.

Institutional theory can be relied upon for other purposes; indeed, it can assist understanding of law in action, and the limitations of law, in a variety of ways, as it may '...help to explain how one can admit the limitations of the judicial process, while still having faith in it as a way of promoting it as a mechanism for accountability' (ibid.). In recent times, roughly four categories of sociology have been identified: professional, critical, policy and public (Burawoy 2007). The latter category, public sociology, is perhaps most useful to this chapter, as it considers the possibility of sociology being used for public good, and specifically for the purpose of improving the lives of groups of people. This bold move from theory, to action, is not completely unknown in socio-legal literature; for example, Rawls' benchmarks for social justice have been pursued in concrete, quantifiable ways (Keeley 1978; Nussbaum 2000; Rawls 1980). The sociological project itself – which has been described as 'more like an anarcho-syndicalist profession with decentralized participation in a system of democratic councils' – starts at a process of understanding interaction, yet through 'participation', however 'decentralized' (Burawoy 2003: 1603). This participation may be distinguished from mere observation or reporting, and carries with it the hope of achieving pragmatic outcomes.

Indeed, what might be described as the modern sociological project was born with trade unions – the ultimate form of pragmatism, and law in action – and the expansion of educational opportunities. As Burawoy explained, '[t]he classical sociology of Weber, Durkheim, Simmel and Pareto arose with the expansion of trade unions, political parties, mass education, voluntary associations at the end of the nineteenth century, just as U.S. sociology was born amidst reform and religious organizations' (2003). The ideas that were introduced by these scholars have developed in ways that develop the original, but also in ways that might better be described as a tribute to the original author. For example, the scholarship interpreting Weber's contribution to sociology has flourished, in many ways in tribute to its richness, and its sheer provocativeness. Has this literature taken on a life of its own, or does it bear resemblance to the original? Perhaps Weber's two most important concepts are domination and legitimation, themes with relevance for workplace equality (Weber 1981: Weber explained that '...domination (*Herrschaft*) does not mean that a stronger elemental force somehow asserts itself; rather, it means that the action of those giving orders is related in meaning to those obeying, and vice versa, in such a way that both *can* ordinarily count on the realization of the expectations toward which they have oriented their action'). Weber treated the process of legitimation seriously, even empirically (Wolin 1981). What is significant for this chapter is the possibility of deploying the legitimation process on expectations of diversity. Put differently, what do we expect a workplace to look like, and what do we expect from it? Additionally, what do we expect a worker's obligations, or daily tasks, to include?

The question has particular relevance to the emergence of the 'sandwich generation', and a generation of women balancing elder care in both their own family, and perhaps in-laws as well, alongside child care, and paid labour in the workplace

(Nichols and Junk 1997; Remennick 1999; Spillman and Pezzin 2000). This example is presented here, to ground the discussion of sociological perspectives on pragmatism. Who may be helped by tax law? Enter a new generation of women labourers, the children of the baby boomer generation, who have presented a challenge to what was understood to be a pre-existing path of development in the relationship between women and work. The embodiment of feminist objectives by governments largely has focused on moving women away from unpaid labour in the home, into paid labour in the marketplace. The idea was that this movement would be self-propelling, for as mothers and housewives left unpaid labour behind, they would need to hire others to perform these tasks. The tax system in both the US and the UK has been used to encourage this movement; and, where possible (and in efforts not always as easy, on economic terms, as it might first appear to be) to make it financially worthwhile for women to exchange unpaid labour in the home for paid employment.

The emergence of the sandwich generation was the unexpected challenge to this movement. Just as, for example, earned income tax credits encouraged this movement into the marketplace on both sides of the Atlantic, an ageing population meant that women's unpaid labour was increased in unexpected ways. On the question of taxing the sandwich generation, the intersection of flexibility, gender essentialism and money within the forum of the 'multiple care giving woman' supports a multiplicity of discourses. What is perhaps most important is the unexpected nature of elder care. The obligations of child care are well known, and in a sense governments had generations to develop the idea of earned income tax credits. The long-living baby boomer generation was less expected – and, when unexpected, unpaid labour emerges, women historically jump to the task. This is the product of the legitimation process. Unpaid work, which exists for all people, is viewed as primarily the obligation of women. Even with the best government programmes possible in place – the best tax initiatives possible – if unexpected, unpaid labour emerges within a family unit, the task is overwhelmingly likely to be performed by women. Put simply, the principle that women may have to work more, and receive less pay, underpins the market economy.

Discourses of tax, gender and expectations and the implications for taxing workers equally

Given the strong connection between women and work for which they are not paid, both the marketplace and the tax system appeared destined not to know how to deal with them. For example, one solution to the problem of unpaid labour might be for husbands to transfer to their wives money which the husband has earned, and for the wives then to be taxed at the husband's lower rate. This might be described as a make-shift acknowledgment by the husband of the unpaid labour which the wife has performed to enable the husband to be in a position to earn. In fact, the law on both sides of the Atlantic would classify this behaviour as tax avoidance (presuming there is full disclosure – at worst, it could be tax evasion). Of course, it is possible for the husband explicitly to pay his wife for these activities, but the market and tax law are ill-equipped to deal with such explicit commodification of the activities of the family – unless, of course, someone outside of the family is hired to perform this work. Tax, work and the classic tax categorization of 'connected persons' do not mix well.

This is one of the reasons underpinning the presumption that the potential for tax avoidance is perhaps higher in a family business, than in a business without the support of family participation. For example, it may be presumed that there is a potential within a family business to exaggerate the extent of the participation of one of the members, simply to take advantage of the others' marginal rates. Similarly, if the business is incorporated, then it may be tempting to allocate shares within a small company to family members; again, for tax purposes. If the family members are not participating significantly in the operation of the business, it could be alleged that the business in economic reality consists simply of a sole trader, who is employing family relationships in an effort to lower his tax obligations. These allegations raise potentially interesting and difficult questions about the interaction between families, tax and work. They also, however, underscore the difficulties of dealing with expectations concerning women within the marketplace. If women were not so intimately connected with the expectations that they will perform unpaid labour, then taxing them within the context of the family business would not be so problematic.

The public discourse on this question, in both the UK and the US, appears to proceed in two, thoroughly separate trajectories, with the twain seldom meeting. Essentially, the battleground, perhaps a refashioning of 1970s feminist debate, involves class and gender. On the one hand, tax avoiders – for this is how, in the UK, Her Majesty's Revenue and Customs construe families who shift a husband's higher earnings into his wife's (almost, statistically, inevitably, because of her gender) lower bracket, through asset transfer – impact the availability of funding for programmes for the poor (who, largely, will comprise women and their children). On the other hand, it is, simply, unjustifiable, for any reasons perhaps other than the tax avoidance as identified by the Revenue, for a wife's income to be lumped with that of her husband, simply because of the fact of her marriage. This clash invokes the debates of 1970s, feminist Marxism, with its inherent rebellion against Marx's suggestion that gender is (just, another) class (*see, inter alia*, Anthias and Yuval-Davis 1983; Gorelick 1991; Hennessy and Ingraham 1997; Scott 1986). Since the 1980s, what has been described as a new, 'materialist' feminism has addressed many of these issues (Hennessy 1993; Jackson 2001; Vogel 1995).

It has not, however, served to provide a common forum for discussion among tax scholars. The critical tax theory movement in the US perhaps demonstrates the difficulty of this. (Not just feminist, but critical race theorists who have written about tax, as well as gay and lesbian legal theorists, have been included within the category of 'critical tax theory'. [Moran and Whitford 1996]) What 'traditional, liberal' tax scholars, and critical tax scholars, often may have in common is support for feminist goals. This is where consensus ends. The issue may be described by the project: is the project the desire to create a perfect tax solution to the problem of women's economic inequality to men, as supported by their lack of representation and equal pay within the workplace? Or, is the project an effort to demonstrate that the tax system is merely representative of a widely unequal market economy, in need of fundamental restructuring? If one agrees with the latter project, then supporters of the former may believe that 'restructurists' detract time and attention away from important, and immediate, goals. There can be surprise when legal theorists start at a common point, but disagree fundamentally about the ways to achieve their objectives (Zelenak 1997: 1527–43).

The surprise can turn the discussion away from that of best methods, and back to the issue of whether a common starting point indeed existed in the first place. Thus, proposals which assist one group of women, but may disadvantage another, may be dismissed as not being part of the feminist 'project' (ibid., 1543–9). Similarly, tax provisions may defeat allegations of sexism if any woman may be seen to have actually benefited from it. ('Gender/race misunderstanding is not only an independent factor, but it also can encourage careless reading [due to the trivialization factor noted previously] as well as influence a person's ultimate preferences and opinions." Ibid., 1611, n.11.) Scholars who perhaps understood each other, no longer seem to; although such misunderstandings may extend to techniques in themselves, as they may stem from the objective of 'trivializing', not an argument, but a perspective (Kornhauser 1997).

Perhaps the reason for this strong reaction to the deployment of tax in diversity and wider equality projects is, as has been suggested, that tax law in particular has been isolated from the challenges posed to other disciplines; that 'tax professors often don't talk to non-tax folks, and the typical law faculty has only a couple of tax teachers' (Jensen 1997, writing of the US). Thus, it made sense that writers would ask why 'critical tax theory', that is, approaches to tax law embracing 'outsider' theory, would 'spread' to a traditionally insulated area of 'liberal' scholarship (Zelenak 1997; and Frug 1983, 1332). It also invokes the wider question of the fate within cultural feminism of liberal ideology, which may be addressed not as a perspective or view of law, but through Bourdieu's theory of ideology as a compilation of actions, thoughts, and a 'structure of feelings' (Skeggs 2004).

Put simply, this is the product of what has been described as cultural feminism, which largely addressed the filters through which objectives, such as diversity, as perceived. A critique of this approach might involve the dismissal that such a textual reading of history amounts to nothing more than a 'decorative sociology', advocating an overly literal reading of cultural history *à la* Bourdieu (Rojek and Turner

2000). Sociological, cultural studies offers an unparalleled platform for investigation of taxation law and practice, especially given the importance afforded to it in the resurgence of fiscal sociology (McLennan 2006). What it does not offer, however, is a suggestion of 'ways around' the lack of progress that has resulted, or, indeed, what to do next.

Filters, diversity and tax

The image of 'filters' has a strong hold on our collective socio-legal consciousness. 'Filters' abound in critical and cultural theory. Mahoney identified the importance of the 'double filter of the senators and the media' to the working public, who were not home to watch the televised hearings, for their perception of the Anita Hill[1] hearings (Mahoney 1991: 1293). For the audience who were away from their televisions from nine to five, the role of the news programmes, and their task in choosing which aspects of the hearings to present (which Mahoney notes significantly did not include Hill's lengthy testimony as to how much she enjoyed her job, and enjoyed working in the law), (ibid.) were important. Television may be the most significant, modern, figurative and literal, filter of cultural consciousness, but in this sense it has only inherited its role from the cinema. Filters have always existed, and in many ways the most significant filter in Mahoney's research is not television, but the fact that some viewers were at work, and other viewers were not.

This adds a new layer to the arguments within this chapter; namely, that whether or not women work within the marketplace affects how they view the world, and, indeed, the definition of terms such as equality, or the meaning of tax laws. While it is widely acknowledged that the gap between popular understanding of tax policy, and the legislation enacting it, is often wide, it is less often mentioned that whether or not one works in the marketplace can affect whether or not one understands tax. Although the family is an uncertain locus of equality-based analyses, generally, it would appear to have the potential to contribute as well to a woman's perception of what it is to be 'equal', or, what 'diversity' means. One of the more moving references in feminist legal literature is Hirshman's line at the end of an essay, '... to say nothing of those poor benighted souls around 1920 who only wanted to vote' (Hirshman 1991: 1012). The Anita Hill hearings, and their now dated impact, are but one example of the historic nature of the dream of consensus in gender equality. Looking backwards, both to the hearings and to the unity surrounding the campaign for women's suffrage, however, is instructive, especially if it serves to emphasize what has not changed, in a sea of change (Goodrich 1998: 185).

Taxation can be described as a linking concept, across historical divides, although the '[t]he success and intensity of the taxation metaphor as a bridging device may be based on a general perception of taxation as negative' (Jones 1998: 685–6). As Jones has explained,

> [t]he degree of reaction against taxation may have some interesting implications for how one reads taxation metaphors. While the small tradition of good words for taxation has been noted, perceptions of taxation are often negative. (ibid.)

A reason for these negative perceptions may be the disconnect between the obligation to pay tax, and a broader, moral context (Honoré 1993: 5). Honore submits that the obligation to pay tax is 'incomplete, or, if one prefers, inchoate, apart from law' (ibid.). This is due to the fact that although a society may agree that taxes are necessary for the 'cooperative', this agreement is meaningless without consensus on amount, or rate (id.). As Honore explains, '[a]n obligation to pay an indeterminate sum is not an effective obligation; it requires only a disposition, not an action' (id.).

There is not even agreement, in either the UK or the US, on the concept of a generally enforced basic income. Indeed, '[c]onsidering the potential a basic income has for promoting gender justice', as McKay and Vanevery have observed, 'the existing literature is disappointingly lacking in rigorous feminist analysis' (McKay and Vanevery 2002: 271). They suggest that a feminist analysis of the concept of basic income would begin with the acknowledgment that the traditional social security or benefits systems tend to benefit men more than women (ibid.). Thus, tax would be considered as just one element in a wider picture of economic equality. With this observation, the chapter has returned to the observation that tax is just a factor, or an element, in the interaction between equality and the workplace. It is not a solution. As a filter for identifying the problems in the relationship between women and the marketplace, however, it is enormously effective.

Conclusion

There should be no need for tax law to demonstrate its social value, in particular in analyses that engage questions of tax and gender equity. Its merit should more or less be a given. As tax law is important, and thus deserving of forms of protection, then is it a question of keeping policy out of tax legislation? If so, why is this a difficult question?

Sociology has its roots in a search beyond the limits of law, or beyond the understanding of social interaction that law offers (with its emphases on rules/limitations, and actions/reactions). Turning to sociological literature, such as institutional sociology, offers the possibility of understanding law as an actor within a greater pattern. Given the importance of tax law to the paid marketplace, it becomes a factor – whether there is fiscal legislation addressing workplace diversity, or not – in the achievement, or the absence, of a diverse workplace with equality of opportunity for employees from a wide range of backgrounds.

This chapter has analysed whether affirmative action in some cases proved to have something in common with tax instrumentalism; or, using tax advantages to influence economic choices of business – put simply, using tax to make it profitable for a business manager to 'do the right thing'. Additionally, it considered, on the question of tax, the relative importance of the fact that business managers are accustomed to pursuing profit, and not necessarily to distinguishing between a 'real' profit, and a tax motivated profit. These questions, briefly addressed, were necessary for analysis of the success of governments largely to focus on moving women away from unpaid labour in the home, into paid labour in the marketplace. Yet, just as earned income tax credits encouraged this movement into the marketplace on both sides of the Atlantic, an ageing population meant that women's unpaid labour was increased in an unexpected way.

On the question of taxing the sandwich generation, the intersection of flexibility, gender essentialism and money within the forum of the 'multiple care giving woman' supports a multiplicity of discourses, many of which are continuing to be developed, or to unfold. This compares to the obligations of child care, which by contrast are well known. Yes, the long-living baby boomer generation was less expected – and, when unexpected, unpaid labour emerges, this chapter has suggested, women historically jump to the task. There is significance in this issue beyond women, however, and with relevance for a wider, workplace diversity. Unpaid work exists for all people. The question is how the contributions of individuals are recognized. Tax may assist in this process.

Note

1. Currently professor of social policy, law and women's studies at Brandeis University. She testified at Clarence Thomas' 1991 Supreme Court confirmation hearings that Thomas had sexually harassed her in the workplace. Available at: http://en.wikipedia.org/wiki/Anita_Hill.

References

Anthias, F. and N. Yuval-Davis (1983) 'Contextualizing feminism: gender, ethnic and class divisions', *Feminist Review,* 15: 62–75.

Burawoy, M. (2003) 'Public sociologies: contradictions, dilemmas, and possibilities', *Social Forces,* 82: 1603–18.

—— (2007) For public sociology. *2007. Public sociology: fifteen eminent sociologists debate politics and the profession in the twenty-first century,* Berkeley: UCLA, 23–65.

Campbell, J. L.(2006) Institutional analysis and the paradox of corporate social responsibility', *American Behavioral Scientist,* 925–938.

Cotterrell, R. (1987) 'Power, property and the law of trusts: a partial agenda for critical legal scholarship', *Journal of Law and Society,* 14(1): 77–90.

Dignam, A. and M. (2008) Galanis 'Corporate governance and the importance of macroeconomic context', *Oxford Journal of Legal Studies*, 28(2): 201–43.

Frug, G. (1983) 'Ideology of Bureaucracy in American Law', *Harvard Law Review*, 97(6): 1276–388.

Goodrich, P. (1998) 'Laws of love: literature, history and the governance of kissing', *The New York University Review of Law & Social Change*, 24: 183–231.

Gorelick, S. (1991) 'Contradictions of feminist methodology', *Gender and Society*, 5(4): 459–77.

Grosser, K. and J. Moon (2005) 'Gender mainstreaming and corporate social responsibility: reporting workplace issues', *Journal of Business Ethics*, 62(4): 327–40.

Hennesy, R. (1993) Materialist *feminism and the politics of discourse*. NewYork: Routledge.

Hennesy, R. and C. Ingraham (1997) *Materialist feminism: a reader in class, difference, and women's lives*. London: Routledge.

Hirshman, L. (1991) Book of A. *Texas Law Review*, 70: 971.

Honore, T. (1993) 'The dependence of morality on law', *Oxford Journal of Legal Studies*, 13(1): 1–17.

Jackson, S. (2001) 'Why a materialist feminism is (Still) possible – and necessary', *Women's Studies International Forum*, 24(3–4): 283–93.

Jensen, E. (1997) 'Critical theory and the loneliness of the Tax Prof', *North Carolina Law Review*, 76: 1753–76.

Jones, C. (1998) 'Mapping tax narratives', *Tulane Law Review*, 73: 653–98.

Keeley, M. (1978) 'A social-justice approach to organizational evaluation', *Administrative Science Quarterly*, 23(2): 272–92.

King, J. (2008) 'Institutional approaches to judicial restraint', *Oxford Journal of Legal Studies*, 28(3): 409–41.

Kornhauser, M. (1997) 'Through the looking glass with Alice and Larry: the of scholarship', *North Carolina Law Review*, 76: 1609–28.

Mahoney, M. (1991) 'Exit: power and the idea of leaving in love, work, and the confirmation hearings', *South Carolina Law Review*, 65: 1283–320.

McBarnet, D. (2006) 'After Enron will "Whiter than White Collar Crime" still Wash?', *British Journal of Criminology*, 46(6): 1091–109.

McKay, A. and J. O. Vanevery (2002) 'Gender, family, and income maintenance: a feminist case for citizens basic income', *Social Politics: International Studies in Gender, State & Society*, 7(2): 266–84.

McLennan, G. (2006) *Sociological cultural studies*. Basingstoke: Palgrave.

Menkel-Meadow, C. (1989) 'Exploring a research agenda of the feminization of the legal profession: theories of gender and social change', *Law & Social Inquiry*, 14(2): 289–319.

Moran, B. and W. Whitford (1996) 'Black critique of the internal revenue code', A. *Wisconsin Law Review*, 751–820.

Mumford, Ann (2007) Inheritance in socio-political contest', *Journal of Law and Society*, 34(4): 567–93.

Nichols, L. and V. Junk (1997) 'The sandwich generation: dependency, proximity, and task assistance needs of parents', *Journal of Family and Economic Issues*, 18(3): 299–326.

Nussbaum, M. (2000) 'Women s capabilities and social justice', *Journal of Human Development*, 1(2): 219–47.

Pound, R. (1943) 'Sociology of law and sociological jurisprudence', *University of Toronto Law Journal*, 5(1): 1–20.

Purdie-Vaughns, V. and R. Brooks (2007) 'The supermodular architecture of inclusion', *Harvard Review of Law and Gender*, 30: 379–87.

Rawls, J. (1980) 'Kantian constructivism in moral theory', *The Journal of Philosophy*, 77(9): 515–72.

Remennick, L. (1999) 'Women of the "sandwich" generation and multiple roles: the case of Russian immigrants of the 1990s in Israel', *Sex Roles*, 40(5): 347–78.

Rojek, C. and B. Turner (2000) 'Decorative sociology: towards a critique of the cultural turn', *The Sociological Review*, 48(4): 629–48.

Scott, J. W. (1986) 'Gender: a useful category of historical analysis', *The American Historical Review*, 91(5): 1053–1075.

Skeggs, B. (2004) 'Exchange value and affect, Bourdieu and the self', *Feminism after Bourdieu*, L. Adking and B. Skeggs (eds), Oxford: Blackwell, 75–95.

Spillman, B. and L. Pezzin (2000) 'Potential and active family caregivers: changing networks and the "Sandwich Generation"', *Milbank Quarterly*, 78(3): 347–74.

Thomas, R. (1990) 'From affirmative action to affirming diversity', *Harvard Business Review*, 68(2): 107–17.

Van Drenth, A., T. Knijn and J. Lewis (1999) 'Sources of income for lone mother families: policy changes in Britain and the Netherlands and the experiences of divorced women', *Journal of Social Policy*, 28: 619–41.

Vogel, L. (1995) *Woman questions: essays for a materialist feminism*. London: Routledge.

Weber, M. (1981) 'Some categories of interpretive sociology', *Sociological Quarterly*, 22: 151–80.

Williams, W. (1984) 'Equality's riddle: pregnancy and the equal treatment/special treatment debate', *New York University Review of Law & Social Change*, 13: 325–80.

Wolin, S. (1981) 'Max Weber: legitimation, method, and the politics of theory', *Political Theory*, 9(3): 401–24.

Zelenak, L. (1997) 'Taking critical tax theory seriously', *North Carolina Law Review*, 76: 1521–80.

7
Prosecuting disability hate crime

Peter Alldridge

Introduction

This chapter will deal with the confluence of two relatively recent legal phenomena. One is the development of disability discrimination law in general, and the imposition in the public sector of the positive duty to promote equality in particular. The other is the development of a body of criminal law dealing with 'hate crimes'. Some of these provisions deal with the definition of crimes and some with putting in place provision for imposition of higher sentences. A hate crime is 'Any incident, which constitutes a criminal offence, which is perceived by the victim or any other person as being motivated by prejudice and hate' (Association of Chief Police Officers 2005).

> Hate crime legislation must be seen as an important part of ongoing process of the identifying and articulating the values, sensibilities and ground rules of vibrant, multicultural societies, including the public recognition and affirmation of the right to be different. (Jacobs 2002)

Legal definitions and the social model of disability

The social model of disability holds that it is the societal response, and not the impairment itself, that is the problem. It distinguishes clearly between the medical condition (if there is one), which it calls the 'impairment' and the societal response, which it calls the disability. A person who requires a hearing loop is disabled by its absence, a person with a visual impairment is disabled by absence of tactile signage,

107

a wheelchair user is disabled by buildings or transport that do not afford step-free access and so on. If the societal reaction can be changed (e.g. by the provision of ramps) then the disability (not being able to get the wheelchair up the steps) goes away. The social model of disability is a social constructivist thesis which has been both an enormously powerful tool in the instantiation of Disability Studies as an academic discipline and in the generation of political pressure for the rights of people with disabilities (Barnes et al. 1999; Priestley 1998).

This does not mean that impairments are not themselves unpleasant. Those whose physical manifestation involves pain are perhaps the most obvious that are. Nor does it mean we should celebrate disability as we might celebrate other aspects of diversity. Impairments which involve the inability to do something one would like to do are obvious examples. It might mean, as Tom Shakespeare has put it, that being disabled is more like being poor (as opposed to rich) than it is like being a member of a particular disadvantaged race, or having a particular gender, age or sexuality.

When it comes to legal definitions, however, in all the equality and diversity strands there is argument as to the precise contours of the group in question and a tension in setting definitions between essentialism and social construction. The fact that the social model of disability underpins much of the political move for the rights of people with disabilities does not mean, therefore that a constructivist definition of disability will or need be chosen, or will have much value in a legal context. It may very well be that a legal definition that says, for example, that someone suffering from cancer is disabled, is quite justifiable. Nor, in the legal context, need there be one definition of disability. It may very well be, as we shall see, that something is to be said for different legal definitions of disability for the purposes of discrimination and hate crime. The distinction between essentialism and constructivism nonetheless throws up two cases to which any definition of the group for the purposes of discrimination law in general and hate crime in particular must address. They are the case where the disability is not known and the case of mistaken belief that there is a disability. To these the chapter will return.

Disability equality schemes

Compared to race and gender, disability was late to arrive on the equality and diversity agenda. There had been various efforts to treat disability as giving rise to differential treatment, in particular the quota rules on employment and various benefits, but disability was not really treated as giving rise to anything that could be identified as a strand within the legal discourse of equal opportunities in the UK with the enactment of the Disability Discrimination Act 1995, which first conferred (limited) legal rights not to be the victim of discrimination on the basis of disability. The 2005 Act went significantly further, for the first time fully embracing the 'social model' of disability and imposing duties upon public sector bodies to be proactive in promoting the equality of people with disabilities. The legislation has been a qualified success.

The position of people with disabilities has now been granted equivalent status to the other strands in equality and diversity law. The abolition of the Disability Rights Commission and the integration of its functions within the Equality and Human Rights Commission is a clear, if controversial manifestation of that assimilation. Disability equality now informs international movements for equality. The United Nations' Convention on the Rights of Persons with Disabilities and its Optional Protocol came into force on 3 May 2008. Among other rights, the Convention confers upon disabled people the right to be free from exploitation, violence and abuse (Article 16) and the right to be free from torture, inhuman or degrading treatment or punishment (Article 3). International agreements are required to standardize requirements for assistance to air passengers.

Under the Disability Discrimination Act 1995 as amended by the 2005 Act, one of the critical means by which implementation of the general equality duty is effected is by the imposition of a duty upon public bodies to publish and operate of a Disability Equality Scheme (Disability Discrimination Act 1995 (section 49A(1) and Disability Discrimination (Public Authorities) (Statutory Duties) Regulations 2005). All public bodies governed by the Act had to have such schemes in place by November 2006. The scheme was to include a statement of how disabled people have been involved in developing it, an action plan that includes practical ways in which improvements will be made, and information about the arrangements in place for gathering information about how the public sector organization has done in meeting its targets on disability equality. All public service providers have an explicit duty to 'eliminate harassment of disabled people', and this applies in respect of employees, clients and any other groups with whom they might reasonably foreseeably interact. Every year a report must be produced on the operation of the scheme. It should contain a summary of the steps the organization has taken to fulfill the duty, the results of the information-gathering exercise, and how the information has been used. This sounds, and can be, tedious, but it is the constraints imposed by the requirement of maintenance of records and the publication of the report that forces minds actually be applied to the questions in point. It is too early to have clear evidence of the efficacy of the operation of the schemes across a broad range of public sector activities, but while anecdote suggests a patchy rate of compliance and review, the use of targets and milestones is our best hope.

Disability and crime

Crime against people with disabilities is a microcosm of the treatment of disabled people more generally, in the workplace and elsewhere. People with disabilities are vulnerable to crime. Some crimes are more easily committed against people with certain disabilities than against their able-bodied counterparts. Some crimes are committed against people with disabilities where, historically, the governing assumption seems to have been either that it 'doesn't count' at all or 'doesn't count as much as it would were the victim not disabled' (Quarmby 2008). Notable among those are many instances of homicides of people with disabilities that might today be regarded more seriously (Scope 2008: 9). Leaving aside the numbers of people with disabilities killed in the Holocaust, the fact that somebody is thought annoying, or thought to have a worthless life (Shakespeare 1994), or thought to be an impediment to the wishes of others to lead different lives, has from time to time been regarded as a mitigating factor on a charge of killing of a person with a disability.

It is a reasonable assumption that people with disabilities are disproportionately, compared to the population as a whole, victims of crime. It is, however, difficult to generate reliable data on crime against disabled people because there will always be dangers of underreporting (OPM 2009: 51 et seq). Disability hate crime is often hidden. Disabled people face particular barriers when reporting hate crime and getting action taken. There will be offences that the disabled person does not recognize to be an offence (perhaps through learning difficulties). Disabled victims are commonly advised to ignore the perpetrators of offences against them (OPM 2009: 44), and when they do not act upon the advice they are frequently ignored or misclassified. Nonetheless there is now significant evidence that people with disabilities are disproportionately victims of crime. In Living in Fear, 90 per cent of people with learning difficulties reported harassment including physical attacks (Mencap 1999). One quarter of all disabled people say they have experienced hate crime or harassment (Cabinet Office 2007). Properly taking account of abuse in the home might raise that figure (Mason 2005).

There are a number of reasons for the disproportionality in victimization of people with disabilities, and they vary according to the type of offence and the type of disability in point. The causes of crime against people with disabilities might include active dislike of that person, or perception of threat expressed through hostility, or the actual or perceived vulnerability of the disabled person, or the fact that perpetrators think they can get away with the offence, or issues of control or unequal power structures (OPM 2009: 31).

Another distinction which is of importance throughout the literature of disability and which bears here is that between visible and invisible disabilities. In the case of victims of crime who are hitherto unknown to the criminal, the invisible disability will not usually give rise to hate crimes. There may, however, be cases where the attack is made against someone presumed to have HIV because s/he is presumed to be gay. The kinds of hate crime that may be related to invisible disability will be those where the victim is known to the criminal, for example those associated with domestic abuse or abuse by the staff of hospitals or homes. Of the cases reported to the Metropolitan Police it does not appear that there are many of invisible disability (Metropolitan Police 2008). It is important that these cases be not excluded.

How does this disproportionality affect the way in which police, prosecutors and courts should view such offences? It may be argued that crimes committed against vulnerable people are more serious (in the senses of generating a stronger claim to policing and prosecution, and perhaps, heavier penalties), because of the vulnerability of the victim, or because the perpetrators have seen the victim, on account of his/her impairment, as worth less than themselves or than other human beings or because the offences appears wholly or partly motivated by prejudice and hostility towards people with disabilities. Alternatively, it might be responded that offenders will commit offences for some reason or other and there is little reason to privilege an attack on someone, for example, because they are disabled and the attacker hates disabled people over an attack because they support Arsenal, or some other identifier. This chapter adopts the former position.

There always have been non-specific laws in place which are in principle adequate to deal with violence against people with disabilities (Bridges 2001). What has from time to time been lacking is enforcement will. Only recently has the idea been given recognition in English criminal law, which has traditionally had a (problematic) commitment to the irrelevance of motive (Horder 2000), that the particular status of the victim might generate a reason for differential treatment in the courts. This chapter will deal with a narrower group of crimes against people with disabilities – those that have come to be called 'hate-crimes'. In recent years a 'fashion' (Dixon and Gadd 2006: 312) has arisen for making express legislative provision for hate crime (and see Woods [2008] for problems associated with the use of the word 'hate' in this context).

The criminal law may give formal recognition to the wrong done in hate crime in two further ways. They are:

(i) The introduction of specific crimes criminalizing behaviour which engenders what is usually called 'hatred'. 'Incitement to hatred' crimes are clear examples; and

(ii) Provisions that enable higher sentences to be imposed in respect of offences that embody particular attitudes.

So far as concerns the first, most societies most of the time can and should put up with a good deal of free speech, including speech which incites hatred against particular groups. There has been a crime of incitement to racial hatred since 1965 (Race Relations Act 1965). This was amended in 1986 (Public Order Act 1986) and new provisions were added dealing with religious hatred (Racial and Religious Hatred Act 2007). A crime of incitement to hatred in respect of sexual preference was put in place recently (Criminal Justice and Immigration Act 2008) but attempts to amend it so as to deal also with disability failed (Scope 2009: 9). This chapter will leave more general arguments about the legitimacy and justifiability of hate crime legislation side (see e.g. Hurd 2001; Hurd and Moore 2003; Jacobs et al. 1996). The second approach – express provision for aggravated sentencing – will form the focus of this chapter.

The 'hate' aspect of the crime may, then, be treated as a matter of aggravation speaking to sentence. In this regard, as in some others, disability law follows the law on race and ethnic minorities. What is the justification for giving especial legal recognition to motive in a case like this? There are two major reasons. In retributive terms we might find it particularly grievous to act from the more reprehensible motive, and we might consider that hatred of people with disabilities is more reprehensible than, for example, greed. In consequentialist terms we might be more concerned about what might happen if such behaviour were thought to be tolerable. Violence against people with disabilities, just as much as violence against particular racial or ethnic minorities, can lead to genocide. Allocating higher punishments to these offences might militate against a general devaluation of the lives of the victims.

To some extent at least, in this area race equality legislation has provided the template for the development of the law. In the context of race hate legislation Iganski has argued that the major benefit generated by the offences is the impetus to law enforcement for the establishment and maintenance of records (Iganski 1999). The same may well be true for disability law. Racially motivation as an aggravating factor when dealing with sentence first gained statutory recognition in sections 29–32 of the Crime and Disorder Act 1998 (Burney 2003; Burney and Rose 2002; Malik 1999). When the House of Lords considered the width of these provisions (R v Rogers 2007), Baroness Hale cited, as the justification for treating such conduct more severely than the basic versions of these crimes, the summary by Hare (Hare 1997: 416–7):

> The case of principle for an explicit response to the phenomenon rests fundamentally on the realization that crimes motivated by hatred for the group to which the victim belongs are in some sense of a qualitatively distinct order of gravity. This perception arises from intuitive feelings of retribution and from awareness of the impact such offences have on the immediate victims and on society as a whole. In addition to being the target of an act of violence the victim is likely to feel a sense of injustice at having been discriminated against on the basis of his membership of, or association with, a particular group. The more general strain of the argument is that hate crimes entail a threat to public welfare which makes it appropriate to punish them more severely.

The 'basic' offence is racially or religiously aggravated within the meaning of section 28(1) of the 1998 Act if either of two different circumstances exists:

(a) at the time of committing the offence, or immediately before or after doing so, the offender demonstrates towards the victim hostility based on the victim's membership (or presumed membership) of a racial or religious group; or

(b) the offence is motivated (wholly or partly) by hostility towards members of a racial or religious group based on their membership of that group.

One limb of the provision is concerned with the outward manifestation of racial or religious hostility, the other with the inner motivation of the offender. The House of Lords held that by calling the victims 'bloody foreigners' and telling them to 'go back to your own country' the defendants had demonstrated hostility based on their membership of a racial group as defined in the 1998 Act, even though the remarks on their face exhibit a xenophobia without designating the particular group to which the offenders took exception (Para 18).

Baroness Hale held that the statute should be interpreted in a 'flexible, non-technical' way to address the:

> ... [m]ischiefs of racism and xenophobia. Their essence is the denial of equal respect and dignity to people who are seen as 'other'. This is more deeply hurtful, damaging and disrespectful to the victims than the simple versions of these offences. It is also more damaging to the community as a whole, by denying acceptance to members of certain groups not for their own sake but for the sake of something they can do nothing about. (Para 12)

The same sentiments apply in disability hate crime. Statutory provisions dealing with aggravation in respect of disability and sexual orientation were enacted by Criminal Justice Act 2003, section146, which states:

Increase in sentences for aggravation related to disability or sexual orientation

(1) This section applies where the court is considering the seriousness of an offence committed in any of the circumstances mentioned in subsection (2).

(2) Those circumstances are –
   (a) that, at the time of committing the offence, or immediately before or after doing so, the offender demonstrated towards the victim of the offence hostility based on –
      (i) the sexual orientation (or presumed sexual orientation) of the victim, or
      (ii) a disability (or presumed disability) of the victim, or
   (b) that the offence is motivated (wholly or partly) –
      (i) by hostility towards persons who are of a particular sexual orientation, or
      (ii) by hostility towards persons who have a disability or a particular disability.

(3) The court –
   (a) must treat the fact that the offence was committed in any of those circumstances as an aggravating factor, and
   (b) must state in open court that the offence was committed in such circumstances.

(4) It is immaterial for the purposes of paragraph (a) or (b) of subsection (2) whether or not the offender's hostility is also based, to any extent, on any other factor not mentioned in that paragraph.

(5) In this section 'disability' means any physical or mental impairment.

One limb of the provision is concerned with the outward manifestation of hostility towards people with disabilities, the other with the inner motivation of the offender. There was little discussion in the Parliamentary debates, and there is no help in the explanatory notes, as to the purpose of the provisions. The obvious outstanding question is whether the principal concern of the section is with the overt hostility of the offender to members of the group the legislation protects, or is it with attitudes to people with disabilities more generally?

It is clear that the motivation referred to in the section need not be the only motivation (DPP v Woods 2002). As with racial aggravation, it always has been the case that even before statutory recognition was conferred, disability was able to be treated as an aggravating factor (R v Goodall 2002). There are three main reasons why this should be. First, in retributive terms, there is something particularly repugnant about the motive as against the 'regular' motive for crime. Second, the risks of contagion: there are particular forms of crime that are more likely to generate 'copycats'. In the case of racial assaults this is something that will play into general devaluation of the victim grouping. Third, the basis of the offence in hatred speaks to the selection of the defendant, and an appropriate response to the danger to members of that group thus created may be enhanced penalties.

Defining 'disability' in section 146

It might be entirely appropriate that there be more than one definition of disability for each of a number of different legal purposes. For example, a person might be regarded quite legitimately as disabled for the purposes of deciding whether or not she has been the victim of a disability hate crime, but not for the purposes of deciding whether or not she has been the victim of discrimination in employment.

It is also appropriate that the standards set for the appropriate treatment of people with disabilities by providers of services might vary according to the nature of the interaction between the service provider and the person with impairment. In the case where there is to be one isolated interaction between the person with the impairment and the service provider, the standard to be required of the service provider can only be a one-size-fits-most minimum. This is the way, for example, for mass transport to be regulated so as to accommodate persons with impairments affecting their mobility, where bespoke service is impracticable. In the case, on the other hand, where the relationship is a continuing one (employment, most obviously), it is possible, and may be important that the accommodations be tailored to the particular impairment and the individual job.

Where a regulation of the one-size-fits-most sort is being laid down, it is relatively easy for it to state accurately and exhaustively in advance what must be done. It is easy to say what a person needs to avoid doing in order to escape criminal liability for speeding. In the same way, the dimensions required by the Building Regulations of a wheelchair-accessible lavatory cubicle in a public building may be expressed in millimeters. No further evaluation is necessary. A statement of exactly what a person needs to do in order to avoid liability for negligence is far more difficult to make in advance. Exactly what might or might not amount to a reasonable accommodation in the case of a request by an employee for it is typically of the latter category, and something that will usually be decided ex post.

One difference between the criminalization of hate speech and the use of aggravated penalties is that when dealing with criminalization, the Rule of Law requires that the actor should have access to information giving a clear notion that the group against which s/he incites hatred is protected by the offence in question. In the case where the rule speaks to sentence, and ex hypothesi a crime is being committed, the requirement of certainty is not so important. There is no serious prospect that someone considering a hate-aggravated attack would be influenced against it by the prospect of the additional sentence. Nor is there much prospect that they would be influenced by knowledge that the person in question has a qualifying disability. If the sort of hate crime with which we are to be concerned is isolated, there should be a clear definition of disability.

The Disability Discrimination Act 2005, and to a yet greater extent the Commissions charged with its implementation, explicitly embrace the 'social model' of disability. For the purposes of the Disability Discrimination Act 1995 (as amended) the definition of disability is as follows:

(1) Subject to the provisions of Schedule 1, a person has a disability for the purposes of this Act if he has a physical or mental impairment which has a substantial and long-term adverse effect on his ability to carry out normal day-to-day activities.
(2) In this Act 'disabled person' means a person who has a disability.

Schedule 1 sets out various more specific rules, dealing with the meaning of impairment, long-term effect and day-to-day activities, making it clear, for example that cancer and HIV are covered. Without departing from the 'social model' (indeed by adopting it expressly so far as concerns the case where the victim is believed to have an impairment s/he does not in fact have – section 146(2)(ii)), the definition of disability in the Criminal Justice Act 2003 is as follows: '146 (5) In this section "disability" means any physical or mental impairment.' There is no further explanation. The Criminal Justice Act (CJA) notion of disability is wider than that in the Disability Discrimination Act (DDA) definition in two important respects. First, the DDA requires the effect must be substantial. An impairment without a substantial effect (e.g. a minor disfigurement) can (and should) provide the focus for aggravation for the purposes of section146. Second, the DDA requires that the effect must be long term. Transient impairments (like a broken leg) 'count' (again quite rightly) for the purposes of the aggravated offence but not for the DDA. (EU Regulation No.

1107/2006, dealing with the responsibilities of airports in respect of passengers with disabilities, extends its protection to people with transient injuries.)

There is a suggestion in the CPS Policy document (CPS 2007) dealing with the prosecution of disability hate crime that the definition of disability for the purposes of section 146 does not include a number of conditions, including AIDS and cancer. This is not correct. The DDA is explicit about illnesses like AIDS and HIV: they are covered (DDA 1995 Sched 8 Para 8). The provisions in the first schedule to the DDA speak to the question whether or not the impairment has a substantial effect, not to whether they constitute an impairment. However, both HIV and AIDS are (and should be) disabilities for the purposes of section 146, which must be taken to have been written against the background of the DDA.

It is important that this misunderstanding be rectified. Transient and insubstantial impairments are among those most likely to attract hate crime, and it would be inappropriate that they be excluded from the ambit of the aggravated sentence provisions. AIDS and HIV are particular examples of impairments that are likely to give rise to hate crime, and it would be quite inconsistent with the general policy introduced in the 2003 Act to exclude these impairments. If impairment is given this wide a reading nothing further need be done to shift the definition so that it more clearly encompasses crime within a continuing relationship motivated by hostility in respect of an impairment.

How does the public law duty to promote equality apply to enforcement of section 146 by the police and CPS?

Section 146 provides a test for the courts to apply in passing aggravated sentences, but also provides part of the background against which for both the police and the prosecuting authorities to act in the implementation of their positive duties to promote equality. Just as the idea of aggravation on the basis of disability uses as its model the racial aggravation provisions of the 1998 Act, so too does the public law context relating to the enforcement of the law of disability hate crime. The MacPherson Report (1999), and in particular the finding of 'institutional racism' against the police, gave rise to the imposition of the positive duty to promote equality, first expressed in the Race Relations (Amendment) Act 2000. The underlying idea is that the conferment of individual private law rights, and their correlative reactive duties, could only advance the equality and diversity agenda so far, and that proactive public law duties upon various bodies would assist. It was from this template that the positive duty to promote equality of people with disabilities was written (Alldridge 2006; Fredman 2005).

The duty to promote equality applies to all public sector bodies, including those responsible for the enforcement of the 'hate crime' legislation. Thus it extends to the

Police and the Crown Prosecution Service (CPS), both of whom have had to put in place Disability Equality Schemes to govern their own activities. They must have regard to this positive duty in the discharge of their functions. The most important features of those schemes for present purposes are that they have in place appropriate reporting procedures for the identification of what are described as disability 'hate incidents', and that they should publish reliable data and report to groups that represent.

Since it is the duty of each police force under the DDA to produce a disability equality scheme, and since those forces are charged with the enforcement of the law on disability hate crime, this duty covers the preparation and promulgation of a disability hate crime policy, involving monitoring and reporting of disability hate crime. This will include provision for recording cases identified by the police as a disability-related incident and monitoring its performance in respect of those cases. The Metropolitan Police website provides for various means of collecting the information. It states:

Disability Hate Crime

A disability hate crime is a criminal offence motivated by hatred or prejudice towards a person because of their actual or perceived disability. If you have been verbally or physically attacked because of your disability or because someone thinks you are disabled, then please report this to the police, through one of your local third party (or non-police) reporting sites. Alternatively you can report this crime online. All boroughs have Community Safety Units, which have specially trained officers who will support you and investigate your allegation. It is vital that we know about these cases so that we can improve our service delivery to you, prevent other hate crimes occurring and to identify and arrest hate crime perpetrators.

That is, the principal filter in the collection of these data is the reporter. One problem with the early reports in the Metropolitan area is that about a third of cases were wrongly reported or classified. Not all crimes against people with disabilities are qualifying hate crimes: conversely, not all incidents with might be qualifying hate crimes are so reported. This is something to which proper methodology needs to be brought to bear. If the police are increasingly to use the website as its means of informing itself of trends in the commission of offences, attention needs to be given to the way in which online forms are written. Early identification by the police of the incident as being a hate crime is crucial. The magazine *Disability Now* has produced a dossier of cases nationwide that might have been classified as disability hate crimes but were not (*Disability Now* 2009). The dossier includes a number of offences which might be thought to be 'just' crimes with victims with disabilities, but a substantial number of others, grouped by disability, which appear on the face of it to have been hate crimes and have not been so classified. An anecdotal suggestion has been made that a common alternative classification is of offences against vulnerable persons. Attempts are in train to improve the performance of police forces throughout the country in this regard.

Once categorized as an appropriate case with which for the CPS to deal, the file is passed from the police to the CPS. Further investigation needs to be conducted into that procedure for disproportionate dropping of cases in which there is a victim with a disability. Once seized of the issue, so far as concerns disability, the matter then falls to the CPS. In compliance with its Disability Equality Scheme and the more general duty to promote equality, the Crown Prosecution Service also has obligations. The principal exigencies are as follows: produce a disability hate crime policy; monitor and report disability hate crime; monitor performance; report on performance to 'communities'; establish hate crime scrutiny panels; identify specific victim and witness case issues. The key outcomes towards which this activity is intended to militate are the promotion of equality of opportunity, elimination of discrimination and the elimination of harassment. The police and CPS are both obliged to work in partnership with, and report to, affected groups.

In any given case, the critical decision for the CPS is whether or not to bring criminal proceedings. The Code for Crown Prosecutors requires the satisfaction of the evidential test (i.e. that there be a realistic prospect of conviction, usually interpreted as involving a 51 per cent chance of a conviction) and then the 'public interest' test (that there is a public interest in the bringing of the prosecution). There is no suggestion in the current guidance that the 51 per cent hurdle may be relaxed in cases of hate crime (CPS 2009), but the 'public interest' decision will be affected by the aggravating features, and it is suggested that proper implementation of the positive duty will lead to the view that the fact that a particular offence is a hate crime such that the aggravated sentencing provisions may come into play is something that will always militate towards the bringing of a prosecution. Respond, a pressure group for people with learning difficulties, has argued that, 'In applying the Code for Crown Prosecutors' public interest test, the Crown Prosecution Service must be especially mindful of the negative consequences for society of not prosecuting cases of disability hate crime' (Respond 2008). There is much to be said for this. The whole thrust of the move embodied in section 146 ought to be towards raising the profile of these offences.

So far as concerns disability the key findings of the first annual CPS Hate crime report (2007–08) were that in the year ending March 2008, 183 defendants were prosecuted for 'disability incidents'. In 2007–08, 77 per cent of cases resulted in a conviction. In 2007–08, the guilty plea rate was 72 per cent. Acquittals accounted for more unsuccessful outcomes than victim issues, similar to racist and religious incidents and homophobic and transphobic crimes. Eighty-two per cent of defendants prosecuted were men. Offences against the person were the most common offences. Burglary, theft and handling were also common (CPS 2007). These are very small numbers from which little can be inferred, save perhaps to emphasize once more the possible deficiencies in reporting and classification. A wider understanding of the notion of disability will not in itself be sufficient to raise the profile of crime against people with disabilities in general, and disability hate crimes specifically.

Witnesses with disabilities

The Scheme to which prosecutors and police are subject will not be confined in their application to the case where the person with a disability is the victim. The two further cases that will need to be dealt with are those where the disabled person is a witness and where s/he is the defendant. Special Measures Directions are available under Part II of the Youth Justice and Criminal Evidence Act 1999. These create opportunities for the evidence of a person with a disability to be received in criminal proceedings when it might not otherwise, or for it to be received in circumstances that its value as evidence will be amplified (Hoyano 2000; and see R v Camberwell Crown Court 2005). Again, the instantiation of the Code in the light of the positive duty should give rise to increased levels of special measures directions in respect of disabled witnesses. The obligation to monitor and count will prove critical if change is to be secured.

How might the investigation of alleged offences by, or prosecution of people with disabilities be done in such a way as for the police and the CPS thereby to discharge their positive duty to promote equality? So far as concerns the treatment of persons in custody and the rest of the conduct of investigations, this will depend largely upon the observations of the standards for the treatment of disabled defendants aid down in the PACE Codes of Practice. It is conceivable that the sorts of submissions which are made by the CPS in respect of sentence may need to be qualified to comply with the duty. For example, there are some cases of driving offences where disqualification is not mandatory, or, even when mandatory, is subject to some overriding discretion. It may be that prosecutors in cases with disabled defendants should make modifications to their submissions on sentence.

Conclusion

Section 146 is not the answer to crime against people with disabilities, and nor would be the introduction of an incitement to hatred offence. It is difficult to believe that these provisions will have much direct impact upon the incidence of hate crime against people with disabilities. These developments create some unease too, especially for liberals who believe in general that prisons are too full, that sentences are too long, and that the criminal law is better when dealing with people's actions than their motives. Nonetheless, aggravated sentencing provisions are legitimate forms of sentencing law. In general, the sentencing function of the judge is an executive one and arguments against this kind of Parliamentary guidance, stemming from an overextended notion of judicial independence, are frequently overstated. The fact that police and prosecutors have had to develop a monitoring system for hate crimes will raise the profile of those offences in their activities. Arguments from specific and general deterrence are more tenuous (Dixon and Gadd 2006: 317) and while the denunciatory effect of the instantiation of hate crimes is not to be dismissed (Dixon and Gadd 2006: 320), the profile of these offences is more importantly raised by these bureaucratic activities. Raising the profile of crime against disabled people will bring benefits.

Postscript

This chapter was written before the Equality Act 2010 and the consequential replacement of Disability Equality Schemes by Single Equality Schemes. Schedule 1 reenacts the definition of disability for the purposes of the Disability Discrimination Act. The Criminal Justice Act 2003 is not affected.

Table of cases

DPP v Woods (2002) EWHC Admin 485
R v Hinks (2000) UKHL 53
R v Rogers (2007) UKHL 8
Regina v Camberwell Green Youth Court (2005) UKHL4
R (on the application of E) v Governing Body of JFS and the Admissions Appeal Panel of JFS and others (United Synagogue) (2009) UKSC 15

References

Alldridge, P. (2006) 'Locating disability law', *60 Current Legal Problems*, 289–318.
Barnes, C., M. Geoff and T. Shakespeare (1999) *Exploring disability: a sociological introduction*. Malden, Mass: Polity Press.
Bridges, L. (2001) 'Race, law and state', *Race and Class*, 43(2): 61–76.
Association of Chief Police Officers (2005) http://www.acpo.police.uk/pressrelease.asp?PR_GUID=%7BF3F9B5C1-E88A-499E-9E42-12F8C982E7D6%7D
Burney, E. and G. Rose (2002) Racist offences – how is the law working? The implementation of the legislation on racially aggravated offences in the Crime and Disorder Act 1998 Home Office Research Study 244.
Burney, E. (2003) 'Using the law on racially aggravated offences', *Criminal Law Review*, 28–36.
Cabinet Office (2007) Fairness and Freedom: The Final Report of the Equalities Review.
Crown Prosecution Service, CPS Annual Hate Crimes Report (2008) Available at: http://www.cps.gov.uk/publications/docs/CPS_hate_crime_report_2008.pdf
Crown Prosecution Service, Crown Prosecution Service, Code for Crown Prosecutors. Available at: http://www.cps.gov.uk/victims_witnesses/prosecution.html#05.
Crown Prosecution Service, Policy for Prosecuting Cases of Disability Hate Crime Equality Impact Assessment Report (Initial Assessment) (2008) Available at: http://www.cps.gov.uk/Publications/docs/equality_eia_dhc.pdf
Disability Now (2009) Hate Crime Dossier. Available at: http://www.disabilitynow.org.uk/the-hate-crime-dossier
Dixon, B. and D. Gadd (2006) 'Getting the message? "New" Labour and the criminalization of "hate"', *Criminology and Criminal Justice* 6(3): 309–328.
Fredman, S. (2005) 'Does disability equality challenge the existing anti-discrimination paradigm?', In C. Gooding and A. Lawson (eds), *Disability Rights in Europe*. Oxford: Hart, p. 199.

Hare, I. (1997) 'Legislating against hate – the legal response to bias crimes', *Oxford Journal of Legal Studies,* 17: 415–40.

Horder, J. (2000) 'On the irrelevance of motive in criminal law', In J. Horder (ed.), *Oxford essays in jurisprudence* (4th series). Oxford: Oxford University Press pp. 173–91.

Hoyano, L. (2000), 'Variations on a theme by Pigot: special measures directions for child witnesses', *Criminal Law Review,* 250.

Hughes, B. and Paterson, K. (1997) 'The social model of disability and the disappearing body: towards a sociology of impairment', *Disability and Society,* 12(3): 325–40.

Hurd, H. M. and M. S. Moore (2003) 'Punishing hatred and prejudice', *Stanford Law Review,* 56(Spring): 1081.

Hurd, H. M. (2001) 'Why liberals should hate "hate crime legislation"', *Law & Philosophy,* 20: 215–32.

Iganski, P. (1999) 'Why make "hate" a crime? *Critical Social Policy,* 19(3): 386–95.

Jacobs, J. (2002) 'Hate crime: criminal law and identity politics', *Theoretical Criminology,* 6(4): 481–4.

Jacobs, J. B. and J. S. Henry (1996) 'The social construction of a hate crime epidemic', *Journal of Criminal Law and Criminology,* 86(2): 366–91.

James B. J. and K. Potter (1998) *Hate Crimes: Criminal Law & Identity Politics.* Oxford and New York: Oxford University Press.

MacPherson, Sir W. (chair) (1999) The Stephen Lawrence Enquiry February 1999 Cm 4262-I Chapter 6.

Malik, M. (1999) ' "Racist Crime": Racially Aggravated Offences in the Crime and Disorder Act 1998 Part II', *Modern Law Review,* 62(3): 409–24.

Mason, G. (2005) 'Hate crime and the image of the stranger', *British Journal of Criminology,* 45(6): 837–59.

MENCAP (1999) *Living in Fear.* London: Mencap.

Ministry of Justice Disability Equality Scheme. Available at: http://www.justice.gov.uk/publications/docs/disability-equality-scheme.pdf

MPS Equalities Scheme (2008) Disability Annual Report.

OPM (Office for Public Management) (2009) Disabled Peoples' Experience of Targeted Violence and Hostility.

Phillips, S. and R. Grattet (2000) 'Judicial rhetoric, meaning-making, and the institutionalization of hate crime law', *Law & Society Review,* 34: 567–606.

Priestley, M. (1998) 'Constructions and creations: idealism, materialism and disability theory', *Disability & Society,* 13(1): 75.

Quarmby, K. (2008) 'Unequal before the law', *Disability Now,* April.

Read, J. and Luke, C. (2004) 'Demonstrably awful: the right to life and the selective non-treatment of disabled babies and young children', *Journal of Law and Society,* 31(4): 482–509.

Respond (2008) 'From hurting to healing', Available at: http://www.respond.org.uk/campaigns/disability_hate_crime.html

Scope (2009) *Getting away with murder.* London: Scope.

Shakespeare, T. (1994) 'Cultural representation of disabled people – dustbins for disavowal', *Disability & Society,* 9(3): 283–99.

Vincent, F. R., K. Jarman, N. M. Agnieszka and M.-K. Rallings (2009) *Hate crime against people with disabilities a baseline study of experiences in Northern Ireland.* June. Belfast: Institute for Conflict Research.

Woods, J. B. (2008) 'Taking the "Hate" out of hate crimes: applying unfair advantage theory to justify the enhanced punishment of opportunistic bias crimes', *UCLA Law Review,* 56(2): 489.

8

Resources and constraints of diversity and equality officers
Theoretical and practitioner reflections

Ahu Tatli and Sanchia Alasia

Introduction

Despite the academic interest in equality and diversity, there has been only a few studies which have explored the power, resources and constraints that shape the day-to-day agency of diversity and equality officers (for examples of studies which focus on equality and diversity practitioners please see: Lawrence 2000; Parker 1999; Tatli 2008; Tatli and Ozbilgin 2009). Such a lack of academic engagement with the agency of this group of professionals is surprising given their central role in the design, implementation and monitoring of the organizational diversity and equality initiatives and programmes. In this chapter, we aim to fill this gap in the literature by casting a critical eye on the resources and constraints that diversity and equality professionals face when they do their job. In order to achieve this aim, we present theoretical and practitioner insight into the agency of diversity and equality practitioners. The chapter first conceptualizes their agency with reference to different forms of capital that impact upon their actions and decisions, and then offers a practitioner account of the job of managing equality and diversity.

In the first section we provide a theoretical framing of the power and resources of diversity and equality professionals as bearers of different forms of capital. Our conceptualization here is informed by French sociologist Bourdieu's (1977, 1990, 1998) notion of capitals. His theory of human agency is based on a dynamic,

122

relational and strategic understanding of individual action:

> Social agents are not 'particles' that are mechanically pushed and pulled by external forces. They are rather bearers of capitals, and depending on their trajectory and on the position they occupy in the field by virtue of their endowment (volume and structure) in capital, they have a propensity to orient themselves actively either toward the preservation of the distribution of capital or toward the subversion of this distribution. (Bourdieu and Wacquant 1992: 108–9)

After presenting our interpretation of Bourdieu's notion of different forms of capital in relation to diversity and equality professionals, we offer a practitioner account of the day-to-day realities of a diversity and equality professionals' job. This second section of the chapter is narrated by one of the co-authors who currently works as a diversity manager in a health sector organization in the UK. The narration draws a real-life picture of the resources and constraints that diversity and equality practitioners face in their actual organizational settings.

Theoretical reflections: different forms of capital as sources of power and constraints

Contrary to the human capital theories' focus on individual skills and qualifications obtained through education, training and experience in explaining workplace careers and agency (Becker 1975), Bourdieu (1977, 1984, 1987, 1990, 1998) offers a relational theory of capitals. Human capital approach is criticized for creating an illusion of 'free choice', isolating the individual from the socio-economic context, and, in turn, providing an ideological justification of status quo (Crompton 1986; Witz 1992, 1993). Bourdieu's notion of capital goes far beyond the simplistic conception of merit-based human capital theories which legitimize the inequalities in the workplace and reduce the understanding of agency at the workplace to individual factors by ignoring the macro- and meso-level structural factors.

Borrowing from the Marxist terminology, he defines capital as 'accumulated labour (in its materialized form or its "incorporated", embodied form) which, when appropriated on a private, i.e. exclusive, basis by agents or groups of agents, enables them to appropriate social energy in the form of reified or living labour' (Bourdieu 1986: 241). In addition to economic capital which is mainly measured by the income level, Bourdieu (1987) proposes three other forms of capital: cultural, social and symbolic capitals. 'Cultural capital' which is also named as informational capital by Bourdieu refers to factors such as taste and consumption patterns, art, education and forms of language, and has three forms; embodied, objectified and institutionalized (Bourdieu and Wacquant 1992; Mahar et al. 1990). 'Social capital' which refers to relations with significant others, 'is the sum of resources, actual or virtual, that accrue to an individual or a group by virtue of possessing a durable network of more or less institutionalized relationships of mutual acquaintance and recognition' (Bourdieu and Wacquant 1992: 119). Finally, 'symbolic capital', which is the most complex of all, is the form that other forms of capital take once they are recognized and legitimized within a given context (Bourdieu 1987: 4). Consequently, symbolic capital refers to attributes such as prestige, status and authority (Bourdieu 1990).

In line with the Bourdieuan framework, we argue that understanding the resources and constraints that diversity and equality professionals face requires an analysis of different forms of capital owned by them. Therefore, indicators of each form of capital and their impact on the actions of the diversity and equality professionals need to be explored in order to understand the dynamics governing their agency. We will now present a conceptual explanation of cultural, social and symbolic capitals as they relate to diversity and equality officers.

Cultural capital

Indicators of cultural capital include cultural and demographic background as well as traits which traditionally refer to human capital, that is, formal education, training and work experience. Education, experience and training that are relevant to the job, are without doubt essential for establishing a professional legitimacy in an organizational setting. For example, Lawrence (2000) found that the role of diversity and equality officers requires knowledge of legislation, industrial relations and human resource management procedures, as well as traits such as patience, persistence and resilience, which are developed through previous work experience. Furthermore, previous research on the issue revealed that work experience in the form of on-the-job learning has been attached more significance by diversity officers than formal educational qualifications because it provided access to the insiders' knowledge, that is, knowledge of the formal and informal rules and day-to-day working, and authority and power structures of the organization (Ozbilgin and Tatli 2008).

In addition to the human capital traits such as experience, education and training, other factors contribute to the accumulation of social capital. Particularly for the case of diversity and equality practitioners, cultural background can be an important source. Diversity and equality officers need to understand the values and experiences of individuals from dominant and subordinate groups for successful implementation of equality programmes, to respond to resistance and promote organizational change (Elmes and Connelley 1997). Agocs points out to the diffused nature of institutionalized resistance that may face change agents and she argues that 'it is embedded in and expressed through organizational structures and processes of legitimation, decision making and resource allocation' (Agocs 1997: 918). Furthermore, she says:

> Effective advocacy for change in the face of institutionalized resistance is an activity that requires expert knowledge, research and communication skills, commitment to the change project, personal courage (Agocs 1997: 929).

However, she cautions that expertise and skills are not in themselves effective if they are not accorded legitimacy by the organization and particularly by the power holders in the organization (Agocs 1997: 925). For that reason, aspects of cultural capital that are closely linked to human capital, that is, education, experience and training, are not alone enough for gaining the necessary organizational legitimacy, but diversity and equality officers require what we call relational and cultural intelligence on the issues of equality structures, perceptions and dynamics. An important source of this aspect of cultural capital resides in the cultural and demographic background of the diversity and equality officers themselves.

For diversity and equality officers it is essential to have a deep understanding of disadvantage in order to make sense of the legitimacy claims of different organizational actors and their reactions towards diversity and equality projects. Diversity and equality officers' personal experiences of disadvantage or their proximity to discriminated groups is an invaluable source of cultural capital since it provides them with insights into the dynamics of disadvantage and privilege and an understanding of the perspectives of the discriminated groups (Lawrence 2000; Meyerson and Scully 1995). In that sense, cultural capital plays a key role for the ability of diversity and equality managers to do their day-to-day job in two distinct ways. First, it helps them to communicate with and gain support from the members of subordinate groups in the organization. As Acker (2000) argues incongruence between the interests of various groups in the organization and lack of collaboration on the side of those who are in power may undermine the change efforts. In such cases, she claims, change agents may be required to mobilize the involved employees to 'achieve changes that challenge the interests of relatively powerful organizational participants' (Acker 2000: 628).

Second, it provides them with the resilience and patience to do their job which can be more often than not a challenging task before the institutional resistance. Importance personal values and standing such as political commitment to social justice (DiTomaso and Hooijberg 1996), commitment to human rights (Lawrence 2000) and personal identification with disadvantaged groups (Meyerson and Scully 1995), for diversity and equality officers have been cited in the literature. The job of managing equality and diversity is in its nature value based in that values of fairness and equality, and career aspirations are closely intertwined. At the same time, diversity and equality officers' direct and indirect experience of disadvantage impacts on their values and mindsets, shaping their personal commitment to the principles of equality and diversity.

Symbolic capital

In an organizational setting, individuals' status and authority within the organizational hierarchy are most visible indicators of the level of symbolic capital at their disposal. For diversity managers, this translates to their job role and position, and authority of the diversity office within the organization, as well as organizational support for diversity and equality initiatives. The position that diversity and equality staff occupy within the power matrix of the organization may reinforce or debase their efforts towards creating an organizational change. Parker (1999) indicates that seniority is of crucial importance for the influence of equality officers. On the other hand Acker (2000) uncovered in her research that equality officers most of the time lack the organizational standing and status to effectively monitor and influence line managers in relation to meeting the equality and diversity targets and objectives.

In addition to the individual position of the diversity or equality professionals, the availability and position of separate diversity and equality office and its relationship to other functions in the organization establish an essential source of legitimacy to achieve the goals set out by the diversity and equality policies and illustrates the level of centrality of these policies for the organization (Jones, Jerich, Copeland et al. 1989). In other words, positioning of the diversity or equality office within a clear management structure has a crucial impact on the effectiveness of the implementation of diversity or equality policies (Lawrence 2000). The role of the position of diversity office for effective implementation of diversity and equality policies has been stated several times in the anecdotes from practitioners. For instance, Monica Boyle, Director of Changing Workforce for McDonalds Corporation, says:

> At McDonalds, top management is very involved in what we do; I report directly to top management. Our department, affirmative action/changing workforce is not part of personnel and training. Management feels that it is an important department that affects everything we do at McDonalds.... The first person who sees any new program is the chairman of the board; if he doesn't have time to see it, then it isn't worth doing. I think you have to have that kind of commitment from your top people... You can help them see it in a positive way and show them how it can actually make their job easier. That's where you get the buy-in; that's where you get people excited about it. (Jones et al. 1989: 21)

Therefore, the prestige of the diversity and equality office in the organization provides an important site and sign of legitimacy while the lack of it indicates that diversity and equality issues are not high on the organizational agenda, thus limiting the scope of the agency of equality personnel. At a more informal level, an indication of symbolic capital is the support from organizational actors for diversity and equality objectives. Of all different organizational actors, the influence of senior managers has been cited most often in relation to the success of diversity and equality initiatives (Cox and Blake 1991; Dobbs 1996; Joplin and Daus 1997; Muir 1996). The words of an HP diversity representative from Bristol illustrate the enabling role of senior management support:

> Here we've never had to fight battles for diversity because our general manager and functional managers have been very supportive. These are the people who have the power and

the ability to mobilize resources for initiatives ... At other sites, the picture might be quite different – a lack of senior and middle management support and a paucity of funds can be major barriers to effecting change, no matter how enthusiastic about and committed to diversity one is. (quoted in Brimm and Arora 2001: 119)

To summarize, symbolic capital which is accumulated through the status and prestige of the equality staff and the diversity and equality office within the organizational hierarchy and through support of and commitment from senior management provide important clues about the resources that diversity and equality officers have at their disposal as well as the barriers and constraints that they need to overcome in order to implement equality projects. Furthermore, the symbolic capital of diversity and equality managers cannot be understood solely on the basis of micro-level explorations of the personal qualifications and characteristics, but positioning of diversity and equality agenda across organizational power relations needs to be taken into account.

Social capital

Agocs (1997: 929) proposes several strategies that change agents can utilize in order to be effective. Some of these strategies reside within the organization such as convincing 'authorities that change is in their interest', while other are located in the wider society including promoting 'change from outside the organization by seeking improved legislation and regulation, support from other institutions, and public understand and support'. The strategies offered by Agocs are closely linked to the amount of social capital at the disposal of change agents, in our case diversity and equality officers. Social capital at the disposal of these officers emanates from intra- and extra-organizational sources and is accumulated through involvement in formal or informal groups and networks.

Internally, membership in various organizational networks and relationships with organizational members from different groups is essential for diversity and equality officers for building up their social capital. The amount of social capital at their disposal then shape their ability as negotiators or facilitators between different groups including employees, trade unions, senior management and line managers. It has been frequently cited in the literature that success of diversity and equality projects depend on organizational buy-in across different levels and functions (Dobbs 1996; Gilbert and Ivancevich 2000). Therefore equality staff need to have allies who represent both majority and minority perspectives. Commenting on tempered radicals, Meyerson (2001a) suggests that having allies from dominant groups is beneficial for several reasons including gaining access to insiders' knowledge, establishing legitimacy and accessing resources.

In order to gain senior management commitment and ownership, diversity and equality officers increasingly have to rely on business case justifications in addition to legal case arguments. For example, Barbara Jerich, Director of Workforce Diversity at Honeywell, emphasizes the importance of making business case for diversity:

> In many cases the organizations that have seen the most change have done so only after what I'd call galvanizing events. A class-action lawsuit or a takeover attempt will cause a quicker culture change than just about anything. ... If Honeywell has a chance at success in achieving a truly diverse workforce, it's because executive management is behind it a hundred percent. They believe in it. They're really committed to seeing it through, and have invested a lot of time and a lot of money, not just because it's the right thing to do, but because it makes business sense. (Jones et al. 1989: 17)

What becomes apparent from the literature and anecdotal evidence is that positive impact of diversity and equality on the business outcomes is one of the most important motivations for organizational commitment to equality agenda (Dobbs 1996). In fact with the increasing popularity of managing diversity approach, bottom-line justifications increasingly substitute the emphasis on ethics and justice that used to frame the equal opportunities efforts. In this new scene, even the ethical reasons that enforce diversity and equality agenda are explained with reference to the positive public image associated with running an ethical business and being an equal opportunities employer (Gilbert et al. 1999).

Thus diversity and equality professionals may stick to a pragmatic attitude as a part of their strategy to build up change, by using discourses of inclusion and methods of negotiation rather than conflict strategies in order to gain acceptance and support of as many organizational members as possible (Parker 1999). As a diversity representative in HR puts:

> One has to be careful of how one puts one's vision across. Characterising 'white men' as the dominant power group, if done carelessly, will alienate them. They are part of the solution and not part of the problem. We have to guard against presenting diversity as a women's issue and painting white men into a corner. Inclusiveness is critical. (quoted in Brimm and Arora 2001: 116)

The use of strategies of inclusion may be also beneficial through providing diversity and equality officers with an access to 'the advice of insiders who know just how hard to push' (Meyerson 2001b: 100). Brimm and Arora's (2001: 122) account of diversity practitioners illustrates the importance of insider's knowledge for this group of professionals:

> One diversity representative says she 'keeps her ears to the ground' and finds out who, among senior and top management, is sympathetic. Another says she always 'tests the water' before launching an initiative. She finds out what managers are ready to hear and puts her messages across in as non-threatening a way as possible.

In addition to intra-organizational sources, diversity and equality professionals accumulate social capital also through extra-organizational relationships and involvement, particularly through membership in diversity and equality networks and groups outside of their organizations. Such outside involvement has several benefits for diversity and equality officers (Meyerson and Scully 1995). To start with, the extent of their external networks and contact increase their professional credibility and legitimacy in the organization. Furthermore, relationships with equality officers from other organizations provide a sense of solidarity and validation of their commitment to and views about equality and justice (Braithwaite 1992, cited in Parker 1999). Such groups also may function as support networks which diversity and equality officers may turn to for advice and information when they experience barriers and challenges in their organizational settings (Meyerson and Scully 1995).

Thus, social capital is accumulated through involvement in networks and groups both within the organization and outside of the organization. It is essential for diversity and equality professional to have social capital in order to practice their job because social capital when transformed to symbolic capital provides them with the legitimate basis of status and power to enact organizational change strategies.

Case study: day-to-day challenges of managing diversity and equality

The position of diversity professionals within an organization is one of the first challenges of managing diversity successfully. Where the role of a diversity manager is aligned alongside the corporate structures of an organization, the employees are more likely to recognize diversity as an important feature of the organization's mission and values.

Diversity practitioners can be placed within various directorates within an organization, each of which will have their own benefits. Working within a Human Resource department gives the diversity officer a clear focus on workforce issues and influences on policy matters to do with recruitment, maternity and flexible working to name a few. However if based within the senior management section of the organization vital links can be developed by having access to building equality into the strategic aims and objectives of an organization. Some organizations choose to put resources into establishing an equality directorate that has a pivotal position across all sections of an organization and where practitioners can have success in mainstreaming diversity. Wherever the diversity officer is placed, it is vital that there are linkages made throughout the organization. An organization that has done particularly well in this regard is Tower Hamlets Council, who has invested a significant amount of resources into equality. In 2006 the council was awarded the highest level of the Equality Standard for Local Government at level five. Only two other boroughs have reached this standard out of the 388 nationally. It is a nationally recognized framework which is used to measure progress in mainstreaming equality and diversity. In order to reach this level Tower Hamlets Council has a full-time employed directorate equality liaison officer within each of their directorates. Their role is to lead on equalities issues within their directorate. The Council also has a substantial corporate equalities team which lead on strategic work within the chief executives directorate, submit

---

work for the Stonewall Equality Index (of which in 2009 they were seventh out of 100) and pull together the work that takes place within the various directorates.

In order for the diversity manager to be successful, the senior management teams or the people at the top of the organization must support the diversity agenda. When the people who are at the top of an organization are on board with the diversity agenda, the difference is clearly noticeable especially when they are prepared to go beyond the minimum level of legal compliance. Top level support is crucial, for example, when as a diversity manager you wish to pilot positive action programmes for under-represented groups of staff. Their support is also essential for embedding diversity throughout the organization. Their commitment filters down to their senior management teams, through to middle managers and junior staff. Where those at the top of the organization also accept that others at their level should be diverse and supports programmes to achieve this, it demonstrates to the employees their commitment to the equality agenda. Where those at the top of the organization are not on board or do not see the need to engage with the equality agenda, then this presents great challenges to the diversity manager, because only a limited amount of success can be achieved.

Usually any policy or programme being developed to take forward the diversity agenda in an organization requires senior management agreement. Advancing the diversity agenda within an organization that has management resistance is challenging and can be de-motivating. If diversity practitioners have a strong sense of character and an interest in social justice issues, this can provide the momentum to continue in their roles. Similarly the diversity practitioners' role is challenged, if staff at the lower levels of the organization are not engaged with the equality and diversity agenda. Staff within the organization have a role in highlighting the inequality and discrimination that occurs, so that action plans and programmes can then be built around the actual needs of the organization, rather than the perceived effects of discrimination.

Designing and delivering diversity training provides the next challenge. It is difficult to design a diversity course that will meet all the needs of those who will receive the training. Some will need general awareness, whereas others, especially managers will need more in-depth information about equality law and how to manage diverse groups of staff. However frequently it is not practical to come up with a multitude of courses, so practitioners are often faced with designing, delivering or commissioning a course with a one-size-fits-all approach. Organizations that are proactive to diversity issues will provide these courses for their staff as a matter of course. Those who are less convinced are usually swayed by the vicarious liability argument, which is where organizations have to demonstrate their commitment to equality throughout the whole organization, when discrimination claims are made against them.

Staff networks consisting of employees from the diverse groups can have some success in advancing the diversity agenda. These groups are quite frequent within the public sector, such as Transport for London, Home Office, Cabinet office and many other government departments. Private sector organizations establish these groups also including, Shell, KPMG and Ernst and Young. Usually a separate group is organized for each protected equality group. There are usually networks for women, Black, Asian and Minority Ethnic staff, disability, religion and belief, age and lesbian, gay, bisexual and transgendered staff.

Two important factors increase these group's chances of success. First, support from the organization in terms of resources for the group. If the organization can provide assistance in establishing staff network groups, suggesting terms of reference and setting up regular meetings, then this can give such groups the solid foundation that they need to last. Secondly, momentum from staff themselves to get engaged within the networks. There should be commitment from staff to give up time, for example in their lunch hour to attend meetings, put forward their views and assist in carrying out actions that supports the groups aims. If staff within the organization do not feel the need for a network group to support them within the workplace place, the sustainability of the group is limited.

A high-level diversity champion that supports staff network groups and indeed diversity within organizations can be extremely useful. In supporting network groups, they can have a role in speaking at network meetings, which in turn can attract further membership to the group and provide the group with credibility. Staff network groups that have had particular success have been the Black and Asian staff network group at Ernst and Young, who have helped to address race diversity by working with the organization to set targets to double Black and Asian representation at Board level by 2010. Similarly, KPMG's Islamic society has helped to address the needs of their growing Muslim staff and client base and have introduced the use of Islamic business models to gain new business worth in excess of £500k in fees. Imperial as one, which is a race equality group within Imperial College, has the support of the College's rector and Management Board who actively undertake the role of equality champions.

The role of a diversity champion can be important, in spearheading the diversity agenda and making the diversity practitioner role easier to fulfil. In the public sector, where the appointment of diversity champions is a common feature, their role has two main functions. The first is to be a role model and signal positive images of diversity to employees within the organization. The second is to give reassurance to the relevant diverse groups within the workforce, that there is someone senior within the organization who is willing to speak up on issues that affect them. Diversity champions can also have success in gleaning from the various protected equality groups, what their particular concerns are that they may not have necessarily have found out otherwise. They can set examples by attending equality training in lieu of their busy schedules and briefing their senior management teams on the importance of engaging with the diversity agenda.

Diversity champions can also have a role in establishing good practice within organizations, by acting as role models that underpin the value of diversity (Kandola 2009: 134). By demonstrating appropriate behaviour and setting an acceptable standard, this could help to diminish inappropriate actions. This is particularly important for other leaders within organizations to grasp and model for their staff groups.

There is a moral argument to treat people equitably within the workplace, however practitioners over the last decade have more frequently outlined the benefits for their organization to gain further buy in. Practitioners may use the business case for diversity as a leverage to overcome the difficulties of mainstreaming equality within organizations. The practitioner's role here is to encourage people to engage with the diversity agenda. This can be done by outlining how establishing diversity networks within their companies and placing diversity at the heart of the business can contribute to an increase in profits and expansion of customer base. Business Link a government business advice and support service outlines why business should widen their choice of employees to improve competitiveness. There is nothing mentioned about the moral imperatives:

- having a wider range of resources, skills and ideas among your employees that you can tap into
- improving staff retention, leading to lower recruitment and training costs
- increasing employee efficiency and lowering stress due to cross-functional teams, i.e. employees are capable of a variety of roles thanks to their different backgrounds and skill sets
- avoiding claims of unfair treatment or discrimination
- building a reputation as a diverse business
- building a competitive edge in recruitment and retention as you can select from a bigger pool of candidates
- how customers with different religious beliefs or from different backgrounds might react to your business or product
- problems that customers may have, for example language barriers and poor access for disabled people

The success of any diversity manager's role can be enhanced by networking externally. Being a member of several network groups comprising of diversity professionals within higher education and the public, private and voluntary sector, can help diversity practitioners overcome some of the challenges of tackling new and complex areas of diversity. These networks can prove invaluable in sharing knowledge and the provision of advice and guidance about setting up diversity initiatives or tackling complex issues. These networks can provide support in quite a lonely field and reassurance that some of the issues the practitioner is expected to provide guidance on have been faced by others elsewhere.

The volume of diversity legislation within the UK has been a challenge for diversity practitioners to grapple with. Since the year 2000, a lot of new equality legislation has been introduced, which the diversity practitioner is expected to know and be able to advise on. The practitioner needs to be conversant with race, sex and disability legislation, in addition to sexual orientation, religion and belief and age regulations. The practitioner needs to be able to keep up to date with the legislation and articulate its meaning and implications to those at all levels within organizations. This is a pivotal role especially as the legislation is constantly being updated and interpreted by the tribunals. As discussed earlier within this chapter, on-the-job learning is the method by which many diversity practitioners gain this legal knowledge. There is no one course or legal seminar that can teach a practitioner about all aspects of equality law, as well as the nuances and difficulties that come with trying to apply this in a workplace setting. Being from an under-represented group can help, however the practitioner best attains this knowledge through journals, magazines, legal updates and networking with other practitioners. The protection given to protected equality groups is not the same and this presents another challenge, which the Single Equality Bill aims to address. The Single Equality Bill will be a single point of reference, as opposed to the many different discrimination Acts that are currently in place. All of the equality strands will be levelled up, resulting in all equality target groups being afforded the same level of protection. The Bill will not necessarily however, make it any easier for diversity practitioners to deal with the issues of competing rights and responsibilities, particularly in the areas of sexual orientation and religion and belief. When two protected groups want opposing outcomes, this requires skill and tact to resolve. The higher education sector has usually promoted freedom of speech, thought and expression. Equality law does limit this, if this will cause others to be deeply offended. Universities can find it difficult to grapple with this concept, which goes against the principles they set out to achieve. The diversity practitioner should have the skill to carefully balance their roles and responsibilities, particularly when it comes to providing advice and guidance. Often when advising those of issues that arise with individuals or groups that are protected by the legislation, one needs to have tact and sensitivity as well as persuasion and diplomacy skills to find an amicable solution.

What equality legislation has done for diversity practitioners, is provide them with the power to use it as a tool to convince those within organizations, that it is within their best interests, to fulfil its various requirements. Although most organizations have a diversity strap line or equality policy, the fact that equality legislation requires public sector organizations to produce equality schemes and proactively promote equality between different groups of people, has helped to move the diversity agenda forward. The equality schemes have accompanying action plans, which prompt the thought of how the organization can put programmes and initiatives in place that can begin to effectively tackle institutional discrimination.

The challenge facing diversity professionals in this area is the amount of time it takes to produce equality schemes for gender, disability and race. The required consultation with relevant staff and student groups and the development of action plans is time consuming. As well as equality schemes, data has to be produced annually on promotions, recruitment, retention and training. The compilation of these various reports, which can have varying reporting periods, can make it difficult to find the time to monitor those who have said they will complete actions and develop ways of proactively fostering good relations between different groups, which is also legally required. The disappointing aspect of the law to date has been the lack of enforcement. There has been very little repercussion in practice to organizations that do not fulfil the legal requirements. Because there are so many public sector organizations to monitor, it would be impossible for the Equality and Human Rights Commission to individually monitor them all. Consequently organizations that do not fulfil the requirements, are usually not reprimanded and so do not necessarily feel a sense of urgency, to engage with all aspects of the legal requirements.

Conclusion

In this chapter, we offered theoretical and practitioner reflections on the resources and constraints that shape the power and influence of diversity and equality officers. We first discussed cultural, social and symbolic capital owned by these officers and identified the specific sources of different forms of capital. Diversity and equality officers have these three types of capital in varying configurations depending on their individual dispositions and social and organizational context within which they operate. Cultural capital is the sum of human capital attributes and cultural and demographic characteristics. Social capital is accumulated through involvement in formal and informal diversity and equality networks within and outside of the organization. Finally, symbolic capital is associated with the positional authority and prestige of the person of the diversity and equality officers and the diversity office as well as organizational support for diversity and equality objectives.

After providing our theoretical reflections, we offered a practitioner account of the challenges of the job of managing equality and diversity as a real life case study. Diversity and equality officer are but one group of stakeholders that exerts influence on the organizational diversity and equality efforts (Tatli 2008). Green and Kirton (2009) emphasize the importance of line-managers, trade unions and employees, as well as diversity managers in terms of their impact on equality and diversity programmes. For the same reason, social, symbolic and cultural capital at disposal of diversity and equality practitioners with respect to each of these stakeholder groups acts as a crucial resource or a hindrance when they do their day-to-day job. Thus, we discussed the strategies used by diversity officers to increase their success in gaining high-level support, so that organizations would take diversity more seriously. In that sense, our case study does not only reveal the negative impact of lack of certain capitals on the agency of diversity and equality practitioners but also demonstrates the creative and strategic ways in which practitioners seize opportunities and use different strategies to influence organizational actors and structures.

Our discussion in this chapter implies that diversity and equality officer's move strategically within the organizational power field and their capacity for manoeuvre is framed by the amount and configuration of different forms of capital at their disposal. Furthermore, they employ discourses of inclusion and business case as strategic resources in order to increase legitimacy and organizational support for the equality agenda. For that reason, human capital attributes such as competencies and skills based on education, experience and training, are insufficient for understanding the power and influence of diversity and equality staff. On the contrary, their professional effectiveness is shaped by organizational and social context as well as individual competency attributes. Both social structures such as legislation and institutional frameworks and organizational structures such as organizational culture and formal governance and diversity dynamics, need to be take into account in order to make sense of the capacity of diversity and equality officers to affect organizational change towards progressive, egalitarian, fair and inclusive organizational practices.

We believe that the arguments and examples we put forward in this chapter has important implications for diversity and equality research and policy. As the most visible actors in the diversity management processes, diversity and equality officers deserve more research attention if we are to understand and conceptualize the failure and success of organizational diversity and equality policies and programmes true to their complexity. In terms of organizational, regional and national policy, there is a need for initiatives such as training and networking frameworks, organizational structures of legitimacy and authority for diversity and equality personnel, in order to empower the practitioners.

References

Acker, J. (2000) 'Gendered contradictions in organisational equity projects', *Organization*, 7(4): 625–32.

Agocs, C. (1997) 'Institutionalised resistance to organisational change: denial, inaction and repression', *Journal of Business Ethics*, 16: 917–31.

Becker, G. S. (1975) *Human capital*. Chicago: University of Chicago Press.

Bourdieu, P. (1977) *Outline of theory of practice*. Cambridge: Cambridge University Press.

—— (1984) *Distinction: a social critique of the judgement of taste*. London: Routledge.

—— (1986) 'The forms of capital', In J. G. Richardson (ed.), *Handbook of theory and research for the sociology of education*. New York, London: Greenwood, pp. 241–58.

—— (1987) 'What makes a social class? On the theoretical and practical existence of groups', *Berkeley Journal of Sociology*, 32: 1–18.

—— (1990) *The logic of practice*. Stanford: Stanford University Press.

—— (1998) *Practical reason: on the theory of action*. Cambridge: Polity Press.

Bourdieu, P. and L. Wacquant (1992) *An invitation to reflexive sociology*. Cambridge: Polity Press.

Brimm, L. and M. Arora (2001) 'Diversity management at Hewlett-Packard, Europe', In M. A. Albrecht (ed.), *International HRM: managing diversity in the workplace*. Oxford: Blackwell, pp. 108–24.

Cox, T. H. and B. Blake (1991) 'Managing cultural diversity: implications for organisational competitiveness', *Academy of Management Executive*, 5(3): 45–56.

Crompton, R. (1986) 'Women and the "service class"', In R. Crompton and M. Mann (eds), *Gender and stratification*. Cambridge: Polity Press, pp. 119–36.

DiTomaso, N. and R. Hooijberg (1996) 'Diversity and the demands of leadership', *Leadership Quarterly*, 7(2): 163–87.

Dobbs, M. F. (1996) 'Managing diversity: lessons from the private sector', *Public Personnel Management*, 25(3): 351–67.

Elmes, M. and D. L. Connelley (1997) 'Dreams of diversity and realities of intergroup relations in organisations', In P. Prasad, A. J. Mills, M. Elmes and A. Prasad (eds), *Managing the organisational melting pot: dilemmas of workplace diversity*. London: Sage, pp. 148–67.

Gilbert, J. A. and J. M. Ivancevich (2000) 'Valuing diversity: a tale of two organizations', *Academy of Management Executive*, 14(1): 93–105.

Gilbert, J. A., B. A. Stead and J. M. Ivancevich (1999) 'Diversity management: a new organisational paradigm', *Journal of Business Ethics*, 21: 61–76.

Green, A. and G. Kirton (2009) *Diversity management in the UK: organizational and stakeholder experiences*. London: Routledge.

Jones, R. T., B. Jerich, L. Copeland and M. Boyle (1989) 'Four by four: how do you manage a diverse workforce', *Training and Development Journal*, 43(2): 13–21.

Joplin, J. R. W. and C. S. Daus (1997) 'Challenges of leading a diverse workforce', *Academy of Management Executive*, 11(3): 32–47.

Kandola, B. (2009) *The value of difference: eliminating bias in organisations*. Oxford: Pearn Kandola publishing.

Lawrence, E. (2000) 'Equal opportunities officers and managing equality changes', *Personnel Review*, 29(3): 381–401.

Mahar, C., R. Harker and C. Wilkes (1990) 'The basic theoretical position', In R. Harker, C. Mahar and C. Wilkes (eds), *An introduction to the work of Pierre Bourdieu: the practice of theory*. London: Macmillan.

Meyerson, D. E. (2001a) *Tempered radicals: how people use difference to inspire change at work*. Boston, MA: Harvard Business School Press.

—— (2001b) 'Radical change, the quiet way', *Harvard Business Review*, October: 92–100.

Meyerson, D. E. and M. A. Scully (1995) 'Tempered radicalism and the politics of ambivalence and change', *Organization Science*, 6(5): 585–600.

Muir, C. (1996) 'Workplace readiness for communicating diversity', *The Journal of Business Communication*, 33(4): 475–86.

Özbilgin, M. and A. Tatli (2008) *Global diversity management: an evidence based approach*. London, New York: Palgrave.

Parker, C. (1999) 'How to win hearts and minds: corporate compliance policies for sexual harassment', *Law and Policy*, 21(1): 21–48.

Tatli, A. (2008) *Understanding the agency of diversity managers: a relational and multilevel investigation*, unpublished PhD Thesis, University of London.

Tatli, A. and M. Özbilgin (2009) Understanding diversity managers' role in organizational change: towards a conceptual framework, *Canadian Journal of Administrative Sciences*, 26(3): 244–58.

Witz, A. (1992) *Professions and patriarchy*. London and New York: Routledge.

—— (1993) 'Women at work', In D. Richardson and V. Robinson (eds), *Introducing women's studies*. London: Macmillan.

9

Flexibility and equality
Friend or foe?

Hazel Conley

Introduction

The concept of labour flexibility has dominated academic and policy debates concerned with the changing nature of work since the 1980s. However, rather than becoming more precise, the term has been stretched to cover qualitatively different aspects of labour market activity. Early definitions of flexible work were at least united in their negative analysis of the impact on the quality of working life. However, adding to the conceptual complexity, more recent theories have attempted to cast flexibility in a more positive light. Management discussions of flexibility treated the concept as unitary, that is containing no essential conflicts, by stressing the positive aspects as juxtaposed to rigidity (Blyton and Morris 1991). Later analyses, largely stemming from European social policy debates on 'flexicurity' have taken more pluralistic approach that seeks to ameliorate the negative impacts of labour market flexibility.

This chapter starts by providing a brief summary of the early flexibility debates and more recent debates on the positive aspects of labour market flexibility before considering segmentation theories and the relationship between flexibility and inequality. Segmentation theorists argue that working practices that deviate from a full-time, permanent 'norm' are linked to labour market segregation and are instrumental in the inequality suffered by disadvantaged groups of workers, while adherents of flexicurity contend that the same working practices offer valuable access to work for the same groups of workers. It is argued that these two divergent positions have led to tensions and contradictions in social policy, which on one hand extol the virtues of a flexible labour market and on the other require the introduction of protective legislation for 'non-standard' workers. These tensions are also played out within organizations where employment policies that extend and encourage certain types of flexible working are often at odds with equality and diversity policies. The chapter draws on existing research literature, secondary analysis of European labour market data and primary qualitative data to provide a clearer understanding of the links between flexibility and equality at work to interrogate the proposition that flexicurity can help rather than hinder the labour market prospects of disadvantaged groups.

Flexibility revisited

Felstead and Jewson (1999: 2) highlight the proliferation of terms that have arisen to encompass what they choose to call flexible labour. Other terms include atypical employment, non-standard work, the insecure workforce, precarious work, contingent labour and vulnerable work. These concepts, including flexibility, are themselves multifaceted covering various arrangements that are considered to deviate from a standard of full-time, permanent employment. Rodgers (1989) includes temporary, casual, part-time, disguised illegal wage employment, homeworking, 'moonlighting', self-employment and out-working in the category of 'atypical' employment. There are however important conceptual differences between these forms of work and that heterogeneity makes generalization difficult. Felstead and Jewson note that the precursor of the multiplication of terms used to refer to non-standard employment has been 'a lack of theoretical precision characteristic of research in this area' (1999: 2). In collecting national statistical data on temporary work, the Labour Force Survey (LFS) and the European Labour Force Survey (ELFS) measures four aspects of temporary work: fixed-term contract, agency work, casual work and seasonal work, and it is these forms that are the focus of this chapter.

Flexibility, as a descriptor for work, arose after a number of arguments stressed that the declining prosperity of mature economies results largely from rigidities in labour markets and production processes (Hirst and Zeitlin 1989; Piore and Sabel 1984). Such rigidities were identified at both macro- and micro-levels and were closely related to the post-war growth in job security (Cousins 1999). In brief, macro-level influences were largely considered to be the over-regulation of national and international labour markets, while micro-level rigidities resulted from employer practices that relied heavily on static internal labour markets. Trade union organization has also been implicated in maintaining working practices that some have considered added to rigidity (Hayek 1980; Metcalf 1988).

In the UK the concept of flexibility became the centre of debate after Atkinson (1984, 1985) developed the model of the 'flexible firm' (Cousins 1999). According to Atkinson (1985) flexibility falls into three categories: functional, financial and numerical. Non-standard work falls into the latter category of numerical flexibility, which requires that a certain segment of the workforce must be easily dispensable.

The model was further developed to include the concept of a core and peripheral workforce. Core workers are regarded as the stable component and are considered to possess skills unique to the firm. They therefore represent valuable assets and hence are highly regarded and rewarded by the employer. There are two groups of peripheral workers. The first group has skills that are needed at certain times but which are not specific to the firm and are available in the external labour market. The second group consists of workers who have limited skills or are unskilled. To achieve numerical flexibility the latter two groups are likely to be employed on a temporary basis either via the use of fixed-term and temporary contracts, staffing agencies or directly hired casual work.

The major criticisms of the flexible firm model are to be found in the edited book *Farewell to Flexibility?* (Pollert 1991). The editor's main criticisms firstly consider that the model of the flexible firm is based on flawed economic theories and equally tenuous concepts of post-Fordism and the 'post-industrial society'. In contrast to these theories Pollert contends that the flexible firm model offers a prescriptive device for work intensification linked to Taylorist work practices. Secondly, it is argued that the model does not 'fit the facts' in many important respects. The main contention is that there is little empirical evidence for the existence of a core/periphery model and no clear-cut distinction between core and periphery workers. It is argued that, while legislation has reduced the rights of vulnerable workers, high unemployment and the reduction of trade union power has disciplined and disempowered the core workforce.

Pollert's arguments are extended in the final chapter by Hyman (1991) who considers that the flexible firm model raises the constant contradiction in industrial relations between trust and constraint in the need to establish both consent and control. Hyman makes the observation that employers are likely to use a different mix of strategies for different workers. This in itself would seem to indicate the beginning of a core/periphery model. However, like Pollert, Hyman argues that the 'flexible firm' also inhibits core workers as they become locked into internal labour markets. Status as a core worker therefore removes the ability to 'exit' while the demand for loyalty and individuality as opposed to collectivity removes the 'voice' of core workers. Lastly, both Hyman and Pollert contend that flexibility is inherently political. For example, Pollert considers that the model is linked to changes in the role of the State and its endorsement of neo-classical economics. Hyman argues that flexibility is synonymous with the interests of capital as the basic goal is to transfer risk and costs from the enterprise to the worker.

The above points raise some interesting questions relating flexibility to issues of control and the role of the State. Houseman and Osawa (2003) note that flexibility and the adoption of 'non-standard' work has followed different patterns in developed economies. Although debates in the UK have polarized flexibility and security (Healy 2006), the European Union (EU) has actively promoted 'flexicurity', which is defined as 'an integrated strategy to enhance, at the same time, flexibility and security in the labour market' (EC 2007: 10). The rationale for flexicurity is that it should help Member States to meet the Lisbon Strategy[1] for 'more and better jobs'. It is also argued that flexicurity will provide access to the labour market for disadvantaged groups:

> Flexicurity should reduce the divide between insiders and outsiders on the labour market. Current insiders need support to be prepared for and protected during job to job transitions. Current outsiders – including those out of work, where women, the young and migrants are over-represented – need easy entry points to work and stepping-stones to enable progress into stable contractual arrangements. (EC 2007: 20)

The general idea is that Member States could reduce employment protections (in those States that had any) to allow a freer use by capital as long as provisions are put in place to support workers between 'transitions'. It is clear that the underlying principle is to reduce worker expectations of permanent employment and to provide capital with a workforce that is reliant on the State for support between intermittent spells of employment rather than secure employment In this sense flexicurity is still quite compatible with Pollert's and Hyman's earlier critique of flexibility. What is different between earlier flexibility debates and the newer concept of flexicurity is the idea that the latter can reduce rather than deepen labour market inequality. The following sections examine the relationship between flexibility and equality to ascertain how far this proposition might be viable.

Flexibility, segmentation and segregation

Dex and McCulloch (1997: 87) argue that 'flexible work is not evenly distributed in the British economy. It is disproportionately experienced by individuals with certain characteristics'. These findings accord with international statistical summaries in which Rodgers (1989) found that women, young people and immigrant workers are more likely to hold precarious forms of work. It has been argued that what is often described as flexibility are, in effect, 'typical patterns of female employment and not widespread adoption of a flexible workforce' (Ackers et al. 1996: 14). Taking a global perspective, Standing (1999) also argues that flexibility and feminization are closely related. However he maintains that flexibility is widespread and feminization affects men as well as women. Figure 9.1 provides European data on women and men in temporary jobs. The analysis shows that there is wide variation between countries, both in terms of the number of temporary workers and the gap between men and women. However in most countries the share of women in temporary jobs is larger than for men.

Dex and McCulloch (1997: 69) have shown, using UK Labour Force Survey data, that the highest percentages of temporary jobs are found among women in the 'Black and Other group' and that women from ethnic minority groups are far more

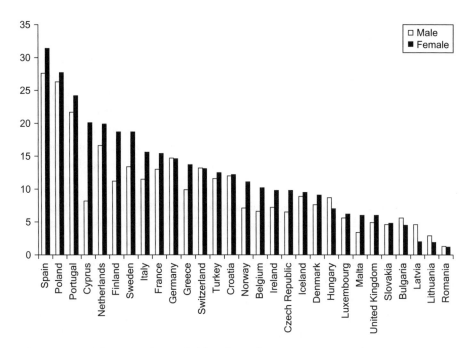

Figure 9.1 Employees aged 15 and older: share of temporary contracts by sex, 2008

Source: Author's Graphical Representation of statistical data contained in European Labour Force Survey Annual Results 2008

likely than white women to hold full-time temporary as opposed to part-time jobs. Similarly, Cassirer (2003) found that black women in America are over-represented in temporary jobs but less likely than white women to work part-time. In the UK data on migrant workers also strongly support Rodgers (1989). A report complied by the UK government, based on its worker registration scheme, monitors the work activities of migrants from the 'A8' countries.[2] In 2007, 52 per cent of all workers who registered worked in temporary jobs.

Young people are also particularly likely to work in temporary jobs. In 2005, 30 per cent of men and women under the age of 30 in the EU 25 were working in fixed-term employment, which was more than double the amount of those over the age of 30 (Eurostat 2008). The figures varied widely within the EU 25 with the highest being Spain with over 50 per cent of men and women under 30 working on fixed-term contracts and the lowest Romania with less than 5 per cent. In both these countries the majority of temporary work is involuntary, but this again varies among EU countries.

The links between labour markets segregated along ethnic and gender lines and labour market segmentation and divisions in the terms and conditions of groups of workers, have long been drawn. Doeringer and Piore's (1971) theory of dual labour markets was originally developed to explain the racial segregation and the poorer terms and conditions of black workers in American labour markets. Based on dual labour market theory, Barron and Norris (1976) noted that women are more likely than men to occupy marginal and precarious jobs. Other segmentation theorists have identified the interaction between part-time work and temporary employment contracts which may explain why 'women returners in particular are likely to be found in temporary jobs' (Rubery and Fagan 1992: 157). My research in this area (Conley 2002, 2003) found a strong association between temporary work and part-time work in UK public services. Similarly Casey et al. (1997: 62) found a positive correlation between employer's use of part-time workers and the use of short-term contract work, stating:

> ... high users of part-time employees were much more likely (three times) to be high users of short-term contract workers than either low part-time users or non-users of part-timers.

Kalleberg et al. (1998) noted that a combination of gender, ethnicity and industrial sector of employment were strongly correlated with the incidence and quality of non-standard work arguing that 'women of all races and ethnic groups are highly concentrated in the lowest quality types of non-standard work. As a whole, men who do non-standard work are concentrated in the higher quality types of work. However non-white men are overrepresented in low quality non-standard jobs and under represented in high quality jobs' (ibid.: 8). In my more recent research (Conley 2003, 2006, 2008) I argue that temporary work in the UK is clustered into a small number of industrial sectors, most notably the public sector, where women and ethnic minority workers are predominantly employed (see Figure 9.2).[3] The UK government

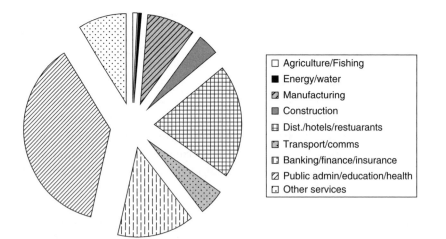

Figure 9.2 UK Temporary work by Industry Sector

Source: Author's graphical representation of statistical data contained in Labour Force Survey 2007 Q4

report on A8 migrant workers indicates that 'in many cases A8 nationals are supporting the provision of public services in communities across the UK' (Home Office 2007: 2) and the same report shows that the majority of these workers do so in temporary jobs. Similar patterns of clusters of temporary workers in public services are found in other EU countries (Ashiagbor 2006: 81) and worldwide (Rani 2008).

Flexibility and equality

It is clear that the interplay between labour market segmentation and segregation means that there is no shortage of women, ethnic minorities and migrants in non-standard work, in line with EU claims that it is needed for 'easy entry' into labour markets. However, in order to reduce inequality flexible work should close the gap between 'insiders' and 'outsiders'. It is therefore worrying that Kalleberg et al. (1998) identify poor quality non-standard work with already disadvantaged groups of workers. Similarly the International Labour Organization (ILO) (2008) highlights that non-standard employment is a factor in rising global income inequality. They argue that there is no clear link between employment growth and income inequality because growth has largely been achieved by the creation of poorly paying non-standard work. Their data show that in Europe temporary jobs pay on average 20 per cent less than permanent jobs; in Latin America informal work pays 43 per cent less than formal work and in India casual workers earn 45 per cent less than 'regular' employees (ibid.:115). Interestingly, their conclusion, in direct opposition to EU thinking, is that national policy makers should *avoid* the duality between standard and non-standard employment.

Non-standard employment has been implicated in one of the major social inequalities in the US – between those who have healthcare insurance and those who do not. Ditsler et al. (2005) found that in 2001, while 74 per cent of workers in standard (full-time, permanent) jobs had employer provided healthcare, only 21 per cent of non-standard workers did. Even when employer sponsored healthcare was available, less than 40 per cent of non-standard workers took it up because they either could not afford it or because they relied on a partner's cover. Ditsler et al. (2005) argue that the rise in non-standard employment in the US is in part related to employers' seeking incentives to avoid the burden of providing healthcare insurance. Their article raises the important point that while governments and employers seek labour flexibility, social structures and institutions for the provision of financial services such as pensions and healthcare insurance, are still largely geared to servicing workers with standard jobs (see also Fredman 2004).

Migrant workers in non-standard jobs have experienced particularly high levels of exploitation in poor quality jobs. TUC (2007) draws data from a number of sources to show that migrant agency workers in the UK suffer poorer health and safety conditions: low pay (sometime illegally low); are provided with less training;

are rarely paid holiday, sick pay or overtime payments and have spurious deductions made from their pay.

Poor work is implicit in the concept of flexicurity where the argument is that non-standard work is a stepping stone that will lead to better things. There is mixed evidence on how far this is actually the case. Starting with Buchtemann and Quack (1989) the debate has focused on whether non-standard work provides a bridge to better quality/more secure work or whether it simply succeeds in trapping disadvantaged groups in poor work. A number of studies have found strong between country differences.[4] In a comparison of outcomes for temporary workers in UK, France, Denmark and Germany, Gash (2008) argues that although, on the whole, temporary work does provide a bridge to more permanent work rather than *unemployment*, there are a number of variables where it might also lead to a trap. For example, temporary workers in the UK, France and Denmark are more likely to enter education, become economically inactive or take another temporary job than are they likely to gain permanent employment. The opposite is true for temporary workers in Germany. Other important variables that are strong predictors of transitions into permanent work were higher educational qualifications (but only in Germany and the UK); the occupational category – with temporary manual workers in France and Denmark less likely to enter permanent work while in the UK and Germany higher grade occupational groups were less likely to enter into permanent contracts; temporary workers in the private sector in France and Germany are more likely to enter permanent work than temporary workers in the public sector. Gash (2008: 662) argues that the risk of unemployment for temporary workers is greatest when the temporary work is preceded by spells of unemployment, stating 'This suggests that a proportion of the temporary workforce is engaged in cycles of unemployment and temporary employment.'

The risk of unemployment for temporary workers is also likely to increase dramatically during times of economic crisis. Certainly in the UK the largest job losses announced at the beginning of the current crisis disproportionately affected temporary workers.[5] The Organization for Economic Co-operation and Development (OECD) (1996) raises an important point specific to temporary work in the UK. In contrast to most other OECD countries, temporary work in the UK appears to be economically 'pro-cyclical'. The report describes the links thus:

> ... if temporary work arrangements are allowed, in particular when they imply a lower cost and/or easier procedures of hiring and firing, economic growth might lead to employment growth mainly through such [temporary] jobs. In a slump employers would tend to let these workers go first. During upturns, the bulk of hirings would then be in the form of temporary work arrangements. The incidence of temporary work should thus increase in upturns and decrease in downturns. (ibid.: 8)

This seems to imply that temporary work in the UK stems largely from cost-based decisions furnished by limited employment protection for workers. It is difficult to see from this economic model how flexibility could help temporary workers into permanent jobs.

Gendered and ethnicized experience of temporary work

The preceding sections have drawn on macro analyses of large-scale national and international surveys to illustrate the links between flexibility and inequality. Felstead and Jewson have noted the dominance of the statistical analysis over theoretical concerns in the academic treatment on non-standard work. One result is that definitions have been developed largely as a result of the pragmatic requirements of statistical data collection and remain 'untheorized' (1999: 5). Secondly, it means that the experience of temporary workers has been left largely unconsidered. The aim of this section is to draw on literature and primary qualitative research data that has sought to explore the day-to-day experience of temporary workers to further understand how flexibility becomes gendered and ethnicized. The primary data is drawn from a study of fixed-term contract work in UK local government conducted between 1997 and 2000 (Conley 2000).[6]

A number of qualitative studies have highlighted the gendered nature of temporary work. In their study of work place discrimination Collinson et al. (1990: 118) note that women were considered by managers to be more suitable for temporary work because of their 'divided responsibilities between home and work, which meant that they could be treated first and foremost as wives and mothers, easily laid off, replaced and /or re-engaged'. Henson (1996) has also noted the strong links between gender and temporary agency work in the US. Temporary agency work is traditionally gendered, a feature that was reflected in the names of the early agencies, most notably 'Kelly Girl'. Henson argues that temporary work is portrayed as providing flexibility for female workers that is directly linked to child care responsibilities both present and past by targeting the 'devoted mom' and the 'gregarious grandma' (ibid.: 27). However he maintains that the reality is similar to that argued by Collinson et al. above:

> Temporary employment, with its intermittent work availability and without a promotional track, fit well with an existing national ideology that assumed that women's labour activity was transitory, impermanent and secondary. (Henson 1996: 8)

However women temporary workers, in contrast to their employers, often do not see their work or commitment to it as transitory:

> If you are working on a full-time contract they seem to think that you have made this commitment and that you have been working in the same place for x amount of years. And they take up my records and they say 'you have been over there, you have been over here'... I have heard the manager say this in passing 'Oh Pamela has been with us a long time now, but she has never really made that full commitment'. And I think that's a

bloody cheek. If I have been working two years here and two years there, what is it! (Black woman, temporary residential social worker)

Even if some women do take temporary work because traditionally gendered family arrangements meant that it was feasible, economic situations and orientations to work change:

> I was not the main breadwinner in the household so part-time suited. But my circumstances have changed. My kids have gone to university and that is a major expense for us. My husband's circumstances have changed. Whereas before, I didn't have to work, now I am looking at a secure income albeit part-time I am looking towards it because that income is used now. (White woman, temporary teacher)

The quantitative analyses have identified that once in temporary work it is not always easy to escape it. One problem with the quantitative data is that it does not research causality in any great depth. In contrast, the qualitative data above reveal how, coupled with a male bread-winner model, the 'trap' of temporary work becomes gendered even when this model no longer pertains (Fredman 2004).

Another problem with the quantitative data on temporary work is that it often aggregates statistics to include a number of qualitatively different forms of temporary work. While the qualitative data above research the experiences of directly hired fixed-term contract staff, other qualitative studies (Casey and Alach 2004; Kirkpatrick and Hoque 2006; Tailby 2005) have researched staff hired via staffing agencies and found that their experience and expectations can be quite different. All of these studies indicate that agency staff actively chose to undertake this form of work instead of permanent work. This is a preference that is often picked up from quantitative data. However the qualitative studies uncovered complex, often gendered reasons behind these choices. For example, Tailby's (2005) study of agency and bank nurses revealed that this form of work was often held in conjunction with a permanent post and used essentially as a better paying form of overtime to supplement relatively low pay and which could be more easily combined with childcare. Casey and Alach (2004) and Kirkpatrick and Hoque (2006) highlight that agency work is often chosen as a way of exerting more control over the type and location of work undertaken, which provides a way of avoiding the most unpleasant aspects of certain jobs. However this strategy is only possible in tight labour markets or occupations suffering acute skill shortages, and immediate benefits can be outweighed by loss of pensions and other 'deferred' income.

There has been far less qualitative research that has examined ethnicity and temporary work. I have previously (Conley 2000, 2002) noted that the low status of temporary work is associated with undervaluing of language skills of ethnic minority workers and to the weak labour market position of migrant workers:

> There are so many Bengali people from Bangladesh who are living in this country. Most of them are doing restaurant jobs. And if you want to work for [a] restaurant you don't

need to get any skill to get this job. You can get this job straight away and you can stay long by doing this work. But I didn't like to do restaurant work and my lack of communication skill, not only mine but other people from back home, lack of communication skill is why they couldn't get any other job other than restaurant jobs. And you can find most of the people working in restaurants. There isn't anything else because they didn't get any job skill from back home. When this job came up that is why it was very important to me. (Bangladeshi male, temporary language instructor)

These experiences highlight the devaluation of the language skills possessed by minority ethnic workers in the UK and their segregation into stereotyped jobs as a result. In reality this instructor's competency in the Bengali language was a scarce and valuable skill in the school in which he worked. However this was not reflected in his terms and conditions of work or in his own feelings of worth. He considered that the insecure terms of his employment contract was a price worth paying to escape the stereotyped work usually available to Bangladeshi migrant workers.

Conclusions

The analysis in this chapter highlights that non-standard work tends to add to rather than alleviate the disadvantage experienced by vulnerable groups of workers. The EU, in its endorsement of flexicurity, has opted for the social policy solution. While flexicurity is conceptualized as a method of turning non-standard work from a trap to a bridge, the evidence is mixed and not very encouraging. Furthermore, the EU position on legislative protection is somewhat contradictory (Ashiagbor 2006: 92). Explicit in the idea of flexicurity is that regulation should be limited so that employers can hire and fire labourers more freely and that workers should not expect stable employment. The corollary of reduced regulation is that the State should step in and provide support for 'transitions' between jobs. However, much of the EU legislation stemming from the social chapter of the Maastricht Treaty, such as the directives on part-time workers, fixed-term employees and agency workers, has been aimed at providing employment protection for non-standard workers. The legislation has been heavily contested and the agency workers directive, at the time of writing, is still not implemented into UK law. Even where directives have been implemented, there is as yet no evidence that the resulting legislation has had any great impact on the position of non-standard workers (Conley 2008). Analysis of quantitative data from the European Labour Force Survey highlights that the numbers of and the outcome for temporary workers varies widely across different nation states. The impact on equality for disadvantaged groups is also likely to be variable. Not all EU states have embraced flexicurity or interpreted it in the same way. In this respect the conclusion of Barbieri (2009: 5) 'that institutions matter' is important.

Contrary to the promises of flexicurity, rather than social policy providing for smoother transitions between flexible jobs, pension and national insurance structures trap women into jobs that are part of an out-dated male-as-breadwinner model of household income generation (Fredman 2004). Furthermore, Fredman (2004) contends that the current configuration of the law means that non-standard workers, particularly those who move between paid work in the public sphere and unpaid work in the home, are considerably marginalized. The qualitative data reviewed in this chapter support this view. In short only one side of the flexicurity bargain is achieved: employers have more freedom in the use of non-standard workers but the State, in many cases, has failed to reconfigure social structures or legislation to temper the negative affects on already disadvantaged groups.

Notes

1. For a full summary see: http://www.eurofound.europa.eu/areas/industrialrelations/dictionary/definitions/lisbonstrategy.htm
2. The eight European countries admitted to the EU in 2004.
3. Although the data contained in Figure 9.2 represent a snapshot of temporary work by Standard Industrial Classification for only one quarter of 2007, these proportions have not changed substantially since 1984 when statistics on temporary work were first collected in the UK.
4. See Barbieri (2009) for a useful summary of research in this area.
5. 23 October 2008, *Peterborough Evening Telegraph*, 70 temporary workers laid off at Perkins Industry shipbuilders; 16 February 2009, *Times On-line* BMW make 850 temporary agency workers redundant; 29 November 2008, *The Scotsman*, Rolls Royce make 40 temporary workers redundant.
6. Funded by ESRC research grant R00429634355.

References

Ackers, P., C. Smith and P. Smith (eds) (1996) *The new workplace and trade unionism: critical perspectives on work and organisation.* London: Routledge.

Ashiagbor, D. (2006) 'Promoting precariousness? The response of EU employment policies to precarious work', In J. Fudge and R. Owens (eds), *Precarious work, women and the new economy. The challenge to legal norms.* Oxford: Hart Publishing.

Atkinson, J. (1984) 'Manpower strategies for flexible organisations', *Personnel Management*, August: 26–9.

—— (1985) *Flexibility, uncertainty and manpower management.* Brighton: Institute of Manpower Studies.

Barbieri, P. (2009) 'Flexibility employment and inequality in Europe', *European Sociological Review*, on-line advance access published 4 May 2009.

Barron, R. D. and D. M. Norris (1976) 'Sexual divisions and the dual labour market', In D. L. Barker and S. Allen (eds), *Dependence and exploitation in work and marriage.* London: Longman.

Blyton, P. and J. Morris. (1991) 'A flexible future: aspects of the flexibility debates and some unresolved issues', In P. Blyton and J. Morris (eds), *A flexible future? prospects for employment and organization.* Berlin: De Gruyter.

Buchtemann, C. and S. Quack (1989) '"Bridges" or "traps" ? Non-standard employment in the Federal Republic of Germany', In G. Rodgers and J. Rodgers (eds), *Precarious jobs in labour market regulation: the growth of atypical employment in Western Europe*. Brussels: International Institute for Labour Studies.

Casey, C. and P. Alach (2004) 'Just a temp? Women, temporary employment and lifestyle', *Work, Employment and Society*, 18(3): 459–80.

Casey, B., H. Metcalf and N. Millward (1997) *Employers' use of flexible labour*. London: Policy Studies Institute.

Cassirer, N. (2003) 'Work arrangements among women in the United States', In S. Houseman and O. Machiko (eds), *Non-standard work in developed economies. Causes and consequences*. Michigan: Upjohn Institute.

Collinson, D. L., D. Knights and M. Collinson (1990) *Managing to discriminate*. London: Routledge.

Conley (2000) 'Temporary labour in the public sector: employers' policies and trades union responses in social services and schools', Unpublished PhD Thesis University of Warwick.

—— (2002) 'A state of insecurity: temporary work in the public services', *Work, Employment and Society*, 16(4): 725–37.

—— (2003) 'Temporary work in the public services: implications for equal opportunities', *Gender, Work and Organization*, 10(4): 455–77.

—— (2006) 'Modernisation or casualisation? Numerical flexibility in the public services', *Capital & Class*, 89 (Summer): 31–57.

—— (2008) 'The nightmare of temporary work: a comment on Fevre', *Work, Employment and Society*, 22(4): 731–6.

Cousins, C. (1999) *Society, work and welfare in Europe*. Basingstoke: Macmillan.

Dex, S. and A. McCulloch (1997) *Flexible employment: the future of Britain's jobs*. Basingstoke: Macmillan.

Ditsler, E., P. Fisher, C. Gordon (2005) *On the fringe: the substandard benefits of workers in part-time, temporary and contract jobs*. The Commonwealth Fund. Available at: www. cmwf.org

Doeringer, P. B. and M. Piore (1971) *Internal labour markets and manpower adjustments*. Lexington, MA: D.C. Heath.

EC (2007) 'Towards Common Principles of Flexicurity: More and Better Jobs through Flexibility and Security' COM (2007) 359 Luxembourg: Office for Official publications of the European Communities.

Eurostat (2008) *The life of men and women in Europe. A statistical portrait*. Luxembourg: European Commission.

Felstead, A. and N. Jewson (1999) 'Flexible labour and non-standard employment', In A. Felstead and N. Jewson (eds), *Global trends in flexible labour*. Basingstoke: Macmillan.

Fredman, S. (2004) 'Women at work: the broken promise of flexicurity', *Industrial Law Journal*, 33(4): 299–319.

Gash, V. (2008) '"Bridge or Trap"? Temporary workers transitions to unemployment and to the standard employment contract', *European Sociological Review*, 24(5): 651–68.

Hayek, F. (1980) *Unemployment and the unions*. London: Institute of Economic Affairs.

Healy, G. (2006) 'Flexicurity – the UK Picture', unpublished paper for ETUI/SALTSA project How Secure is Flexicurity?

Henson, K. (1996) *Just a temp*. Philadelphia: Temple University Press.

Hirst, P. and J. Zeitlin (1989) 'Flexible specialisation and the competitive failure of UK manufacturing', *Political Quarterly*, 60(2): 164–78.

Home Office (2007) *Accession Monitoring Report May 2004–September 2007.* Available at: http://www.ukba.homeoffice.gov.uk/sitecontent/documents/aboutus/reports/accession_ monitoring_report/report13/may04sept07.pdf?view=Binary

Houseman, S. and M. Osawa (eds) (2003) *Nonstandard work in developed economies.* Michigan: Upjohn Institute.

Hyman, R. (1991) 'Plus ca change? The theory of production and the production of theory', In A. Pollert (ed.), *Farewell to Flexibility?* Oxford: Blackwell.

ILO (2008) *World of work report income. Inequalities in the Age of Financial Globalization.* Geneva: ILO.

Kalleberg, A., E. Rasell, N. Cassirer, B. F. Reskin, K. Hudson, D. Webster, E. Appelbaum and R. M. Spalter-Roth(1998) *Nonstandard work, substandard jobs: flexible work arrangements in the US.* Washington: Economic Policy Institute.

Kirkpatrick, I. and K. Hoque (2006) 'A retreat from permanent employment? Accounting for the rise of professional agency work in UK public services', *Work, Employment and Society,* 20(4): 649–66.

Metcalf, D. (1988) *Trade unions and economic performance: the British evidence.* London: London School of Economics.

OECD (1996) Employment outlook. Paris: OECD.

Piore, M. and C. Sabel (1984) *The second industrial divide: possibilities for prosperity.* New York: Basic Books.

Pollert, A. (1991) 'The orthodoxy of flexibility', In A. Pollert (ed.), *Farewell to flexibility?* Oxford: Blackwell.

Rani, U. (2008) *Impacts of changing work patterns on income inequality.* Geneva: International Institute for Labor Studies.

Rodgers, G. (1989) 'Precarious work in Western Europe: the state of the debate', In G. Rodgers and J. Rodgers (eds), *Precarious jobs in labour market regulation: the growth of atypical employment in Western Europe.* Brussels: International Institute for Labour Studies.

Rubery, J. and C. Fagan (1992) Does feminization mean a flexible labour force?, In A. Ferner and R. Hyman (eds), *Industrial relations in the New Europe.* Oxford: Blackwell.

Standing, G. (1999) 'Global Feminization through flexible labor: a theme revisited', *World Development,* 27(3): 583–602.

Tailby, S. (2005) 'Agency and bank nursing in the UK National Health Service', *Work, Employment and Society,* 9(2): 369–89.

TUC (2007) *Migrant agency workers in the UK.* London: TUC.

10

Gender, ethnicity and migration in black women's business start-up resourcing

Cynthia Forson

Introduction

The aim of this chapter is to examine, from an intersectional perspective, the business start-up experiences of black women in relation to the acquisition of human and social capital for business start-up. Policy discourse has highlighted the benefits of small business ownership and entrepreneurship for the labour market participation of underrepresented and disadvantaged groups such as women and ethnic minorities (DTI 2003). Yet academic research consistently emphasizes that in some respects women experience business ownership differently from men. Fewer women than men have growth-oriented businesses, women generally start with lower levels of capital and women's businesses are confined to 'female' sectors such as catering, social enterprises and personal services. However, much of the work on women's business ownership has either focused on the experiences of white women or considered them as a homogenous group (De Bruin et al. 2006). Comparatively very little work has engaged with the dynamics of black and minority ethnic (BME) women's businesses although more recent works include details about this group (see e.g. Dawe and Fielden 2005; Dhaliwal 2000; Forson 2006, 2007a).

Work on ethnic minority business ownership (mainly focused on men) has argued that there seem to be more differences between ethnic minority groups than between BMEs as a group and their white counterparts (Smallbone et al. 2003). For example, social class has been cited as one of the differentiating structures in the experiences of groups. Ram and Barrett (2000) have suggested that the differences between the motivations to self-employment of Pakistanis and Bangladeshis on the one hand and African-Asians and Indians on the other, may be put down to differences in educational backgrounds and affluence. Yet there seems to be a consistent lack of research differentiation between BMEs in terms of the diversity of the group and the experiences of Africans and Caribbeans in business is seldom investigated. Further, with a few exceptions (e.g. Bradley and Boles 2003; Forson 2007b) the differences within groups of BME people are also rarely examined, for example in relation to gender, class, or migrant status.

Against this background and in the context of the Black Hairdressing sector in London, the overall aim of this chapter is to examine the ways in which gender, ethnicity and migration, and the intersections of these identities impact on the resource mobilization experiences of black women in business. The chapter highlights ways in which the intersectional experience can lead to complex and sometimes unique outcomes for black women, compared to their white or Asian counterparts, and between African and Caribbean women. The chapter focuses particularly on the strategies the women employ in resourcing their businesses within the context of a society and labour market that is stratified by ethnicity and gender.

The chapter draws on the data of a wider study on the business experiences of black women in London. It begins with a discussion of the position of black women in the entrepreneurship and small business literature, followed by an examination of current research on resource mobilization and start-up experiences and questions whether the existing literature adequately reflects the experiences of black African and black Caribbean women in the United Kingdom. The methodology employed is then outlined followed by a contextualization of the study through a discussion of the nature of the subject sector. Finally, the findings of the study are discussed in the light of the impact of the intersections of gender and ethnicity.

Positioning black women in business

Although theoretical developments in research on female business owners is still immature compared to that on men (De Bruin et al. 2007; Marlow et al. 2009), there is ample evidence to suggest that in many respects entrepreneurship and business ownership is a gendered process and experiences of business ownership demonstrate gender influences . Although there are several feminist perspectives, feminist writers' main arguments focus on the differences in the ways in which men and women have experienced business ownership.

A feminist standpoint emphasizes the gender roles which favour men over women and focuses on the disadvantages that women face in starting and growing their business reflected in the under representation of women in small business ownership and their limited access to social financial and human capital for their businesses (Belle and La Valle 2003; Fielden and Davidson 2005). Others centre on the role of culture in privileging the male experience and emphasize the androcentric nature of extant discourse on small business ownership (Ahl 2004).

However, with racism as a substantive force in the lives of black women, especially those living outside of Africa (Amos and Parmar 1997; Hooks 2000), standpoints that rely solely on gender in explaining women's experiences do not adequately cater to the experiences of black women. Gender analysis is unable to take on how multiple oppressions crisscross and interlace, making black women's experiences qualitatively different from those of white women while not denying that they also suffer the effects of patriarchal structures as well. Studies on ethnic minority women in business ownership have acknowledged the relevance of ethnicity *and* gender in defining and shaping their experiences, for example, in relation to the gender-specific nature of ethnic resources and the differential access to these resources in the ethnic economy (Anthias and Mehta 2003; Bradley and Boles 2003).

Patriarchal analysis on its own limits the possibility of taking into account the historical and contextually related ways in which gender divisions are manifest. Many feminists have called for feminist theorizing to move beyond the abstract concept of patriarchy to more grounded levels of analysis embedded in women's everyday lives (Gottfried 1998), that are able to encompass the multiplicity of women and their lives. This requires a discussion on black women in business in a historical and contemporary context that incorporates the impact of race, ethnicity, class, structural poverty, economic exploitation *as well as* gender; a discussion that transcends gender specificity.

Previous research on black women in business

Start-up experiences of women in business centre on raising capital – human, social and financial. These are primary factors in the successful transition from thinking about self-employment to actually becoming self-employed. However, this chapter concentrates on social and human capital.

Human capital, education and training

Human capital consists of achieved attributes that lead to increased levels of efficiency and output (Becker 1993). Human capital can be obtained from several sources which include, but are not limited to, investments in formal education, job experience and general and specific training (Carter et al. 1997). However, Pierre Bourdieu (1986) envisages human capital as an institutionalized form of the broader concept of cultural capital which also includes dispositions, attitudes and ways of thinking. Dollinger (1994) has argued that entrepreneurial capital extends to judgment, insight, creativity, vision and intelligence.

Research on women business owners has demonstrated that they are generally not less qualified than men but lack business specific-skills such as marketing, accounting and so on, reflecting women's vulnerability to discrimination in terms of securing employment and gaining promotion to managerial positions (Bradley et al. 2007), where they are likely to gain on-the-job training in business and management skills. This has been known to create a lack of confidence in women when they start-up their own businesses (Carter and Cannon 1992).

Further, although there is no difference in the propensity of men and women business owners to undertake relevant training in the early stages of the business, some government-sponsored initiatives have been found to have effectively discriminated against a considerable number of women (Richardson and Hartshorn 1993). In addition, reviews of many of the programmes designed to support and train unemployed and underemployed persons have shown that BME people have lower participation rates and lower outcomes compared to the majority population (Atkinson et al. 2003).

Research on entrepreneurship and self-employment has established the importance of role models in the choice of self-employment as a career (Delmar and Davidsson 2000). Research also suggests that not only the presence of self-employed parents but also how positively their status or performance is perceived influences the children's intentions to become self-employed (Davidsson 1995). Thus, self-employed parents are probably important if they are perceived to be successful. This effect may be stronger for males than for females (Matthews and Moser 1995) and might reflect the fact that most of the role models studied have been men. Applying this to ethnic minority groups Butler and Cedric (1991) noted that the effect of role models is particularly strong when combined with an anticipation of higher rewards than those available in employment.

There is little discussion on the educational and training circumstances of BME entrepreneurs. Whitehead et al. (2006) have noted that BME entrepreneurs have higher educational credentials than the self-employed population as a whole. With the high deployment of family labour and the small firm as training ground for would-be BME entrepreneurs (Ram et al. 2000), many BME entrepreneurs have learned the skills they employ in their businesses from apprenticeships in their parents' or other family members' businesses. Further, Asian women business owners (Dhaliwal 2000) and would-be business owners (Fielden et al. 1999) also train in their family firms. Yet at the intersection of gender and ethnicity, black female entrepreneurs may have fewer opportunities as the proliferation of Asian businesses has not been replicated in the African and Caribbean communities.

As such black women may need to rely on alternative sources of human capital to the formal provision available. Research in the United States revealed that self-employed African-American women, whose business ownership experiences are often compared to black people in the United Kingdom, desire training in traditional areas such as management, accounting and marketing (Lownes-Jackson 1999). However, other areas identified by the research indicated they also desire training in growth and expansion, global opportunities, corporate procurement, computers and technology, recruitment and health insurance issues.

The above-mentioned skills may not be available to BME and specifically black women through the normal channels. As such, black women may need to devise their own strategies to acquire the skills they need for their businesses through the use of informal channels and social networks.

Networking and business support

Studies on business networking have stressed the importance of networks of both dense and loose ties for the success of women's (Kovalainen 2004) and men's enterprises. Advocates of the positive impact of networking have found that networking aids the acquisition of information and advice (Shaw 1997) and in Ireland it has been found to contribute to innovation in the firm (Birley et al. 1991). Weak ties (business networks) at the personal level facilitate access to resources beyond the entrepreneur's immediate friends and family (Chell and Baines 2000) such as social and financial capital. For women in particular, networking offers opportunities for overcoming isolation, exchanging information, gaining experience, business contacts and clients, advice and support, accessing mentors and informal advisors (Atkinson 2001). Women have been found to have a high level of other women and kin in their networks (formal or informal) (Renzulli 1998, cited in Renzulli et al. 2000) because they tend to be left out of men's informal networks (Aldrich and Sakano 1998). Renzulli et al. (2000) contend that the high level of kin in women's social networks is disadvantageous in their bid to raise human and financial capital for their businesses.

Social networks can also work against certain groups of women in specifically racialized and gendered ways. First, access to such cheap family labour remains gendered (Dhaliwal 2000). Some groups of BME men seem to have unlimited access to the labour of their wives in their businesses but there is limited reciprocity in that regard as a result of cultural norms. Second, such family employment can lead to the exploitation of women's labour without an acknowledgment of the contribution they make to the success of the business (Apitzsch 2003). The contribution that these women make to the business can be better understood when measured in financial terms, especially when the financial constraints of BME businesses are evaluated.

Further, Asian women who experience discrimination in the formal labour market that acts as a push factor for self-employment find that tight social networks, which would normally provide socialization mechanisms that encourage entry into the small-business community (Ward and Jenkins 1984), create specific difficulties in becoming self-employed in their own right, as access to that support is highly gendered (Dawe and Fielden 2005). Finally, the assumption that certain minority women have automatic family support from older female relatives has been challenged by Rana et al. (1998). They argue that cultural norms dictate that a woman's place is in the home, and there is sometimes a lack of understanding by family members about the demands of women's work outside the home that makes child-care assistance not so readily forthcoming. Ram et al. (2001) highlight how the literature on the importance of family in self-employment masks the negative effects of power relations based on gender, generation and status.

How well are these findings replicated in the experiences of black women with their higher rates of lone parenthood embedded in more egalitarian family structures? The evidence is scarce. However, in view of the fact that black feminists (Anthias and Mehta 2003; Mirza 2003) have argued that the black domestic space, and the actors within it may not have the same dynamics as the white home, it is reasonable to argue that black women's social networks may provide different support than that experienced by white women and Asian women.

Social networks provide social support and reduce the costs of self-employment. However, work on social networks supposes the availability of social networks as given, but with their past and present experiences of migration, African and Caribbean women are sometimes embedded in shifting cultural and geographic networks. These conceptualizations of embeddedness need to take into consideration – to borrow a phrase from Palriwala and Risseeuw (1996) – the 'dynamic interrelationships between domains, the historical processes of change and the negotiated quality of relationships' (p.16) resulting in 'shifting circles of support' and constraint.

Relationships take time and effort to create and maintain, and loss of the benefits from one's network that is occasioned by migration takes time to recreate and rebuild. Many black migrant women have left 'old' family and friends in their countries of origin and are in the process of creating 'new families' and friends in new territories while at the same time maintaining (sometimes) an intercontinental network of ties of reciprocity and obligation that have profound implications for their business decisions and are simultaneously impacted on by these business decisions. At the same time, for migrant women the move to the United Kingdom frequently results in a downslide in the family's economic situation, which means that women are expected to contribute to the family's maintenance without the support of the social networks that made economic activity possible while they were in their home countries.

Many women who find themselves caught between the pressures of finding adequate childcare and working outside the home rely on family members to help out with childcare responsibilities. Married women have greater access to family support of career (Rogers 2005). How about women who are unmarried or whose husbands have no interest in their career? Rogers (2005) posits that non-married women may seek support from extended family. Caribbean and African women have traditionally relied on extended family, kinship and female support for help with both domestic and work-related effort (Bryan et al. 1985; Dunne and King 2003). In Britain, black women often find themselves as heads of families, with limited or non-existent male support, and have to work to support their families.

For some women, particularly Caribbean women, lone parenthood combined with family structures that are more egalitarian make reliance on family members a challenge.

Methodology

The data analysed for this chapter are part of a wider study that examined the self-employment experiences of African and Caribbean women in the United Kingdom, specifically London. The study focused on London as a field of enquiry for black women because a vast majority of Africans and Caribbeans live in London. They make up about 10 per cent of London's population (ONS, 2005). The study included a scoping exercise with key black female informants, interviews with policy makers and implementers, a documentary review of policy documents in the hairdressing and legal sectors and 50 (15 lawyers and 35 hairdressers) in-depth interviews with black African and black Caribbean women business owners in London in the black hairdressing sectors. The black hairdressing sector is a traditionally feminized, ethnicized and low-income sector. Regulation in the sector is low and it is characterized by an informal culture. The sector is seen as a 'safe space' (Kirton and Healy 2004) for black women. In that regard, it is a sector where business owners, employees and clients are mostly black women. The next section outlines and discusses the findings of the research, examining ways in which gender and ethnicity intersect in the start-up resource mobilization experiences of the participants of the study.

The study participants

The demographic characteristics of the 35 African and Caribbean women hairdressing salon owners in this sample indicated that 20 of the women were either born in the UK or had come to the country as children and therefore were primarily educated and acculturated in the UK. The rest (15 women), on the other hand, arrived in the UK as adults with education and work experiences from their home countries and therefore had a shorter length of residence in the country. As will be noted later, although the women participants experienced similar issues, at the intersection of migration and ethnicity, the migrant or non-migrant status of the women had an impact on the strategies they pursued in accomplishing the task of business start up. In some cases, the differences were quite profound. All the hairdressers were engaged in hairstyling. Half of them also offered nail and beauty services (massage, facials and various body therapies) and had product retail sections in their salons. A few (four) of the hairdressers had also diversified into unrelated products such as party planning, party furniture hire and money transfer businesses on the premises.

Raising capital – structures of enablement and constraint

This section presents the interview findings on the participants' experiences of raising capital (cultural, social and economic) for their businesses. It examines the micro-level strategies the women employed in acquiring resources for their businesses and their rationale for the pursuit of such strategies.

Cultural capital

Embodied cultural capital – cultural and ethnic resources

The availability of ethnic and cultural resources to ethnic minorities has been cited as one of the essential attributes of ethnic minority business success in Western nations (Light and Rosenstein 1995). Previous research has shown that many self-employed people are influenced by an exposure to role models at an early age. Inevitably the majority of these role models have been men. A notable finding of this study is the number (16) of women who had *female* self-employed role models in their families – mothers, grandmothers and sisters. An intersectional lens reveals that the matriarchal configuration of West African and Caribbean families which facilitates the economic independence of women in an otherwise patriarchal society (Dunne and King 2003) provided ethnic resources (female self-employed role models) for the participant women, which are not always available to Asian or white women.

Further, an examination of the nexus of gender, ethnicity and migration provides additional insight. Of the 16 women who had female role models, 13 were migrant women. Only three of the non-migrant women had self-employed role models in their families. Olivia's and Beryl's father and mother were business owners from whom they had taken over their hairdressing businesses and Adjoa's parents owned a dry cleaner's shop in [West Africa]. Compared to this group, ten migrant women cited their mothers as self-employed, three had self-employed sisters, one had a self-employed grandmother and three had self-employed fathers. Clearly, the history of black people in the UK combined with UK culture reconfigures the dynamics of the black family.

Examining the intersection of migration, ethnicity and gender further, the data revealed that ten of the migrant women had also been self-employed themselves before they came to Britain and this had consequences for the confidence with which they approached business start-up and the way in which they mobilized resources for their businesses. The high level of previous self-employment among the migrant women is a reflection of the high self-employment activity found amongst women in the countries that typically send migrants to Britain as a result of a traditional culture of high economic activity rates among women coupled with women's limited access to jobs in the formal employment sectors of those countries. Much of the research on women's and ethnic minorities' entrepreneurship tends to focus on their experiences in the host countries without a consideration of prior experiences of migrants and how these may affect their behaviour and perceptions of self-employment.

So as Rachel put it, 'I know a lot before I start my business ... before I came to this country ... I know a lot about setting up and doing a business as well'.

Many of these activities were conducted in countries where state provision of business support is non-existent and therefore these women have learnt to be self-reliant and also reliant on their networks for survival (Chamlee-Wright 1997). One of the issues that came to the fore during this investigation was the difference between the non-migrant women and the migrant women by the way in which they employed business support provision for their businesses. A considerable number (9) of non-migrant women had sought and sometimes employed different forms of business advice and support. Some, like Bambi, had gone through the formal channel of Business Link and 'spoke[n] to colleagues at the college', while others such as Zoe had used qualified friends and family members to understand the business start-up process. The non-migrant women, perhaps because most of them were hairdressing tutors, had very good links with the hairdressing colleges that enabled them to get advice and access to skilled staff.

In contrast, as several of the migrant women either had personal experiences of self-employment or family histories of 'trading', they had a self-sufficiency that bordered on disdain for business advice. When she was asked what sources of business advice she had used in starting her own business Ellen, typifying the norm said: 'I don't think there is any advice to be given as to how to start a shop. You know what you want to do. You get the funds and you open the shop ... get the basic infrastructure and that's it.'

It would seem that business advice became important only when things went wrong or after the women had run their businesses for a while and had realized that the 'experience'" from their home countries was inadequate to sustain them in a more corporatist environment. The issue for these women was not the awareness of the availability of or access to business support and training but their perceptions of its importance given their prior experience. It would seem therefore that black women's level of embeddedness in the British society influences their perception of the necessity of training and business support as resources for their businesses, at least in the start-up phase and for migrant women in this sample, business support was deemed important only after the start-up phase.

Institutionlized cultural capital-accumulating human capital

Non-migrant women were very experienced hairdressers with higher qualifications in the hairdressing industry, ten of them with teaching qualifications in hair care, contrasted by general lack of business experience. Perhaps in recognition of their lack of business skills and experience, non-migrant women tended to rely on formal training to start their businesses. Many of them had actively sought business training on a variety of courses ranging from two-day crash courses to six-month business management programmes. Sarah, a 56-year-old Caribbean woman had taken the business course that was part of the hairdressing programme of study at the time she was training for her hairdressing qualifications because she always knew she would open her own business. Many of the non-migrant women actively engaged in on-going training, particularly in hairdressing skills at the colleges.

Several of the migrant women, on the other hand, had abandoned their chosen careers and retrained to enter the hairdressing industry in the United Kingdom and their resourcefulness in raising human capital for their businesses is noteworthy. Although Henrietta was aware of her lack of relevant human capital, her attempts to rectify this by enrolling in a course were frustrated by a pregnancy which forced her to abandon her plans for a period. However, she continued her 'training' by volunteering her services at other hairdressing salons. More importantly, she also provided hairdressing services for her friends and family in her home to build up her experience. In her own words, 'Weekends my house is packed with friends and I do their hair, facials, waxing and stuff like that. This helped me to know how to do hair properly'.

In exchange, however, many of those who charged for their services found that they were unable to charge the same prices as high street salons. In addition, several women recall having to make meals, tea/coffee for their friends and family coupled with a general lack of privacy, which sometimes motivated them into starting their formal businesses earlier than they had envisaged. Several of the migrant women used family and friends to build their human capital in the form of experience in the craft of hairdressing and adjust to the host country before embarking on business ownership in the formal sector. Many migrants who are ineligible for state benefits have to rely on the jobs outside the mainstream in order to survive in the host country.

Social capital – entrepreneurship as a 'collective' activity

Ethnic minority businesses' access to cheap unskilled labour in the form of family members to run their businesses has been noted as being at the heart of their success in small business, something which African and Caribbean businesses lack (Ram and Jones 1998).

Social capital benefits of group membership

Zoe and Olivia employed their mothers as receptionists (a non-core activity) in their businesses. This would seem to support the contention that the professional nature of the businesses limits the extent to which Africans and Caribbeans can employ cheap family labour (Ram and Jones 1998). The support given by families extended to financial advice from Olivia's brother, a professional financial advisor and free accounting services provided by the husbands of Fola, Henrietta, Adjoa and Ellen. Bambi's and Zoe's daughters, Fola's sister and Henrietta's and Adjoa's husbands would take over the management of the businesses if the women were unavailable for any reason – all non-core activities. Contrary to much literature on the disadvantage experienced by African and Caribbean business people as a result of a lack of family support, families played an important role in both the start-up and management of the interviewees' businesses. Shirley's brother had provided 100 per cent of her start-up capital and she said she would turn to her mother for capital to try something new in the business. Henrietta, Martha, Ellen, Rachel, Fola and Lillian had sought and gained finance from or through family members for start-up purposes.

Families were also pivotal in the indirect support they gave the businesses in the context of a loss of social networks resulting from migration. Therefore, while Caribbean women were able to rely on available family support in the UK, both Lillian and Martha (black Africans) were very reliant on their mothers for free childcare services, on an intercontinental basis. Lillian's mother had given up her job to come and live with her from Africa while Martha had sent her children to her mother in Africa while she took her hairdressing course and they had only returned to the UK when they were of school-going age.

Some commentators on social capital in relation to entrepreneurship have bemoaned the lack of wider networks available to women and ethnic minorities as the reason for the dependence on tighter networks of kinship and friendship. Such lack has been explained in terms of the wider frameworks of racism and sexism – that, women and ethnic minorities lack access to wider, information rich networks. But many of these women come from cultures where social networks are very fluid and informally structured and organized around kinship and co-residential ties. To interpret the behaviour of these women outside of cultural influences is to determine entrepreneurship as occurring and existing in a vacuum. These women bring culture into the market place and some of their behaviour is a reflection of their cultural backgrounds. As such, a reliance on co-ethnic, kinship and female networks may not necessarily be a reaction to racism or sexism, or the consequences of the loss of wider networks due to migration but a reflection of the way business is done in their countries of origin and operation in an ethnic niche.

When a consideration is made of the financial cost of the range of support involved in these activities provided by family members and friends it is clear how fluid capital can be (Bourdieu 1986). Thus families are heavily relied on as social networks that directly provide capital (social and economic) and labour, albeit on an intermittent basis, for the business and indirectly facilitate the acquisition of human capital. Families also provide other intangible assets such as encouragement and moral support for fledgling businesses.

This communal resource and cultural dynamics was also observed in the participants' day-to-day running of their businesses. Almost 80 per cent of the participants did not operate an appointment system because of customers' attitudes to punctuality. As such, the salons were run on a first-come-first-served basis. This meant that customers usually had long waiting periods in the salons to get their hair done creating a camaraderie fostered by an informal atmosphere, which benefited the hairdressers. At a couple of salons waiting clients were observed engaging in physical work for the salon such as making tea/coffee for each other, or sweeping the salon floor when the premises got really busy.

Of particular interest is the tension played out between self-interest and altruism in the dynamics of the acquisition of resources through social networks. The women were acutely aware of the differences between their (black) salons and those of white women and they wanted to redress the derogatory stereotypical image of black hairdressing salons because of the lack of professionalism associated with black salons. There was a sense in which they believed that their salons were a representation of the *black community* to the 'world out there' expressed in their sentiments thus:

> You know when you walk into a white lady's salon, you can tell the difference. The environment is not like this; it's so beautiful and well decorated, spotlights everywhere, wooden floor because they have backing and they know what they are doing. They are born into this system; they know which button to press. (Fola)

From an intersectional perspective, Fola touches on three important aspects of 'difference' between the business experiences of black and white women. In talking about the environment of a black woman's salon, she is referring to the difference in class between white women and black women as a group. Second, the statement also has an ethnic dimension as Fola is also aware that white women in business are culturally aware, 'they know what they are doing' as they have the cultural capital (disposition and judgment) required to succeed in business. Third, 'they know which button to press' is an acknowledgment of her migrant status and the attendant lack of networks that entails. Harriet, on the other hand, underscores the wealth of knowledge, insight and critique among black women themselves about the ways in they can use business ownership to overcome some of the resulting configurations of racism, sexism and class in their lives and experiences:

> I've seen black people … they walk in a shop and then they compare other shops to your shop. Meanwhile when you go to those shops their toilets are not clean, most of the black shops. When I first opened this shop people said it's a white shop. I said, 'No, why do you think so?' They ask, 'Who is the owner of this shop?' I say, 'Me'. They say, 'It's yours?' They think I work here. I say, 'No, it's mine'. They say, 'Yours?' I say, 'Yes'. You always thought it was for a white person. Even black people say so. Why do we have to have a mind like that? Because the shop is so clean? We have to believe in ourselves. At the end of the day we can do it ourselves. We can do it. (Harriet)

As such the human capital and labour benefits that the women could potentially gain from membership in the black community were not always welcome. In order to distance themselves from the perceived lower class status of black hairdressing salons, some participants actively discouraged the informality noted above in order to create a professional atmosphere. Zoe said she wanted to show that black hairdressers were not about sitting around and gossiping. Zoe, Shirley and Bambi all operated appointment systems. Shirley had a sign in her salon that said 'This is a business premises; if you are not here on business please do not sit about'.

Although Jocelyn had begun to train both her daughter and son to take over her business when she retired other women interviewed rejected the idea of their children's involvement in the hairdressing business. This was particularly true of the migrant women who saw their own involvement in the hairdressing sector as a contingency plan that evolved through the unexpected experiences of migration. They had better aspirations for their children and therefore limited their children's involvement in the business. The women were rejecting gender-segregated work that operates in ways that reproduce economic exploitation. Lillian's narrative makes it clear that from the perspective of one who has suffered from gendered, class-based racism this is not a viable option for her daughter if she is to avoid her mother's experience. As such, the mother rejects the benefits she may gain from her social capital in order to give her daughter a chance to enter a better profession.

The caring roles women participants played were not confined to their immediate families alone. Women are usually responsible for the care of elderly relatives and with particular regard to migrant women from cultures as those found among the participants of this study such roles do not cease simply because one has left one's country of origin. In as much as the women were able to call on extended family to help them with childcare and other responsibilities even on an intercontinental basis, so too did their care of elderly relatives also extend across continents. Ashi explains, 'Because we have families back home to cater for, even if you go on income support how much will they give us? We still have to cater [financially] for our parents back home'.

Indeed, like in the case of other women, families were not always a positive resource but sometimes placed a constraint on the business intentions of some of the women, particularly those with children. Henrietta had had the opportunity to open a second shop in the West End of London but had shelved her plans because she felt that running two businesses would place too much of a burden on her family relationships.

Almost all the salon owners only hired co-ethnic employees, initially suggesting a deliberate strategy to employ members of the black community as is the case in many ethnic minority businesses. However many bemoaned the lack of professionalism perceived in staff, demonstrated in their perceived tardiness, disloyalty and lack of skills. Interviewees seemed to view the disloyalty and tardiness, as a 'black people's' problem. Typical comments by participants included, 'With the black stylists it's a whole lot of problems. We are not reliable. That is a shame. That is a shame to our own people' (Ellie).

However sectoral constraints created difficulties in seeking employees outside the co-ethnic pool. Ellie felt it was 'a shame you don't get any other race to learn the black hair because whatever we do [employees] are predominantly black. You don't get any other race to be so proficient on our hair', and Mary had 'not come across a European doing black hair', the implication here being that given the choice participants would have no loyalty to the 'black community' in terms of hiring policies. The co-ethnic employment practices were born out of necessity rather than any altruistic intent and ethnic ties did not appear to be a significant feature of participants' recruitment practices. The composition of the workforce was a product of sectoral structures and they ultimately shaped and underpinned the existing employment characteristics of the businesses (Ram and Jones 1998).

Individual social capital

Migrant hairdressers also relied on friends and other hairdressing colleagues for essential information on premises, supplies and labour. Lillian reported finding her premises through a tip from her colleague's barber and a supplier through a hairdresser friend. These narratives were multiplied in other women's interviews. Bambi 'spoke to *colleagues* at the college and ... an ex-boyfriend ... gave [her] a lot of business advice because he works as a business advisor' while Zoe had two of her friends provide the labour for refurbishing her salon.

Interestingly the secondary role played by husbands of migrant *women* in these businesses is in direct comparison with the female 'silent contributors' of South Asian family businesses (Dhaliwal 1997) demonstrating differences between the two groups at the intersection of ethnicity and gender. Many of these husbands have jobs of their own but these 'invisible men' come home at night and take care of children or work on the administrative side of the businesses. Fola described her husband's life:

> The little time that he is off from his work I want to dump the children on him, you know. When he comes back from work from seven o'clock we are there. He has to do the children's homework. While I am cooking he is helping them to do the homework. So he has no life. He cannot go out, he can't do anything. On the weekends when he is free, Saturday, that is my busiest day in the salon. I am in this shop every Saturday for fourteen good hours. From eight o'clock in the morning to ten o'clock in the evening. So Saturday I don't see my children because they will be sleeping before I leave home. He does the child-minding, so he hasn't got a life, no friends, nobody, because of the business.

What is interesting here is that unlike Asian businesses where the 'silent contributors'' work is perceived as secondary or trivial back office work the women in this study seemed to elevate the importance of the work their husbands did for their businesses:

> Everything is my husband, my husband ... to be quite honest when it comes to the accounts I don't have a clue ... When it comes to banking he does it. When it comes to paying the girls, we've got an accountant who does it and he (my husband) sends everything to the accountant so I don't know anything about that. In a way I've been spoilt a little bit but ... you know ... it's one of those things. I don't know it so he's the one who takes on everything for me. (Henrietta)

However, as a caveat to the above optimistic picture of these hairdressers having supportive husbands who facilitated the work–home interface, none of the husbands had changed their lifestyles in relation to any of the 'lower' domestic tasks such as cleaning and cooking. Husbands seemed quite agreeable to take on 'clerical' and 'intellectual' tasks such as accounting for the business and 'doing homework with the kids' but not the tasks on the lower end of the scale, so to speak. This negotiated quality of social exchange, recurring in the lives of Corinne, Rachel, Fola, Martha, Lillian, Sarah, Collette, Moronike, Carol, Sharon and Hyacinth is glaring in the following extended extract of the interview with Corinne:

> *Cynthia*: How do you manage to combine your family life with running the business?
>
> *Corinne*: As a hairdresser I work six days a week. On Sunday I go to church. From church I go to the market to do shopping and I cook the whole day. So I don't really have time at home but I still have time for the family to prepare the food. I cook the food and I put them in the freezer so anybody can pick it up and warm it. I do that on Sundays.
>
> *Cynthia*: Do you think other members of your family have had to change their lifestyle because of your business? For example does your husband cook more or help with the cleaning in the house or anything?
>
> *Corinne*: All he does is come back from work and eat and sleep. African men don't like to cook.
>
> *Cynthia*: Does he help with the business in any way?
>
> *Corinne*: Yeah, when I travel he do come in to see about the business, check the stock and collect whatever they make to bank it.

In terms of formal networks, none of the hairdressers belonged to any organizations and 14 of them went to trade shows regularly but did not actively participate as stand holders, mainly because of the cost of participation. Some of the participants however, viewed networking as a 'waste of time' and resources, particularly business networks that were not sector-specific. In this regard, the women were rejecting the political undertones that black business networks tend to develop due to the history of black organizing in Britain. However, others felt that formal networking was important for survival. Lillian compared the hairdressing industry to that of black retailers in Dalston market and lamented the failure of black hairdressers to develop a network that would help them in business. It was quite clear, however, that hairdressers' strategies in acquiring social capital inclined towards the use of close kinship and friendship ties as opposed to formal networking and at the intersection of gender, ethnicity and migration, their experiences were qualitatively different from white or Asian women.

Conclusion

This chapter has argued that an analysis of women's entrepreneurial experiences that only takes gender into consideration as most literature on the subject does, fails to understand the nature of the influences of varying structures in the lives of different groups of women. It has argued for an intersectional analysis that takes into consideration the qualitatively different outcomes that may emerge from the entrepreneurial start-up process of black women due to the effects of gender, ethnicity and class and in some cases, migration, as well as the choices these women make within such structures.

Through an intersectional lens, the chapter has demonstrated that, within the context of the hairdressing sector, black women's experiences of human and social capital resourcing for their businesses can be qualitatively different from white women. The participants' use of social capital was circumscribed by the gendered and ethnicized perceptions of the wider society. For example, although all women are reliant on their social ties for resourcing their business start-ups, black women's ability and willingness to use the social capital that these ties bring is shaped by their rejection of racialized perceptions of black hairdressing. The need to develop a 'professional' business environment, arguably meaning governed by white, as well as male norms, limited their willingness to use available social capital

Further, at the intersection of gender and ethnicity, more complex differences were evident between the two groups of black women. Being less embedded in British corporatist culture, black African women's strategies, shaped by their cultural understandings of entrepreneurial capital, actively rejected the importance of business support and training in the start-up process. On the other hand, black Caribbean women engaged with the start-up experience from a perspective that demonstrated their embeddedness in British culture. However, the tendency of business support mechanisms to lump all ethnic minority women together in designing support systems fails to recognize the importance of such differences in women's behaviour based on ethnicity.

In this study at least, the black Africans' embeddedness in family networks meant they were able to rely on husbands and children to help with the businesses. Indeed the (African) women embedded in tighter family structures were more dependent on their informal social network than non-migrant (Caribbean) women. Initially, without external structures in place to create and develop formal resource and exchange organizational networks, black women migrants, are reliant on informal social ties. As they become more assimilated into the dominant culture, they then acquire the cultural capital required to assist them in their pursuit of self-employment – in the words of one of the participants, by then 'they know which buttons to press'.

It is clear from this study that although black women seek to gain control over their labour market participation through self-employment, the all-pervasive gendered, ethnocentric and class-based structures they encounter in employment rear up in self-employment as well. The rhetoric of some of the female and BME entrepreneurship literature about self-employment as the answer to the inequities minorities face in the labour market denies the hurdles black women have to overcome in setting up and running their businesses. However, within this framework, individual women in confront and negotiate within and between themselves and different social structures, often do grasp opportunities around them and forge forward their own life agendas but this must not blind us to the experiences of the majority who do not and sometimes cannot do so.

References

Ahl, H. (2004) *The scientific reproduction of gender inequality: a discourse analysis of research texts on women's entrepreneurship.* Malmö: Liber.

Aldrich, H. and T. Sakano (1998) 'Unbroken ties: how the personal networks of Japanese business owners compare to those in other nations', In M. Fruin (ed.), *Networks, markets, and the pacific rim: studies in strategy.* New York: Oxford University Press.

Amos, V. and P. Parmar (1997) 'Challenging imperial feminism', In H. S. Mirza (ed.), *British black feminism: a reader.* London: Routledge

Anthias, F. and N. Mehta (2003) 'The intersection between gender, the family and self-employment: the family as a resource', *International Review of Sociology*, 13(1): 105–16.

Apitzsch, U. (2003) 'Policies and their paradoxes: gaining autonomy in self-employment processes. The biographical embeddedness of women's and migrants' business', *International Review of Sociology*, 13(1): 163–82.

Atkinson, C. (2001) 'With a little help from my friends: networking and mentoring among entrepreneurs for personal business and professional development', WEI Working Paper 18, Pontypridd, University of Glamorgan Business School.

Atkinson, J., C. Evans, R. Willison, D. Lain and M.Van Gent (2003) 'New deal 50plus: sustainability of employment', The Institute for Employment Studies for the Department for Work and Pensions, London.

Becker, G. S. (1993) *Human capital.* Chicago: University of Chicago Press.

Belle, A. J. La Valle (2003) *Combining self-employment and family life.* Cambridge: Polity Press and Joseph Rowntree Foundation.

Birley S., S. Cromie and A. Myers (1991) 'Entrepreneurial networks: their emergence in Ireland and overseas', *International Small Business Journal*, 9(4): 56–74.

Bourdieu, P. (1986) 'The forms of capital', In J. G. Richardson (ed.), *Handbook of theory and research for the sociology of education.* New York: Greenwood Press, pp. 241–58.

Bradley, F. and K. Boles (2003) *Female entrepreneurs from ethnic backgrounds: an exploration of motivations and barriers.* Manchester: Manchester Metropolitan University Business School.

Bradley H., G. Healy, C. Forson and P. Kaul (2007) *Ethnic minority women and workplace cultures: what does and does not work.* London: Equal Opportunities Commission.

Bryan, B., S. Dadzie and S. Scafe (1985) *The heart of the race: black women's lives in Britain.* London: Virago.

Butler, J. S. and H. Cedric (1991) 'Ethnicity and entrepreneurship in America: toward an explanation of racial and ethnic group variations in self-employment', *Sociological Perspectives*, 34(1): 79–94.

Carter, N. M., M. Williams and P. D. Reynolds (1997) 'Discontinuance among new firms in retail: the influence of initial resources, strategy and gender', *Journal of Business Venturing*, 12(2): 125–45.

Carter, S. and T. Cannon (1992) *Women as entrepreneurs.* London: Academic Press.

Chamlee-Wright, E. (1997) *The cultural foundations of economic development: urban female entrepreneurship in Ghana.* London and New York: Routledge.

Chell, E. and S. Baines (2000) 'Networking, entrepreneurship and microbusiness behaviour', *Entrepreneurship & Regional Development*, 12(3): 195–215.

Davidsson, P. (1995) 'Determinants of entrepreneurial intentions', Paper presented to RENT IX Conference, Piacenza, Italy, 23–24 November.

Dawe A. J. and S. L. Fielden (2005) 'The experiences of Asian women entering business start-up in the UK', In S. L. Fielden and M. J. Davidson (eds), *International handbook of women and small business entrepreneurship.* Cheltenham: Edward Elgar, pp. 120–32.

De Bruin, A., C. G. Brush and F. Welter (2006) 'Introduction to the special issue: towards building cumulative knowledge on women's entrepreneurship', *Entrepreneurship Theory and Practice*, 31(3): 585–93.

—— (2007) 'Advancing a framework for coherent research on women's entrepreneurship', *Entrepreneurship Theory and Practice*, 31(3): 323–39.

Delmar, F. and P. Davidsson (2000) 'Where do they come from? Prevalence and characteristics of nascent entrepreneurs', *Entrepreneurship and Regional Development*, 12: 1–23.

Dhaliwal, S. (2000) 'Asian female entrepreneurs and women in business – an exploratory study', *Enterprise and Innovation Management Studies*, 1(2): 207–16.

Dollinger, M. J. (1994) *Entrepreneurship strategies and resources.* Burr Ridge, IL: Irwin.

DTI (2003) 'A strategic framework for women's enterprise', Department of Trade and Industry, London.

Dunne, M. and R. King (2003) 'Outside theory: an exploration of the links between education and work for Ghanaian market traders', *Journal of Education and Work*, 16(1): 27–44.

Fielden, S. L. and M. J. Davidson (eds) (2005) *International handbook of women and small business entrepreneurship.* Cheltenham: Edward Elgar.

Fielden, S. L., A. J. Dawe, M. J. Davidson, and P. J. Makin (1999) 'Women's economic growth in Heywood Middleton and Rochdale', UMIST Working Paper Series, 9906.

Forson, C. (2006) 'The strategic framework for women's enterprise: BME women at the margins', *Equal Opportunities International*, 25(6): 418–32.

—— (2007a) 'Intersectionality, context and "choice": the career choice influences of self-employed black women', In M. Ozbilgin and A. Malach-Pines (eds), *Career management and entrepreneurship: a research companion.* Cheltenham: Edward Elgar, pp. 548–80.

—— (2007b) 'Social embeddedness, "choices" and constraints in small business start-up: black women in business', PhD thesis presented to School of Business and Management, Queen Mary, University of London, London.

Gottfried, H. (1998) 'Beyond patriarchy? Theorising gender and class', *Sociology*, 32(3): 451–68.

Hooks, B. (2000) 'Black women: shaping feminist theory', In J. James and T. D. Sharpley-Whiting (eds), *The black feminist reader*. Oxford: Blackwell Publishers, pp.131–45.

Kirton, G. and G. Healy (2004) 'Shaping women's trade union identities: a case study of women-only courses in MSF and TGWU', *British Journal of Industrial Relations*, 42(2): 303–23.

Kovalainen, A. (2004) 'Rethinking the revival of social capital and trust in social theory: possibilities for feminist analysis'. In B. L. Marshall and A. Witz (eds), *Engendering the social. Feminist encounters with sociological theory*. London: Open University Press, pp. 155–70.

Light, I. and C. Rosenstein (1995) *Race, ethnicity and entrepreneurship in urban America*. New York: Aldine de Gruyter.

Lownes-Jackson, M. (1999) 'Training and educational needs of African-American female entrepreneurs (research notes)', *International Advances in Economic Research*, 5(3): 399.

Marlow, S., C. Henry and S. Carter (2009) 'Exploring the impact of gender upon women's business ownership: introduction', *International Small Business Journal*, 27(2): 139–48.

Matthews, C. H. and S. B. Moser (1995) 'Family background and gender: implications for interest in small firm ownership', *Entrepreneurship and Regional Development*, 7(4): 365–78.

Mirza, H. S. (2003) ' "All women are white, all the blacks are men – but some of us are brave": mapping the consequences of invisibility for black and minority ethnic women in Britain', In D. Mason (ed.), *Explaining ethnic differences: changing patterns of disadvantage in Britain*. Bristol: The Policy Press, pp. 121–38.

ONS (2005) *Region in figures: London*. Vol 9, Winter 2004/05, London: Office of National Statistics.

Palriwala, R. and C. Risseeuw (1996) *Shifting circles of support: contextualising kinship and gender in Sub-Saharan Africa*. London: Sage.

Ram, M. and G. Barrett (2000) Ethnicity and enterprise. In S. Carter and D. Jones-Evans (eds), *Enterprise and small business: principles, practice and policy*. Harlow, Essex: Prentice-Hall.

Ram, M. T. Jones (1998) *Ethnic minorities in business*. London: Small Business Research Trust.

Ram, M., B. Sanghera, T. Abbas, G. Barlow and T. Jones (2000) 'Ethnic minority business in comparative perspective: the case of the independent restaurant sector', *Journal of Ethnic and Migration Studies*, 26(3): 495–510.

Ram, M., T. Abbas, B. Sanghera, G. Barlow and T. Jones (2001) 'Making the link: households and small business activity in a multi-ethnic context', *Community, Work and Family*, 4(3): 327–48.

Rana, B. J., C. Kagan, S. Lewis and U. Rout (1998) 'British South Asian women managers and professionals: experiences of work and family', *Women in Management Review*, 13(6): 221–32.

Renzulli, L. (1998) 'Small business owners, their networks and the process of resource acquisition', Master's thesis presented to Department of Sociology, University of North Carolina, Chapel Hill.

Renzulli, L. A., H. Aldrich and J. Moody (2000) 'Family matters: gender, networks and entrepreneurial outcomes', *Social Forces*, 79(2): 523–46.

Richardson, P. and C. Hartshorn (1993) 'Business start-up training: the gender dimension in businesses', In S. Allen and C. Truman (eds), *Women in business: perspectives on women entrepreneurs*. London: Routledge.

Rogers, N. (2005) 'The impact of family support on the success of women business owners', In S. Fielden and M. Davidson (eds), *International handbook of women and small business entrepreneurship*. Cheltenham: Edward Elgar.

Shaw, E. (1997) 'The real networks of small firms', In D. Deakins, P. Jennings, and C. Mason (eds), *Small firms: entrepreneurship in the 1990s*. London: Paul Chapman Publishing.

Smallbone, D., M. Ram, D. Deakins and R. Baldock (2003) 'Access to finance by ethnic minority businesses in the UK', *International Small Business Journal*, 21(3): 291–314.

Ward, R. and R. Jenkins (eds) (1984) *Ethnic communities in business*. Cambridge: Cambridge University Press.

Whitehead, E., D. Purdy and S. Mascarenhas-Keyes (2006) *Ethnic Minority Businesses in England: Report on the Annual Small Business Survey 2003 Ethnic Boost. Small Business Service*, Sheffield.

11

The use of quotas in the most equal region

Politics and corporate boards in the Scandinavian countries

Cathrine Seierstad

Introduction

Occupational sex segregation is a global phenomenon that exists everywhere, even though forms and patterns vary considerably between countries and regions (Anker 1997). While the Scandinavian countries[1] are perceived as the most equal in the world on international rankings (World Economic Forum 2005, 2008) with a variety of political strategies promoting equality, including the woman friendly (Hernes 1987), social democratic (Esping-Andersen 1990) welfare model in addition to a variety of affirmative action (AA) strategies; the labour markets are characterized by occupational sex segregation, both horizontal and vertical.

This chapter explores these paradoxes with respect to women in the three Scandinavian countries: Denmark, Norway and Sweden. It begins by situating the Scandinavian experience in an international setting. This is done in order to illustrate the relevance of macro data in a comparative context to uncover patterns of equality and occupational sex segregation, both of a regional and country specific nature. Further on, the Scandinavian countries use of political strategies will be investigated as this will affect labour market patterns for women and men and thereby equality. In addition, this chapter will present the Scandinavian countries use of quotas in two occupational groups; politics and corporate board of directors as well as the gender representation in the respective groups in order to provide some meso-level trends within the countries. This chapter draws on primary and secondary data, including data gathered with Tore Opsahl looking at the changes within Norwegian board of directors from 2002 to 2009 (Seierstad and Opsahl unpublished).

This chapter identifies two key points; first, the success of the gender equal Scandinavian countries is more complex than the international rankings suggest. In addition, the Scandinavian countries though often clustered together (e.g. Esping-Andersen 1990) show significant differences in relation to political choices (e.g. while Sweden and Denmark are members of EU, Norway has on two occasions, 1972 and 1994 in referendum voted against this path), equality, welfare and the use of AA strategies. Consequently, these points indicate the need for country-specific focus as Scandinavian countries have significant differences, which affect the view and patterns of equality.

Equality, global patterns and trends

Looking at global data on gender equality, it is noticeable that equality between the sexes is not achieved anywhere (the World Economic Forum 2005, 2008; UN Human Development Report 2007–08). Yet, the data show great differences between countries and regions and suggest that the Scandinavian countries are getting closer and leading the way.

The World Economic Forum

The Global Gender Gap examines four critical areas (economic participation and opportunity, educational attainment, political empowerment and health and survival) for measuring inequality between men and women globally. In 2008 Norway passed Sweden as the most equal country in the world, and the 2008 ranking also reveals that the four most equal countries are the Nordic countries Norway, Finland, Sweden and Iceland, while the third Scandinavian country Denmark is ranked number seven as shown in Table 11.1. Compared to the 2006 and 2007 rankings there has been some small movements between the Nordic and Scandinavian countries with Norway currently positioned as the most equal country.

Another influential approach is the Human Development Report, which provides a global assessment of countries' achievements in different areas of human development. Related to equality, important insights can be found from female economic activity rate, gender-related development index (GDI)[2] and gender empowerment measure (GEM).

It is evident from Table 11.2 that in no country do you find female economic activity rate equivalent to that of men. Nonetheless the table indicates that the Scandinavian countries have amongst the highest female economic activity rates

Table 11.1   World Economic Forum 2008, Global Gender Gap 2008

Country	World Economic Forum: The Global Gender Gap Index 2008 Rankings		
	2008	*2007*	*2006*
Norway	1	2	2
Finland	2	3	3
Sweden	3	1	1
Iceland	4	4	4
New Zealand	5	5	7
Philippines	6	6	6
Denmark	7	8	8
Ireland	8	9	10
Netherlands	9	12	13
Latvia	10	13	19
Germany	11	7	5
Sri Lanka	12	15	13
United Kingdom	13	11	9
Switzerland	14	40	26
France	15	51	70
United States	27	19	20

Source: World Economic Forum (2008)

with Sweden's and Norway's female economic activity rate being 87 per cent of men's, while Denmark's is 84 per cent. Norway and Sweden are ranked first and second on the GEM rank, with Denmark fourth. The GDI ranking shows that Norway is ranked first, while Sweden is fifth and Denmark eleventh.

Both the World Economic Report and the Human Development Report indicate that equality in the Scandinavian countries is relatively high, higher than other regions, and that women in these countries are in a unique situation with (arguably) greater equality than other countries and regions.

Occupational sex segregation in the Scandinavian labour markets

Though, the Scandinavian countries are perceived as the most equal countries in the world, international comparative studies also illustrate that the Scandinavian countries are characterized by a high level of occupational sex segregation (e.g. Anker 1997; Charles 1992; Charles and Grusky 2004), both horizontal and vertical. When it comes to the concept of equality and occupational segregation, there are no guarantees that a country scoring high on equality in society in general

Table 11.2 Human Development Report 2007–08 Economic activity rates, gender empowerment and gender development index

Country	Female economic activity rate	GEM rank (2005)	GDI rank (2005)	HDI rank
Norway	87	**1 (1)**	**3 (1)**	2
Sweden	87	**2 (2)**	**5 (4)**	6
Finland	86	3	8	11
Denmark	84	**4 (3)**	**11 (13)**	14
Iceland	86	5	1	1
Netherlands	77	6	6	9
Belgium	73	7	14	17
Australia	80	8	2	3
Germany	77	9	20	22
Canada	84	10	4	4
Spain	66	12	12	13
Austria	76	13	19	15
United Kingdom	80	14	10	16
United States	82	15	16	12
France	79	18	7	10
Ireland	74	19	15	5

Source: Human Development Report, 2005, 2007–08

Note: *GDI: female economic activity rate, gender-related development index, *GEM: gender empowerment measure

will have a low level of occupational segregation. Charles and Grusky (2004) point out that different and surprising patterns exist in other countries as well, and conversely some of the countries that are commonly viewed as examples of more conservative gender tradition, such as Japan and Italy, do not show up as particularly segregated, while Sweden, characterized by having egalitarian and family friendly policies, remains deeply segregated (Charles and Grusky 2004: 6). Anker also points out that occupational segregation is lower in Asia than in Europe and within Europe it is actually highest in the Scandinavian countries (1997: 334).

The reasons that these patterns of unequal gender distribution are particularly visible at organizational level in the Scandinavian countries are neither clear nor logical. In addition, there are studies that point to great variations between the Scandinavian countries. An example is Nermo (2000) who argues that occupational sex segregation is stronger in Norway than Sweden (Denmark was not part of this study). Healy and Seierstad (2007) argue that Scandinavian academia are highly segregated, yet with variations between the countries both related to share of female professors as well as experiences of inequality. Acker (1994, 2006c) found in her study of Swedish banks that gender is part of the organizing processes of gender regimes. Seierstad (2010) takes the position that in Norway different gender inequality regimes are present in politics, the private sector and academia where women in general are underrepresented in senior positions and women experience barriers in the hierarchical ladder.

Acker (2006b) argues that much of the social and economic inequality in the US and in other industrial countries is created and maintained within the organizations, in the daily activities of working and organizing the work. Acker (2006b: 443) expresses the opinion that 'all organisations have inequality regimes, defined as loosely interrelated practices, processes, actions, and meanings that result in and maintain class, gender, and racial inequalities within particular organisations'. An especially interesting factor Acker (2006b: 443) points out is that 'even organisations that have explicit egalitarian goals develop inequality regimes over time'. This is particularly interesting in the case of the Scandinavian countries where attempts for gender equality, both from organizational and state level have been on the agenda for decades.

Employment patterns

Looking at employment patterns in public and private sectors within the Scandinavian countries, it is clear that women are, to a greater extent than men, employed in the public sector (for example, women are especially overrepresented in caring occupations such as nursing and as kindergarten teachers).

The share of women employed in the public sector is high in all the Scandinavian countries, which is most likely related to the social democratic welfare approach (see Table 11.3). As illustrated by Alvesson and Due Billing (2009: 56) 'much of the success of the Nordic countries is attributed to the comprehensive welfare system with a gender division of labour with most women working in the public sector'. Nevertheless, consequences of this include lower status, fewer possibilities for

Table 11.3 Public and private sector employment trends in Scandinavia

	Patterns of employment, Public and Private (per cent)			
	Men		Women	
	Public	Private	Public	Private
Denmark 2005	20	80	46	54
Sweden 2003	19	81	51	49
Norway 2005	37	63	69	31

Source: Norway: Equality Report 2005; Denmark: Holt, Geerdsen, Klitgard et al. 2006; Sweden: Government Statistics 2004b

Table 11.4 Proportion of executives in Scandinavian private sector by sex

	Executives in the private sector (per cent)	
	Men	Women
Denmark	96	4
Sweden	81	19
Norway	78	22

Source: Denmark, Danish Gender Equality Centre 2005 ; Norway, Equality Centre 2005, The equality report; Sweden, National Statistics 2005

progression and lower pay than in men's jobs: consequences tend to be greater in the private sector (Alvesson and Due Billing 2009: 56).

Furthermore, in relation to education there has been a recent tendency, for example in Norway, for women to choose traditionally male dominated areas such as medicine, finance, and management, but men are not to the same extent choosing the traditionally female dominated areas (see Teigen 2006).

Considering vertical segregation trends, even though the statistics provided earlier by The Human Development Report and World Economic Forum indicate a relatively high level of equality in Scandinavian societies; the division between the sexes in top positions in the private sector shows a different reality.

Table 11.4 based on national equality data undoubtedly indicates that the Scandinavian countries have high level of vertical segregation in the private sector. Denmark has the lowest and this indicates a very low share of female executives, while Norway and Sweden have a higher share of female executives in the private sector compared to Denmark.

Political strategies to equality

Looking at the different approaches for challenging inequality and occupational sex segregation, Chang (2000: 1662) argues that to realize cross-national variation in patterns of occupational sex segregation one has to recognize the institutional context within which these sex segregation regimes exists. State feminism has been important in the Scandinavian equality approach, also in the development of the 'woman friendly' welfare state (Hernes 1987). The concept 'state feminism' was introduced by Scandinavian feminist Hernes (1987) and describes the political alliance between the feminist groups as well as the political arena. It is based on the idea that the women friendly potential in a relationship between feminist groups at the bottom (the women's movement) as well as political decision makers at the top that together creates a woman friendly state (Freidenvall, Dahlerup and Skjeie 2006).

State feminism has been a type of utopia, where the idea of the women friendly society was drafted theoretically with the goal of creating a society where different treatments and opportunity on the basis of sex can disappear (Skjeie and Teigen 2003: 34).

Chang (2000) argues that there are two areas where state intervention into the characteristics of women's labour force participation is likely to take place. The first area is equality of access, which means that states can intervene in the public sphere by introducing legislation that either promotes or inhibits women's access to participate in all occupations. The second area is related to substantive benefits, which means that the states can interfere in the private sphere by taking over some of the responsibilities of families (e.g. child care, cash support) (2000: 1662–3). Arguably, both these areas of strategies are highly relevant and important in the case of Scandinavia. Political strategies, both related to equality of access as well as welfare has major impacts on the situation for both women and men in society, in the labour market and in the private sphere and are therefore important factors for equality between the sexes. The Scandinavian social democratic (Esping-Andersen 1990) welfare approach is characterized by having substantive childcare coverage, parental leave and is built around the idea of egalitarianism and universalism. Nevertheless, there are differences in welfare provision between the Scandinavian countries as well (see Ellingsæter and Leira 2006).

Equality strategies

Freidenvall et al. (2006) argue that to a great extent, the Nordic discourse can be described as an incrementalist discourse of empowerment which is built on the idea that gender equality develops gradually, and where state involvement can assist in progressive movement of equality in the right and required direction. Nevertheless, even though equality is the political goal for countries, there is great disagreement of why and how to achieve this. Where to interfere and the difference between state involvement and organizational level strategies are important factors for countries as well as occupational groups' strategies.

The Scandinavian countries have throughout the years had a great deal of focus on equality between the sexes and have a variety of strategies and laws in place. In 1978, Norway established the Gender Equality Act, which was amended in June 2005. The purpose of the Act is that it shall promote gender equality and aims in particular at improving the position of women. Women and men shall be given equal opportunities in education, employment and cultural and professional advance (Norwegian Government 2005). In June 2009, the Swedish Government presented a new strategy for improving gender equality in the labour market and the business sector. The strategy contains specific measures aimed at promoting equal opportunities for women and men to develop their potential in these areas (Swedish Government 2009). In Denmark, the Danish Ministry of Equality introduced in February 2009 an action plan with 15 specific areas for improving equality between the sexes. The areas include reduction in income differences, encouragement of fathers to take more parental leave and challenging traditional choices in relation to education and the aim is to improve equality between men and women by 2015 (Danish Government 2009).

All the Scandinavian countries have over the last decades encouraged greater gender balance in the labour market and the political arena. In order to enhance the female representation in corporate bodies a law was passed in Norway in the 1980s, which was shortly followed by the other Nordic countries requiring greater gender balance in all public committees (Freidenvall et al. 2006: 62). As illustrated by Freidenvall, Dahlerup and Skjeie (2006: 62) "these laws demand that the appointing minister or organ[3] shall see that all public committees rather vaguely acquire a 'gender balance, or set up a minimum-maximum of 40/60 for both sexes'.

Equal right to equal participation is, according to Skjeie and Teigen (2003: 216), the state feminisms fundamental belief. While they argued that equal pay has been the unsolvable equality problem, quotas has been a key tool on the way to 'the land of equality' (Skjeie and Teigen 2003: 165). Yet, there have been different approaches between the Scandinavian countries. While Skjeie and Teigen (2005: 188) pointed out that gender quotas have played a prominent role in Norwegian equality policies – they also emphasized that this is the case in Norway possibly more than in the other Scandinavian and Nordic countries. Skjeie and Teigen (2003) point to the fact that a diverse set of (re)distributive regulations have over the past 30 years been put in place. This includes national laws to regulate the gender composition of publicly appointed boards and committees at state and municipal levels, as well as the newly introduced gender composition of the boards of public and private companies which the following section will illustrate further. In addition, all the countries have strategies focusing on other areas of inequality, such as ethnicity, sexuality, religion, disability and age which has become more and more important over the last years.

This chapter has shown there are some differences in outlook between the Scandinavian countries as well as within them, the next section will explore patterns of gender representation and the use of AA strategies in two occupational groups.

The use of affirmative action and gender representation in politics and on board of directors

Collinson et al. (1990: 192) argued that their UK study found that 'despite anti-discrimination legislation in the mid-1970s a substantial number of employers many of whom publicly subscribe to equal opportunities, are still "managing to discriminate on the grounds of sex through a variety of recruitment practices". Several authors, such as Acker (2006) set out AA as a potential 'solution' to the problem of inequality; yet, Acker (2006) recognizes that these strategies often fail.

Turning to the meso-level analysis, the next sections will illustrate how specific AA strategies are in use in the two occupational groups. In addition, the female representation in the respective groups is discussed. The justification for focusing on politics and board of directors on public limited companies lies in the nature of these groups. They are both important, high-profile and high-status institutions within a country. In addition, there are significant differences that also make them particularly interesting for comparison. In particular, the use of AA in these groups as well as between the Scandinavian countries varies considerably which consequently will affect the share of representation of women.

Politics

In 2003, Rwanda, maybe surprisingly passed Sweden and became the number one country in the world in terms of women's representation in parliament (Dahlerup 2006b). Dahlerup (2006b) points to the fact that Rwanda is part of a new global trend to use electoral gender quotas as a 'fast track' to more gender balance within the political arena. Nevertheless, the approach and the use of quotas as well as the share of women in parliaments vary considerable between countries and regions. Dahlerup (2006b) argues that gender balance among political representatives is important for various reasons. In an international setting, she points to the fact that only 16 per cent of the world's parliamentarians are woman, and according to feminist movements as well as to feminist theory the lack of women in political institutions might have serious negative consequences. This can be in relation to the political agenda, for the communication of women's interest, and for the legitimacy of democratic institutions (Dahlerup 2006b). Moreover, the lack of women (as well other minority groups) may influence how these groups are viewed and perceived by themselves and others. Dahlerup (2006a) illustrates that globally there is now a focus on improving gender balance and around 40 countries have introduced gender quotas in elections to national parliament. This has been done either by legal gender quotas mandated by the Constitution like it is in Burkina Faso, Nepal, the Philippines and Uganda, or by electoral law as in many parts of Latin America, Belgium, Bosnia–Herzegovina, Serbia and Sudan (Dahlerup 2006a: 19–21). In addition, in more than 50 other countries, most political parties have voluntarily set out quotas such as Argentina, Bolivia, Ecuador, Germany, Italy, Norway and Sweden. In addition, in many other countries, only one or two parties have chosen to use quotas (Dahlerup 2006a,b). The use of quotas in politics, as in other areas of the labour market, are often seen as controversial, as the use of quota as a tool can make significant changes in women's representation and thereby affect the situation for women as well as men. Nevertheless, Dahlerup (2006a) argued that this is becoming a global trend ranging from the perceived equal countries to the more gender traditional countries.

What also makes politicians' a special and interesting occupational group is the fact that they are elected by the people to represent the people. Thus, the idea of democracy is important and arguments for social justice are particularly salient in this area.

The use of quotas in Politics in Scandinavia

In Scandinavian politics, there have been different approaches to the use of quotas. Table 11.5 clearly shows that there are significant variations both between and within countries, and consequently the political parties' use of equality strategies diverge considerably.

In Danish politics, there has been a step away from the use of voluntary quotas and currently, no political parties operates with this strategy, while in both Norway and Sweden, voluntary quotas have been and are important strategies for a great share of the political parties. None of the Scandinavian countries operate with legal quotas in relation to gender balance in the elected political bodies, which can be seen as a paradox as equality between the sexes is a key national strategy.

Table 11.5 Use of quotas in Scandinavian politics

Norway	Sweden	Denmark
Social Left Party: 40% (1975)	Social Democratic Labour Party: 50% (1987)	The Socialist Peoples Party: 40% (1977–96)
Labour Party: 40% (1983, now 50%)	Left Party: 50% (1987)	The Social Democratic Party: 40% (1977–96)
Centre Party: 40% (1989)	Green Party: 50% (1987)	The Left Socialist Party: 50% (1985-party no longer exists)
Christian Party: 40% (1993)		
Liberal Party: 40% (1975)		

Source: Freidenvall et al. 2006

Gender representation in politics

The representation of women in the political arena fits well with the information provided by World Economic Forum (2005, 2008) and the Human Development Report (2005, 2007–08) with the assumption that the Scandinavian countries are relatively equal with women well represented in public life. It comes as no surprise that the countries that to all appearances come across as the most equal ones have the highest representation of women in the political arena as seen in Table 11.6.

The case of the Scandinavian and the Nordic countries stands out with a particularly high female representation in the political life, both in the parliament and government. In 2005, there was even a slight majority of women in the Swedish government.[4]

Table 11.7 shows the percentage of women in Scandinavian Parliaments in 1975, 1995 and 2005. This demonstrates the development from the 1970s to 2005. In the mid-1970s, there was no voluntary quotas, while various strategies have been in use in the Scandinavian countries over the last decades. Even so, international literature on women in politics often referred to the Scandinavian countries as having a large number of women in politics due to quotas. This point is somewhat flawed as there are no legal quotas for the political arena in these countries where voluntary party quotas were not introduced until the 1980s when women already occupied 20–30 per cent of the seats, which were also at that time the highest in the world (Freidenvall, Dahlerup and Skjeie 2006). Looking at the share of women in 1990 it is

Table 11.6 The share of women in Scandinavian politics

Country	Women in government at ministerial level 2005 (Total percentage)	Seats in parliament 2005 (Total percentage)
Sweden	**52.4**	**45.3**
Finland	47.1	37.5
Norway	**44.4**	**38.2**
Netherlands	36	36.6
Denmark	**33.3**	**36.9**
United Kingdom	28.6	18.1
Iceland	27.3	30.2
Canada	23.1	21.4
Ireland	21,4	13.3
Belgium	21.4	34.7
Australia	20	24.7

Source: Human Development Report 2005: 316–17

Table 11.7 Share of women in Scandinavian parliaments

	Women's seats in parliament (in percentage)		
	1975	1990	2005
Sweden	App. 20	38	45.3
Norway	App. 15	36	38.2
Denmark	App. 15	31	36.9

Source: Human Development Report 2005: 316–17

clear that there was a massive increase from 1975 to 1990 and again an increase, but not as rapid from 1990 to 2005.

The use of AA strategies in politics in Scandinavia demonstrates the considerable variations between the countries' use of quotas. It is noteworthy that Denmark which chose to stop the use of quotas in the mid-1990s is the country with lowest percentage of women in parliament, while Sweden in which most parties follow a 50-50 quota policy is also the country with the highest share of women in politics.

Board of Directors

Organizational barriers for women's career advancement have been an important area for organizational research over the last decades (e.g. Acker 1990, 2006a, b; Collinson et al. 1990; Kanter 1977). Singh and Vinnicombe (2004: 479) found that women are almost completely absent from the very senior positions in the FTSE 100 companies, and they argue that 'male directors form an elite group at the top of the UK's corporate world, and few women break through this glass ceiling into this elite, despite making inroads into middle management'. British women made up approximately 11 per cent of the directorships in 2007 (Sealy et al. 2009). Similar patterns are also present in the rest of Europe as well as in the US where women held approximately 14.6 per cent in 2006 (Joy 2009: 15). This indicates that gender on the boards of directors in large companies is a barrier for career advancement (Singh and Vinnicombe 2003: 349). Singh and Vinnicombe (2004) argued that this is an issue of concern, as women's talents are not being fully utilized. In addition, Huse and Solberg (2005) argued that women make and can make valuable contribution on corporate boards and they are therefore beneficial to boards in many ways. The private sector has traditionally been an area where state intervention in relation to gender representation has been avoided. Yet, the absence of women in the decision-making processes, especially on top corporate boards has become a key concern and there has been a growing international interest in women on corporate board of directors (Burke and Vinnicombe 2008), both for the state and policymakers as well as researchers. Huse et al. (2009: 8) point to the recent crisis in confidence in large corporations globally and argue that this has given renewed attention to the areas of corporate social responsibility (CSR), corporate governance and the composition and roles of board of directors. As a result, the inclusion of women and employee elected members on boards are important in the contemporary debates (Huse et al. 2009).

In recent years, there has been a growing awareness of the fact that corporate boards are mainly composed of male directors. The awareness has led to the identification of three stakeholder approaches to increasing women's representation in various countries. Burke and Vinnicombe (2008) identify three approaches: The coercive approach, which supports the use of government legislation, has been observed in Norway (enacted legislation), Sweden (proposed legislation) and Spain (parliamentary discussions). Second, the liberal approach, which assumes that organizations will voluntarily consider appointing women to corporate boards because it is the right thing to do. This has been the primary attitude in the US and Canada. Third, the collaborative approach which emphasizes cooperation among various stakeholder groups and has been the main approach observed in the UK (Burke and Vinnicombe 2008: 3). Therefore, while Norway, Sweden and Spain are open to the use of quotas and gender targets on boards, it is an unlikely approach in the majority of other countries (Burke and Vinnicombe 2008: 3).

This section will examine the use of AA strategies on boards of directors on public limited companies, first in a Scandinavian setting, and then the focus will be on Norway. The case of Norway is particularly interesting, being the first country in the world to introduce a gender representation law in the private sector.

The use of quotas on Board of Directors

As illustrated in Table 11.4, data from 2005 revealed that the share of women in executive position in Scandinavia was low. In two of the Scandinavian countries, Norway and Sweden, over the last years, there have been national debates and initiatives for introducing quotas also in the private sector. Norway decided to introduce a gender balance law in 2003, which has been referred to as one of the most radical equality laws. The Swedish government did not however support this approach after a change in government. Nevertheless, the Swedish government appointed a special group to report on this issue and evaluate if this should potentially be implemented in Sweden as well (email correspondence Lundgren, Swedish Government, 2006) and Sweden has recently proposed a mandatory 25 per cent participation rate for women (Burke and Vinnicombe, 2008: 3). Denmark has not sought to increase the share of women in senior positions by legal means.

The gender representation law in Norway

As seen in Table 11.8, Norway stands out having introduced what has been described as a radical gender representation law. The first Bondevik[5] Regjering proposed the idea of gender quotas on company board of directors which was officially suggested in June 2003 by the Bondevik II[6] Regjering and ratified by the Storing December 2003. The law affects several types of companies and the legislation on gender representation on boards will apply to all publicly owned enterprises (including, state-owned limited liability and public limited companies, state-owned enterprises, companies incorporated by special legislation and inter-municipal companies) and all public limited companies in the private sector. There are no rules for privately owned limited liability companies because most of these companies in Norway are small family enterprises and the owners are themselves members of the board. Public limited companies normally have a broader spread of shares and less personal involvement in the management. Norway has approximately 205,000 limited liability companies (Norwegian Government 2008).

For publicly owned companies the law came into force on 1January 2004, with a two-year implementation period. In the case of the public limited companies, it was a dialogue between the Norwegian Government and the private sector where it was agreed that the amendment for a gender balance on public limited companies' board of directors should be withdrawn if the companies voluntarily complied by July 2005. However, this was not the case as the proportion of women was only 16 per cent in 2005 (The Norwegian Government 2008). Therefore, the law was introduced in January 2006 with a two-year implementation period ending in January 2008.

Table 11.9 shows the minimum percentage of each sex that is required by the law to be represented on boards of different sizes (employee representatives are not included in the law). This indicates roughly a gender balance of 40 per cent over all.

Table 11.8 Use of AA strategies on board of directors in Scandinavia

Norway	*Sweden*	*Denmark*
Public firms (ASA) require a gender balance of at least 40 per cent from 01.01.2006 with a two- year grace period.	Suggestion of a 40 per cent quota, but change in government let to withdrawal of law. Proposed legislation of 25 per cent minimum gender representation	No law on gender balance in boards. No initiative to gender balance

Source: Norway: Norwegian Government 2008; Sweden: Burke and Vinnicombe 2008: 3

Table 11.9 The requirement for representation of both sexes on public limited companies' board of directors by the gender representation law in Norway

Size of Board	Required representation of each sex	Effective minimum per cent
2	1	50
3	1	33
4	2	50
5	2	40
6	3	50
7	3	43
8	3	37.5
9+	40%	40

Source: The Norwegian Government 2008

The use of gender quotas within the private sector has been controversial. In particular, strong and conflicting opinions from the media, politics and the private sector have challenged the image of Norway being an equal country. Although strong arguments were raised by the opposing side, both in politics and other areas of society, the Norwegian Government (2008) argued for introducing gender representation rules based on several reasons both related to justice and utility. The Government argued from a justice point of view pointing to the importance of democracy as equality between the sexes, a fairer society, and a more even distribution of power between the sexes as important factors for introducing the law. In addition, several arguments in line of utility and the business case were used. One argument is that the legislation is important for the Norwegian economy. The demands for gender balance on company boards ensure that Norway makes use of all the human resources in the country, not just half of it. As women are more likely to access higher education it is important that their talent and competences are used. In addition, business case arguments were used related to diversity as having a positive impact on the companies' bottom line. Hence, recruiting more women to the boards will increase the diversity, and thereby influence the bottom line (Norwegian Government 2008).

Gender representation on Board of Directors

The private sector is characterized as powerful, influential, financially important, and generally not controlled by the state. Historically, the private sector, including board of directors, has been male dominated where men have controlled the majority of high-level positions and especially those related to power. Consequently, patterns of vertical sex segregation in the private sector have been present in all three countries as illustrated in Table 11.4.

Building on data from European Professional Women's Network Board Woman Monitor 2008,[7] Figure 11.1 illustrates the trend for eight European countries in relation to gender trends on board of directors.

Figure 11.1 illustrates how Norway is a frontrunner for improving the share of women on board of directors but also how Sweden and Denmark have a significantly higher share of women on boards than United Kingdom, Germany and France.

Table 11.10 illustrates the proportion of female directors within the boards of listed companies at the stock exchange in Norway, Sweden and Denmark. From this table it is clear that even though the share of women has risen from 2004 to 2007 in all the countries, the case of Norway stands out with a significantly higher share of women in 2007, after the implementation of the law.

Looking at Scandinavian countries listed on the stock exchange in Table 11.10 it is also evident how the share of women has been low, and how the case of Norway stands out.

This indicates that through regulations Norway managed to increase their share of women on corporate boards and have a more balanced composition of men and women as directors than Sweden and Denmark in particular. The next section will illustrate some of the changes that have occurred on Norwegian boards throughout the last six years.

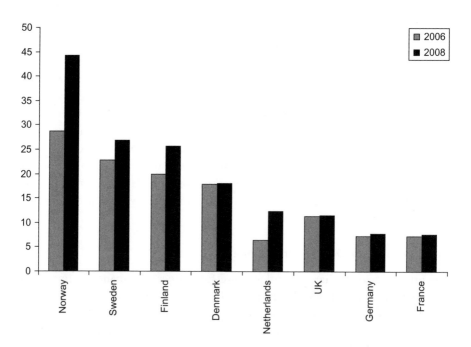

Figure 11.1 Share of women on company boards in eight European countries
Source: EPWN 2008

Table 11.10 The proportion of female directors in listed Scandinavian companies by stock exchange

	Copenhagen Denmark	Stockholm Sweden	Oslo Norway
2004	8.5	16.1	15.9
2007	10.0	19.2	37.0

Source: Hoel 2009: 84

The case of Norway; changes within the composition of board of directors

In an attempt to study the early effects of the gender representation law on various parameters of equality, we aimed to explore the impact on equality among directors on the boards of companies affected by the law (Opsahl and Seierstad[8]). We argue that equality goes beyond representation, and understand equality as the ability to influence. In this context, we looked at different parameters of influence in addition to female representation on corporate boards. Although it is given by the law that the share of women must increase we looked at whether companies have continued to increase the proportion of female directors beyond the minimum requirement. Moreover, we assessed the extent to which it has affected the most senior positions, such as the gender of the chair as well as the directors' prominence (i.e., possession of multiple directorships) and social capital (i.e., ability to funnel and control the flow of information).

When the legislation came into force and became applicable to all public limited companies in January 2008, most of the public limited companies in Norway had complied with the law (The Norwegian Government 2008). Table 11.11 illustrates the percentage of women on boards as well as the percentage of women on boards excluding the employee representatives.

We found that a substantial increase in the proportion of female directors occurred only during the implementation period, and especially towards the end of the period. This suggests that the law has challenged the under representation of women on public limited companies' boards of directors, and made the boards appear more democratic and equal. This indicates that the hard strategy of legislation was a successful tool for improving the gender balance, which could guide international policymakers. It also indicates that even though companies have complied with the law, it is also evident that companies have reached their minimum target for gender representation, but it is noteworthy that the female share is not above the minimum. This could suggest that companies are simply complying with the law, and not moving towards further equality between the sexes. Consequently, gender still seems to be a barrier as the proportion of female directors has not exceeded the minimum requirement of 40 per cent.

Table 11.11 Share of women on Norwegian Boards with and without employee representatives

Date	Percentage of women on board	Percentage of women on boards excluding the employee representatives
January 2003	9	8.1
January 2004	9.7	9.1
January 2005	11.7	11.4
January 2006	16.9	17.1
January 2007	25.3	25.7
January 2008	36	36.8
January 2009	40.1	41.1

Source: Opsahl and Seierstad unpublished

Looking at the most senior position within the board, the chair position, it is apparent that these positions are still highly male dominated.

Table 11.12 shows that few boards are chaired by a woman. During our observation period, the proportion of boards led by a female chair has increased from 2 per cent to 4 per cent. However, two-thirds of this increase occurred before the implementation period (January 2006). This suggests that the law has had a marginal effect on the gender of the chair and the boards appear internally segregated. As women have not gained a substantial increase in access to the most influential position on the corporate boards in the period of the law, this might be an indication that there are still gender barriers for women at the organizational level as only the minimum requirements for female representation are met and men control the top position within the boards.

The gender representation law has been the centre of attention for the media, both in Norway and internationally. The media has highlighted that certain female directors have attained a large number of directorships. These directors have been labelled the 'Golden Skirts' by newspapers like the *Financial Times*.

Looking at directors sitting on multiple boards we found that the number of prominent directors has increased substantially during our observation period. More specifically, the number of prominent directors rose from 91 to 224. Moreover, the maximum number of directorships that a single director holds has increased dramatically and the maximum number has doubled. More specifically, in May 2002, one female and two male were the most prominent directors by being members of four public limited companies' boards each, whereas in August 2009, one female director held eight directorships. The gender balance amongst the prominent directors has also changed. At the beginning of our observation period, only 7 of the 91 prominent directors were women, and at the end of the period, 107 women and 117 men were prominent directors. Thus, the increase in prominent directors is

Table 11.12 Share of female Chairs on Norwegian
boards 2003–09

Date	Percentage of female chair on Boards
January 2003	2.7
January 2004	2.9
January 2005	3.1
January 2006	3.4
January 2007	3.5
January 2008	4
January 2009	4
July 2009	4

Source: Opsahl and Seierstad unpublished

mainly driven by an increase in the number of female directors, which has led to a substantial change in the gender balance among prominent directors. More specifically, if only considering directors with at least three directorships, 61.4 per cent of them are women. When considering directors with seven or more directorships, all of them are women.

Discussion and conclusion

As illustrated by Alvesson and Due Billing (1997, 2009) 'our point, hardly original, is that gender patterns are complex, often contradictory'. This argument seems especially true in the Scandinavian countries being perceived as the most equal, yet showing strong pattern of occupational sex segregation, both horizontal and vertical. While Norway, Sweden and Denmark have experienced a mass entry of women to the labour market and consequently have a high female economic activity rate, patterns of occupational sex segregation are also indeed present. This indicates that gender structures, also in the Scandinavian countries, are remarkably resilient. It is a paradox that the Scandinavian countries that are ranked high on equality and have a high share of women in politics, at the same time have surprisingly few women in senior positions in the private sector and in academia (Healy and Seierstad, unpublished).

It is an irony that parliaments place legal restrictions on areas in both the public and private sector, yet in the political arena none of the countries operate with legal gender quotas. While quotas are in use in Norwegian and Swedish politics, this is of a voluntary character. On board of directors of public limited companies the Scandinavian countries have different approaches. Norway introduced a gender representation law of a minimum of 40 per cent of each sex in 2006, while Sweden that had considered this approach decided not to but have now opted for a minimum gender representation of 25 per cent (Burke and Vinnicombe, 2008: 3). Denmark does not operate with quotas on board of directors. Hence, both in politics and board of directors the Scandinavian countries do not present a uniform model in the use of quotas either voluntary or compulsory. Norway is the most AA strategy friendly country, closely followed by Sweden, while Denmark has less use of hard strategies. This indicates that while Norway and Sweden operate with strategies focusing more on equality of outcome; Denmark has chosen the approach focusing more on the idea of equality of opportunity.

In the case of Norwegian boards, we suggest that the gender representation law has successfully challenged the under-representation of women on public limited companies' boards of directors, and made the boards appear more democratic and equal (Opsahl and Seierstad unpublished). This is a signal that the hard hiring strategy of legislation was a successful tool for improving the gender balance. However, while we found that the minimum representation level has been met, the share of women has not increased further and women are not represented at the highest level within the boards. This might indicate that there are still organizational barriers women meet that men do not. In addition, our analysis indicates possible counter-effects of the law. Although more women have entered the boardrooms, our study finds that differences amongst directors have risen when looking at additional proxies for influence on corporate boards. The maximum number of boards that a single director is part of has increased considerably which has led to the concentration of the benefits associated with prominence to a select few. Since this benefit is only enjoyed by a few directors and associated with a particular gender, the intention of the Norwegian Government in creating a more equal setting can be questioned as a new elite of 'golden skirts' has emerged. This indicates that even though the gender representation law has improved the share of women on boards, it has had unintended effects which indicates that an equal setting is not yet achieved.

The Scandinavian countries have managed to get women into organizations, but both the nature of the organizations and positions inside organizations varies. As all the Scandinavian countries show pattern of horizontal and vertical sex segregation the idea of equality might still be more of an aspiration than reality. While the woman friendly social democratic welfare states have helped women to get important rights, there is scope for further improvements. The use of AA strategies in the Scandinavian countries are somehow weaker than the national goals of equality suggests. As a result, there might be a need for greater use of strategic AA, such as quotas as where quotas are in use the gender representation has risen significantly, while in areas of encouragement and suggestions there has only been minor improvements. Skjeie and Teigen (2003: 200) pointed to the fact that the Norwegian equality debate has changed from the main argument used in relation to justice, to the business case and utility being more and more important, which has been especially clear in relation to the private sector. Studies show that patterns of inequality and discrimination also exist in the Scandinavian countries which points to the importance of maintaining social justice arguments. As Teigen (2000) argued, it is a need to remove AA from the discrimination/antidiscrimination debate as the question should not be 'why women', but 'why not women'. As long as women are meeting barriers men are not, it will result in uneven distribution of power and influence within society; therefore the need to reframe the debate of AA.

It is disappointing that the 'most equal' region still has far to go in its quest for equality. Nevertheless, despite their flaws, the use of AA strategies are yielding some benefits and resulting in greater visibility of women in public life.

Notes

1. The Scandinavian countries include Norway, Sweden, and Denmark. The Nordic countries are the Scandinavian countries and Finland and Iceland.
2. GDI measures the same variables as the Human Development Index (HDI) except that the GDI adjusts for gender inequalities in the three aspects of human development (longevity, knowledge and a decent standard of living). The difference is that the GDI adjusts the average achievement of each country in life expectancy, literacy and gross enrolment, and income in accordance with the disparity in achievement between men and women (Human Development report 2005:270–1). GEM measures gender inequality in economic and political spheres of activity and is made up of two dimensions. First, economic participation and decision making are measured by the percentage of female administrators and managers, and professional and technical workers; and second, political participation and decisionmaking are measured by the percentage of seats held in parliament (Human Development report 2005:270–1). The GEM measure is most relevant to vertical sex segregation.
3. In this context, the word organ refers to body or committee
4. There will be some variations in these numbers throughout the periods due to change within the governments.
5. Bondevik's first term as Prime Minister was from 1997 to 3 March 2000 and it was a coalition cabinet consisting of the Christian Democratic Party, the Centre Party and the Liberal Party.
6. Bondevik's second period in office was a coalition cabinet consisting of the Christian Democratic Party, the Conservative Party and the Liberal Party 2001–05.
7. Survey methodology for EPWN 2008: The survey was carried out by Egon Zehnder International using data provided by BoardEx which is based on publicly available information. It focuses on the 300 largest companies in Europe by market capitalization and is sorted based on the worldwide headquarters home country. The top European companies were based on the FTSEurofirst 300 Index. In addition, for all countries, at least six companies were included to make sure the data is significant (EPWN 2008: 7).
8. To test our hypotheses, we collected a list of all the 384 public limited companies in Norway (Allmennaksjeselskap or ASA) that were available online through the Norwegian Business Register on 5 August 2009. Based on the list of companies, we collected all official announcements made to the register that were online. These announcements contain changes to the composition of the boards of directors since 1 November 1999.

References

Acker, J. (2006a) *Class questions: feminist answers*. Lanham, MD: Rowman & Littlefield Publishers Inc.

——(2006b) 'Inequality regimes: gender, class, and race in organizations', *Gender and Society*, 20: 441–64.

——(1994, 2006c) 'The gender regime of Swedish banks', *Scandinavian Journal of Management*, 10(2): 117–30.

Alvesson, M. and Y. D. Billing (1997) *Understanding gender in organisations*. London: Sage Publications Ltd.

—— (2009) *Understanding gender in organisations*. London: Sage Publications Ltd (2nd edition).

Anker, R. (1997) 'Theories of occupational segregation by sex: an overview', *International Labour Review*, 136: 315–39.

Burke, R. J. and S. Vinnicombe (2008) 'Women on corporate boards of directors: international issues and opportunities', In S. Vinnicombe, V. Singh, R. J. Burke, D. Bilimoriam and M. Huse (eds), *Women on corporate boards of directors*. Cheltenhan: Edward Elgar Publishing Limited.

Chang, M. L. (2000) 'The evolution of sex segregation regimes', *American Journal of Sociology*, 105(6): 1658–701.

Charles, M. (1992) 'Cross-national variation in occupational sex segregation', *American Sociological Review*, 57 (4): 483–502.

——(2003) 'Deciphering sex segregation. Vertical and horizontal inequalities in ten national labour markets', *Acta Sociologica*, 46: 267–87.

Collinson, D., D. Knights and M. Collinson (1990) *Managing to Discriminate*. London: Routledge.

Dahlerup, D. (2006a) *Women, quotas and politics*. New York: Routledge.

—— (2006b) http://www.quotaproject.org/aboutQuotas.cfm).

Danish Gender Equality Centre (2007) http://www.lige.dk/

Danish Government (2009) http://ligeuk.itide.dk/files/PDF/gender_action_plan_2009.pdf

Ellingsæter, A. M. and A. Leira (2006) *Politicising parenthood in Scandinavia – gender relations in welfare states*. Bristol: The Policy Press.

Esping-Andersen, G. (1990) *The three worlds of welfare capitalism*. London: Polity press.

European Professional Women's Network, European PWN BoardWoman Monitior (2008) Available at: http://www.europeanpwn.net/files/3rd_bwm_2008_press_release_1.pdf

Freidenvall, L., D. Dahlerup and H. Skjeie (2006) 'The Nordic countries: an incremental model', In D. Dahlerup (ed.), *Women, quotas and politics*. New York: Routledge.

Healy, G. and C. Seierstad (2007) *Gender segregation in Scandinavian countries – the case of academia*. Proceedings of the International Labour Process Conference, Amsterdam, Netherlands.

Hernes, H. (1987) *Welfare state and women power – essays in state feminism*. Oslo: Norwegian University Press.

Hoel, M. (2009) 'The quota story: five years of change in Norway', In S. Vinnicombe, V. Singh, R. J. Burke, D. Bilimoriam and M. Huse (eds), *Women on corporate boards of directors*. Cheltenhan: Edward Elgar Publishing Limited.

Holt, H., L. Geerdsen, C. Klitgard and M. Lind (2006) *Det konsopdelte arbeidsmarked*. Copenhagen: socialforskningsinstituttet.

Human Development Report (2005) http://hdr.undp.org/statistics/data/indic/indic_246_1_1.html

Human Development Report (2007–2008) http://hdrstats.undp.org/en/indicators/#G

Huse, M. and A. G. Solberg (2006) 'Gender-related boardroom dynamics: how Scandinavian women make and can make contributions on corporate boards', *Women in Management Review*, 21(2): 113–130.

Huse, M., S. T. Nilesen and I. M. Hagen (2009) 'Women and employee elected board members, and their contributions to board control tasks', *Journal of Business Ethics*, 89(4): 581–97.

Joy, L. (2009) 'Women board directors in the United States; an eleven year retrospective', In S. Vinnicombe, V. Singh, R. J. Burke, D. Bilimoriam and and M. Huse (eds), *Women on corporate boards of directors*. Cheltenham, UK: Edward Elgar Publishing Limited.

Kanter, R. M. (1977) *Men and women of the corporation*. New York: Basic Books.

NAV http://www.nav.no/page?id=328 attained 26.08.09

Nermo, M. (2000) 'Models of cross-national variation in occupational sex segregation', *European Societies*, 3: 295–333.

Norway: Equality report Likestillingssenteret (the Centre for Equality). Available at: http://www.likestilling.no

Norwegian Government (2005) The Act relating to Gender Equality. Avilable at: http://www.regjeringen.no/en/doc/Laws/Acts/The-Act-relating-to-Gender-Equality-the-.html?id=454568

—— (2006) Rules on Gender Representation on Norwegian Company Boards. Available at: http://www.regjeringen.no/nb/dep/bld/tema/likestillingsomradet/Hand-out-Gender-on-Boards.html?id=416864

—— (2008) Representation of both sexes on company boards. Available at: http://www.regjeringen.no/en/dep/bld/Topics/Equality/rules-on-gender-representation-on-compan.html?id=416864

Sealy, R., S. Vinnicombe and V. Singh (2009) 'The pipeline to the boards finally opens; women's progress on FTSE 100 boards in the UK', In S. Vinnicombe, V. Singh, R. J. Burke, D. Bilimoriam and M. Huse (eds), *Women on corporate boards of directors*. Cheltenham, UK: Edward Elgar Publishing Limited.

Seierstad, C. (2010) *Gendered structures and gendering practices in Norway: The case of politics, academia and board of directors*. Proceedings of Gender Work and Organisation, University of Keele.

Seierstad, C. and T. Opsahl (2009) *A change in representation on Norwegian Boards of Directors: compliance, prominence, and women's experience*. Conference paper presented at the Equal Opportunity International, Istanbul.

Singh, V. and S. Vinnicombe (2003) 'The 2002 female FTSE index and women directors', *Woman in Management Review*, 18 (17): 349–58.

—— (2004) 'Why so few women directors in top UK boardrooms? Evidence and theoretical explanations', *Corporate Governance: An International Review*, 12(4): 479–88.

Skjeie, H. and M. Teigen (2003) *Menn imellom*. Oslo: Gyldendal.

—— (2005) 'Political constructions of gender equality: traveling towards a gender balanced society?', *NORA – Nordic Journal of Feminist and Gender Research*, 13 (3): 187–97.

Swedish Government (2004a) http://www.regeringen.se/sb/d/258/a/26350

—— (2004b) http://www.scb.se/templates/tableOrChart____27569.asp

—— (2009) Strategy for gender equality in the labour market. Available at: http://www.sweden.gov.se/sb/d/4096/a/130290. Data obtained 26.08.09.

Teigen, M. (2000) 'The affirmative action controversy', *Nora nr*, 2(8): 63–77.

—— (2003) *Kvotering og kontrovers – om likestilling og politikk*. Norway: Unipax.

—— (2006) *Det kjønnssegregerte arbeidslivet -En kunnskapsoversikt*. Oslo: Institutt for Samfunnsforskning.

World Economic Forum (2005) *Women's empowerment: measuring the Global gender Gap*. Availbleat:http://www.weforum.org/pdf/Global_Competitiveness_Reports/Reports/gender_gap.pdf

—— (2008) *The Global Gender Gap Report 2008*. Available at: http://www.weforum.org/en/Communities/Women%20Leaders%20and%20Gender%20Parity/GenderGapNetwork/index.htm

12

Relevance of US and UK national histories in the understanding of racism and inequality in work and career

Franklin Oikelome

Introduction

This chapter provides insight into the relevance of national histories in the understanding of racism and inequality at work and career in the UK and US and the institutional responses in both countries. It explores conceptual, historical and contemporary contexts of racism and inequality in work and career in both countries and shows the importance of common historical links that have led the different contemporary contexts. The chapter seeks to highlight the importance of national histories in understanding the structure of inequalities and also considers various institutional responses. The rationale for the chapter is based on the premise that modern discriminatory practices often combine with historical patterns (Jenkins 2007). Given the ubiquitous nature of the term 'racism' and its tendency to be often used in a loose and an unreflective way, it is sometimes necessary to consider the context. As Davy Smith states, 'There are forms of social influence – racism and its effects – that are experienced almost exclusively by members of minority ethnic groups ... racism cannot be taken to be a given feature of society; its historical roots and current social origins need to be explored (2000:1696).

Knowledge of national histories would enable an understanding of some of the complexities of diversity in different countries as well as grasp the uniqueness of racism and structural inequality which are often a response to a country's historical, political, demographic and social conditions. Without a historical understanding one cannot fully understand the nature of inequalities both globally and nationally.

Understanding how racism and inequality has evolved in a historical sense is thus important to any meaningful appreciation of current practice of racial discrimination and inequality. For example, Jenkins (2007) notes that black neighbourhoods of New Orleans would not have been disproportionally affected by the Hurricane Katrina of 2005 but for the segregation of the 1960s whereby black men and women were concentrated in low-lying neighborhoods and public-housing developments. This illustration is an example of how important social justice and equality are towards addressing the problems of social exclusion which generally manifests in low income and poverty; pertinently, there is a relationship between poverty, racial segregation and access to employment (Quillian and Redd 2006).

One of the earliest definitions of racism was by Benedict who defines it as 'the dogma that one ethnic group is condemned by nature to congenital inferiority and another group is destined to congenital superiority' (1945: 87). Van de Berghe defines it as 'the belief that organic, genetically transmitted differences (whether real or imagined) between human groups are intrinsically associated with the presence or the absence of certain socially relevant abilities or characteristics, hence that such differences are legitimate basis of invidious distinctions between groups socially defined as races (1967: 11). A more concise definition was advanced by Schaefer (1990) as '...a doctrine of racial supremacy, that one race is superior'.

These definitions suggest a link between racism and slavery which is not surprising given the history of the evolution of slavery. The notion of 'white supremacy' and 'belief in a superior race' was an underlying catalyst of the slave trade even though economic reasons fuelled slavery to some degree (Clarke and Hamby 2005: 132). This barbaric practice which entails the degradation and inhumane treatment of humans by other humans was justified based on a warped rationalization that slaves were inferior or less than humans.

Subsequent sections in this chapter will explore the historical roots of racism and slavery in the US and the UK and how their legacies continue to manifest in contemporary practice. The forms of racism and patterns of segregation in the two countries as well as the different patterns of inequality and exclusion in different sectors of the economy of both countries will be considered. In essence, the analysis moves from national macro context through to meso organizational level to the micro level of the individual worker and at each level demonstrates the importance of different histories. The evidence used is based on a combination of reports, studies and anecdotes drawn from a variety of sources including journal articles, textbooks and news reports. Overall, the value inherent in providing comparative insights will ensure that caution is exercised in any assumptions made regarding common antecedents and meanings to the same or similar events.

Racism and inequality in the United States

History of racism

The history of racism in America is somewhat complex. Waters (2004: 20) notes that the history of race and ethnic divisions in the United States is essentially characterized by the slavery and forced migration of Africans as well as the expansion of the US through conquest of Native Americans. Actually, racism and the unequal treatment of racial minorities in the United States goes as far back as the beginning of colonization, predating the period of black-white relations and the implementation of the institution of slavery (Hurst 2006). Hurst points out that the early days of settlement witnessed discrimination against Native Americans whereby religious and ethnocentric criteria rather than colour or racial distinction were used to initially separate groups into superior and inferior categories. However, as time went on, settlers needed labour power to fully utilize the land and this eventually resulted in slaves being imported and traded for over two centuries. The colonial and independent periods witnessed land grabs and imposition of hardships through a long series of wars, massacres and forced displacement with the primary objective of obtaining the resources of Native Americans (Brescia 1982: 8). Brescia also noted that the ideological expansionist justification included stereotyped perceptions of all Native Americans as savages. According to Castillo (1998), Indians in California in particular were subjected to enslavement before the Indian Citizenship Act of 1924 granted US citizenship to all Native Americans and formally legalized equality.

In their account, Clarke and Hamby (2005) pointed out that the first black Africans were brought to Virginia in 1619. Interestingly, it was noted that the first black Africans brought to the US did not expect to end up as slaves for the rest of their lives:

> .... Initially, many were regarded as indentured servants who could earn their freedom. By the 1660s, however, as the demand for plantation labor in the Southern colonies grew, the institution of slavery began to harden around them, and Africans were brought to America in shackles for a lifetime of involuntary servitude. (19)

Clarke and Hamby also note a social rift in every aspect of colonial American culture; only the wealthiest Americans owned slaves whereas in contrast, poor whites recognized that slavery devalued their own labour:

> Although the 1860 census showed that there were nearly four million slaves out of a total population of 12.3 million in the 15 slave states, only a minority of Southern whites owned slaves ... three-quarters of Southern white families, including the 'poor whites', those on the lowest rung of Southern society, owned no slaves. (p. 132)

However, the observation that only the rich owned slaves did not mean that those who didn't opposed the slave trade institution. It was just simply that they could not afford to. Clarke and Hamby states:

> The yeomen and poor whites supported the institution of slavery as well. They feared that, if freed, blacks would compete with them economically and challenge their higher social status. Southern whites defended slavery not simply on the basis of economic necessity but out of a visceral dedication to white supremacy. (132)

In 1863, the formal institution of slavery ended by decree with the Emancipation Proclamation. However, despite the end of the Civil War in 1865, black men and women were still denied the rights and opportunities provided to whites in the US at the end of the American Revolution. Bell (2007) notes that legalized discrimination and segregation did not actually end with the end of slavery and that racism and discriminatory practices continued in post-emancipation America. The existence of Jim Crow laws between 1865 and 1964 – which mandated de jure segregation in all public facilities, with a supposedly 'separate but equal' status for black American – ensured that educational disparities and widespread criminal acts against people of colour abounded with the implication that the progress of black people, particularly in the South, were severely impeded.

The 1930s and 1940s saw a hardening of institutionalized racism and legal discrimination against citizens of African descent in the US. During the period, prominent African American activists clamoured for civil rights, organizing protest marches and seeking government concessions. The 1950s and 1960s witnessed the peaking of the American Civil Rights Movement, characterized by boycotts, demonstrations and the organizing of widespread protests across the nation under a younger generation of leaders (Takaki 1993). The uprising led to the Civil Rights Act of 1964 and executive orders for affirmative action, which signified a change in the social acceptance of legislative racism in America and was to result in a profound increase in the number of opportunities available for people of colour in the US.

A post-racial era?

While the passage of the Civil Rights Act was a significant milestone in the history of race relations in the US, the election of the first ever African-American president of the United States arguably in 2008 represents a water-shed in the history of the country. The development heralded what many observers hoped was a new dawn in America's race relations. The new president won an overwhelming proportion of the black vote as well as securing a broad support of white voters thereby signalling the willingness of America to draw a line under its inglorious racial past. Could this be the beginning of a post-racial era in America or just a blip in the wider scheme of things? Of course in the long term, the answer remains to be seen but current evidence suggests the latter might be the case.

Minority groups make up a quarter of the US population and despite the progress of black people in the US since the Civil Right Act came into existence; they are still faced with serious challenges as they pursue the American dream. In particular, their experiences at work and in relation to career opportunities have been a major focus of the debate concerning racial disadvantage and inequality. Two types of discrimination were identified by Bell as occurring at the organizational level. 'Access discrimination' occurs when people are denied employment opportunities or access to jobs based on their race, sex, age or other factors while "treatment discrimination' occurs when people are employed but are treated differently and not in accordance with job-related criteria (2007: 107). Studies have shown that black people experience varying forms of treatment discrimination at work. For example, one study found the prevalence of lifetime experiences of racial discrimination among black workers (Krieger et al. 2006). In other cases, less overt forms of racism have replaced blatant racism. For example, Deitch et al. (2003) found that black people's experience of racism is manifested at work in the form of subtle acts of mistreatment.

A study by the National Urban league (2009) found that black people were twice as likely to be jobless and more likely to be denied access to employment compared to white people. Even when in employment, they are more likely to be earning less than their white counterparts. In an earlier study, Grodsky and Pager (2001) found that black men working in the most highly paid private sector jobs (i.e. insurance sales, securities and financial services sales, actuaries, lawyers and physicians) earned 20 per cent less than similar white workers; the racial disparity was found to be even greater in lower paid jobs (i.e. upholsterers, bus drivers, hotel clerks, woodworking machine operators) leading the authors to conclude that increases in occupational mobility will not necessarily result in racial earnings equality for black men.

Disproportionate disparities also exist between white and black people regarding poverty. Black households have considerably lower wealth than white households (Blau and Graham 1990); education brings lower returns in terms of income, occupational status and avoidance of unemployment among black than among white people (Hacker 1995) and the purchasing power of black people is less than that their white counterparts with respect to food, housing and other necessary expenditures (Williams and Collins 1995). The National Urban league (2009) report also notes that black Americans trail whites on income and education while the US Census Bureau (2008) paint a similar scenario (see Table 12.1).

Furthermore, the United States remains a residentially segregated society in which black and white people inhabit different neighbourhoods of vastly different quality (Sethi and Somanathan 2004). Black people are increasingly more likely than whites

Table 12.1 Black and white American population on selected indicators

Factor	Black	White
Total median family income	$34,218	$55,530
Poverty rate	24.7%	8.6%

Source: US Census Bureau 2008

to find themselves living in high-poverty neighbourhoods with limited resources and limited options. This makes it far more likely for concentrated high-poverty communities to be cut off from pathways out of poverty such as quality schools and affordable consumer credit and other.

Institutional response

The United States has several legislative provisions aimed at promoting a fair and tolerant society. The cornerstone of all legislative provisions is the Civil Rights Act of 1964 which makes it unlawful to discriminate against any individual in matters relating to employment and also protects individuals against racism in every sphere of life.[1] The provision prohibits not only intentional discrimination but also neutral job policies that disproportionately affect persons of a certain race or colour and that are not related to the job and the needs of the business. The Equal Employment Opportunity Commission (EEOC) is the body which enforces all Federal laws prohibiting job discrimination and also provides oversight and coordination of all federal equal employment opportunity regulations, practices and policies. In a recent report, the EEOC (2007) noted that race-based charges brought against employers in the country rose by 12.4 per cent from 26,740 in 2005 to 30,510 in 2007; conversely the number of resolutions within the same period has fallen by 6 per cent from 27411 in 2005 to 25882 in 2007 (Table 12.2). How should these figures be interpreted? Could it be that the fewer resolutions are indicative of a less effective institutional mechanism for enforcing racial equality in employment or are other factors accountable?

One major spin-off from the Civil Right Act is the Affirmative Action (AA) policy which is intended to promote access to education or employment for minority groups and women. The major motivation for AA programmes is to redress the effects of past discrimination and to encourage public institutions to be more representative of the population. The intuitive appeal of AA policies arguably derives from the notion that by giving preferential treatment to minority applicants through targeted recruitment efforts, the historical disadvantage that these groups have been subjected to is being fairly and legitimately addressed. However, its critics believe that overt preference for applicants from particular racial background over better or equally-qualified candidates from other racial backgrounds only

Table 12.2 Race-based charges: 1997–2007

	2005	2006	2007
Receipts	26,740	27,238	30,510
Resolutions	27,411	25,992	25,882

Source: Equal Employment Opportunity Commission 2007[2]

serves to perpetuate racial division instead of minimizing the importance of race in American society (JAMA 1990). More about this will be discussed in the conclusion but suffice to say at this juncture that current evidence suggests that much of the legacy of racism still haunts contemporary American society. While there is little doubt that black people have made significant progress since the days of the civil rights movement, the evidence on persisting racial inequality in almost every facet of life is a testament to the enduring heritage of the dark era. Changes in the political landscape may be discouraging overt forms of racism, but evidently, it has not eradicated subtler manifestations of racial prejudice. Attitudes die hard, and since racial attitudes account for discriminatory acts, it is changes in racial attitudes that are needed to bring about a truly post-racial America.

Racism and inequality in the United Kingdom

Historical context

The UK also has a long history of racism which still influences contemporary thinking in the country. In medieval times before the period of slavery, an apartheid-like system had existed in early Anglo-Saxon England. For more than 300 years from the middle of the fifth century, native British were prevented from mixing with those of the Anglo-Saxon population and the latter also had a substantial social and economic advantage over the natives (BBC 2002; Thomas et al. 2006; Vince 2006). Post-medieval Britain can be defined by its preoccupation with the consolidation of an Empire and engagement in slave trade, the legacy of which remains till today. One example of this legacy is the Commonwealth, the successor of the British Empire. Interestingly, the objectives of the Commonwealth include the promotion of individual liberty, the pursuit of equality and opposition to racism. This in the very least suggests that Commonwealth countries are resolved to preventing history repeating itself. However, it is arguable whether their erstwhile colonial master will be able to rid itself of the ignominious memory of the atrocities perpetrated during the colonial era. Indeed, Gilroy (2004: 100) suggests that the history of Britain's Empire is source of shame that undermines its moral legitimacy and damages its national esteem.

Immigration is one area in which Britain's brutal colonial history continues to cast its long post-colonial shadow. Tensions over immigration date back to the period when it was originally engendered by hostility towards Irish immigrants, Jews and immigrants from Russia and Eastern Europe. Skellington (1996: 96) notes that Irish migration started in 1840, the Jewish immigration before World War I and migration by New Commonwealth subjects after World War II. Initially, most of British subjects in the colonies and dominions retained a legal right to enter and settle in Britain but since the 1960s Britain has been imposing very strong limits on immigration through legislation particularly targeted at members of the Commonwealth who had previously been able to migrate to the UK under the British Nationality Act 1948. The Immigration Act 1971 further tightened the noose by virtually ending all legal immigration especially primary immigration, into the UK.

Interestingly, black people have actually lived in the UK for centuries during which period they were subjected to slavery and exploitation (Sandhu 2003). In essence, migrants helped built the United Kingdom and contributed towards making it what it is today. It is thus not surprising that the perceived injustice coupled with Britain's racialized politics have generated ethnic tensions which have often boiled over in various uprisings and riots by immigrant and minority populations in the country as far back as the early 1908s and more recently in the 1950s (BBC 2004). The riots, which were reportedly sparked by societal racism, discrimination and poverty, also occurred in 1980, 1981, 1982, 1982 and 1985.[3]

Racism and inequality in contemporary Britain

In recent times, successive governments have tried to promote racial harmony and ensure equality and fairness in the society. Considering that ethnic minorities make up a significant proportion of the UK population (currently at 8 per cent), it would appear that the government not only recognizes the promotion of racial equality as a matter of social justice imperative but also one of political expediency. Allegations of institutional racism are usually treated seriously because of the potential political implication and negative publicity. However, while governments and businesses often express their unequivocal commitment to equality and diversity and would usually reaffirm this official policy whenever there are accusations of racial discrimination, the rhetoric often fall short when examined against the backdrop of existing evidence.

Evidently, there is still widespread ethnic segregation, residentially, socially and in the workplace in Britain. According to a UK National Survey of Ethnic Minorities, Britain remains a place of inequality, exclusion and isolation (CRE 2007). The study notes that ethnic minorities in Britain are more likely to be stopped by police and excluded from school. Other studies indicate experiences of racial harassment and discrimination among ethnic minority people (Virdee 1997). A Home Office Citizenship Survey found a perceived increase in racial prejudice (Kitchen et al. 2006). A similar survey found that around 30 per cent of those of working age viewed themselves as racially prejudiced in 2003 (Heath and Cheung 2006). Qualitative investigations of experiences of racial harassment and discrimination have found that for many people, experiences of interpersonal racism are a part of everyday life and the way they lead their lives is constrained by fear of racial harassment, daily racist abuse, being made to feel different is routine and expected and having belongings damaged or experiencing violence (Virdee 1995). Trevor Phillips, the head of the Equality and Human Rights Commission (EHRC) in the UK, warned that the country is 'sleepwalking toward apartheid' and breaking up into 'literal black holes into which no one goes without fear and trepidation and nobody escapes undamaged' (*Times* 2005). In the same newspaper article, He warns: 'you can get to the point as they have in the U.S. where things are so divided that there is no turning back'.

As far as employment and economic matters are concerned, studies indicate that ethnic minorities are less likely to be invited for interviews, selected after the interview process, earn less than their white colleagues, have less income left over than their whites after their basic needs had been taken into account, experience higher rate of unemployment, are less likely to be in management positions, are less likely to gain promotion or advance on the career ladder at work and are worst off compared to whites on a range of quality-of-life measures (Bajekal et al. 2004; Berthoud 1998; Blackaby et al. 1994, 1996, 1997; Carmichael and Woods 2000; Frijters et al. 2005; Heath and Yu 2005; Jowell and Prescott-Clarke 1970; Modood 1997; Platt 2006; Virdee 1997; Wood 2009).

Other studies which have focused on deprivation found that minorities were more deprived compared to whites (Gordon et al. 2000; Pantazis et al. 2006). Platt's (2007) study indicates that minority ethnic groups have higher rates of poverty than the average for the population and this cut across children, working-age adults and pensioners (Table 12.3). The study not only showed that minority groups are relatively worse off than whites, but also that Pakistanis and Bangladeshis face more risks of poverty. This within-group difference is noteworthy because it illustrates how some particular ethnic groups face more risks than others. Similarly, Kenway and Palmer's (2007) study indicates that around two-fifths (40 per cent) of people from ethnic minorities – twice the rate for white people – live in income poverty (Table 12.4). They also showed that income poverty rate varies substantially between

Table 12.3 Poverty rates by ethnic group in Britain (%)

Ethnic group	All individuals	Children	Working-age adults	Pensioners
White	19	25	17	19
Mixed	32	40	28	36
Indian	28	32	25	30
Pakistani or Bangladeshi	59	65	55	48
Black or black British	38	46	35	27
– of which				
Black Caribbean	30	37	28	26
Black non-Caribbean	46	54	41	31
Chinese or other	37	44	36	26
All	39	48	46	31

Source: Platt (2007): Households below Average Income Data, the data is the average for 2002/03 to 2004/05 2002/03 and is calculated after housing costs

Table 12.4 Overall income distribution according to ethnic groups

Ethnic group	% in the poorest quintile	% in the 2nd quintile	% in the middle quintile	% in the 4th quintile	% in the richest quintile	Total
White British	18	20	21	21	20	100
White other	25	16	16	15	28	100
Indian	27	18	19	17	19	100
Black Caribbean	30	22	19	17	12	100
Black African	45	20	14	13	9	100
Pakistani	52	30	9	4	5	100
Bangladeshi	66	21	7	3	2	100
All groups combined	20	20	20	20	20	100

Source: Kenway and Palmer 2007: Households below Average Income; the data is the average for 2002–03 to 2004–05 and is after deducting housing costs

the ethnic minority groups with Pakistani and Bangladeshi households being more likely to experience income poverty.

Institutional response

Over the years, various legislative acts have been enacted by the British government as a response to the problems of racism and inequality. The Race Relations Act 1968 made it illegal to refuse housing, employment or public services to a person on the grounds of colour, race, ethnic or national origins.[4] This was succeeded by the 1976 Race Relations Act (RRA) which in addition to forbidding discrimination on the grounds of 'colour, race, nationality or ethnic or national origins' also established the Commission for Race Equality (CRE). In 1975, the Equal Opportunities Commission (EOC) was established as part of a Sex Discrimination Act (SDA). The CRE and EOC had legal mandate to investigate discrimination relating to employment in the country. In 2000, the RRA was amended and extended existing legislation by placing key public bodies, including all Government departments, under a statutory general duty to promote race equality. This duty means that public authorities must have due regard to the need to eliminate unlawful discrimination, promote equality of opportunity and good relations between people of different racial groups. The general duty is supported by a series of specific duties, applicable to both employment and service delivery and requires that each authority have a Race Equality Scheme which sets out the ways in which the organization will meet the requirements outlined in the specific duties. Recently, the laws received an overhaul with the introduction of the 2007 Equality and Human Rights Act (EHRA) which brings together six equality strands, sex, race, disability, age, religion, sexual orientation. The EOC and CRE are merged into the EHRC which deals with all six strands.

These policies have had some impact on the effort to combat inequalities. At the very least, they have generated a heightened state of awareness concerning the issues so much so that it has become less likely for blatant or overt racism to occur without going unchallenged. Nevertheless, the persistence of inequalities is a reminder that serious obstacles remain. There is evidence that equal opportunities polices have failed to have sustained impact on the experiences of minority ethnic nurses (Culley 2001) and doctors (Esmail and Everington 1997). Beishon et al.'s (1995) study found very significant gaps between written policies and the actual practices undertaken in the workplace. Furthermore, Blackaby et al. (1994) found that equal opportunities legislation has been less successful in reducing the white/ non-white pay differential between white and black and minority ethnic nurses. Shields and Wheatley Price (2002) support this finding by suggesting that the substantial differences between the disparities in the amount of training received by minority ethnic workers compared to white workers represented a failure of equal opportunities policies.

Conclusion

The United States and Britain both have a history of racism and inequality whose legacies remain strong and inextricably linked through empire and slave trade. The expansion of the United States has resulted from successive waves of migration, the conquest of indigenous Native Americans and the slavery of African-Americans. Similarly, black people have been exploited by Britain via the slave trade and have contributed to the expansion of the British Empire even if they and other minorities have been subjected to various forms of restrictions in terms of migration. In a sense, the national histories of both countries have influenced the current focus of respective national debates regarding race relations such that issues related to migrants have dominated the discourse in the UK whereas non-migrants issues have driven the debate in the United States.

In the United States, racism has a history which dates back to the period of slavery and racial segregation and the legacy of slavery has determined many African-Americans' contemporary circumstances. Similarly, in Britain, the current racism directed towards immigrants goes as far back as the 1800s during which tensions over immigration were originally engendered by hostility towards the Irish, black and Jewish immigrants from Eastern Europe. Although public expressions of white supremacy in the UK have now been limited to far-right political parties, immigrants and migrants are still viewed with deep suspicion and media stereotypes of them as scroungers and a drain on the economy of Britain is not uncommon. This plays into the hands of organized fascists groups like the BNP, a far-right and anti-immigration group which gained its first ever seats on the London Assembly in 2005 and the European Parliament in 2009. Apparently, the BNP exploited public unease about issues such as rising unemployment and council flats accommodation coupled with media stereotypes of immigrants as scroungers depriving white Britons of their rights as citizens. While far-rights groups also exist in the United States, the election of the first ever African-American President in 2008 suggests that the country as a whole has made significant progress in race relations.

In both countries, minorities have been excluded from avenues that would enable their economic advancement and upward mobility. The patterns of discrimination against minority groups in the United States exist in many forms and institutions and dates back to the inception of slavery. In particular, the disparities in wealth between black and white people are largely the result of differences in inheritance due to slavery and the legacy of discrimination (Bell 2007). This observation is supported by a 2006 census report which suggests that the wealth gap according to race is not just a story of merit and achievement but also a story of the historical legacy of race in the United States.[5] In Britain, the resilience and perpetuations of racial inequality and racial segregation has remained consistent for centuries. Trevor Philips, the chairman of the EHRC puts it succinctly:

> How is it that 50 years after the first wave of colonial migrants arrived on the *Empire Windrush*, we can predict with certainty that a black British man is now twice as likely to see the inside of a jail cell as he is ever to sit in a university tutorial? And why are young ethnic minority Britons twice as likely as their elders to have a circle of friends which completely excludes whites? (*Times* 2004)

The relevance of poverty and racial segregation to the discourse on workplace and career inequality is underpinned by the link of the former to racial differences in employment and earnings. Social capital explanations have been used to appreciate the endurance of major disparities in poverty rates among racial and ethnic groups (Wilson 1987; Quillian and Redd 2006). Mainly, most explanations has hinged on the notion that higher rates of group poverty is fuelled by a reduced stock of a type of social capital which is occasioned by a disadvantaged racial or ethnic groups' structural position in social networks. According to Wilson (1987), the persistent poverty of urban minorities derives from their isolation from social contact with middle-class persons. In the same vein, Quillian and Redd (2006) argued that racial differences in poverty outcomes may be explained by the fact that lower income non-whites often reside in urban neighbourhoods with low levels of 'collective efficacy' and that employment and wage gaps of non-white jobseekers is often a result of exclusionary job networks. They concluded that the evidence for these explanations is mixed, but that the stronger evidence in accounting for racial poverty gaps are the contextual disadvantages from disadvantaged neighbourhoods and peer groups, which contribute especially to crime and delinquency problems in minority communities. Indeed, the importance of job networks has been demonstrated in that they are important (Royster 2003) and job contacts are mostly racially homogeneous (Mouw 2002). Quillian and Redd (2006) notes:

> If many black and Hispanic job seekers have job networks that provide less information and influence toward acquiring a job than the networks of white job seekers, and these connections are an important advantage in gaining employment, then it could be that job networks are an important factor contributing to racial gaps in employment. (13)

Given that the debate on race relations in the United States is seemingly dominated by a focus on African-Americans for the most part, it is necessary to stress that Native Americans are also among the most economically disadvantaged groups in the country. It is also pertinent to note that their current circumstance has its roots in the experiences of their ancestors at the hand of the early settlers. Even within minority groups in the UK, there are degrees of differences in inequality. Minority groups such as the Bangladeshi and Pakistanis have been found to be relatively worse off than others although it should be noted that human capital (e.g. educational qualifications) has been found to partly account for this (see Platt 2005).

The approach of equality legislation within the United States is defined essentially by affirmative action. Anti-discrimination enforcement aims to ensure equal access to affirmative action programmes and the jobs to which they lead. In the UK, equal treatment or 'positive action' is the overriding philosophy of equality legislation whereby under-represented groups are identified and action is taken to improve their representation. The UK used to have a multi-agency approach in which separate agencies representing different strands of diversity enforces legal protection for minorities. This has now been replaced by a combined approach in which all strands are embedded within the EHRC, mirroring the EEOC in the US.

Despite an extensive legal framework that enshrines racial equality and protects against discrimination in both countries, ethnic minorities continue to lag behind whites. The UK boasts of a plethora of legislative and policy initiatives aimed at combating racism and inequality but it appears these have had limited impact. Similarly, the discrepancy appears to also challenge America's view of itself as a society of equal opportunity where the spotlight on affirmative action has intensified in recent times. It should be pointed out that while affirmative action would be considered illegal in the UK, the country's equality legislation supports positive action which allows for employers to take proactive steps to encourage more representation of minorities in their workforce. This means that employers can act to improve the representation of underrepresented groups through encouraging applications from underrepresented groups or sending them on training courses, albeit on merit.

The supporters of affirmative action in the US argue that it is necessary to compel employers to adopt the programme in order to ensure that the racial status quo is not perpetuated indefinitely. In other words, social justice requires it. Sceptics however, consider the programme to be reverse racism which also flies in the face of social justice. The question is: who has the strongest claim to the moral high ground? While it is generally acknowledged that discrimination is a prime cause of inequality, perhaps it is time for black men and women to shoulder greater responsibility for fixing their own problems. In what appears to be a clear indication of a backlash against affirmative action, on 29 June 2009, the Supreme Court ruled that white fire-fighters in New Haven, Connecticut were unfairly denied promotion by the city of New Haven due to their race.[6] The impact which this ruling is likely to have on future affirmative programmes and indeed the implications it posits for future race relations, remains to be seen.

In summary, this chapter has demonstrated the importance of national histories in understanding the structure of inequalities and prevalence of racism in the US and the UK and the institutional responses to them. It has shown how different forms of racism and segregation in the two countries and patterns of inequality and exclusion in different sectors of the economy conspire to prevent ethnic minorities from availing themselves of opportunities to achieve economic prosperity and upward mobility. Furthermore the study reinforces the observation that racial inequality in the workplace is still very much alive despite the progress that has been achieved in the back of anti-discrimination and equality legislation in both countries.

Notes

1. Source: http://www.eeoc.gov/types/race.html
2. Source: http://www.eeoc.gov/stats/race.html (Accessed 18 August 2008).
3. 'A different reality: minority struggle in British cities', University of Warwick. Centre for Research in Ethnic Relations. Accessed 18 August 2009.
4. 'The Race Relations Amendment Bill': http://www.parliament.uk/commons/lib/research/rp2000/rp00-027.pdf (Accessed 27 August 2009).
5. 'Census report: Broad racial disparities persist', 14 November 2006. http://www.msnbc.msn.com/id/15704759/ (Accessed 4 August 2009).
6. http://documents.nytimes.com/supreme-court-opinion-ricci-v-destefano

References

Bajekal, M., D. Blane, I. Grewal, S. Karlsen and J. Nazroo (2004) 'Ethnic differences in influences on quality of life at older ages: a quantitative analysis', *Ageing and Society*, 24: 709–28.

BBC (2002) 'English and Welsh are races apart'. Available at: http://news.bbc.co.uk/1/hi/wales/2076470.stm. Accessed 17 August 2009.

—— (2004) 'The Scarman Report'. Available at: http://news.bbc.co.uk/1/hi/programmes/bbc_parliament/3631579.stm

Beishon, S., S. Virdee and A. Hagelli (1995) *Nursing in a multi-ethnic NHS*. London: Policy Studies Institute.

Bell, M. P. (2007) *Diversity in organizations*. Mason: Thompson South-Western.

Benedict, R. F. (1945) *Race and racism*. London, England: Routledge and Kegan Paul.

Berthoud, R. (1998) 'The incomes of ethnic minorities', ISER Working Paper 98. Colchester: Institute for Social and Economic Research, University of Essex.

Blackaby, D., K. Clark, D. Leslie and P. Murphy (1994) 'Black-white male earnings and employment prospects in the 1970s and 1980s', *Economics Letters*, 46: 273–9.

Blackaby, D., S. Drinkwater, D. Leslie and P. Murphy (1997) 'A picture of male and female unemployment among Britain's ethnic minorities', *Scottish Journal of Political Economy*, 44: 182–97.

Blackaby, D. H., K. Clarck, D. G. Leslie and P. D. Murphy (1996) 'The changing distribution of black and white earnings and the ethnic wage gap: evidence for Britain', Paper presented at the Conference of the European Association of Labour Economics, China, September 1996.

Blau, F. D. and J. W. Graham (1990) 'Black-white differences in wealth and asset composition'. *Quarterly Journal of Economics*, 105: 321–9.

Brescia, W. (1982) 'French-Choctaw Contact, 1680s–1763', In W. Brescia (ed.), *Tribal government, a new era*. Philadelphia, Mississippi: Choctaw Heritage Press.

Carmichael, F. and R. Woods (2000) 'Ethnic penalties in unemployment and occupational attainment: evidence for Britain', *International Review of Applied Economics*, 14(1): 71–98.

Castillo, E. D. (1998) 'Short overview of California Indian history', California Native American Heritage Commission.

Clarke, G. and A. L. Hamby (2005) *Outline of US history*. New York: Nova Science Publishers.

CRE (2007) *A lot done, a lot to do – our vision for an integrated Britain*. London: Commission for Racial Equality.

Culley, L. (2001) 'Equal opportunities policies and nursing employment within the British National Service', *Journal of Advanced Nursing*, 33(1): 130–7.

Davy Smith, G. (2000) 'Learning to live with complexity: ethnicity, socioeconomic position, and health in Britain and the United States', *American Journal of Public Health*, 90: 1694–8.

Deitch, E. A., A. Barsky, R. M. Butz, S. Chan, A. P. Brief and J. C. Bradley (2003) 'Subtle yet significant: the existence and impact of everyday racial discrimination in the workplace', *Human Relations*, 56(11): 1299–324.

Frijters, P., M. A. Shields and S. Wheatley Price (2005) 'Job search methods and their success: a comparison of immigrants and natives in the UK', *The Economic Journal*, 115(507): F359–F376.

Esmail, A. and S. Everington (1997) 'Asian doctors are still being discriminated against', *The British Medical Journal*, 314(1619): 4.

Gilroy, P. (2004) *After empire: melancholia or convivial culture*. London and New York: Routledge.

Gordon, D., R. Levitas, C. Pantazis, D. Patsios, S. Payne, P. Townsend et al. (2000) *Poverty and social exclusion in Britain*. York: Joseph Rowntree Foundation.

Grodsky, E. and D. Pager (2001) 'The structure of disadvantage: individual and occupational determinants of the black-white wage gap', *American Sociological Review*, 66(4): 542–67.

Hacker, A. (1995) *Two nations: black and white, separate, hostile, unequal*. New York, NY: Ballantine Books.

Heath, A. and S. Y. Cheung (2006) *Ethnic penalties in the labour market: employers and discrimination*. DWP Research Report 341. Leeds: Corporate Document Services.

Heath, A. and S. Yu (2005) 'Explaining ethnic minority disadvantage', In A. Heath, J. Ermisch and D. Gallie (eds), *Understanding social change*. Oxford: Oxford University Press, pp. 187–224.

Hurst, C. (2006) *Social inequality: forms, causes, and consequences* (6th edition). Boston: Allyn & Bacon.

JAMA (1990) 'Black-white disparities in health care', *JAMA*, 263(17): 2344–6.

Jenkins, A. (2007) 'Inequality, race, and remedy', *The American Prospect*. Available at: http://www.prospect.org/cs/articles?article=inequality_race_and_remedy

Jowell, R. and P. Prescott-Clarke (1970) 'Racial discrimination and white-collar workers in Britain', *Race*, 11: 397–417.

Kenway, P. and G. Palmer (2007) 'Poverty among ethnic groups how and why does it differ?' Joseph Rowntree Foundation, London: New Policy Institute.

Kitchen, S., J. Michaelson, N. Wood and P. John (2006) *2005 citizenship survey: race and faith topic report*. London: Department for Communities & Local Government.

Krieger, N., P. D. Waterman, C. Hartman, L. M. Bates, A. M. Stoddard, M. M. Quinn et al. (2006) 'Social hazards on the job: workplace abuse, sexual harassment and racial discrimination – a study of Black, Latino and White low-income women and men workers in the United States', *International Journal of Health Services*, 36(1): 51–85.

Modood, T. (1997) 'Employment', In T. Modood , R. Berthoud, J. Lakey et al. *Ethnic minorities in Britain: diversity and disadvantage*. London, England: Policy Studies Institute, pp. 83–149.

Mouw, T. (2002) 'Are black workers missing the connection? The effect of spatial distance and employee referrals on interfirm racial segregation', *Demography*, 39(3): 507–52.

—— (2003) 'Social capital and finding a job: do contacts matter?' *American Sociological Review*, 68: 868–98.

National Urban League (2009) 'State of Black America 2009: Message to the President' New York: http://www.nul.org/newsroom/publications/soba

Pantazis, C., D. Gordon and R. Levitas (eds) (2006) *Poverty and social exclusion in Britain: the millennium survey*. Bristol: The Policy Press.

Platt, L. (2006) 'The intergenerational social mobility of minority ethnic groups', *Sociology*, 39: 445–61.

—— (2007) 'Poverty and ethnicity in the UK', Joseph Rowntree Foundation, University of Essex.

Quillian, L. and R. Redd (2006) 'Can social capital explain persistent racial poverty gaps?', National Poverty Center Working Paper Series, No. 06-12. Available at: http://www.npc.umich.edu/publications/working_papers/

Royster, D. (2003) *Race and the invisible hand: how white networks exclude black men from blue-collar jobs*. Berkeley, CA: University of California Press.

Sandhu, S. (2003) *London calling: how Black and Asian writers imagined a city*. Glasgow: HarperCollins.

Schaefer, R. T. (1990) Racial and ethnic groups. (4th edition). City, IL: Scott Foresman/ Little Brown Higher Education.

Sethi R. and R. Somanathan (2004) 'Inequality and segregation', *Journal of Political Economy*, 112: 1296–321.

Shields M. A. and S. W. Wheatley Price (2002) 'The determinants of racial harassment at the workplace – evidence from the British nursing profession', *British Journal of Industrial Relations*, 40(1): 1–2.

Skellington, R. (1996) *Race in Britain today*. London: Sage.

Takaki, R. (1993) *A different mirror: a history of multicultural America*. New York: Little, Brown & Co.

Thomas, G., M. Stumpf and H. Harke (2006) 'Evidence for an apartheid-like social structure in early Anglo-Saxon England', *Proceedings Biological Sciences*, 273(1601): 2651–7.

Times (2004) 'Face facts: race inequality persist'. Availble at: http://www.timesonline.co.uk/tol/comment/article500305.ece

—— (2005) 'Britain urged to wake up to race crisis'. Available at: http://www.timesonline.co.uk/tol/news/uk/article569491.ece

US Bureau Census (2008) 'Income, poverty and health insurance coverage in the United States: 2008', Available at: http://www.census.gov/hhes/www/poverty/poverty08.html

Van de Berghe, P. (1967) *Race and racism: a comparative perspective.* New York: John Wiley and Sons.

Vince, G. (2006) ' "Apartheid" slashed Celtic genes in early England', *New Scientist.* Available at: http://www.newscientist.com/article/dn9575-apartheid-slashed-celtic-genes-in-early-england.html

Virdee S. (1995) *Racial violence and harassment.* London, England: Policy Studies Institute, p. 199.

—— (1997) 'Racial harassment', In T. Modood, R. Berthoud, J. Lakey et al. (eds), *Ethnic minorities in Britain: diversity and disadvantage.* London, England: Policy Studies Institute, pp. 259–89.

Waters, M. C. (2004) 'Race, ethnicity and immigration in the United States', In F. Devine and M. C. Waters (eds), *Social inequalities in comparative perspective.* Oxford: Blackwell Publishing.

Wilson, W. J. (1987) *The truly disadvantaged: the inner-city, the underclass, and public policy.* Chicago: University of Chicago Press.

Williams D. R. and C. Collins (1995) 'US socioeconomic and racial differences in health: patterns and explanations', *Annual Review of Sociology,* 21:349–86.

Wood, D. (2009) 'Racial inequality continues to rise', *Human Relations.* Avilable at: http://www.humanresourcesmagazine.com/news/871839/Racial-inequality-continues-rise/ Accessed 28 August 2009.

13

The labour market context and its effect on women's participation in independent business and professional networks

A comparative study in the UK and Germany

Nicole Avdelidou-Fischer

Introduction

The United Kingdom and Germany are among the largest and most financially power-ful countries in the European Union (IMF 2008) that increasingly face similar chal-lenges: ageing populations, lower marriage and higher divorce rates, 'postponement' of childbirth and dramatically falling fertility rates. Both countries maintain a process of integration in the European Union and have increasing numbers of women in ter-tiary education and in paid employment. Also on a national level, the United Kingdom and Germany have been legislating to ensure equality of opportunity and treatment regardless of gender, and over the last years, new strands of law have come into force, to extend the Sex Discrimination Act in the UK and assemble Germany's scattered anti-discrimination directives into the General Act on Equal Treatment. However, investment in education does not seem to offer women equal returns as for men and an important factor behind women's numerical growth in the labour force is said to be part-time work. Women in the UK and Germany appear concentrated in less presti-gious, lower income occupations, and continue to do much of the unpaid work at home.

Within this contradictory context, the increase of women-only business and pro-fessional networks in the UK (McCarthy 2004) and Germany (Lenz 2008), raises the question of whether those networks are an effect of positive developments in the public sphere and legislation or of negative conditions under which women's employment takes place. Research in this area is rather sparse (Travers and Pemberton 2000), mono-national (e.g. Bock 2002), and tends to treat women-only networks as parts of the same overarching category, no matter if they are informal corporate networks, formal long-established societies, specialized industry groups or profession-related associations (e.g. Frerichs and Wiemert 2002). Among this variety of networks, there is one form that has not yet been a focus of study on its own: independent networks for business and professional women (henceforth women's independent networks – WINs). Focusing on WINs by employing a comparative approach, this chapter will provide insights into a neglected setting, and make an original contribution to the literature of gender equality and women's networks.

In line with the above, the objective of the chapter is to compare the differences or similarities of women's position in the contemporary UK and German labour markets in the form it exists inside official governmental and other monitoring agencies' reports, contrast these to WIN women's own interpretations of the context and find relations to their participation in WINs.

Research methods

WINs are formally organized member-based societies for working women. WINs are different from women's professional associations because they are not industry or profession-related, and their members come from different sectors, have different occupations or hierarchical positions, and can be salaried employees or self-employed. The term 'independent' means that they are not internal to any corporation, or part of any trade union or feminist organization, and so do not demand political or ideological consensus of their members. In this study, participants were voluntary members of four WINs:

AURORA, launched in 2000, aims to increase the number, growth and success of women-owned businesses in the UK through online business. In 2008, the network reported having 28,000 members.

BPW UK, founded in 1938, aims at helping business and professional women achieve their full potential in all aspects of their life. It has 44 local clubs around the UK and over 1500 members.

Its German counterpart, BPW DE, dates back to 1931. Its purpose is to promote women's development and equal treatment in employment and education, and has 38 local clubs across the country, with 1700 members.

BFBM was founded in 1992 with the aim of promoting equality and acceptance for women in employment and society. The network consists of 16 local clubs around Germany, with over 350 members.

Primary data were gathered via 55 semi-structured interviews, 10 observations of monthly local meetings and annual national conventions, and a research diary. Secondary data were collected via OECD, EUROSTAT and other relevant reports and databanks. The target population was members at all ranks and levels of organizational involvement, came from a variety of sectors and had diverse occupations; their demographic characteristics are summarized in Table 13.1.

The position of women in the UK and German labour markets

This section deals with the macro level of analysis to discuss the empirical context of women's employment position in the UK and Germany. According to Walby

Table 13.1 Demographic characteristics of participants

	United Kingdom	Germany
Age range	30–84	32–66
Ethnic origin		
Native-born	70.36%	89.66%
Foreign-born	29.64%	10.34%
Highest level qualification		
O-levels to below Bachelor	23.08%	41.38%
Bachelor degree	46.15%	24.14%
Master degree	26.92%	31.03%
Doctoral degree	3.85%	3.45%
Marital status		
Single	23.08%	10.34%
Cohabiting	15.38%	13.79%
Married	53.85%	62.08%
Divorced	7.69%	13.79%
Dependant family members		
0	74.07%	34.48%
1	18.53%	17.24%
2	3.70%	44.83%
3	3.70%	3.45%
Employment status		
Salaried employee	33.34%	31.03%
Self-employed	51.85%	68.97%
Unemployed	3.70%	0.00%
Retired	11.11%	0.00%

(1990) there are three main empirical features of gender relations in employment: (i) gender employment rates, (ii) gender pay gap and (iii) gender segregation. In general, these agree with van der Lippe and van Dijk's (2002) most frequently used indicators of women's employment in comparative research. Although these indicators will be presented separately, it must be noted that they relate to and influence each other.

Gender employment rates

In all age groups a higher percentage of men (UK 80.8 per cent; DE 77.4 per cent) than women (UK 68.1 per cent; DE 65.2 per cent) are employed in the United Kingdom and Germany, although the female population slightly outnumbers men in both countries (EUROSTAT 2009). But in all categories the gap between male and female employment rates is narrowing, which is due to the fact that the proportion of adult women who are economically active is rising. The largest increase occurred in 1991 for German women in the age group 25–54, as a result of the reunification of Germany (OECD. Stat 2009).

When isolating the former East Germany, employment rates are almost equal and in 2006 men formed 50.2 per cent and women 49.8 per cent of the labour market (Wagner 2007). Albeit the reunification imposed a male breadwinner model and brought high unemployment rates in the east (van Hoven 2002), the effects of state policies on women's full participation in the labour force are still obvious. However Rueschemeyer and Schissler (1990) warn against understanding the East's 'forced emancipation' as equality, because women in East Germany were segregated to a considerable degree in traditionally female occupations and were rarely found in the highest leadership positions in the workplace, the union or the party and the government. But still, Ferree (1995) argues that state policies have played a major role in systematically shaping women's experiences of paid work, marriage and motherhood, which further influences the interpretations of oppression and freedom that women construct.

On the whole, full-time employment rates are more dissimilar between genders than between countries. What is particularly noticeable, is that the pattern of women's workforce participation in standardized age groups (Figure 13.1) resembles an M-known as the 'M-curve' (Stockman et al. 1995). Although the graph does not represent employment over life course, it is still telling a clear story. Once graduating from high school or university, women's entry to the labour market produces the M's first peak. After the age of 29, the line turns downwards as women get married and have children. Some women return to full-time employment after the child-rearing years and in the UK the M visibly heads for its second peak after the age of 44. In Germany, one can presume a second peak at the 50–54 age group but it generally remains flatter. The line descends with every following group more and more as women start retiring from the workforce.

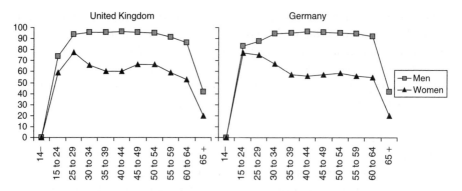

Figure 13.1   M-curve of full time as a percentage of total employment 2008

According to Hakim (1995) the increase in female employment in Europe and among married women, has been the most pervasive myth in feminist sociology. She argues that all change has actually consisted of a conversion of full-time to part-time jobs. In 2007, women made up 77.4 per cent of part-time employees in the UK and 80.7 per cent in Germany, and the share of involuntary part-timers as a percentage of part-time employment, is lower for women than for men in both countries (OECD. Stat 2009). By means of part-time working women reconcile family and work life, and this prevents women's market capital from depreciating (Drobnic et al. 1999). In the attempt to explain patterns of women's employment, Hakim (1998, 2000) developed Preference Theory, which argues that work-lifestyle preferences are at least as import-ant – if not more – as the social and economic context in determining those patterns. Hakim postulates that there are substantive differences between the priorities and values of women that produce three different categories of: (i) home-centred women, who prefer not to work but prioritize family and children, (ii) adaptive women, who prefer to combine work and family and (iii) work-centred women, whose main pri-ority in life is employment. For Hakim, this heterogeneity is reflected in women's diverse employment patterns and translates into moving in and out of the labour market, phases of part-time employment, or uninterrupted full-time employment. Next to accepting the notion of 'genuine preference' without question, many authors (e.g. Lee and McCann 2006) seemingly find it difficult to believe that every single woman is provided with chances to do otherwise and that gender-roles are primar-ily negotiated at a micro level. Even if – as Hakim claims – 'adaptive women' choose part-time jobs with the awareness that they are low-paid and low-status but also fit their domestic and family role, it is hard to infer that all these women see their genu-ine preferences reflected in their work arrangements (Lee and McCann 2006).

Gender pay gap

The UK and Germany legislate to ensure equal pay for equal work regardless of gen-der. The first legal basis for equal pay between men and women constituted Article

119 of the EC Treaty of Rome, which came into force in 1958 (Fontaine 2004). The EC confirmed and expanded the provisions of Article 119 in 1975 with the Equal Pay Directive (75/117), which introduced the principle of equal pay for 'work of equal value' between genders (Mazey 1998).

The UK introduced its Equal Pay Act in 1970, three years before it joined the EC (Fontaine 2004). Interestingly, it wasn't until 1980 when a compliance law for equal pay was introduced in Germany, although it has been an EC grounding member. This shows that German civil servants initially felt that the EC law was adequate, while the UK's aspiration to EC membership proved – at least in theory – more efficient to take action on a national level (Mazey 1998).

Median wages for men are higher than those for women in both countries (Figure 13.2). The unadjusted Gender Pay Gap represents the difference between average gross hourly earnings of male paid employees and of female paid employees as a percentage of average gross hourly earnings of male paid employees. In 2007, the gender gap in median earnings of full-time employees was 23.0 per cent in Germany, and 21.1 per cent in the UK, with both values being above the EU 27 average which was 17.4 per cent (EUROSTAT 2009). The widest income gap for all adults exists in Great Britain, in retirement, where women receive 47.0 per cent less than men, which is in a large part due to the effect of time out of the workforce raising children or working part-time (EOC 2006).

According to Blackburn et al. (2002) the pay gap is a self-reproducing way for conceptualizing a vertical dimension in gender segregation. Partners find it economically rational to prioritize the employment of the higher earner, which is usually the man (Becker 1985). Without career breaks, men increase their human capital and so continue to earn more. Even though through childcare and housework women require and develop skills which have marketable value, it is claimed that domestic work does not contribute to the growth of an individual's human capital. As a result women may settle for poorer jobs, and if they keep the primary responsibility for housework and care, they 'choose' to enter the labour market part-time or in full-time jobs that are less demanding and so less rewarded. This way a segregated

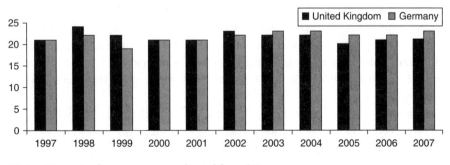

Figure 13.2 Gender pay gap in unadjusted form (%)

labour market is sustained (Blackburn et al. 2002). This theory of 'human capital' and its extension in 'rational choice', have been very popular among economists (e.g. Becker 1985). However, they neglect that money is an essential but not the only reward from employment. Furthermore, supporting the gender division of labour cannot be 'rational' because there can be no guarantee for an enduring partnership or for a concurring management of the finances. For Ferree and Hall (1996), it is the gender norms that discount women's earnings and define the extent to which women control their incomes or are entitled to a family wage. They claim that location in the economic system alone does not explain women's social standing since money does not translate into power and autonomy at the same rate for women as for men. In view of that, Ferree and Hall (1996) advance Acker's (2003) argument of the abstract and disembodied worker, stating that also money should be questioned as an abstract, objective measure of economic power. This is an important feminist critique because it points out that women's social position is generated by multiple dimensions of stratification.

Gender segregation

Gender segregation remains one of the major sources of gender inequality in the OECD labour market (Coré 1999). Horizontal segregation is when certain jobs of a similar level are dominated by one gender and vertical segregation is when one gender is prevailing at higher levels within organizations (Daniels and Macdonald 2005: 2).

While the participation of women in economic and political life has increased significantly across Europe over time, their representation in key positions of power and influence is still far below that of men (EUROSTAT 2008). In the UK and Germany, there are more men than women managing businesses, irrespective of whether they own them or not and according to EUROPA (2009), there is little sign of either of these gaps narrowing over recent years. The relative number of self-employed is only a partial indicator of those running businesses because many business managers, especially in larger companies, are salaried employees of the enterprises they work for rather than self-employed; therefore, it is equally important to consider, the relative number of men and women classified as company directors or senior executives and as managers of small enterprises (EUROSTAT 2008). The gap between women and men is widest at the highest level managerial positions, that is, directors and chief executives of companies, where the proportion of men occupying these positions was, on average, about three times that of women.

Comparing the employment distribution of women with that of men, women tend to be concentrated in fewer sectors of activity, with the larger proportion working in services; this concentration seems to be increasing rather than falling over time (EUROSTAT 2008; Oswald 2007). In the UK and Germany during 2005, women dominated in 6 out of 62 occupations, them being: health care and social work, retail trade, education, public administration, business activities and hotels and restaurants. These 6 sectors accounted for 69.2 per cent of women's employment in the UK and 60.5 per cent in Germany. For men, the degree of concentration is lower, and the 6 most important sectors accounted for 44.8 per cent of men's employment in the UK and 38.7 per cent in Germany. Hence, there are about three times more male-dominated occupations than female-dominated ones. It appears that women enter a more restricted range of professions than men, but Blades (2006) warns that this could also be a statistical illusion because occupations that are typically chosen by men appear in a more detailed breakdown.

Still, what is no illusion, is the cross-national similarity of women's occupations that are attributable to prevailing cultural definitions of femininity, historically rooted in the domestic division of labour (Charles 1992). According to Witz and Wilson (1982), the marked separation between the types of jobs that are performed by gender, is the single most important feature of the structuring of male and female participation in the workforce. Witz and Wilson (1982) argue that the increase in female labour force participation relates closely to the post-war expansion of service employment because for many employers women were a pool of available, cheap workers who already possessed appropriate skills. Most of these skills reflect domestic skills and represent human capital acquired outside the labour market and consequently there is no cost of training (Witz and Wilson 1982: 46). The two aspects which emerged in service industries are also dominant characteristics of female employment. The first is the sex-typing of skills, that means, men collect higher pay and status when utilizing these same skills. The second is women's confinement to secondary labour markets, characterized by low wages, few fringe benefits, low status, few training and advancement prospects, and part-time or generally unstable employment (Witz and Wilson 1982).

Adding to the above argument, Bradley (1999) states that gender segregation is persistent but not fixed, because sex-typing is specific to particular times and places – like in the case of post-industrialism, when men lost jobs in manufacturing and the feminization of the service sector occurred. As a result, gender identity mixes with occupational identity and fewer men are attracted to the jobs, now seen as lacking status (Cockburn 1991). Subsequently, feminization and the devaluation of a job go hand in hand. There is, though, also the view that the marginal status of a function explains why so many women are in a field (Hon 1995). An industry which is seen as a 'soft' one attracts women because they can play an acceptable role, for example, a caring role. This is consistent with the data from EUROSTAT (2008) where the top six female-dominated occupations involve the supply of services and are not only identical between UK and Germany, but also in the EU-25 – while there are 62 occupations in total. Men are less concentrated in a few sectors of activity compared with women and the sectors concerned vary more between countries (EUROSTAT 2008).

Women's interpretation of the labour market and the need for separate organizing

This section turns to the micro level of analysis to explore WIN members' own accounts of their situation within the UK and German labour market contexts described above and to investigate if they consciously choose to organize autonomously and separately as women, and why.

While one of the participants in Britain and four in Germany discovered after joining the WIN, that their situation as a woman in the UK and German labour markets was not unique, for the majority, being with 'women like myself, who are going through the same sort of thing' was the origin for consciously choosing a women-only instead of a mixed business network. For Charlotte (AURORA) 'women like myself' were female solo entrepreneurs, for Heidi (BPW UK) they were working mothers, for Gaby (BFBM) 'the only female director in a male board', for Sabine (BPW DE), 'a female technician in a male-dominated corporation'. Members made clear references to how the masculine culture in business, the double-burden, the vertical and horizontal sex segregation of the UK and German labour markets, presented in the previous section, affected their involvement in gender-specific networks.

They also made clear references to the category of 'being a woman' and consequently different from men, but sameness was seen to derive from their current marginality (Liff and Wajcman 1996) in the UK and German labour markets, while the variation between the meanings they assigned to 'women like myself' challenges the belief of a women's shared identity. Incidentally, all four WINs had the same amount of women (about one fifth) who were also members of their occupational association. There was generally of the view that occupational associations do not have to be women-only because hard information (e.g. latest statistics, new laws) is often transmitted in impersonal ways; profession-related knowledge is not specific to gendered experiences, and higher numbers of members mean higher chances that somebody has an answer to a question. The decision to choose an independent women-only over a mixed-sex network was a qualitative one and based on the anticipation of positive features of WINs, added to the evading of negative features of mixed networks. WIN members in both countries had faced obstacles to their career advancement and they wanted them addressed among women because they believed that: (i) only women can empower, support the right way, (ii) it is easier to identify with female role models and mentors, and (iii) mixed business networks have an aggressive culture. These career obstacles can be grouped under four separate headings:

Being female in a male context
Low self-esteem/lack of confidence
Work-life balance
Discrimination

Being female in a male context

One third of the members in the UK and half in Germany perceived the masculine organizational culture in their workplace as one of the biggest obstacles. They described it as 'very competitive and aggressive', 'very sort of macho', 'boys' club atmosphere', where 'it can be a disadvantage if you are a capable woman'. UK members have added class – next to ethnicity and gender – related impressions, with the most frequent examples being 'public school boys', and 'Oxbridge buddies'; accordingly UK members said 'you must be a white middle-class man to climb the hierarchy', while German members simply mentioned the sex, for example, 'management is for men only'.

Half of the self-employed women and one third of the salaried employees were represented in this category. For the self-employed members this masculine culture was chiefly the reason they started their own business and some salaried employees thought about doing the same or retiring as they 'cannot take it much longer'. Regarding the high-ranked women among them, I found similar dynamics to Marshall (2000): mothers who felt like they were living two half lives instead of one complete life, and women who had fought hard for each achievement and do not want to battle for much longer.

However, my analysis reveals that some women took this masculine culture for granted and learned 'how to play the corporate game'. Klaudia (BPW DE) was an ambitious Financial Controller. In the first company announcement for a Chief Financial Officer post, her departmental manager refused to include her application for the position in their internal recruitment process, without telling her why. When a second call was sent out, she decided to skip her departmental manager and gave her application directly to the personnel manager, with whom they re-wrote the job description so that she perfectly fitted it, and had a meeting with the CEO to persuade him of her loyalty to the company and commitment to the job; shortly after she became CFO. 'It doesn't work otherwise' she said laughing loudly. She added that 'working in a male-dominated sector is exhausting' and she did experience harassment, but she said she was tough and had BPW, where she could talk about all these crazy incidents with women who have experienced the same and so keep her sanity. In the above case, Klaudia took (what Kram and Hampton 2003 call) an integrating approach and turned strains to opportunities.

Kram and Hampton (2003) claim that this is the only response that frees women from cultural traps, especially vis-à-vis leadership styles, as in some organizations strong and competitive women may be criticized for being insufficiently feminine, while caring and collaborative women in masculine environments may be criticized for being insufficiently leader-like. The authors argue that when implementing the integrating approach, women examine reactions of their behaviour, others' needs and values, and systemic forces, and adapt their style accordingly. This is indeed a very liberal approach where the white middle-class male as normal assumption remains unchallenged, and women seem to lack the cunningness that would render them skilled to compete in the business world. Strategies geared toward fixing women's purported deficiencies are faulty because they do not address the underlying problem of society's lack of appreciation of women, and in so doing they 'narrow our understanding of what might constitute the full range of effective leader behaviour' (Ely 2003: 154). Besides, some women in my study who were – like Klaudia – eager to change themselves in order to assimilate more effectively into the masculine culture, told me that others' expectations can be so contradictory that it is 'impossible to reach them without a split personality'; the same person who appointed them because he was convinced they 'would be able to handle the boys', criticized their behaviour the next day and complained that he thought 'bringing a woman in would soften the male team'. 'There's no way you can do it right as a woman' chuckled some BPW UK members humorously, during an observation. As in past research (Kelly and Breinlinger 1996; McCarthy 2004), by sharing frustrating workplace incidences, BPW members brought to the surface the gendering processes that disadvantage women and received the reassurance that they are 'not going mad'.

Low self-esteem/lack of confidence

Half of the members from the UK and half from Germany are represented in this category, making personal deficiencies the most frequently mentioned obstacle. Ten women from the UK and six from Germany believed that their lack of self-esteem has been an obstacle for their career advancement. The members wished they had received more support and guidance by their parents, career advisers and teachers.

This result is not unique. There is an array of studies (Anderson 2004; Ely 1995; Mallon and Cassell 1999) where women talk about how their low self-confidence is slowing down their careers, as well as management research that relates high self-confidence with hierarchical advancement (Yukl 1989). Also in comparison to men, women are often found rating themselves lower on confidence (McCarthy 2004; Parker 2002), a trend that is reinforced in male-dominated environments (Ely 1995). However, the relationship between girls' low self-esteem and later socio-economic achievements could not be confirmed in research, and the positive association between men's high self-esteem and socio-economic achievement was trivial in practical terms (Mahaffy 2004). These results suggest that an individualistic approach fails to educate people about the social structural factors that deflate self-esteem and perpetuate gender inequality, and implies that women's perceived deficiencies are more consequential than structural arrangements (Mahaffy 2004).

Although most women in my study perceived men and women as inherently different, only few UK women believed that men are more self-confident. Several very successful entrepreneurs and some high-ranked managers in both countries tended to mix up their perfectionism with low self-confidence, which is again telling about the image gender roles impose on women. Stereotypical assumptions may discourage individuals from describing their behaviour in ways that deviate from traditional norms (Rhode 2003) and as women do not enjoy the presumption of ambition, precision, endurance and other agentic attributes to the same extent as men, perceivers have difficulty encoding them as such (Scott and Brown 2006). One could doubt that women in high positions lack self-esteem but for many WIN members heightened visibility meant more scrutiny and criticism from their surroundings (known as the 'visibility-vulnerability spiral' in Kram and Hampton 2003). They reported having burned themselves out 'trying to compete with the guys', 'having to work ten times harder than a man', 'always having to prove yourself in leadership'. Overall, for most women their alleged low self-esteem was connected with specific regrets, for example, an opportunity they did not grasp or a negative event they did not react to.

Self-esteem is not only a subjective self-judgment – that may or may not reflect one's objective image – but is relational, and actually, public events that are associated with appreciation – when a person succeeds, is praised, is loved – are said to have a greater impact on self-esteem than private ones (Leary and Baumeister 2000). Many of the WIN members in this category felt their parents and teachers have not encouraged them to establish a strong sense of self-confidence and independence – the way some did with their brothers or male classmates. A similarity between BPW members in both countries was that they actively tried to change this for the next generation of women. Some said conditions for women have worsened since the years 'we couldn't have careers or reach high positions because we weren't allowed to earn the qualifications'; they were perplexed with the fact that girls today perform better than boys at school, make up more than half of new graduates, then 'get pregnant and without a second thought, they interrupt or even quit their careers because it's best for the family'; a couple of members asked me during the interview if I knew whether this is due to biological needs or societal pressures. At least half of BPW members believed Young BPW (the group for members under age 35) should target girls while they are at the last school year and recruit them as soon as they have entered academic education or vocational training programmes, so that girls enter early enough an encouraging and reassuring community. These members motivated girls to network in every possible chance.

One quarter of members in the UK and equal parts in Germany, wished they had known early enough how important it is to have a mentor or a role model, which was something they found through their participation in WINs. When asking the salaried employees if they tried to find a woman mentor within their work organization, numerous participants tried to explain to me that 'it is not the wisest thing to do' because female mentoring relationships are highly visible and so under constant scrutiny; when the relationship is harmonious it is supposed 'a conspiracy against men', when there is an argument between the two women, 'men rub their hands together in self-satisfaction'. Yet, for some of the interviewees, cross-gender mentoring relationships were out of the question because they could 'get interpreted as sexual'. On the basis of this and prior research (Gallese 1993), while the female mentor-female protégé relationship avoids perceived sexual tension, it entails the greatest 'risk' of all mentor-protégé combinations to be inhibited by the masculine corporate system itself because men tend to view evidence of women forming intimate alliances as a threat. Additionally, not all women in the senior ranks are willing to become a mentor to a female protégé. Two German members portrayed the only female executive in their corporation as the hardcore career person, single and childless, who envies them for being ambitious and married with children – sociologists label these women as Queen Bees (Rhode 2003; Wilson 1995). Joining an autonomous women-only network, solves these problems because this setting 'has the highest possible concentration of successful women', and pairs can be matched in relation to professional background or personality and not just based on biological sex. Besides, female mentoring relationships are not seen as exotic, and take place within a nurturing, supportive environment.

Work-life balance

Most WIN members in both countries confirmed being the ones who carried out the majority of the household chores, and had the career breaks in order to take care of children. Hence, it is not surprising that for one third of the women in the UK and for over half in Germany, reconciling work and family was one of the biggest obstacles for their career advancement. Almost two thirds of these women were self-employed, which agrees with Parasuraman and Simmers (2001) that business ownership is not a panacea for balancing work and family role responsibilities. Several interviewees were aware that parental leave provisions were more generous in Germany than in the UK, but many German women felt this left them no choice other than to foster the male breadwinner model. As a result, the family life cycle had a stronger impact on employment patterns of German than of UK WIN members. Just as in the M-curve presented earlier, a cross-national typical female employment pattern consisted of full-time work until marriage and children, a career break until a market or other childcare solution was found, and the return to the labour market via part-time or self-employment, for better reconciliation of work and family. The second most-mentioned reason for a career break (although merely 15 per cent of the respondents) was the spouse's job relocation.

The above results are generally at one with information presented in a previous section, but what is striking is that, at first glance, they seem to imply that women's employment decisions are profoundly structured by domestic circumstances. Most women in my study felt their partner considers their job to be as important as his, but only a tiny minority enjoyed a symmetrical responsibility for family and home-related tasks. That was because some women considered their own job as secondary since they were earning less or did not have career ambitions. An interesting element of these answers was that these women still characterized themselves as emancipated because it was their decision – and not that of their husbands – to perform household tasks. Additionally, I soon discovered that to some women a supportive partner was simply the one who did not stop them from going to work. Some other women, who had spouses willing to 'help', complained that men have 'a different sense of order and temperatures', which made it impossible to perform the caring role right; the husband would 'let the toddler daughter go out and play in the snow wearing a cotton skirt and without pantyhose on', or 'he first thinks that something is dirty when even a sight-impaired person can see it', etc.

It is doubtless true that an important factor in women's disadvantage in work is their disproportionate responsibility for domestic work, including care for the young, old and ill (Cockburn 1991), however the deeper question is, which structures make women take over or be assigned these responsibilities. In the above examples, none of the UK or the German women answered that they wanted to be the ones who take care of home and family because they liked it. In contrast, all of the answers point to the lack of better alternatives. Even in cases where women claimed to be doing domestic work voluntarily, it appeared they did so given restricted options of 'what is best for the family', for example, 'he needs one hour to iron one shirt so what's the point?', 'he has a very demanding job and works 24/7', 'he is the higher earner', 'he would not be able to run a house even if he wanted!', 'he is after a promotion and a break would be very damaging for his career'. Hence, women's household commitment exists because of patriarchal social structures within which women make their choices (Walby 1990); in view of that, it is not the family that benefits the most from women's domestic labour, but patriarchal capitalism. Returning to a previous point, even though, superficially, a married woman's employment decisions appear constrained by her domestic circumstances, in reality they are constrained by her husband's employment (Walby 1990).

In the face of these structural barriers, some WIN women have adopted 'the predominant male model of a successful manager' (Wajcman 1998) and subordinated other aspects of life, such as the family, to the demands of the career. However, opposite to most of their colleagues who were married fathers, adopting 'the predominant male model' meant for most of these women renouncing marriage and motherhood. In Hakim's (1998) three-fold typology of women's work-life preferences, these WIN members fall under the 'work-centered' ones, whose priorities are all focused on the public sphere. Employment, for these women, is a continuous activity throughout adult life, from the time of leaving education to retirement (Hakim 1996); many of them are single and even more are childless. I found no 'home-centered' women among the WIN members, who preferred homemaker careers and who abandoned employment permanently around the time of marriage and/or childbirth (Hakim 1998), but this result is self-evident bearing in mind that employment is a condition for WIN membership. Consistent with Hakim's (1998) prediction, the largest amount of my respondents fell under the 'adaptive' women, who made a deliberate choice to combine work and family, and whose employment was a fragmented activity due to domestic breaks or other periods of non-work other than involuntary unemployment (Hakim 1996). Along with the above, both supportive and opposing evidence is found for elements of Preference Theory. First of all, support is found for Hakim's argument that women are not a homogenous group that naturally seeks to combine employment with family work. Accordingly, WIN members did have heterogeneous employment patterns. However, I could find little evidence that these heterogeneous employment patterns were caused by genuine, unrestrained choices and they were not merely results of women's sex-role socialization or differing abilities for overcoming constraints. During fieldwork, I heard several stories from mothers suffering under the perception that they lacked employment commitment and the undervaluation of part-time work. Some women described to me extreme feelings of guilt for having to leave their newborn baby to go back to work; some others told me they went crazy when they had to stay at home and take care of infants. I can understand Hakim's willingness to distance twenty first century women from 'the victim feminism that is fashionable in academic circles' (Hakim 1998) but fieldwork data make it unrealistic to uncritically accept the notion of 'choice' incorporated in Preference Theory.

The difference between welfare and socialist regimes poses another important test on Preference Theory, because the socialist conceptual package of the former East Germany prescribed to women the role of the 'worker-mother' (Ferree 1995). Heike (BFBM), married with three children, who was born and still lives in the former East Germany said that 'all women here have always been working – they had to' and continued to describe how the socialist ethos, which stressed work as a civic duty, still helps preserve encouraging attitudes towards married women's employment. Also Nadine (BFBM), married with two children, who was born in West Germany and now lives in the former East Germany, reported enjoying the extended childcare and the positive public opinion about working mothers. Both interviewees were successful in their job and felt they would have not been able to balance work and family the same way in the old states; in fact, Nadine had children after she moved to the former East Germany and although she worked continuously nobody called her 'Rabenmutter'[1] – something she knew happens in the West. Indeed, several WIN members who lived in the old states told me they had to deal with this characterization when considering having a career break or not, for example, 'my mother said I don't want to be a Rabenmutter and I should take at least a short parental leave'. These cases revealed how political context might define a woman's position in Hakim's typology (which deems Preference Theory unsound in socialist regimes), and how cultural values might reinforce or weaken preferences.

Discrimination

Discrimination can be described as the favouring of one social group over others for no justifiable reason, and is based on the negative stereotypes and decisions that people have made about the other groups (Daniels and Macdonald 2005). When I asked the interviewees directly if they have experienced any form of discrimination at work, only three women from the UK and six from Germany answered 'no' or that they 'don't think so' but some were alert of its possibility in the future, while some have witnessed it on others. The majority said yes; their answers described minor to blatant cases of gender, age, class, ethnic and racial discrimination, and most cases interconnected. In all, these findings show a substantial awareness of discrimination.

The most common reference was to gender discrimination, and in particular how male employers and colleagues were convinced they could predict a woman's career pattern, often before they even worked with her. That means, some women told me they did not get a job because the male boss wrongly prophesized that 'such a good-looking girl will soon find somebody to marry and off she is!', or 'well, you know you are in your mid/late twenties, you are going to be stopping to have a family soon'. Other women did not get a promotion because their gender was assumed incompatible with travel: 'it's going to be scary for a woman travelling alone', or 'it's risky for a woman, many places are not very safe'. In the previous section it was demonstrated how the patriarchal structures turn women's biological and social functions as wives and mothers into obstacles and influence women's exit from and entry into the UK and German labour markets. However, the data in this section suggest that also the hypothetical likelihood of marriage or childbearing can become an obstacle for some women's career advancement. Opposite to Hakim (1995) that women make genuine choices, my findings once again could not rule out that women's employment preferences are constrained. Testimonies in my study, support Healy's (1999) argument that the concept of employment commitment is socially constructed and women's commitment is often viewed in relation to their actual or expected mothering role.

Freely voicing grievances against discrimination proved to be one of the key gains underlying women's involvement in women-only, instead of mixed, professional networks. This was particularly important for two respondents from the UK and two from Germany who felt 'nobody is really listening' inside corporations, they got discouraged to discuss these incidents by being told they 'got it all wrong', or 'it wasn't on purpose'. They told me how the shock of the discriminating experience turned into the realization that they are all alone in this, they became disappointed and 'finally, learned that it is better to pretend it does not happen'; this way they 'don't waste energy for nothing' and their colleagues don't call them 'killjoy' or 'spoilsport' – in German: 'Spielverderber' – if they complained (as in Cockburn 2001). For very few respondents who were single mothers, taking discrimination seriously was not something 'you can afford when raising children on your own'; also Aronson (2003) suggests that dealing with discrimination is a luxury, perhaps even frivolous, when compared with the struggles of combining work and single motherhood. Three quarters of the BME interviewees in Britain and an equal number of the foreign-born in Germany were self-employed, and stated that discriminatory incidences were one of the reasons that eventually pushed them to start their own business, however the situation had not improved as they had wished. For example, Nabinye (AURORA) held that nobody was acknowledging her performance nor listening to her career aspirations in the company she worked for; she left to start her own business but still felt that some bankers and suppliers do not take her seriously in wanting to do business because she is a black woman.

A salient national difference materialized in the women's reactions to the word 'discrimination'. For about half the respondents in Germany, discrimination was perceived as a synonym for sexual harassment and some would answer that they have never been discriminated against because they had not experienced any unwanted touching, with the most mentioned example being 'nobody has grabbed my butt'. Some explained to me that 'the word discrimination is really too harsh' and I should rephrase the interview question using the word 'bullied' – in German: 'mobbed'. Several commented they were 'not the type of person that allows [herself] to be discriminated against'; when I asked them how they manage this, they answered that they 'keep calm and smile', or they 'just ignore it until the bully gets tired and stops'. During a BFBM observation, a member sarcastically called this 'the ostrich approach' and remarked that it never works: 'its success is pure illusion; you just learn not to see it when others screw you!'. In general, 10 per cent of the interviewees in both countries were sexually harassed but only Megan (BPW UK) officially reported the incident; she found the experience very distressing, however was persuaded by a female colleague and friend to do so. The senior manager was reprimanded.

Conclusion and implications

In this chapter, it becomes evident that gender inequalities exist in the UK and German labour markets. In both countries, the corporate world remains heavily male-dominated and positive developments in the public sphere and legislation have not managed to disrupt the structure of gender segregation or dethrone masculine organizational cultures. Fieldwork data are generally at one with this information: one third of the women in the UK and over half in Germany perceived the masculine organizational culture, and the reconciliation of work and family as the greatest barriers for their career advancement. Women were excluded from in-company but also from 'out-of-hours' networking activities, due to the 'old boys' network' and the unequal division of childcare and housework.

Half of the members from the UK and half from Germany believed that personal deficiencies, for example, their low self-esteem has been one of the biggest obstacles. Many of the WIN members in this category felt their parents and teachers had not encouraged them to establish a strong sense of self-confidence and independence – the way some did with their brothers or male classmates. One quarter of members in the UK and in Germany wished they had known early enough how important it is to have a mentor or a role model, which is something they found through their participation in WINs. Additional gains underlying respondents involvement in women-only, instead of mixed networks was the apparent safety to voice women's issues and share frustrating or discriminating workplace incidences to receive understanding and the reassurance that they are 'not going mad'. Thus, the majority of members identified their gender status and the independence from working environments as significant, and as a result consciously chose WINs over other business and professional networks.

The fact that WIN members' separatism is informed by a recognition of the gender-specific character of experience, that is, the cross-impacting of their occupational and family work, and the power relations in both spheres, has important implications for our understanding of WINs as settings that do not just appear in a vacuum or take shape according to a group's mood, but as fundamentally informed by the social and economic context within which their members perform and experience their gender. Briskin (1999: 544) postulates that separate organizing produces women as a constituency and, at the same time, emerges from the fact that women are already a constituency. This applies to the vast majority of WIN members, who felt bound by structural relations into the category of 'being a woman' and consequently different from men. Having produced an understanding of the/their world as it is, as well as how it should be, they saw potential advantages of a separation from men and their structures.

Fieldwork data further have important implications for our understanding of 'choice'. In arguing against Hakim (1998) in this chapter, I am not denying that women make choices but doubt that these choices are genuine, unrestrained and not influenced by women's gender-role socialization, differing abilities for overcoming constraints or imposed by political systems. Indisputably, interviewees in this study were capable as rational agents to choose from various alternatives, yet their answers often pointed to the lack of better alternatives. In short, choice appears to be primarily a question of ontology and not of personal preference.

To sum up, women in this study, have a growing sense of their own worth; they might have experienced unfairness but did not accept it as natural or inevitable. The stories of the women are not a number of – what Harding (1987: 5) calls – victimologies. Sometimes people expect feminist research to be depressing and heavy, complaining that women are invisible and unheard in the system imposed on them. My interviewees were full of energy and hope. WIN women become increasingly aware and confident of their ability to negotiate new structures and this confidence makes them more vocal and visible within them.

Notes

I would like to thank the University of London Central Research Fund for the financial support to carry out the fieldwork.

1. The literal translation of the word Rabenmutter is Raven-mother, but metaphorically the term is used in Germany to describe the uncaring mother, who abandons her children in an empty nest while she flies away to egoistically pursue a career. Chancellor Angela Merkel, the first woman to lead the country, publicly condemned this centuries-old synonym for bad mother, and placed it at the centre of a new debate on the future of the German working woman (Landler 2006). To her critics, Merkel has appointed Germany's utmost incarnation of the Rabenmutter as minister for family affairs; Dr. Ursula von der Leyen, a physician and mother of seven. The peak of disapproval to her plans for rewriting Germany's family policies so that women do not have to choose between family and career, was the WDR TV-show 'Hard but Fair', where the host Frank Plasberg showed von der Leyen a fictitious newspaper front page, with a smiling photo of her and the headline 'Mama, where were you when I was little?' (Poelchau 2006).

References

Acker, J. (2003) 'Hierarchies, jobs, bodies: a theory of gendered organizations', In R. J.Ely, E. G. Foldy, and M. A. Scully (eds), *Reader in gender, work, and organization.* Oxford: Blackwell Publishing.

Anderson, V. (2004) 'Women managers: does positive action training make a difference? A case study', *Journal of Management Development,* 23(8): 729–40.

Aronson, P. (2003) 'Feminists or "postfeminists"?: young women's attitudes toward feminism and gender relations', *Gender and Society,* 17(6): 903–22.

Becker, G. S. (1985) 'Human capital, effort, and the sexual division of labor', *Journal of Labor Economics,* 3(1): S33–S58.

Blackburn, R. M., J. Browne, B. Brooks and J. Jarman (2002) 'Explaining gender segregation', *The British Journal of Sociology,* 53(4): 513–36.

Blades, D. (2006) *Women and men in OECD countries,* (Report). Paris: Organization for Economic Co-Operation and Development.

Bock, S. (2002) *Regionale Frauennetzwerke: Frauenpolitische Bündnisse zwischen Beruflichen Interessen und Geschlechterpolitischen Zielen.* Opladen: Leske und Budrich.

Bradley, H. (1999) *Gender and power in the workplace: analyzing the impact of economic change.* Basingstoke: Macmillan Press.

Briskin, L. (1999) 'Autonomy, diversity, and integration: union women's separate organizing in North America and Western Europe in the context of restructuring and globalization', *Women's Studies International Forum,* 22(5): 543–54.

Charles, M. (1992) 'Cross-national variation in occupational sex segregation', *American Sociological Review,* 57(4): 483–502.

Cockburn, C. (1991) *In the way of women: men's resistance to sex equality in organizations.* London: The Macmillan Press Ltd.

―― (2001) 'Equal opportunities: the short and long agenda', *Industrial Relations Journal,* 20(3): 213–25.

Core, F. (1999) 'The continuing saga of labour market segregation', *OECD Observer,* (April): 42.

Daniels, K. and L. Macdonald (2005) *Equality, diversity and discrimination: a student text.* London: Chartered Institute of Personnel and Development.

Drobnic, S., H. P. Blosfield and G. Rohwer (1999) 'Dynamics of women's employment patterns over the family life course: a comparison of the United States and Germany', *Journal of Marriage and the Family,* 61(1):133–46.

Ely, R. J. (1995) 'The power in demography: women's social constructions of gender identity at work', *The Academy of Management Journal*, 38(3): 589–634.

——(2003) 'Leadership: overview', In R. J. Ely, E. G. FOLDY and M. A. Scully (eds), *Reader in gender, work, and organization*. Oxford: Blackwell Publishing.

EOC (2006) *Facts about women and men in Great Britain*. Manchester: Equal Opportunities Commission.

EUROPA (2009) *The EU at a glance*, (Report). Brussels: European Union Institutions.

EUROSTAT (2008) *The life of women and men in Europe: a statistical portrait*. Luxembourg: Office for Official Publications of the European Communities.

—— (2009) *Population and social conditions*, (Base Page). Luxembourg: Statistical Office of the European Communities.

Ferree, M. M. (1995) 'Patriarchies and feminisms: the two women's movements of post unification Germany', *Social Politics*, 2(1): 10–24.

Ferree, M. M. and E. J. Hall (1996) 'Rethinking stratification from a feminist perspective: gender, race, and class in mainstream textbooks', *American Sociological Review*, 61(6): 929–50.

Fontaine, P. (2004) *Europe in 12 lessons*. Brussels: European Commission Directorate-General for Press and Communication.

Frerichs, P. and H. Wiemert (2002) *'Ich gebe, damit du gibst'. Frauennetzwerke –Strategisch, Reziprok, Exklusiv*, Opladen: Leske + Budrich Verlag.

Gallese, L. R. (1993) 'Do women make poor mentors?', *Across the Board*, 30(6): 23.

Hakim, C. (1995) 'Five feminist myths about women's employment', *The British Journal of Sociology*, 46(3): 429–55.

——(1996) 'Labour mobility and employment stability: rhetoric and reality on the sex differential in labour-market behaviour', *European Sociological Review*, 12(1): 1–31.

—— (1998) 'Developing a sociology for the twenty-first century: preference theory', *The British Journal of Sociology*, 49(1): 137–43.

—— (2000) *Work-lifestyle choices in the 21st century: preference theory*. Oxford: Oxford University Press.

Healy, G. (1999) 'Structuring commitments in interrupted careers: career breaks, commitment and the life cycle in teaching', *Gender, Work & Organization*, 6(4): 185–201.

Hon, L. C. (1995) 'Toward a feminist theory of public relations', *Journal of Public Relations Research*, 7(1): 27–88.

IMF (2008) *World economic outlook*, (Database). Washington, DC: International Monetary Fund.

Kelly, C. and S. Breinlinger (1996) *The social psychology of collective action: identity, injustice and gender*. London: Taylor & Francis.

Kram, K. E. and M. M. Hampton (2003) 'When women lead: the visibility–vulnerability spiral', In R. J. Ely, E. G. Foldy and M. A. Scully eds), *Reader in gender, work, and organization*. Oxford: Blackwell Publishing.

Lander R. M. (2006) 'Quoth the raven: i bake cookies, too', *The New York Times*, April 23, Frankfurt.

Leary, M. R. and R. F. Baumeister (2000) 'The nature and function of self-esteem: sociometer theory', In M. P. Zanna (ed.), *Advances in experimental social psychology*. San Diego, CA: Academic Press.

Lee, S. and D. McCann (2006) 'Working time capability: towards realizing individual choice', In J. -Y. Boulin, M. Lallement, J. C. Messenger and F. Micon (eds), *Decent working time: new trends, new issues*. Geneva: International Labour Office.

Lenz, I. (2008) *Die Neue Frauenbewegung in Deutschland: Abschied vom Kleinen Unterschied. Eine Quellensammlung*. Wiesbaden: VS Verlag für Sozialwissenschaften.

Liff, S. and N. J. Wajcman (1996) '"Sameness" and "difference" revisited: which way forward for equal opportunity initiatives?' *Journal of Management Studies*, 33(1): 79–94.

Mahaffy, K. A. (2004) 'Girls' low self-esteem: how is it related to later socioeconomic achievements?', *Gender and Society*, 18(3): 309–27.

Mallon, M. and C. Cassell (1999) 'What do women want? The perceived development needs of women managers', *Journal of Management Development*, 18(2): 137–52.

Marshall, J. (2000) 'Living lives of change: examining facets of women managers' career stories', In M. Peiperl, M. Arthur, R. Goffee and T. Morris (eds), *Career frontiers: new conceptions of working lives*. Oxford: Oxford University Press.

Mazey, S. (1998) 'The European Union and women's rights: from the Europeanization of national agendas to the nationalization of a European agenda?', *Journal of European Public Policy*, 5(1): 131–52.

McCarthy, H. (2004) *Girlfriends in high places: how women's networks are changing the workplace*. London: Demos.

OECD.STAT (2009) *Statistics Portal*. Retrieved 8 January 2009, from source http://webnet. oecd.org/wbos/index.aspx.

Oswald, S. (2007) *Sozialversicherungspflichtig Beschäftigte nach Wirtschaftsabteilungen und Geschlecht 1999 bis 2006*, (Beschäftigungsstatistik). Nürnberg: Zentrales Datenzentrum der Bundesagentur für Arbeit.

Parasuraman, S. and C. A. Simmers (2001) 'Type of employment, work-family conflict and well-being: a comparative study', *Journal of Organizational Behavior*, 22(5): 551–68.

Parker, J. (2002) 'Women's groups in British Unions', *British Journal of Industrial Relations*, 40(1): 23–48.

Poelchau, N. (2006) Die Rabenmutter. *Süddeutschen Zeitung*, 26 January: München.

Rhode, D. (2003) 'The difference "difference" makes', In R. J. Ely, E. G. Foldy and M. A. Scully (eds), *Reader in gender, work, and organization*. Oxford: Blackwell Publishing.

Rueschemeyer, M. and H. Schissler (1990) 'Women in the two Germanys', *German Studies Review*, 13 (Special Issue): 71–85.

Scott, K. A. and D. J. Brown (2006) 'Female first, leader second? Gender bias in the encoding of leadership behavior', *Organizational Behavior and Human Decision Processes*, 101(July): 230–42.

Stockman, N., N. Bonney and X. Sheng (1995) *Women's work in East and West: the dual burden of employment and family life*. London: UCL Press.

Travers, C. and C. Pemberton (2000) 'Think career global, but act local: understanding networking as a culturally differentiated career skill', In M. J. Davidson and R. J. Burke (eds), *Women in management: current research issues, volume 2*. London: Sage Publications.

Van Der Lippe, T. and L. Van Dijk (2002) 'Comparative research on women's employment', *Annual Review of Sociology*, 28: 221–41.

Van Hoven, B. (2002) 'Experiencing democracy: women in rural East Germany', *Social Politics*, Fall: 444–70.

Wagner, A. (ed.) (2007) *Analytikreport der Statistik: Analyse des Arbeitsmarktes für Frauen und Männer*. Nürnberg: Statistik der Bundesagentur für Arbeit.

Wajcman, J. (1998) *Managing like a man: women and men in corporate management*. Cambridge: Polity Press.

Walby, S. (1990) *Theorizing patriarchy*. Oxford: Blackwell Publishing.

Wilson, F. M. (1995) *Organizational behaviour and gender*. New York: McGraw-Hill Publishing Co.

Witz, A. and F. Wilson (1982) 'Women workers in service industries', *Service Industries Journal*, 2(2): 40–55.

Yukl, G. (1989) 'Managerial leadership: a review of theory and research. *Journal of Management*', 15(2): 251–89.

14

Exploring the intersections of gender, sexuality and class in the transport and construction industries

Tessa Wright

Introduction

Occupational gender segregation has been identified as one of the three main causes of the continuing gender pay gap. Reducing the gender pay gap has been a priority of the current government (Government Equalities Office 2008: 2) and part of this has involved measures to counteract gender segregation and encourage women to enter traditional male sectors that have been resistant to change. A number of initiatives have been taking place in the UK at national and local level to address occupational gender segregation, with a focus on getting women involved in the construction of the Olympic 2012 site in London. This makes it an interesting time to examine the experiences of women in male-dominated sectors.

I argue that an intersectional approach – that explores how gender, sexuality and class are interwoven – can offer useful insights into occupational gender segregation. A better understanding of the heterogeneity of women's experience in male-dominated occupations may assist in the recruitment and retention of women in traditional male work sectors, thus supporting policies to reduce occupational gender segregation. This chapter thus presents some preliminary findings from research into the experiences of heterosexual, lesbian and bisexual women in skilled manual and professional occupations in two of the most heavily male-dominated industrial sectors in the UK, transport and construction.

The chapter first sketches the UK context in relation to occupational segregation and the construction and transport industries in particular. It then shows how previous research on women in non-traditional female work, while recognizing the importance of sexuality when women enter male-dominated work, tends to overlook the specific experience of lesbians in this type of work, despite suggestions that they may be more attracted to gender atypical careers. The theoretical basis for an intersectional approach to analysing inequality in organizations is outlined, and some early research findings are then presented, based on analysis of a small selection of interviews with women working in transport and construction.

Non-traditional female work: The UK context

Occupational gender segregation and unequal pay

In the UK the Labour government from 1997–2010 paid considerable attention to reducing the persistent gender pay gap – women's average hourly pay (excluding overtime) is still 16.4 per cent less than men's pay for full-time employees and 20.2 per cent for all employees including part timers (National Statistics 2009). Occupational gender segregation has been identified as one of the three principal causes of the gender pay gap, alongside the unequal impact of women's family responsibilities and pay discrimination (EOC 2001). Occupational segregation describes both 'horizontal' segregation in which women are concentrated into just 10 occupations – predominantly low paying ones – and 'vertical' segregation which limits women's progress into higher paid positions.

The Labour Government made reducing the pay gap a priority for the period 2008–11 (Government Equalities Office 2008: 2), which included measures to ensure equal pay contained in the Equality Act, passed in April 2010. Following the recommendations of the Women and Work Commission (2006), set up to examine the issue of women's pay, the government allotted money to tackle occupational segregation, with £40 million funding for improving women's skill levels, with a focus on male-dominated occupations, including training for women returning to work, prioritizing engineering, construction, transport and logistics, and providing work opportunities in preparation for the London 2012 Olympic Games (DCLG 2007). It is therefore an interesting moment at which to investigate the experiences of women in traditional male occupations when there may be the possibility of movement in sectors previously resistant to change.

The construction and transport sectors

This research focuses on the two most heavily male-dominated industrial sectors in the UK – construction (where 90 per cent of workers are male) and transport (76 per cent of workers in transport, storage and communication are men) (EOC 2006: 21).

Construction has seen no improvement in the proportions of women in employment since 1972 (EOC 2006: 21), despite efforts by the industry to train and recruit more women (Gurjao 2006: 1). In the UK construction industry, women make up only 13 per cent of the workforce and less than 2 per cent of those in manual occupations (LFS 2008–09, personal communication from ConstructionSkills, 27 July 2010). More than 80 per cent of women in the construction industry work in skilled administrative, professional, technical and clerical occupations and less than 5 per cent are employed in skilled construction and related trades, so they are much more likely to be employed in professional and associate occupations (14 per cent) or as managers (13 per cent) than in manual occupations (Briscoe 2005: 1003).

Transport shows a similar pattern, with women representing only 9 per cent of all transport occupations, but most likely to be found in leisure and travel service occupations (56 per cent of those employed) or in administrative roles as transport and distribution clerks (30 per cent of employees) (Hamilton et al. 2005: 52). Only 11 per cent of managers in transport are women and they account for only 4 per cent of transport drivers and operatives. The proportion of women bus drivers in London is only 6 per cent and Transport for London has set an objective of increasing this to 12 per cent by 2012 (LDA 2007).

Women in non-traditional work

The study of women who enter traditional male spheres of work is of interest to those who wish to break down occupational gender segregation, as the presence of women in jobs traditionally said to require 'masculine' traits or attributes challenges the supposed 'naturalness' of the association of these traits with men. As Reskin and Padavic (1988: 538) argue, it challenges the ideology of inherent differences that justifies male dominance, and they ask how man's work can serve as a 'rugged test of manhood' if women can do it.

Despite attempts to become 'one of the boys' – a common strategy for women in male-dominated work – they are constantly reminded of their physical difference from men, their possession of a female body, through comments about appearance, bodies and their reproductive capacity (Cockburn 1991; McDowell 1997). Indeed, women are seen as 'one of the maternal sex' even when celibate or childless (Cockburn 1991: 76). Embodiment and sexuality are thus particularly significant in heavily male-dominated and masculinized workplaces. Sexual harassment may be more extensive for women in traditional male occupations (Collinson and Collinson 1996). Even in everyday relations, women are seen in sexualized terms, with the roles available to women fairly limited, as one of McDowell's female traders in an investment bank observes: 'If you are seen as feminine or desirable they think you're available, and if you are not they call you a dyke' (McDowell 1997: 141).

My own research on the UK fire service (Wright 2008: 107), where only 3 per cent of fire-fighters are women (DCLG 2008), found similarly restrictive roles, with some commenting that women were seen as either 'fire tarts or lesbians'. Cockburn observed that lesbianism can be 'used as a category with which to control heterosexual women' (1991: 196), a form of control also noted in other studies (Colgan, Johnstone and Shaw 1996: 265, Henwood 1998: 45, Martin and Jurik 2007: 44). Thus, 'the lesbian' is clearly present as a figure in organizational discourses. However it is notable that as a real-life woman she is mostly absent from these studies.

The small number of exceptions include Chetkovich's (1997) study of race and gender in a US fire service, which found that a number of women were openly lesbian. This was advantageous in some respects and disadvantageous in others. While the environment was described as socially conservative and homophobic with homosexuality a frequent topic of humour, it was also said that an open lesbian was able to tease and joke with her colleagues without suggesting that she was open to sexual advances. Martin and Jurik (2007: 74) found that lesbian police officers faced homophobic attitudes from both colleagues and the public.

The neglect of lesbian experience from most studies of non-traditional female work was remarked upon by a writer on lesbian sexuality of her own earlier work. In an introduction to an earlier article on women in manual trades in the US, Kath Weston (1998) points out that she made no direct references to sexuality in her original piece, nor are there any in her earlier book on the subject (1982). Yet she acknowledges the salience of sexuality in the later article, pointing out that 'no doubt substantial numbers – perhaps disproportionate numbers – of lesbians have pursued blue-collar work over the years, although there are no statistics on the subject' (Weston 1998: 96).

In the UK, Christine Wall (2004) reflects on her experiences of the manual trades during the 1970s and 1980s. She notes that even though the organization representing tradeswomen, Women and Manual Trades, must have been made up of at least 50 per cent lesbians:

> The prospect of being an 'out' lesbian in the macho world of construction was never a great ambition for any of us. In 1978 when I started at a Skillcentre on a carpentry and joinery course I had been 'out' and living an openly lesbian lifestyle for three years, but had absolutely no qualms about wearing conventionally feminine blouses, letting my hair grow a little longer and passing as straight while I was training at the Skill centre. (ibid: 163)

Wall's comments reflect the importance of context in women's decisions about when to disclose their sexuality. Despite her willingness to be out in other aspects of her life at the time, a male-dominated training environment was not considered a safe place to be openly lesbian. As we will see later, social attitudes concerning sexuality have changed significantly in recent decades.

Theoretical approach: intersectionality and inequality regimes

Black feminist writers, particularly in the US, have been highly influential in drawing attention to the heterogeneity of women's experience (Collins 2000; Crenshaw

1991; Hooks 1981 [1990] 2004) and in providing crucial insights and conceptualizations of the nature of intersecting oppressions. Crenshaw (1991) describes how structural intersectionality, which places women of colour at the intersection of race and gender, makes their experience qualitatively different from that of white women. But both Crenshaw (1991) and Collins (2000), while primarily exploring intersections of gender and race, note that the concept of intersectionality can be expanded to include other social divisions such as class, sexuality, religion, age and citizenship. Healy et al. (2008) argue convincingly that an 'intersectional sensibility', a term used by Kimberle Crenshaw (1991: 1243), can be valuable in alerting us to the differences in women's experiences.

Central to Yuval-Davis's (2006) conceptualization of intersectionality is the understanding that it is a constitutive, rather than an additive process. This represents a rejection of a view of oppression as simply cumulative, such that a black woman might face a 'double oppression' based on both her gender and race, and a black lesbian might experience a 'triple oppression' based on gender, race and sexual orientation. She argues that an individual cannot simply be said to suffer oppression 'as black', 'as a woman' or 'as a working class person' because:

> Being oppressed, for example, as 'a Black person' is always constructed and intermeshed in other social divisions (for example, gender, social class, disability status, sexuality, age, nationality, immigration status, geography, etc.). (Yuval-Davis 2006: 195)

In discussing gender, sexuality and class, I will therefore avoid an additive approach and examine instead the complex processes that constitute gender, sexuality and class in work organizations.

However, translating concepts of intersectionality into concrete analysis of social practice is not an easy task, but Joan Acker (2006a: 40) recommends starting with the material conditions of life and the relations involved in their production. To do this, she extends her notion of 'gendered processes' within organizations (1990, 1992) to include class and race, and devises a conceptual framework of 'inequality regimes', defined as: 'Loosely interrelated practices, processes, actions, and meanings that result in and maintain class, gender, and racial inequalities within particular organizations' (Acker 2006b: 443).

While organizations vary in the extent of these disparities, she identifies six characteristics of inequality regimes: the bases of inequality; the shape and degree of inequality; organizing processes that create and recreate inequalities; the invisibility of inequalities; the legitimacy of inequalities; and the control and compliance that maintain inequalities. These are described more fully in Chapter 1.

Acker's framework thus provides a useful way of systematically describing the variety of processes and dynamics that produce inequality in organizations at all levels, which also allows for the variability of inequality in different organizations, at different times and on different grounds, whether gender, race or class. She notes that sexuality, while significant in processes of inequality, is not as thoroughly embedded in organizing processes as gender, race, and class. However, I would argue that sexuality – and in particular dominant heterosexuality – has a central place in organizational processes and is deeply entwined with gender. Acker noted that in considering the visibility or degree of awareness of inequality in organizations, non-heterosexual sexuality is almost always invisible to the heterosexual majority. On the other hand, I have argued above that in male-dominated workplaces 'the lesbian' may be present in organizational discourses, even though she may not always be visible as an actual worker. Thus, sexuality is distinct from other forms of inequality, and requires specific attention to uncover these processes of 'invisibilization'. The dimension of control and compliance in Acker's framework, for example, invites analysis of informal interactions and people's internalized beliefs, as well as formal hierarchies and relations. It will be argued later that informal interactions are very important in sustaining gendered and sexualized work cultures for both heterosexual women and lesbians.

Methodology

The research is using a qualitative approach, collecting data by means of semi-structured interviews, focus groups, observation of events for women in non-traditional work and analysis of company or industry documentation related to the recruitment of women.[1] This chapter presents some initial findings based on the analysis of six of the interviews with women working in transport and construction – three from each sector. Three are heterosexual and three are lesbians. It also draws on interviews with selected experts on the employment of women in non-traditional female work.

Findings

Motivations for choosing non-traditional work

We have seen earlier the small numbers of women entering traditional male roles within the transport and construction sectors, so it is relevant to understand the reasons why the small minority of women who make gender atypical occupational decisions choose to do so. For one of the interviewees, Karen, the motivation was simple: pay.

> So basically I looked at the highest starter wage, if you like, that I could still retain a job in London [...] I was looking at starter jobs £14–£15,000 and [the current organization] was £18,000, back in 2000. So that was purely my drive really.

Karen had done bar work and worked as a croupier and was keen to get out of the casino industry, but only had a basic education and needed to support herself living alone. Therefore, her options were limited, but a job in a typically male industry – working in a station ticket office – offered better pay than more traditional female work. Her domestic circumstances were also important in her decision, as she was single, rented a flat and therefore needed to support herself.

For those in professional roles, pay was also better than average for women. Fiona noted that as a building consultant she earned more than her female friends outside the construction industry. For Fiona too financial security was important:

> I wanted to have a profession, to have something I could always fall back on, so I think it's more security rather than money [...] being financially independent was always absolutely huge. I saw my mother being financially dependent and the inequalities that that sets up within a relationship.

During the interview, Fiona expressed a clear feminist consciousness, and recognized the connections between work choices and relationships for heterosexual women, and the effect on personal relationships that lack of individual income produces. Fiona chose not to live with her male partner of several years, and therefore required financial independence. For lesbians too, choices about work and personal life are intertwined, and were significant in Nadia's feelings about promotion at work:

> It's important to develop my skills and progress. Maybe this is a sexuality issue [...] but I don't have the option of marrying and settling down in the conventional way. I mean it's always said that women earn less than men, so if you're a lesbian and even if you do meet somebody, you're probably going to be on less as a household than a straight counterpart, so I think I'm a bit more driven in that sense.

For another lesbian interviewee, work was essential to her sense of independence, despite a previous partner offering to support her. Lesley recalled her ex-partner's expectations when they moved for her job, and Lesley's own reaction:

> She says, 'well I don't really want you to work when we move down, because I'll be doing long hours, it's probably best if you stay at home and just look after the house [laughs]. We'll have more than enough money, no need for you to work'. I said right OK; let's just think about this sensibly now. I left school when I was 16, always had my own wages, I'm not reliant or dependant on anybody, and I'm not gonna start now, I'll find a job.

Her partner's attitude in fact gave Lesley extra motivation to find a job and 'put her brain to use'. Having previously worked in retail, Lesley was determined to try something different and took a job as a station assistant, from where she applied to be a train driver, saying:

> I've never, ever, ever done anything like this in my life before. I've always been in retail just doing in sales. Working at the station as a customer services assistant was completely different, but to go operational was something completely alien. I thought I have to try it, if it doesn't work then I'll come back and I'll go for supervisor. I have to give it a go, and it's the best thing I ever did.

Lesley emphasized the confidence doing a traditional male job gave her and, she believed, could give other women:

> I think it's good for women in general [...] because I think it proves to a lot of people that women can actually do the same job as a man, sometimes better. [...] because I think they would feel better about their self, because they've got a sense of achievement. It is a very hard job to get. It's probably one of the hardest.

Sexuality was also felt to be important in making non-traditional career choices. For Jo, being a lesbian was empowering in her ability to make a non-typical career choice. Discussing her lesbian sexuality and its effects, she said:

> You have to actively decide to do it, don't you? You could just go along and just be what everybody else is, or you could make an active choice, and for me that active choice, whatever you choose, [...] it's a choice. And to me, I think that's really powerful, that you have to do that means that you can then think, well actually I'm not going to go off and be a secretary, I'm going to think what I want, if I want to be a secretary I will, but actually, this looks really interesting, I'm gonna do it.

Jo's views support findings from the vocational psychology literature, primarily based on research in the United States, that lesbians tend to demonstrate more non-traditional, androgynous gender roles than heterosexual women and that they are therefore more likely to reject pressure to pursue gender traditional interests and occupations (Croteau et al. 2000; Fassinger 1996; Morgan and Brown 1991). Thus lesbians' day-to-day experience of challenging traditional gender roles may free them to choose occupations that are non-traditional for women, as Jo has indicated here, illustrating the profound connections between gender and sexuality in women's work and life choices. We have also seen here that material considerations, such as educational qualifications and domestic circumstances (whether single or cohabiting, regardless of sexual orientation) also affect women's need for financial independence and impact on their work choices. The comments here also made it clear that, beyond the need for financial support, a non-traditional work choice can be very empowering for women and greatly increase their personal confidence.

Intersecting identities

I have argued that gender and sexuality are deeply intertwined in women's decisions about work, but other identities may also come into play in women's experience of the workplace. The complexity of managing multiple identities in work organizations are amply demonstrated by Nadia in her discussion of employee network groups. As a black lesbian, she realized that she could attend three staff networks: the Women's; Black, Asian and Minority Ethnic (BAME); and Lesbian, Gay, Bisexual and Transgender (LGBT) groups. She had chosen to prioritize the

LGBT group for these reasons:

> I don't have to come out about anything because they can see that I'm a person of colour, they can see that I'm a woman and they already know that I'm gay, so that's probably one of the most comfortable spaces.

She anticipated that in the other groups, all her identities would not be accepted in the same way, fearing, for example, that if she attempted to raise issues related to being a lesbian in the BAME group, they might suggest this was more appropriately discussed in the LGBT group, which she said would feel 'like putting little bits and pieces of yourself in a box'. She explained that her worries about how her sexuality would be received were because 'most of my experience has been with people of colour, so any positive and negative that I've had has been from that group'. Nadia's concerns highlight the need for groups based on one specific form of oppression or identity to also demonstrate an 'intersectional sensibility' as described above (Crenshaw 1991; Healy et al. 2008) to ensure that potential members do not feel the need to put 'bits and pieces' of themselves 'in a box'.

Nadia's comments also point to the invisibility of minority sexual identity in organizations, which makes it distinct from other identities such as those of gender or ethnicity. One of Acker's (2006a,b) characteristics of inequality regimes is the visibility or degree of awareness of inequality in organizations, and she notes that minority sexuality is almost always invisible to the heterosexual majority: 'Heterosexuality is simply assumed, not questioned' (Acker 2006b: 452).

For Nadia and others, though, making her sexuality visible is not simply a matter of choosing when or how to 'come out' to colleagues, as this is made more complex by her awareness of the impact of her other identities on relations with colleagues. This can result in discussion of sexuality being avoided in certain situations:

> It might be that I thought, well I can leave that one [sexuality] because people have preconceptions about me because I am a person of colour, and then in some situations people will think about you in a certain [way] ... because you're a woman, and then to add to that the fact that you are also gay, it's like sometimes you feel like you are just alienating more and more people.

Her comments here presume that the people she may 'alienate' represent the 'norm' from which she is progressively distancing herself with each of her identities – or in Acker's (1990) terms the 'universal worker' who is in reality a man, and here we may add, a heterosexual, white man. She is also recognizing the linked nature of oppression stemming from her intersecting identities.

Thus discussion of the visibility of inequalities also needs to take account of intersecting identities, as individuals' experiences of making visible their sexual identity will vary depending on other factors, such as gender, ethnicity and class, as well as organizational and workplace cultures and formal and informal interactions in the workplace.

Gendered and sexualized organizational culture

The interviewees in traditional male work talked of multiple ways in which the male-dominated culture manifested itself. In some cases, it was simply disbelief that women could do a 'male' job. Jo had previously worked in a bike shop as a mechanic and described the perceptions of some customers: 'And you could stand there absolutely covered in grease and they would still say, "can I talk to the mechanic?" And you'd wonder, "what d'you think this is, has my mascara run?"'

And for Asian women working in construction, it may be even harder to be taken seriously due to stereotypes related to both gender and race. Jasminder, a senior manager in a building firm said:

> Sometimes I've been to conferences where people have said: 'Do you know where I hang my coat up love?' or 'D'you know where we can get tea and coffee?' and then they see me speaking and try and hide their face [laughs].

All three heterosexual interviewees described organizational cultures in the past where nude images of women were on display in areas where they worked, and in one local authority building department the men had a 'porn club' where they contributed money each week to buy pornographic magazines. One woman had also suffered an incident of physical sexual harassment on a building site, which she had managed to report and deal with, at some personal cost. All had been young women when these incidents occurred, and felt that they had had to 'toughen up' as a result, but Karen had chosen to move away from the 'sexist world' of working in a rail station, and found her male colleagues in her current non-operational role more 'gentlemanly'. Jasminder pointed out that comments made to her in a local authority 19 years ago could have led to legal action today, but that 'at the time it was just about keeping your head down and getting on with it'. Fiona also felt that the culture in the construction industry had changed enormously since she had complained about nude calendars 20 years earlier, which would not be acceptable now in offices in construction companies. However, she thought that building sites remained difficult places for women working in the manual trades. In her view, class, as well as gender, differences influenced how she was treated on site: 'If you are on the professional side as opposed to the manual trades, there is still acertain deference from the contractors to you as the professional, so I probably won't get quite as much gyp [as tradeswomen].' As Acker (2006b) has pointed out, gender and class controls are one of the ways in which inequality is produced and maintained in organizations, and sexual harassment is often used as a way of controlling women at work (Cockburn 1991). Even when women chose to remain in the 'sexist world' Karen referred to, their behaviour is modified and they must adapt to male norms. In referring to the prevalence of nude calendars and porn magazines at work when she started as a trainee, Jasminder said 'you don't want to be seen as a spoilsport, so you turn a blind eye'. Although these forms of workplace behaviour are no longer tolerated in the majority of workplaces, sexuality remains present in workplace interactions in male-dominated work. For women whose work involves socializing with clients, there is potential for unwanted interest, and Fiona said she sometimes had to 'take cover along' in the form of a colleague when entertaining a male client to ensure there was no misunderstanding about the nature of the relationship. She also pointed out that this difficulty recedes as you get older, indicating the important intersections of age and gender in relation to sexuality at work.

Lesbians also have to find ways of dealing with sexualized cultures, and even when they are open about their sexuality at work, they may not be immune to flirtation from male colleagues, as Lesley described here in relation to her train driver colleagues:

> They [male colleagues] did start paying me a lot of attention, although they knew that I wasn't interested in them and that they were wasting their time completely, but they still, not in a bad way, they were flirting, but in a nice way. They were having a joke and they knew that, you know, there was nobody crossing a line.

For others, though, their sexual orientation may be a way of avoiding unwanted sexual attention and can make working relationships easier. Jo said that when male colleagues knew about her sexuality, she was:

> Able to be one of the lads, not so much in my head, but it kind of removes a sexual tension that is there if there's a possibility [...] But once you're gay as well, [...] I think it makes you easier to deal with, because you're not trying to get into bed with them. You are actually trying to get them to answer the question.

In environments where sexual banter, or even harassment, is prevalent, open lesbians may be able to avoid some of the unwanted attention faced by heterosexual women. An example may be found in the UK fire service, where some lesbians reported easier working relationships with men, and one heterosexual woman pretended to be a lesbian, initially as a joke, but then found it had benefits in avoiding unwanted advances from male colleagues (Wright 2008).

Informal or internalized (Acker 2006b) forms of control can permeate, for example, through dress codes, in which women are expected to dress in a way that is neither too masculine nor too sexual, as Fiona explained:

> It would be considered unprofessional if you were showing too much cleavage or too much leg, that would be slightly frowned upon, because it's slightly conservative [...] I mean if you went in something terribly male that would be slightly wrong too. It's female rather than feminine.

Dress can also represent one way in which lesbians signify being out at work: Jo was accustomed to being open about her sexuality and her choice of clothing formed part of her lesbian identity. However, she thought that the professional dress required for her job as a consultant in an engineering firm might obscure her sexuality:

> When you make people dress smartly, then it's more difficult to tell, isn't it? [...] I usually wear something vaguely smart and try to keep my hair longer than looking like I've been conscripted [laughs] and not trainers and all the things that you would normally use to, that would normally make you obvious.

Jo was aware in this job that colleagues may not recognize her as a lesbian, and she may therefore need to consciously tell people, something that was unusual for her, as she felt that her sexuality was normally quite obvious to people. Dress may thus have different, but equally significant, meanings for lesbian and heterosexual women in work organizations.

Although Acker (2006b) and others have noted that non-heterosexual sexuality is usually invisible to the heterosexual majority in organizations, heterosexual and lesbian interviewees pointed out the visibility of lesbians and gay men in one metropolitan transport organization, particularly in certain departments or areas. One interviewee, Lesley, had met her female partner while working at a station, where she worked with several gay men and lesbians. Everyone had been aware of the relationship, and she had experienced no problems due to her sexuality. Since then she had transferred to being a train operator, and had invited some of her male colleagues to her 'wedding' to her partner. The LGBT staff network group was felt to be a factor in raising the profile of LGBT staff and signalling the organization's commitment to non-discrimination in this area. Karen, a heterosexual woman, who had worked with quite a few lesbian and gay colleagues while in an operational role, felt that the organizational culture had changed in recent years: 'I think the staff networks have played a big role in that, in promoting, you know the differences, promoting that whole culture, you know of, like, you are who you are, it doesn't matter.' She had also observed racist and discriminatory behaviour in stations in the past, but felt that the organization's high-profile promotion of its equality and inclusion policies, including of the network groups, had lead to definite improvements in workplace culture and expressed attitudes.

Barriers to progress

Although none of the six women interviewed had experienced barriers as a woman to entering their chosen occupations, a number of potential difficulties emerged in relation to progression in their careers.

The male-dominated culture of organizations described above clearly has an effect on the working lives of women, and we saw that Karen decided to leave an operational role in part because of the sexist environment in which she worked. For her, however, this could be seen as a positive career move, as she has progressed up the career ladder in the organization. Nevertheless, she felt strongly that she was limited in how far she could progress by her lack of higher education qualifications,

'I think you need to have formal education behind you to really have a step up, and I think that's my stumbling block at the minute'. She pointed out that those completing the graduate scheme could go straight into her grade, despite not having the years of experience that she has. In this case, gender was not felt to limit progress as much as education. However, Karen did feel different from other women who she saw as succeeding in the organization:

> I think women are very... maybe it's because of the male dominated environment but women are very driven. [...] I'm not that competitive in the work environment, I'm quite happy just for everyone to get along, it's all ok, and I feel that blokes just do their jobs and that's it.

Here she may be suggesting that higher standards are required for women to succeed in male-dominated work and at higher levels in organizations, but her observations also point to the connections between class (in this case represented by educational background) and gender in women's capacity to progress in male-dominated worlds. In her mind, women needed to conform to a particular type (well-educated, ambitious and competitive) in order to succeed.

Fiona believed that her career progression had certainly been limited by gender, but also alluded to class and ethnicity in who got promoted:

> I think it is partly that the face doesn't fit. [...] The area I work in is still very traditional, it's all very suited and booted, it's very golf, it's very football, it's very rugby, it's that sort of thing. And it's that thing that's very hard to pin down, it's not even prejudice, they just don't think of you when they are thinking about promotion. [..] And it's a very specific, fairly narrow type of man that does it. You know he's white, he plays golf.

Thus men, as well as women, make progress in their careers based on informal criteria of 'fitting in', and business networks often play an important role in determining such inclusions, particularly in the private sector. The exclusion of women from networking opportunities that are necessary for career development in some professions has led to the establishment of women's networking groups. A key informant interviewee from one such network, Women in Property, said that women, even senior ones, were simply not invited to corporate social events that provided opportunities to network with people that would advance their careers. A representative of another network, the National Association of Women in Construction, felt that the exclusion was less deliberate, but nonetheless real:

> Every time there's corporate entertainment it's a day out at the rugby and whatever. [..] It always seems to be the nature of events that wouldn't be your cup of tea... after a while you don't to go, because you just think, you know, standing around at the bar at rugby with everyone drinking beer, and you don't go to those eventually, you don't make the contacts.

Such informal exclusionary practices are a further form of organizing processes, identified by Acker (2006a), that sustain inequality regimes, and deny women access to business practices that develop men's careers. Jasminder, however, had consciously decided to get involved in the activities of her professional body when she realized that there would be no opportunities for promotion in the organization where she was working due to low staff turnover. This had resulted in her gaining a high profile in her industry – which she said caused some jealousy among male colleagues – and being headhunted for a senior role. Furthermore, she managed to juggle these additional commitments with work and raising children.

The organization of work and home lives

Jasminder was the only one of the six interviewees discussed here who had children. Fiona thought it was common for women of her generation, those in their late forties and fifties, who had progressed to her level not to have children, a view confirmed by the literature which finds that women in senior or male-dominated roles are less likely to have children than average (Bagilhole 2002: 6; McDowell 1997: 86; Wajcman 1998: 139; Wood and Newton 2006: 338–9). However, she observed a change happening for women currently in their thirties, who were now more likely to stay in their jobs when they had children, which she attributed to societal changes that had impacted on the culture and practices in her workplace.

Jasminder, whose eldest daughter is 18, had brought up two children while working and training as a building surveyor. Her husband had been very supportive and his career had been put 'on the back burner' while hers progressed, and she had become the main earner in the family. She still, however, took responsibility for much of the domestic work of the household, and compared herself to her male colleagues:

> Some of the guys here are doing long hours, and I just say, 'well I haven't got a wife at home who cooks and cleans, I've got to go home and do it myself'. They're alright, they do it because they can, I think that's the main difference, if you haven't got any other commitments, you can do the long hours.

She also commented that in her current firm, the other male managers were sympathetic to the need to get home for childcare as they also took some responsibility for the care of their own children, reflecting the societal changes referred to by Fiona earlier.

While there may be commonly held perceptions that lesbians may be more committed to their jobs because they do not have children (Dunne 1997; Friskopp and Silverstein 1995), it is increasingly common for lesbians to raise children, either as couples or alone (Peplau and Fingerhut 2004). Furthermore, they may have alternative arrangements, such as a commitment to friends' children, as was the case for Lesley. She and her partner were committed to looking after the baby daughter of some friends, a lesbian couple, every Monday and Lesley had had to adjust her shifts to accommodate this.

We have a lot of input in [the baby's] life. And we try and rest now on a Monday together so that we can both spend time with her. And as far as we're concerned, so long as we're in her life, she's in ours. [...] we're committed to her one day a week, and that's a sacrifice we've both had to make, because I need to work a Saturday to rest on a Sunday and a Monday, so that's something that I had to think about.

Nadia, a lesbian aged 28, was also thinking about children in the future, and related this to the need to get promotion at work:

I'd like to have a family at some point, I'd probably adopt. And that is something that's in the mix in terms of finances, how's that going to be financed, yeah, it needs to be paid for in some way and if you have a young child, who's going to stay at home or nursery fees. I mean some of the guys that have children, quite a few of them, their wives are at home [...] if I was to be with somebody who was earning less than me, there'd be no point in me staying at home, so that's even more of a reason why I'd need to be motivated about trying to get promoted and get ahead.

She was taking account of the likelihood of a future female partner earning less than her, based on women's average lower earnings, and was comparing herself to male colleagues with children, most of whom had wives at home. In this sense she was putting herself in the typically male parenting role rather than comparing herself to the more common pattern of heterosexual women in two-parent households who work part time (Glover and Kirton 2006: 7). Minority sexuality can here be seen to provoke less gender-typical ways of thinking about the relationship between domestic and professional lives.

Conclusion

This chapter has argued that to fully understand the experiences of women in non-traditional female work we need to apply an intersectional approach, or sensibility, that explores the interrelated nature of gender, sexuality and class, as well as of ethnicity and age. I have tried to illuminate how such intersections play out in the everyday working lives of six women – three heterosexual and three lesbian – in the transport and construction sectors. These intersecting elements affect women's decisions about choice of career, which is inevitably entwined with considerations based on opportunity, personal and home circumstances, and their day-to-day experience of work. We have seen that in heavily male-dominated environments, both gender and sexuality are to the fore, and lesbians and heterosexual women must find ways of navigating this tricky terrain. The organizational context plays an important part in shaping women's experience, and we have seen that social changes, for example in attitudes to sexual harassment at work or flexible working, have changed the workplace environment considerably in the last 20 years. However the evidence from these interviewees showed the many ways in which organizations still exclude or marginalize women, who are often still considered to deviate from the white, heterosexual, male norm. Class and level of educational attainment were also shown to be barriers to progression in some cases. Joan Acker's (2006b) notion of inequality regimes is useful in helping to reveal these processes. By avoiding an additive approach to inequality, we have seen that minority sexuality may not necessarily create additional problems at work for women in male-dominated work, and can be associated with fewer gendered constraints on work choices.

Attention to women's material circumstances in relation to work choices allowed us to see that whether a woman was single or in a relationship, together with the economic relations within that relationship, were as important factors as their sexuality. The presumption that a heterosexual woman may have a higher-earning male partner to support her, whereas a lesbian will not, was challenged in two ways. First, none of the heterosexual women discussed here relied on a male partner for financial support, and the one married woman earned more than her husband. Second, a lesbian interviewee Lesley described an ex-partner who had expected to be the sole breadwinner while Lesley remained at home, a notion which was, however, firmly rejected by Lesley. Thus, women's own need – or desire – to be financially independent was not solely influenced by the gender of their partner.

However, there were differences observable between the heterosexual women and lesbians in relation to sexual harassment, which had been experienced by all three heterosexual women. The more serious incidents described, though, had occurred decades earlier, and the women felt that sexual harassment was less common now in their industries. Nonetheless, such experiences highlight the close relationship between gender and sexuality in male-dominated work, in which women are constructed in relation to their availability – or not – to men. For one of the lesbians too, flirtation was part of how male colleagues related to her, despite knowing about her sexuality, but she felt that this did not 'cross the line'. For another, though, being open about her sexuality removed the sexual tension from working relationships.

Such diffusion of the sexualized nature of work relationships that (presumed) heterosexual women may face depends, though, on lesbians being open about their sexuality at work. It seems clear that changes in public attitudes towards lesbians and gay men (Cowan 2007: 7), as well as greater legal rights, have enabled many lesbians and gay men to be open about their sexuality at work and have had a positive effect on organizational policy and practice on sexual orientation (Colgan et al. 2006; Stonewall 2008). This may mean that Acker's (2006b: 452) contention that non-heterosexual sexuality is almost always invisible to the heterosexual majority in organizations is becoming less true, at least in large organizations with a commitment to equality and diversity. We saw that in one transport organization this was attributed to the visibility of the LGBT network group and the active promotion of the organization's equality and diversity policy. However, advances in equality are constantly at risk from changing political and economic circumstances, and while currently resources are being put into tackling occupational gender segregation and supporting women into non-traditional roles, political changes at national and regional levels could threaten these, as could economic pressures from the current recession.

Note

1. Data collection includes 40 semi-structured interviews with women working in the construction and in transport sectors (20 in each sector), representing heterosexual, lesbian and bisexual women. The sample contains a balance of women working in professional and manual occupations within the two sectors. Additionally, two focus groups are being carried out in each sector: one with women entering the sector and one with women already working in the sector. Contextual information about the transport and construction industries is being gathered through 12–15 interviews with selected experts on the employment of women in non-traditional female work. They represent industry and training bodies, employers, trade unions, women's networks and voluntary organizations that have an interest in women working in transport and construction. Observations of events aiming to attract women into traditional male work are being made, and analysis of documentation and images produced to attracting women into non-traditional work is being carried out.

References

Acker, J. (1990) 'Hierarchies, jobs, bodies: a theory of gendered organizations', *Gender & Society*, 4(2): 139–58.
— (1992) *Gendering organizational theory. Gendering organizational analysis*. A. Mills and P. Tancred (eds), London, Sage: 248–60.
— (2006a) *Class questions: feminist answers*. Maryland: Rowman & Littlefield.
— (2006b) 'Inequality regimes: gender, class, and race in organizations', *Gender & Society*, 20(4): 441–64.
Bagilhole, B. (2002) *Women in non-traditional occupations: challenging men*. Basingstoke: Palgrave Macmillan.
Briscoe, G. (2005) 'Women and minority groups in UK construction: recent trends', *Construction Management and Economics*, 23: 1001–5.
Chetkovich, C. (1997) *Real heat: gender and race in the urban fire service*. New Brunswick: Rutgers University Press.
Cockburn, C. (1991) *In the way of women: men's resistance to sex equality in organizations*. London: Macmillan.
Colgan, F., C. Creegan, A. McKearney and T. Wright (2006) *Lesbian, gay and bisexual workers: equality, diversity and inclusion in the workplace*. London: Comparative Organisation and Equality Research Centre, London Metropolitan University.
Colgan, F., S. Johnstone and S. Shaw (1996) 'On the move: women in the Toronto public transport sector', In S. Ledwith and F. Colgan (eds), *Women in organisations: challenging gender politics*. Basingstoke; Macmillan, pp. 245–77.
Collins, P. H. (2000) Black feminist thought: knowledge, consciousness and the politics of empowerment. New York: Routledge.

Collinson, M. and D. Collinson (1996) '"It's Only Dick": the sexual harassment of women managers in insurance sales', *Work Employment Society*, 10(1): 29–56.

Cowan, K. (2007) *Living together: British attitudes to lesbian and gay people*. London: Stonewall.

Crenshaw, K. (1991) 'Mapping the margins: intersectionality, identity politics, and violence against women of color', *Stanford Law Review*, 43: 1241–99.

Croteau, J. M., M. Z. Anderson, T. M. Distefano and S. Kampa-Kokesch (2000) 'Lesbian, gay, and bisexual vocational psychology: reviewing foundations and planning construction', In R. M. Perez, K. A. DeBord and K. M. Bieschke (eds), *Handbook of counseling and psychotherapy with lesbian, gay, and bisexual clients*. Washington, DC: American Psychological Association, pp. 383–408.

DCLG (2007) *Towards a fairer future: implementing the women and work commission recommendations*. London: Department for Communities and Local Government.

— (2008) *Fire and rescue service equality and diversity strategy 2008– 2018*. London: Department for Communities and Local Government.

Dunne, G. (1997) *Lesbian lifestyles: women's work and the politics of sexuality*. Basingstoke: Macmillan Press.

EOC (2001) *Just pay: report of the equal pay task force*. Manchester: Equal Opportunities Commission.

— (2006) *Facts about women and men in Great Britain 2006*. Manchester: Equal Opportunities Commission.

Fassinger, R. E. (1996) 'Notes from the margins: integrating lesbian experience into the vocational psychology of women', *Journal of Vocational Behavior*, 48: 160–75.

Friskopp, A. and S. Silverstein (1995) *Straight jobs, gay lives: gay and lesbian professionals, the Harvard Business School, and the American workplace*. New York, London: Scribner.

Glover, J. and G. Kirton (2006) *Women, employment and organizations*. Abingdon: Routledge.

Government Equalities Office (2008) *Delivering the equality PSA 2008-2011*. London: GEO.

Gurjao, S. (2006) *Inclusivity: the changing role of women in the construction workforce*. Ascot: The Chartered Institute of Building.

Hamilton, K., L. Jenkins, F. Hodgson and J. Turner (2005) 'Promoting gender equality in transport', EOC Working Paper Series. Manchester, Equal Opportunities Commission.

Healy, G., H. Bradley and C. Forson (2008) 'Intersectional sensibilities in analyzing inequality regimes in public sector organisations', International Labour Process Conference, Dublin.

Henwood, F. (1998) 'Engineering difference: discourses on gender, sexuality and work in a college of technology', *Gender and Education*, 10(1): 35–49.

Hooks, B. (1981) *Ain't I a woman: black women and feminism*. Boston: South End Press.

— ([1990] 2004) 'Choosing the margin as a space of radical openness', In S. Harding (eds), *The feminist standpoint theory reader*. London: Routledge.

LDA (2007) *London 2012 Olympic Games and Paralympic Games: the employment and skills legacy*. London: London Development Agency.

Martin, S. E. and N. C. Jurik (2007) *Doing justice, doing gender: women in legal and criminal justice occupations*. Thousand Oaks; London: Sage.

McDowell, L. (1997) *Capital culture: gender at work in the city*. Oxford: Blackwell Publishers.

Morgan, K. S. and L. S. Brown (1991). 'Lesbian career development, work behavior, and vocational counseling', *The Counseling Psychologist*, 19: 273–91.

National Statistics (2009) 'Gender pay gap narrows', Published 12 November 2009. Retrieved 16 November 2009, from http://www.statistics.gov.uk/cci/nugget.asp?id=167.

Peplau, L. A. and A. Fingerhut (2004) 'The paradox of the lesbian worker', *Journal of Social Issues*, 60(4): 719–35.

Reskin, B. F. and I. Padavic (1988) 'Supervisors as gatekeepers: male supervisors' response to women's integration in plant jobs', *Social Problems*, 35(5): 536–50.

Stonewall (2008) *Workplace equality index*. London: Stonewall.

Wajcman, J. (1998) *Managing like a man: women and men in corporate management*. Cambridge: Polity Press.

Wall, C. (2004) '"Any woman can": 20 years of campaigning for access to construction training and employment', In L. Clarke, E. F. Pedersen, E. Michielsens, B. Susman and C. Wall (eds), *Women in construction*. Brussels: CLR/Reed Business Information, pp. 158–72.

Weston, K. (1982) *The apprenticeship and blue collar system: putting women on the right track*. Sacramento: California State Department of Education.

— (1998) *Long slow burn: sexuality and social science*. London: Routledge.

Women and Work Commission (2006) *Shaping a fairer future*. London: Women and Work Commission.

Wood, G. J. and J. Newton (2006) 'Childlessness and women managers: "choice", context and discourses', *Gender, Work & Organization*, 13(4): 338–58.

Wright, T. (2008) 'Lesbian firefighters: shifting the boundaries between "masculinity" and "femininity"', *Journal of Lesbian Studies*, 12(1): 103–14.

Yuval-Davis, N. (2006) 'Intersectionality and Feminist Politics', *European Journal of Women's Studies*, 13(3): 193–209.

15

Work-life balance

Attitudes and expectations of young black and minority ethnic graduates

Gill Kirton

Introduction

Work-life balance (WLB) is a topic of considerable interest among policy-makers and academics and it is increasingly a priority for many working people, including the subjects of this chapter – early career graduates (Cousins and Tang 2004; Sturges and Guest 2004). It is well established that gender matters for orientations to WLB, but within most research, 'race'/ethnicity is usually invisible so that little is known about its intersection with family responsibilities, community ties and work (Rana et al. 2007). The evidence that does exist indicates that kinship and community are particularly salient for Asian communities who it is argued face a stronger sense of familial obligation that places pressures on individuals seeking WLB. Further, some 'migratory families' are spread around the world which can add to the difficulties individuals face in achieving balance (ibid.).

Although the contemporary WLB discourse goes beyond the reconciliation of paid work and family responsibilities, there can be no doubt that WLB comes into sharp focus when people become parents. It is clear that women overall, irrespective of race/ethnicity, still largely shoulder domestic and family responsibilities and adapt their career aspirations and behaviour to reconcile work and family (Windebank 2001). Bruegel and Gray (2005), while recognizing that the total time spent on childcare by *men* might reflect 'cultural' factors, found no significant ethnic differences affecting the distribution of *primary* childcare between partners. However, the Time Use Survey they interrogate does suggest a *class* effect with men with more education and in managerial or professional jobs spending more time on childcare than other men (ibid.). Nevertheless, highly qualified women in dual-career couples typically choose to prioritize the male partner's career and earnings potential once they have children (Hardill and Watson 2004). Further, among such couples a traditional gender division of domestic labour remains strong with women overwhelmingly managing parenting arrangements (Windebank 2001). Turning to men, while there remains then a dominant breadwinning conception of father-hood, there are also developing concepts of fatherhood as self-fulfilment and caring fatherliness, meaning that even though on average fathers work longer hours than mothers, some forgo other out-of-work activities to spend more time with their children (Bruegel and Gray 2005). This points to the importance of considering within the WLB debate the role of more fundamental gendered attitudes to parenting.

Duncan et al. (2003: 10) argue that people make decisions about how parenting might be combined with paid work with reference to 'gendered moral rationalities': moral and socially negotiated views about what behaviour is right and proper (i.e. not just with reference to what childcare is available). Duncan et al. (2003) point out that what is considered 'good' parenting varies between social groups. Their study which included African-Caribbean women, found that ethnicity provided a 'major fault line' in mothers' understandings about combining motherhood and paid work. The African-Caribbean mothers, particularly those in professional and manage-ment jobs, were more likely than the white to regard substantial hours in employ-ment as a component of good mothering.

Hakim (2005: 64) attributes ethnic differences in work-family orientations to the differential influence of traditional sex-role ideology. She finds that support for the 'symmetrical gender roles model' of the family is strongest by far among black (African-Caribbean) females and weakest by far among Indian males; also that acceptance of patriarchy is strongest among Indian males and females. Similarly, other authors have argued that in many cultures family roles and strong cultural expectations regarding marriage and motherhood continue to complicate career and WLB choices for some Black and minority ethnic (BME) women (Dale 2005; Hite 2007). Data on labour market participation seemingly support this claim; for example the 2001 UK Census showed that 36 per cent of Pakistani and 40 per cent of Bangladeshi women were full-time homemakers compared with 12 per cent of white women (Dale 2005). Further, there is evidence that Asian women themselves believe that they give much more priority to their family, than white women (Dale et al. 2002). However, the picture is complicated by educational attainment with highly educated Pakistani and Bangladeshi women much more likely to be in employment and less likely than their less-educated counterparts to marry and have children at a young age (Dale 2005). There is also some evidence of national variation in conceptions of the 'good mother'. Based on a French case study it is argued that underpinned by relatively strong childcare provision, French women have 'a certain ability to not feel guilty about the social norms associated with the image of the "good mother"' (Guillaume and Pochic 2007). Thus, the existing literature points to the need to examine WLB from the (gendered) perspectives of different BME groups in different national contexts.

To what extent are these issues, including the gendered attitudinal changes towards parenthood that are clearly evolving, influencing the present generation of *young graduates* as they begin to navigate their work careers and family lives? Again, specifically in relation to young graduates, more is known about the impact of gender than about race/ethnicity. Purcell (2002: 28) notes that three-and-a-half years after graduation 'young women still accept the cultural mandate that has allocated the primary parenting responsibility to females'. Sixty-five per cent of Purcell's sample of young women graduates agreed that they expected to take career breaks for family reasons, compared to only 12 per cent of men. Only 17 per cent of the women said that they would expect their partner to take career breaks, while 41 per cent of the men expected that their partner would do so. Thus, it appears that the 'maternalist' discourses that position women as primarily responsible for domestic work and family care continue to influence the younger generation despite the prevalent discourse of gender equality (Wood and Newton 2006). The question relevant for this chapter is whether we can subsume young BME women and men within the broader gender categories? Or, are there racialized/ethnicized dimensions to young women's and men's WLB attitudes? In a study of young people, similar proportions and only a minority of all (ethnic) groups of girls said they would be happy to stay at home and look after children rather than have a career. Further, despite the belief that there are pressures on some South Asian young women to prioritize family over career, in the same study only 10 per cent of Bangladeshi and 12 per cent of Pakistani respondents said that their parents expected them to get married and have children rather than follow a career (Bhavnani 2006). These findings suggest that while ethnicized, cultural and family-instilled gendered values exist, they are dynamic and liable to generational change.

Turning to WLB and the workplace, authors have argued that while some women might consciously choose a career break or part-time work for a period, because they want to take the time to enjoy motherhood (Hardill and Watson 2004), others might adapt their careers, not because they prefer to do so, but because the structural supports necessary to enable them to carry on working full-time simply are not available to them (Windebank 2001). Thus, the desire for WLB has to be set within prevalent work regimes. There is a growing perception (and probably reality) that in order to succeed in career terms, it is necessary to accept the 'long hours' culture' that has come to dominate working life in British organizations particularly for managers and professionals (Liff and Ward 2001). Indeed, previous research shows that having invested heavily in their future careers, graduates' desire for career success leads them to work increasingly long hours and experience an unsatisfactory WLB (Sturges and Guest 2004). Arguably though, with increased legal provision supporting WLB arrangements the climate in the workplace is now more accepting of people's desire to balance work and family life. Overall the evidence shows an increase in WLB policies in the UK (comparing the 1998 and 2004 Workplace Employment Relations Surveys), but their spread is uneven. For example, the public sector has more generous extra-statutory leave arrangements to support employees with caring responsibilities than the private sector. But, there is a prevalent and worrying attitude among managers that it is up to individual employees to balance their work and family responsibilities: in 2004 two -thirds of managers still believed this to be the case, although this was fewer than in 1998 (Kersley et al. 2004).

This chapter discusses the WLB attitudes and expectations held by young BME male and female business graduates. Two main areas are explored: (i) ethnicized and gendered attitudes towards parenting and work, and (ii) expectations of WLB at the workplace. Although it is accepted that attitudes do not always translate into actual behaviour, this chapter argues that they are important for understanding the multitude of factors, the compromises and dilemmas that are concealed by the apparent choices young BME women and men make in navigating and reconciling their careers and family life. First, in order to provide a framework for understanding the influence of race/ethnicity on WLB attitudes and expectations, there is a discussion of the formation of race/ethnic and gender identities. This is followed by an outline of the study.

The formation of race/ethnic and gender identities

It is argued that identity performs two important functions: first, it provides meaning to life and allows individuals to label themselves; second, it provides normative guidance for behaviour, including how to manage work and family (Bagger et al. 2008: 189). An important criticism of early literature on race and ethnicity is that subjectivity was under-theorized, so that while individuals were placed within the complex interplay of changing processes of racialization and wider socio-economic change, they were rendered passive recipients of those processes (Brah et al. 1999). More recently, authors have developed dynamic, multi-dimensional theories of race/ ethnic identity formation processes. Jenkins' (2004) sociological framework focuses on the interactional constitution of identity; how identity *works* in everyday life through three distinct 'orders'. The individual order 'is the human world as made up of embodied individuals, and what-goes-on-in-their-heads'. The interaction order 'is the human world as constituted in relationships between individuals, in what-goes-on-between-people'. The institutional order 'is the human world of pattern and organization, of established-ways-of-doing-things' (ibid.: 17). Thus a multitude of interacting factors influence people's self-concept, which in turn influences their behaviour in different social settings. Importantly, within Jenkins' framework identity is not a static state of being; rather a continuous process of *identification*, meaning that for individuals and for wider society, the salience of any particular identity can change over time.

In a similar vein, Bradley (1996: 25) outlined three levels of identity: passive, active and politicized. Her concept of 'active identities' is the most useful for understanding the WLB attitudes and expectations of young BME graduates: individuals are conscious of active identities, which are positive, potentially multi-faceted and which provide a basis for individuals' actions. Bradley argues that active identities are often promoted by the experience of discrimination, but in the present chapter it is argued that an active identity can also develop from a more positive self-concept and act as a kind of normative or moral compass in guiding behaviour. This links with the earlier point about the gendered (and ethnicized) moral rationalities that underpin attitudes to parenting.

It is also important to think about how gender intersects with race/ethnicity as it is now widely accepted that not only does ethnicity impact on gender identity, but that gender intersects with and complicates ethnic identity. Ramji (2007), for example, argues that British Asian Muslim identities are usually seen as constructed in relation to culture, religion and ethnicity with a lack of attention to gender dynamics. She shows how gender and class intersect with ethnic identity producing contestation about what constitutes 'good Islamic behaviour' among men and women. Both frameworks outlined above allow for the possibility of individuals having multiple identities. Bradley (1996: 25) argues that people now draw their sense of identity from a broad range of sources and sets of lived relationships including class, gender and ethnicity. In terms of which, among an array of possible identities available to individuals, are most salient, Jenkins argues that identities established early in life are *primary* identities, including ethnicity, kinship and gender. These primary identities are more robust and resilient to change than other identities (ibid.: 19). The chapter draws on these multi-layered concepts of identity and identity formation processes to theorize young BME business graduates' attitudes towards and expectations of WLB.

The study

The research consisted of individual face-to-face interviews with 40 new BME business graduates in June–July 2006 and two focus groups in January 2007 with final-year business undergraduates (four female and two male participants). The fact that the population studied was business graduates should not escape notice. Business is an area where female and BME students are well represented (Connor et al. 2004). Business students are more likely to have chosen their degree for pragmatic reasons and are therefore likely to be more vocationally oriented (Pitcher and Purcell 1998).

A central feature of the method was peer interviewing, the aim of which was to overcome age, racial/ethnic and social barriers that might prevent respondents from being frank and open. This obviously had limitations and it would never be possible to achieve a perfect match between interviewer–respondent characteristics. In the end, for practical reasons, four of the interviewers were of BME backgrounds while one was white; all were female. All the interviewers were new business graduates/ final-year undergraduates in their early twenties.

In order to reduce the risks associated with employing inexperienced interviewers, a fairly structured, but flexible, interview schedule was used. The schedule provided opportunities for respondents to expand, explain or give examples and for interviewers to interject their own probes. Interview questions covered three main themes – family background; reasons for and attitudes to university and degree choice; immediate and future career plans and aspirations. Respondents were also asked to respond using a five-point Likert scale to a number of WLB statements (see Table 15.1). It was significant that the female respondents talked spontaneously about WLB issues throughout the interview, whereas the males had to be asked specific questions. The females typically brought children and family into most of their answers including questions about the sector, occupation and type of organization they would like to work in. Interviews lasted approximately one hour, focus groups about two hours; all were digitally recorded and transcribed. Transcripts were anonymized and coded, using NVIVO, according to the research themes and questions. In the chapter the gender and (self-identified) ethnic background of respondents is indicated against quotes in order to help the reader situate comments. However, the sample size was not large enough to enable any definitive comparisons of the orientations of one ethnic group compared to another. Nevertheless where there seemed to be significant differences in attitudes, perceptions or opinion based on ethnicity, these are commented upon.

Table 15.2 shows selected characteristics of respondents. Males proved less willing to participate in the study. Possibly the one striking feature of the sample is the absence of Black Caribbean and small number of Black African respondents; this is an obvious limitation of the study. This is a reflection of the skewed ethnic composition of the universities from which most respondents were drawn, where Black Caribbean students in particular are under-represented.

For the purposes of a discussion about WLB aspirations, it is interesting to note the occupation of respondents' mothers, since whether or not mothers are in paid work (and in what type of job) is thought to influence BME children's attitudes to gender roles in general and parenting in particular as they grow up (Bhavnani 2006; Dale et al. 2002). In this respect, most respondents came from traditional households: of the respondents' mothers, 23 were described as housewives; 2 helped in the family business; 14 had administrative, sales and personal service jobs; a small minority (7) were in professional or associate professional occupations (e.g. GP, teacher, nurse, accountant).

Table 15.1 Attitudes to WLB

WLB Statement	Strongly agree		Agree somewhat		Neither agree nor disagree		Disagree somewhat		Strong disagree	
	F	M	F	M	F	M	F	M	F	M
I expect to work continuously until retirement	5 (15%)	3 (25%)	6 (18%)	7 (58%)	3 (9%)	0 (0%)	14 (41%)	1 (8%)	6 (18%)	1 (8%)
I expect to take some time out of full-time work for childcare	20 (59%)	1 (8%)	8 (24%)	4 (33%)	4 (12%)	4 (33%)	1 (3%)	1 (8%)	1 (3%)	2 (17%)
I would expect my partner to take a career break for childcare	9 (26%)	5 (42%)	14 (41%)	5 (42%)	6 (18%)	1 (8%)	3 (9%)	1 (8%)	2 (6%)	0 (0%)
I expect to get my main fulfilment from work	3 (9%)	0 (0%)	6 (18%)	2 (17%)	10 (29%)	6 (50%)	9 (26%)	3 (25%)	6 (18%)	1 (8%)
I am extremely ambitious	8 (24%)	6 (50%)	17 (50%)	5 (42%)	7 (21%)	1 (8%)	2 (6%)	0 (0%)	0 (0%)	0 (0%)
I would like to work for a family-friendly employer	23 (68%)	6 (50%)	7 (21%)	5 (42%)	4 (12%)	1 (8%)	0 (0%)	0 (0%)	0 (0%)	0 (0%)
I expect to get my main satisfaction from family life	21 (62%)	3 (25%)	11 (32%)	8 (67%)	1 (3%)	1 (8%)	1 (3%)	0 (0%)	0 (0%)	0 (0%)

F- Females, N = 34; M- Males, N = 12

Table 15.2 Selected characteristics of respondents

	Female (N = 34)	Male (N = 12)	All (N = 46)
Ethnic background[1]			
Black African	4	0	4
Black Caribbean	0	0	0
Chinese	3	1	4
Indian	9	1	10
Bangladeshi	3	3	6
Pakistani	0	1	1
Mixed	5	5	10
Other BME			
Age			
20–21	21	7	28
22–23	10	5	15
24	3	0	3
Marital status			
Married	1	0	1
Live with partner	1	0	1
Single	32	12	44
Children			
Yes	1	0	1
No	33	12	45

Ethnicized and gendered attitudes to WLB?

This section discusses male and female attitudes to parenting and work. To put the discussion in context of *career* orientations, all bar one of the male respondents and nearly three quarters of the female respondents saw themselves as extremely ambitious (see Table 15.2). In order to provide a reference point for the discussion about WLB, respondents were asked what arrangements they imagined they might have in their personal lives in ten years' time. The responses were fairly conventional and perhaps predictable. With the exception of one male respondent, all stated that they expected to be married or living with a partner and have children (by around the age of 31–2).

Male attitudes to parenting and work

Notions of what it means to be a 'good' father, the meaning and place of work and family in their lives emerged quite strongly in the interviews with male respondents; their answers to the WLB statements are shown in Table 15.2. The men expressed a strong family orientation insofar as they nearly all agreed that they expected to get their main satisfaction from family life. However, their views about appropriate parenting revealed a traditional gendered moral rationality. They mostly believed that their role would be as breadwinner and their future female partner's primary role would be as care-giver. This position reflects previous research involving a range of ethnic groups suggesting that fathers in general are still seen by themselves (as well as by other family members) as primarily financial providers (Duncan et al. 2003; Hakim 2005). In line with this, the majority of the men stated that they would expect their partner to take a career break for childcare, with most disagreeing in principle with using professional childcare services. The importance of finding a partner who shared their view of the appropriate gendered division of domestic responsibilities is illustrated by the following quote:

> I'll probably be a full-time working parent and the Mrs will probably, unfortunately, have to work part-time or just look after the kids. My future Mrs will feel the same way as me; she won't want to be working full-time and neglecting her kids. I would like to be the breadwinner. It's not a man thing, but I don't believe in babysitters. (Male, Bangladeshi)

Thus, an active male gender identity became the basis for choice and (future) action. In order to rationalize and position this view as 'natural', respondents often marshalled ethnic and religious identities formed in Jenkins' (2004) terms in the individual and interactive orders in the guise of family-instilled cultural values:

> It's better for a child to be brought up by a woman because to be honest men don't know much about anything like that. The child will get a much better upbringing being brought up by a woman because the woman's been taught those things by her mother; especially in my culture anyway. (Male, Afghan)

Despite the fact that only rarely do men act as primary care-givers, in the UK it has been found that it is fathers, rather than mothers, who are more likely to report conflicting pressures between work and family life (Cousins and Tang 2004). This is no doubt due in part at least to the fact that men who have children work longer hours than other men, but is also a reflection of changing conceptions of the good father and thus changing male gender identities (Bruegel and Gray 2005). The male respondents strongly emphasized the importance of family to them and some did feel that they would strive to make some practical adjustments to their work lives and personal, career sacrifices in order to be a good father, for example:

> I think that at that age, when I'm 31/32 and if I've got kids, I'd start planning towards starting up my own business because I think it's quite important to spend a lot of time with your kids. If I'm working for a big company and I don't have time for my kids, I think I'd look for a better option. (Male, Malaysian)

> 'I know I've talked a lot about how important money is, but I feel it's very, very important to spend time with your family. I would like to get home at a time where I can spend time with my kids. I wouldn't want to work 'til 8, say, get home at 9 and put my kids to bed. I would be willing to make financial sacrifices. (Male, Pakistani)

Some of the males talked about having spent very little time with their fathers when they were growing up, but generally they felt they had reaped the benefit of their fathers' strong work ethic in terms of the financial security provided. Most saw this strong breadwinner figure as a good father and role model and aspired to follow in their fathers' footsteps. In this sense, they indicated the way that their own male gender identity had been formed in the interactive order. However, they indicated that, like their fathers, they would be prepared to forgo other non-work activities in order to give time to their children:

> It would be unrealistic to say that I will only work this many hours because sometimes work does require you to work extra hours. Sometimes my father would come back very late, but I can confidently say that he spent as much time as possible with his family. It's all about your priorities, but if your work requires you to work long hours, then so be it. (Male, Pakistani)

One respondent wanted to break with the past and be a more involved father than his own had been, seeing this as critical to a child's upbringing:

> I've been raised by females and so have most of my friends, but for me I couldn't have children and not be around them – it's not a trend I want to continue. I don't think it's good, especially if you have a son, but even if you have a daughter, I think it's important for them to have a mum and a father around. (Male, Iranian)

This respondent highlights the fact that there is nothing inevitable about the impact of the influences a person is exposed to in the interactive order and that 'what goes on in someone's head' (the individual order) is not predetermined.

In summary, the men demonstrated highly traditional, gendered attitudes towards parenting, which in some cases clearly intersected with race/ethnicity insofar as cultural and religious values were invoked to explain and even to legitimize their views. These attitudes constituted an element of their male gender identity which became a basis for choice and (future) action.

Female attitudes to parenting and work

The evidence shows that a large proportion of women managers are childless and the growth of WLB policies seems to have done little to reverse this long-standing trend (Wood and Newton 2006). At the very least, it is argued that the traditional masculine career pattern and its powerful normative influence requires younger women to postpone motherhood in order to get established in their careers prior to taking maternity leave and/or a career break (Guillaume and Pochic 2007). Despite the fact that my respondents were ambitious, they were not envisaging joining the ranks of childless women managers, but they were planning on delaying motherhood beyond the current average age in Britain of first time mothers of 27 (ONS 2000). All the women in the study expected to have children at some point and the overwhelming majority (32 out of 34) envisaged motherhood by about age 31–2.

Research has found that some women in management believe that the culture of long working hours does not support 'appropriate' parenting (Wood and Newton 2006: 355). This fits with the idea that 'gendered moral rationalities' surround women's views about combining work and mothering (Duncan et al. 2003). Add this to Dale's (2005: 239) finding that Bangladeshi and Pakistani women believe that 'Asians give much more priority to their family' than the white population and a gendered *and* ethnicized moral rationality might be seen to shape the female gender identity and hence career behaviour of some BME women.

The female respondents in my study held quite varied attitudes towards parenting and work and what it means to be a good mother. The majority felt that 'times are changing' for *all* women and that their generation was not expected to sacrifice their careers for their family. Just five respondents stated that they expected to become non-working mothers – their understanding of the good mother meant full-time homemaker. These women's gender identities were strongly rooted in a view that women are morally obliged to privilege caring for their children, and that they therefore face a choice between career and family. They were clear that their children would be put before their careers:

> I think it is far more important to raise a child properly than it is to become a manager in a company. Anyone can gain a qualification, have an ambition and do that, but I think to be a successful parent is far harder and that is underestimated by a lot of people. (Female, Indian)

The idea that paid work, especially full-time, inevitably meant 'neglecting' children was a strong theme in the interviews with these women:

> I think if you have children you should not leave them with other people, even like grandparents. You should take time out and be with them. I wouldn't want them to grow up without me so I would take time out of work. (Female, Indian)

Can these views be explained by reference to race/ethnicity? These respondents tended to see their view as their own choice, rather than as a function of culture, religion or ethnicized family pressure. Many, invoking gender norms, stated that 'like most women' they simply wanted time to enjoy their children. It also seemed that some had been influenced by scaremongering stories in the media about the unreliability or even negligence of paid child carers, meaning that they saw it as an impossible choice, for example:

> I do want a career and I do want children, but I guess I'll have to balance it out. I don't really want childminders. I'm not giving my child to a nanny so she can drop it on its head and not tell me when I get home. (Female, Pakistani)

With regard to how they would provide 'appropriate' parenting, interestingly, hardly any of the women indicated that they anticipated family help with childcare despite some evidence that certain minority ethnic women tend to gain childcare support from the wider family (Bradley et al. 2005). While the vast majority of respondents expected to take a career break for childcare, about two-thirds anticipated that they would combine paid work and primary childcare responsibilities by working part-time. Overall, a number of respondents seemed to feel torn between the possibility of a fulfilling career and being a good mother. The assumption that they would be primary care-givers and therefore the ones to adapt their careers (rather than adopting a more gender symmetrical model) was typically rationalized by reference to the fact that they expected their partners to earn more. However, around two-thirds also said that they would expect their partner to take a career break at some time for childcare so that they could continue with their careers, suggesting some desire for a more symmetrical division of family responsibilities. On the other hand, some respondents, particularly Muslim women, favoured more traditional gender roles and drew on ethnicized 'cultural' values they experienced in the interactive order as the basis for their views:

> I think it's the husband's duty to provide for the family. That's my personal view, but I do think it's based on my religion. In a relationship husband and wife have certain responsibilities and the man simply can't stop work and look after the children. (Female, Bangladeshi)

> Generally men are supposed to be the sole provider, the breadwinner, so I wouldn't expect him to take time off. It's not that I don't think women can be financially independent, but it's my culture, men have to provide for the family. (Female, Malaysian)

Only seven respondents said that they expected to be full-time working mothers. There was no clear ethnic division in this small group; two were Indian and the others were of Malaysian, Black African, Chinese, Arabian, Pakistani backgrounds. They described themselves as very career-minded, for example:

> How would I do that? [Juggle full-time work and children.] God knows! I don't know, I really don't know. Get a nanny! I don't know. At the moment, the way I feel now, I'm like so career minded that I just can't imagine myself stopping. (Female, Indian)

In addition to gender and race/ethnic identities, these women also displayed a strong and active graduate identity and were concerned that their investment in their education and career would be wasted if they gave up work to look after children:

> If I have children, I would be a full-time working parent. The fact that you have worked so hard to get to where you are, I mean if you are in a senior or middle management position, you've worked so hard to get here. I would find it personally hard to let go of that. (Female, Indian)

These respondents were less accepting of the traditional gender division of domestic responsibilities, often wanting to break with the past and the influence of a domestically oriented mother. They anticipated a gendered negotiation taking place to establish the boundaries of shared responsibility for care-giving. A small number had been influenced by mothers who had had full-time careers while they were growing up and this seemed to have instilled a stronger career orientation. These women saw less tension in having a career and being a good mother, again highlighting the multiple influences in the interactive order and multiple possible individual responses:

> Well I think my mum and dad brought me up well and they worked full-time and I think I have grown up healthily and happily, so I think I can manage to do that in the future too. Because of family some [women] give up their career and I don't think that's the right thing to do, so I think women can achieve in a career and be a good parent at the same time. My mum proves it! (Female, Chinese)

It was also clear that many women did not see being a mother and homemaker as a full-time occupation. As in Dale's work on BME women (2005), they talked about work as a means to independence, not wanting to 'sit around all day' and not wanting to marry someone who would expect them to do that. However, some of the Asian women, particularly Muslims, suggested that there was a cultural expectation of marrying and having children relatively young and then prioritizing family by not working. They also said that their own parents were quite liberal and understood that 'the traditional culture' could not be 'forced' upon them, indicating the possibility of some space for re-negotiation of cultural prescriptions. The one respondent who was already a mother of a one-year-old child was a young Pakistani woman working part-time, but who had longer term career aspirations either to start her own business or to shift into a management role once her child was older.

In summary, the women's attitudes to WLB to some extent reflected findings of other research on women graduates in general. However, it was clear that active race/ethnic identities also played a role in shaping attitudes, particularly of those who described themselves as religious (usually Muslim).

WLB and the workplace

The workplace is an important component of the institutional order in which identities are constituted and evolve. Related to this, respondents were asked about the expectations that they had of their future employers in the light of the spread of WLB policies. Although they had little experience of workplace practices and no direct experience of the challenges of combining work and family, this was a topic on which they had plenty to say. Mirroring studies of women already in management positions (Liff and Ward 2001) the women anticipated that having children would have a detrimental impact on their careers. Many were already developing strategies in anticipation of this; in particular they were considering careers that they thought would offer temporal flexibility. One obvious idea that many had was to work in a profession amenable to part-time work. Some cited accountancy as one such profession:

> Basically, I am hoping to get experience, qualify as an accountant and then there is much more flexibility; you can demand the hours that you want to work. There are values that I'd like to teach my children and I don't feel that in a nursery environment they'd get that. (Female, Bangladeshi)

The available evidence indicates that the reality does not match up to this perception and the career progression and pay prospects of women in accountancy who take up flexible working are negatively affected (Smithson et al. 2004). Similarly, one respondent who planned to go into teaching explained that part of the reason was that she believed it would enable her to juggle work and childcare:

> I do want to get married in the next ten years and if I have kids then I want them to be my priority rather than my job. So I probably want to be teaching because at senior management level you've got too much pressure, you're not going to be home looking after your kids. (Female, Pakistani)

What they did not anticipate was the reality that part-time or flexible working infringes the double temporal career norm of long hours and quick upward mobility (Guillaume and Pochic 2007) meaning that it is unlikely to provide a wholly satisfactory solution to career and family balance. Other studies demonstrate that in reality part-time working represents a huge gendered compromise for highly qualified women that many of these respondents were unaware of (Fagan and O'Reilly 1998; Liff and Ward 2001; Smithson et al. 2004). Nevertheless, they believed that part-time work provided the solution to the problem of achieving 'appropriate' parenting and being a good mother.

Most women accepted the 'double burden' of paid and unpaid work and talked about it being a 'reality' that (all) women would find themselves having to step off the career ladder at some point, at least temporarily while children were young. They typically considered this a reality that transcended ethnic and cultural divisions:

> I'd say it is a reality for all women – not just Asian women, but other women as well – because everyone is saying now that women that work, that kids who don't really know their mothers, that it's bad. I mean this affects the white community, the black community, it's not about being Asian; it's about being a woman. (Female, Pakistani)

Therefore it was important to be working in a family-friendly organization that would be accommodating. Whatever sector and field they were aspiring to enter, the majority of women wanted to work for an employer with WLB policies in order to minimize the barriers they anticipated:

> Women face a lot of barriers, especially women with children, so I would want to work in an organization that really emphasizes the whole WLB issue; you know, an understanding employer that would not expect you to choose between work and your children, but family-friendly ones are in the minority. (Female, Indian)

The males were also keen on organizations with WLB policies that they saw as helping them to live out their male gender identity. Their perception was that WLB policies made it easier to take time off for family events such as weddings and funerals and for emergencies, like family illnesses all of which might involve travelling abroad. The Muslim males also felt that an organization with active WLB policies would be more likely to accommodate religious obligations such as prayer, festivals and holidays, pilgrimages, etc. Only one of the male respondents related the family-friendly employer concept to his future children and his ability to be a good father: 'Ideally I want my Mrs to stay at home, just like mum. But, if she feels the need to work, then I would like to be in a company that could offer [nursery] facilities' (Male, Bangladeshi).

In summary, there were gendered differences among respondents even at this early stage in their careers. The women were expressing concerns about whether it was possible to combine management and (to a lesser extent) professional jobs with family life. The men also expressed some concerns, but they focused more on the *quality* of family life, rather than on the day-to-day practicalities about childcare, school hours and holidays, etc. However, the men typically regarded themselves as having a duty of care towards elders, parents and grandparents, with some talking about envisaging a time when they would be involved in their day-to-day care arrangements. As stated, they also expressed concern about getting time off to travel abroad for family events such as weddings and funerals. Thus, the male perspective does indicate that workplace WLB policies are attractive to both sexes, but for different gendered reasons that also contain ethnicized dimensions.

Conclusion:
Evolving contexts, evolving identities?

This chapter has attempted to move race/ethnicity from the margins of the WLB debate to the centre. The above outline of the extant literature and discussion of the study's findings indicate that the social and workplace contexts in which people seek to achieve WLB are evolving; so too are the gender and ethnic identities that guide people in their WLB decisions in the face of these contexts. In other words, it is clear from the findings that race/ethnic and gender identities are formed, as Jenkins (2004) suggests, in the individual, interactive and institutional orders. In terms of the social and workplace contexts, there is a greater acceptance of women's desire to combine work and family life, together with evolving conceptions of the good father and mother. The point to emphasize is that minority ethnic communities are just as susceptible to changing social beliefs and values as white people. In other words, race/ethnic identities are dynamic, particularly across generations.

Reflecting Bradley's (1996) multi-faceted concept of identity, the chapter has shown that gender, ethnic and *graduate* identities intersect to form the basis for attitudes to WLB. In terms of the influence of graduate identity, the young BME respondents revealed some similar attitudes and expectations to their white counterparts (as reported in other studies outlined earlier; e.g. Sturges and Guest 2004). However, WLB attitudes and expectations were also related to their ethnic, cultural and religious identities. Thus, they revealed an active graduate identity: they had invested heavily in their education; they were ambitious and looking forward to career success and this emergent graduate identity was a basis for their attitudes to WLB. Active gender identities came into the picture insofar as most of the female respondents anticipated that their future employment decisions would be made with reference to family responsibilities. Deeply gendered moral requirements to take responsibility for children's needs were expressed by some of the women reflecting arguments in studies that have included both white and BME women (Duncan et al. 2003; Dale et al. 2002). Many women actively wanted to play a significant role in bringing up their children and they felt that full-time work within the prevalent long hours' gender regime would preclude this. Nevertheless, as in Dale's (2005) study most of these BME graduate women were highly committed to their careers at the same time as being committed to a future role as a mother; as graduates they saw their careers as an important aspect of their identity. Interestingly though, the Bangladeshi and Pakistani women in the study were seemingly from less traditional family backgrounds than many of the less well educated young women in Dale's (2005) study. There were no examples of women who would not be 'allowed' to work by their families or who had to argue for the 'right' to work. On the contrary, they had been encouraged by their parents to get a university education and to pursue a career. Thus, it is evident that cultural and ethnic identities are class sensitive and no more fixed than are gender ones. Reflecting previous research (Guillaume and Pochic 2007), some of the female respondents who envisaged sustaining their full-time careers through the family formation stage of their lives valued egalitarian household arrangements, where they would share domestic and family tasks with their partners. Again, this challenges the stereotype of certain BME women as passive and submissive within the family (Rana et al. 2007) and indicates the evolving nature of ethnic identities as a basis for choice and action.

The chapter's analysis of WLB at the intersection of ethnicity and gender has also allowed us to consider what a healthy WLB might be in terms of a broader range of social activities and relationships beyond childcare, something that is rarely considered (Bradley et al. 2005). This study highlighted that although most of the men espoused a gendered breadwinner identity, some young BME men see family life (beyond the nuclear family) and religious obligations as central to their lives and have the hope and expectation that work will be accommodating. A critical mass of male role models working flexibly has been heralded as a particularly effective way of challenging assumptions about gender norms and of providing legitimacy to WLB policies. Perhaps BME men will lead the way in this respect with a possibly stronger family orientation in terms of obligations towards family, care and kinship?

Acknowledgements

This research was funded by a grant from the Nuffield Foundation. All the respondents are thanked for their participation. Thanks also to Azzah Abubacker, Lynsie Chew, Cristina Covelo, Resham Mirza and Noareen Raja for conducting the interviews and focus groups.

Note

1. The ethnic categories are those used by the Office for National Statistics. Respondents were asked to self-identify. The Commission for Racial Equality points out that some groups/individuals might feel that none of these categories accurately describes their ethnicity (www.cre.gov.uk/diversity/ethnicity). Reflecting this criticism, some respondents are placed in the 'other BME' category because they self-identified as, for example, Iranian, Malaysian, Arabian.

References

Bhavnani, R. (2006) 'Ahead of the game: the changing aspirations of young ethnic minority women', *Moving on up? Ethnic minority women and work*. Manchester: Equal Opportunities Commission.

Bradley, H., G. Healy, et al. (2005) 'Multiple burdens: problems of work-life balance for ethnic minority trade union activist women', In D. Houston (ed.), *Work-Life Balance in the 21st Century*. Basingstoke: Palgrave Macmillan, pp. 211–29.

Brah, A., M. Hickman, et al. (1999) 'Thinking identities: ethnicity, racism and culture', In A. Brah, M. Hickman and M. Ghaill (ed.), *Thinking identities: ethnicity, racism and culture*. Basingstoke: Macmillan.

Bruegel, I. and A. Gray (2005) 'Men's conditions of employment and the division of childcare between parents', In D. Houston (ed.), *Work-Life Balance in the 21st Century*. Basingstoke: Palgrave Macmillan, pp. 147–69.

Connor, H., C. Tyers, et al. (2004) *Minority ethnic students in higher education: interim report*. London: Department for Education and Skills.

Cousins, C. R. and N. Tang (2004) 'Working time and work and family conflict in the Netherlands, Sweden and the UK', *Work, Employment and Society*, 18(3): 531–49.

Dale, A. (2005) 'Combining family and employment: evidence from Pakistani and Bangladeshi women', In D. Houston (ed.), *Work-Life Balance in the 21st Century*. Basingstoke: Palgrave Macmillan, pp. 230–45.

Dale, A., N. Shaheen, et al. (2002) 'The labour market prospects for Pakistani and Bangladeshi women', *Work, Employment and Society*, 16(1): 5–25.

Duncan, S., R. Edwards, et al. (2003) 'Motherhood, paid work and partnering: values and theories', *Work, Employment and Society*, 17(2): 309–30.

Fagan, C. and J. O'Reilly (1998) 'Conceptualising part-time work: the value of an integrated comparative perspective', In J. O'Reilly and C. Fagan (eds), *Part-time prospects: an international comparison of part-time work in Europe, North America and the Pacific Rim*. London: Routledge.

Guillaume, C. and S. Pochic (2007) 'What would you sacrifice? Access to top management and the work-life balance', *Gender, Work and Organization*, 1–23.

——(2005) 'Sex differences in work-life balance goals', In D. Houston (ed.), *Work-Life Balance in the 21st Century*. Basingstoke: Palgrave Macmillan, pp. 55–79.

Hardill, I. and R. Watson (2004) 'Career priorities within dual career households: an analysis of the impact of child rearing upon gender participation rates and earnings', *Industrial Relations Journal*, 35(1): 19–37.

Hite, L. (2007) 'Hispanic women managers and professionals: reflections on life and work', *Gender, Work and Organization*, 14(1): 20–36.

Jenkins, R. (2004) *Social identity*. Abingdon: Routledge.

Kersley, B., C. Alpin, et al. (2004) *Inside the workplace: first findings from the 2004 workplace employee relations survey*. London: DTI.

Liff, S. and K. Ward (2001) 'Distorted views through the glass ceiling: the construction of women's understandings of promotion and senior management positions', *Gender, Work and Organization*, 8(1): 19–36.

ONS (2000) http://www.statistics.gov.uk/StatBase/ssdataset.asp?vlnk=6372&Pos=2&ColRank=2&Rank=272 retrieved 16 June 2008.

Pitcher, J. and K. Purcell (1998) 'Diverse expectations and access to opportunities: is there a graduate labour market?', *Higher Education Quarterly*, 52(2): 179–203.

Purcell, K. (2002) *Qualifications and careers: equal opportunities and earnings among graduates*. Manchester: Equal Opportunities Commission.

Ramji, H. (2007) 'Dynamics of religion and gender amongst young British Muslims', *Sociology*, 41(6): 1171–89.

Rana, B., P. Chandra, et al. (2007) *Balance in a Box*. Birmingham: Birmingham City University.

Smithson, J., S. Lewis, et al. (2004) 'Flexible working and the gender pay gap in the accountancy profession', *Work, Employment and Society*, 18(1): 115–35.

Sturges, J. and D. Guest (2004) 'Working to live or living to work? Work/life balance early in the career', *Human Resource Management Journal*,14(4): 5–20.

Windebank, J. (2001) 'Dual-earner couples in Britain and France: gender divisions of domestic labour and parenting work in different welfare states', *Work, Employment and Society*, 15(2): 269–90.

Wood, G. and J. Newton (2006) 'Childlessness and women managers: 'choice', context and discourses', *Gender, Work and Organization*, 13(4): 338–58.

16

What shapes the careers of young black and minority ethnic people?

Geraldine Healy and Harriet Bradley

Introduction

The role of young people in the labour market has been a matter of international concern long before the onset of the recent recession. According to the European Commission, unemployment among young people is more than double the overall unemployment rate in Europe, while young people as a group are particularly at risk of poverty. This is the more troubling since, as the Commission acknowledged,

> young people will be vital in ensuring that the Lisbon goals of more growth and jobs can be met – as the future work force, and the future source of the research capabilities, innovation and entrepreneurship that Europe needs to succeed. However, these goals can only be met if young people are equipped with knowledge, skills and competences through high quality, relevant education and training, and if barriers such as growing up in poverty and social exclusion are removed. (European Commission 2005)

In March 2005, European Heads of State and Government adopted the European Youth Pact with the clear aim of improving the education, training, mobility, vocational integration and social inclusion of young Europeans, while facilitating the reconciliation of family life and working life. At the same time, it is evident that equal opportunities and anti-racism are key pillars of European policy, yet racism and lack of equality of opportunities characterize European labour markets. Moreover, the financial crisis of 2008–09 has had a disproportionately negative effect on the opportunities of young people (ESRC 2009; Local Government Association 2009). This chapter brings together these related concerns by exploring black and minority ethnic (BME) young people's career opportunities.

Newburn and Shiner (2005) remind us that transitions towards employment have been extended in recent decades, as has the period of youthful semi-dependence on adults. While many young people manage successfully to navigate this increasingly complicated transition, others experience significant difficulties along the way. Thus transitions are typically fragmented, interrupted and involve movement between a variety of employment statuses (unpaid, part-time and full-time employment, unemployment, education, training) (Bradley and Van Hoof 2005; Jones 2002). These transitions are more unstable for young people from more disadvantaged backgrounds (Furlong and Cartmel 1997; Roberts 1995). Successful navigation of these transitions will to some extent be shaped by the positive and negative influences on young people.

Young people generally aspire to achieve and researchers suggest that there is little difference in aspiration between young men and women (Tinklin et al. 2005). Minority ethnic young people are more likely to enter higher education, have higher aspirations than white young people and are a heterogeneous body (Connor et al. 2004, with some ethnic groups faring better than others (Heath and Cheung, 2006)). However, on completion of their higher or further education they are still less likely to find employment (Strategy Unit 2003) or they may end up in jobs for which they are over-qualified (Battu and Sloane 2004). Moreover, family is a recurrent theme in influencing career choices (Cregan 1999). Dale et al. (2002) highlight the role of the family and how it may affect the career choices of young men and women from Pakistani and Bangladeshi communities. Young women were more likely than young men (and presumably young white people) to place high consideration on how their career choices and decisions to opt higher education would affect their families. Kirton's study of graduates demonstrates that career plans and aspirations, while not simply reflective of or determined by race/ethnicity, are formulated in the light of self-concepts of ethnicity that interact dialectically with awareness of a racialized, discriminatory labour market (2009: 12).

We begin the chapter by considering the individual enablements in young people's lives; we then reflect on their approaches to labour markets and their attitudes concerning how they are perceived by potential employers as young black and minority people, and finally we reflect on the heterogeneity of the young people in our study. But first, we provide insight into the nature of study conducted.

The study

The chapter draws on an ESF research project on young BME people's entry to the labour market (see Healy et al. 2006). We used a range of methods including: semi-structured interviews, focus groups and a small survey of attendees at a diversity career fair. Some 109 BME young people (between 18 and 30) took part in the qualitative part of the study. Seventy-three young people were interviewed in London, Bristol and Birmingham. The majority were British by nationality but had diverse ethnic origins, including Indian, black Caribbean, African, Bangladeshi and Pakistani. The sample included undergraduates from two pre-1992 universities, as well as those working in or aspiring to work in finance, media, retail, IT, public sector, and transport, along with some who were unemployed. The ratio of men to women was four to five.

In addition five focus groups were held, which involved a total of 36 young people, including students and unemployed. Most were British but again their ethnic origins were diverse: Bangladeshis, Pakistanis, black Caribbean, black African, black British, mixed (white and black African, black Caribbean; black Caribbean and African), Algerian, Albanian/Kosovan, Chinese. These were accessed via two agencies and personal contacts. We also interviewed 15 key gatekeepers and significant actors including people working in agencies and organizations dedicated to working with young black people. We sought to capture a variability of experience in our research subjects by interviewing those who arguably might be most protected from racism with their accumulation of human capital and others who on this count were more vulnerable.

The findings

Key influences

While young people often ascribed success or failure to hard work and the achievements of individuals, in their narratives they freely acknowledged the help and inspirations they had received from 'significant others' in their lives. In line with other studies (Cregan 1999; Dale et al. 2002; Loughlin and Barling 2001), we found that parents were key influences on the young people's choices. The nature of parental support varies according to the resources available to them in terms of cultural and social as well as economic capitals (See Alasai and Tatli in this volume for a full discussion on capitals). In the following comment, the cultural value that parents placed on education was clear, but in this case it was backed up by economic resources to enable the young person to build up her cultural capital: 'Well, if I was to start from home, definitely my parents. They always encouraged me, supported me, I had tuition on a regular basis for Maths just to boost me a little and things like that. They were helpful (Nida).'

Parents' influence was often in the form of young people aspiring to be like them or even aspiring not to be like them. Thus, Paulette had the total support of her parents who constantly pointed out that without education, her future would be one of hard work with few choices:

I think it's mostly the sort of whole, I don't want you to study late, I want you to get all your studies out of the way so that you have as many options as possible. I don't want you to have to go back to school late. My Mum is basically making sure that you don't end up having to do the sort of jobs that she does. (Paulette)

Like Paulette, other young people reported the difficulties their parents had in their working lives and were determined to 'break the cycle' and not end up doing the same thing. For example,

I think because they had such a rough time when they first came here and obviously through the rest of their life, very poorly paid, hardworking labour, full days, 12 hours, 14 hours a day. I think it was that which really affected them and that's why they fight so hard particularly my mother to get us better lives for ourselves. (Ali)

Thus, even where there was no history of higher education, family members were key in encouraging their young people to attend university and 'better themselves' through education. This is a common migrant perspective where children are encouraged to perform well in education to avoid the working experiences of their parents. For many such families, education is seen as *the* key resource that gives choice and economic capital and thereby security. For other more privileged families, educational achievement is also about retaining the status gained by the parents. Thus, cultural and social identity even with respect to degree choices comes into play (Reay et al. 2001), with children of professional parents more likely to make choices that would lead to professional work. In such cases, parents were important role models; for example, among our group we noted the sons and daughters of doctors becoming doctors.

I have to say that my parents did want me to become a doctor when I was younger. But obviously when I was doing my A-levels, they said that I should do what I want, what I think, what I am interested in. But I had already, how do I put it, I had already warmed up to the idea of doing medicine as I grew up so that was my most obvious choice. (Akram)

In this case, families are able to pass on the social capital that will enable young people to understand the nature of the job, the challenges and the rewards, while less-privileged families hope that education will give cultural capital and social capital as well as economic capital.

Aspiration to the professions was often strongly associated with an Asian or African background. Indeed it has become so firmly accepted as part of tradition that it is now the material of jokes. The actor and comedian, Sanjeev Bhaskar, was awarded an honorary doctorate from his *alma mater*, the University of Hertfordshire. When giving his acceptance speech, he turned to his parents who were in the audience and said 'now mum and dad, you finally have your doctor!' The audience fell about laughing. This humour mixed with very real parental aspiration, was evident in our study. This emerged when we asked respondents why they chose to go to university and study medicine or law?

That's a hard one, especially when you are Asian! [laughs] I have always wanted to be a doctor since I was young. I have to say part of the reason is that my Dad is a doctor. (Akram)

Q. Why did you choose to do Law when I guess your passion was English?

A. Again my Nigerian background.

Q. You had to be a lawyer, a doctor or an accountant.

A. Exactly. Very strong influence. You do a profession not a career, I mean not a subject. So that was the driving force behind it.... (Nkomi)

Thus, the cultural capital sought through the acquisition of professional status for their children, was to contribute to the status of the family within their particular ethnic community. This was a separate and important objective linked to the desire for their children to have successful professional careers.

Parents' influence might take different and gendered forms. We noted the belief that childcare might be seen as a good career for a Muslim woman. This was accepted by young Muslim women as a possible influence, but for those we interviewed, it was not necessarily the case. 'Not personally, I didn't do that but I do, I know a lot of Asian girls go into that because their families like them to do that (Naz).'

We noted that while gendered differences in relation to ethnicity influenced career choice, this changes over time. Caribbean women have made an important contribution to the nursing profession. However, our research indicates that Caribbean women are no longer encouraging their daughters to follow their path into nursing (Bradley et al. 2007). Moreover, while Pakistani and Bangladeshi women are encouraged to become teaching assistants, they are less likely to want to become nurses.

Interviewees also stated that there were other key people who provided encouragement and support throughout their educational careers. In addition to her parents, Nida reported other influences:

My friends as well, you know when you have, sometimes you have that kind of competition within your friends, it's like a friendly competition it kind of pushes you and wants you to work a bit more. Well, that's them. And the teachers as well with them being helpful and everything. (Nida)

The discourse around peer groups is often about their negative influences. Our study did note the potential negative influence of peer groups, yet we also found that peer groups can be important enabling influences. Nida's comment is important since positive peer group pressure is less frequently acknowledged in the discussions on young people. In our survey of attendees at ACDiversity Graduate Fair, respondents were asked which individuals had positive, negative or no influence on the career choices (see Williams and Healy 2005). The results may be found in Table 16.1.

The positive influence of peer group was important for 80 per cent of career fair respondents. This is a highly educated sample with 83 per cent educated to degree level or above. Thus we do not claim that these results would be representative of the experiences of BME young people generally. But it is illuminating that *positive* peer influence was seen as marginally greater by this particular sample of young adults than was the influence of the mother and the father.

Table 16.1 Who were the key influences in your life?

Individual	N =	Positive	Negative	Neither
		Influence (%)		
Friends/peers	96	80.2	1.0	18.8
Mother	94	77.1	9.6	12.8
Father	86	74.4	9.3	16.3
Other family members	64	67.2	4.1	28.1
Careers advisors	70	57.1	15.7	27.2
Tutors/teachers	75	68.0	14.7	17.3
Colleagues	62	58.1	14.5	27.4
Others	9	88.3		11.1

Source: Williams and Healy (2005)

The distinction between different types of peer groups is important and commentators need caution in treating peer groups as mainly negative influences. Nevertheless, it was clear that the young people we observed at ACDiversity mentoring events,[1] realized that sometimes difficult peer group choices were necessary. A number of these young people were strategizing on how they could achieve their potential and still remain 'cool'; others shifted their friendship groups in order to achieve their aspirations. Bradley (2007: 26–7) argues that If you want to succeed at school you may need to keep clear of the 'cool' groups of kids and throw in your lot with the 'nerds', a move that needs a certain amount of nerve and will power.

We also found that teachers played a key role in influencing young people. This was often in terms of encouraging the young person to pursue a particular career or inspiring them in a subject and motivating them to continue that subject further. Those that stood out in the interviewees' minds did so because of the way they taught and engaged the class, or because they went out of their way to help and encourage their students:

> Q. So at university who was your most significant influence?
> A. I had one really good tutor. He was really good because he saw I was really keen and had an interest in particular areas of psychology and computing and stuff and he would let me, he would get me access to the computer labs outside hours, give me the password. ... me and another chap, a friend of mine, we used to go in and play around with the computers. So have various experiments, set up various little websites and things like that. (Ben)

Ben shows how a university tutor's actions may have a lasting positive effect (Ben went on to become a web producer). More frequently where interviewees mentioned an influential teacher/tutor they were from secondary school. A number of our interviewees recorded the importance of a particular teacher as an enabling and motivating factor in their lives. One example comes from Sybilla:

> I had a Business Studies teacher who was great and she really inspired me to think, hang on, if you don't buck your ideas up you are going to end up working in a shop somewhere. And I really got engaged with Business Studies, really enjoyed it and found it was something that, you know, I knew I could do well at so then I just progressed. Had it not been for her, I don't know what I would have ended up doing. Which is interesting. (Sybilla)

It was also the case that teachers were blamed for blocking opportunities and not recognizing an individual's potential. Career advisers were particularly castigated. One childcare worker had been steered from law in her careers interview and ended up depressed and wanting to get out of childcare into something which would stretch her talents. Another young woman had been furious at being told to go and apply for factory work: she was now running her own media company! We also noted examples where young BME people felt that they had been unduly harshly treated. In one case, this led to a young woman being unable to complete her honours degree leading to additional years of study and a more difficult early career pathway. Years later, the harshness of the decision was accepted, and the honours' year was offered. By then it was too late.

Significant others are very important in all young people's lives. Families are important but also schools and social networks play their part. Quite often, however, the help of families and schools was insufficient in terms of providing young BME people with information about the range of opportunities on offer; the strategies they would need to achieve a chosen goal, and how to beat off fierce competition at interview and application. Here individual influences may be supplemented by collective actors who can work to enable and empower young people in their path to getting a job.

Getting a job

Getting a job is a lengthy and subtle process that begins during school years as some doors are closed and others opened. Children are told to work hard at school so that they will have a choice of work before them. Open doors are often highly dependent on qualifications. However, in line with Kirton's (2009) study, qualifications are important, but they are not the whole story.

Young people need access to a set of social and cultural capitals that will allow them to access opportunities. Such social and cultural capitals together construct a highly persuasive attribute and enable them to navigate the increasingly complicated course outlined by Newburn and Shiner (2005). Such social and cultural capitals around getting work relate to both tangible and intangible resources. Our gatekeepers reported that the following were critical elements of the job search process:

- the ability to produce a CV that brings out the person's competences
- the ability to identify the dress code for the occupation

- good preparation for the interview including knowledge about the organization
- ability to write and speak good standard English in an appropriate style and syntax
- ability to present well at interview
- ability to communicate attributes to interviewers
- ability to back up claims with evidence
- 'who you know' and networking
- self belief
- resilience in the face of rejection

This list is significantly loaded with what are increasingly called 'soft skills'. Moss and Tilly (2001) argue that the rising demand for 'soft skills' such as communication and people skills, opens the door to discrimination that is rarely overt or even conscious, but is nonetheless damaging to the prospects of minority candidates, and particularly difficult to police. Many of our interviewees sought help in drawing up CVs and advice on job hunting. Some non-graduates acknowledged the help they received from agencies in getting advice and guidance on presenting their skills more effectively. Indeed, some claimed they would not have got their jobs were it not for the agencies, given the failure of previous applications and interviews.

Our interviewees were aware that CVs, while a necessary first step, were not sufficient to get them the job. They recognized the critical role of the interview (a demonstration of 'soft skills') and the preparation for the interview.

> I face difficulties all the time. You know, some people, you could be just have made your CV for two years and still not get an offer. So that's really the most difficult bit. But when you actually get in there, it's all down to you really. Because when you think about it, you have to dress well and you have to understand in most interviews that it's all about the presentation. Maybe sixty to seventy per cent because a lot of jobs like managers that have said that they look at your (self) presentation as soon as you get into the room. (Owen)

There are different norms and cultures in different industries. While it is the case that recruitment and selection is becoming increasingly formalized, this will vary according to sector. For the young BME people we interviewed in the media industry, people accessed work by, as it were, cracking the industry's unwritten codes of entry. This industry is characterized by a glamorous image, highly competitive labour markets, once strong unions and short fixed term contracts. These factors have led to efforts to control the recruitment process through the provision of various resources. Such resources include 'the Knowledge', which lists all the studios and the facilities in the audio-visual industry throughout the world, thus potentially enabling access to the key gatekeepers. However, while this might inform, it is not sufficient. More important and influential characteristics of this industry are, 'who you know' and networking.

Some of the graduates we interviewed were focused on the job search process and highly strategic:

> I have tried to boost my CV where I can and try and do things like the work experience, just the benefits. I try and get involved; I volunteered for like about two years in a [charity] bookshop). I did enjoy it but I was also conscious that it's an extra-curricular activity. And then I tried to take leading roles in things as well just to show that I have, you know, managerial (potential) and I can be independent, I don't mind being given responsibility. (Elena)

But even this highly motivated, well-prepared young woman aiming for a career in law was surprised when she attended a careers event for potential lawyers at her university. She saw this as a means to gain further information, while many of her peers treated this as a networking event and dressed accordingly:

> I came in quite relaxed just wanting some information, but for lots of others it was like a job interview; very smart suits and girls were in their suits as well, looking really keen and talking to the right people. So I think, I wasn't quite like that.... I didn't think that everyone would take it quite so intently at that stage. So I get the impression that people are quite, you know, ambitious. (Elena)

One of the important personal qualities that getting work required of many of our interviewees was perseverance. In the competitive world of law, getting a training contract is very important. This will ensure that your fees are paid for your legal training and you will receive a salary. Elena had invested enormous amount of time to ensure that she got such a contract: 'So it was quite intense, I applied to I think about forty, and out of forty, I think, six interviews so I think that's kind of a difficult thing to get so it's a very, very nerve-wrecking period (Elena).'

To succeed it was necessary to invest the time, persevere and not be knocked back by rejections. It can be very difficult not to take rejections very personally. What we noticed about our successful young people were important qualities of resilience and the ability to 'hang on in there' and by implication, that elusive quality, 'self belief'. Without these qualities, it is easy to become discouraged by initial failures and slide into 'poor work' or long-term unemployment.

Ways of navigating a competitive labour market include internships and agencies and it is to these that we now turn.

Internships are a growing recruitment strategy by employers in the UK and elsewhere. This is a work period giving the intern insight into the nature of the industry, the work and overcome the 'catch 22' of no experience, no job, no job, no experience. While not a new phenomenon, the formalizing and institutionalization of the internship is a relatively recent but increasingly important feature of the youth labour market. A recent survey of graduates found that 34 per cent of undergraduates had completed a work placement or internships (Tysome 2006). Milburn states that internships are now a key route to the professions (2009: 47). The internship allows the employer to get to know the person and may act as an extended recruitment process. It may be unpaid as illustrated by Marianne: 'I worked as an intern for different studios: then, I tried to intern different places for unpaid work basically to try to get my feet within the industry (Marianne).'

The growth in use of the unpaid internship by organizations has led to an acceptance by many young people that this is now part of the process of entering the world of work. We see this as a worrying and highly discriminatory practice. It works on the assumption that the young person can afford to work for nothing. This puts young people who do not come from privileged backgrounds, many of whom are BME, at a severe disadvantage. However, this is not necessarily the norm. The following interviewee did some unpaid legal work, but was also fortunate in getting a paid period of work experience, which was no doubt influential in enabling her to get her training contract.

> There was one week, two weeks with barristers or in a law firm or somewhere in a law firm so I have kind of done quite a lot of work experience…it depends on the size of the firm because the smaller ones don't tend to pay. So I did one small, well, kind of medium-sized commercial law firm and they didn't offer you any pay. And when you do pupillages with barristers in barrister chambers, they don't pay you either. So I did a couple of those. But the firm I got my training contract with, they are like bigger so they, I got paid, I think it was £200 a week for two weeks there so that was good. (Elena)

Despite the fact that it may be unpaid, getting an internship may still be a competitive process; equally, social networks gained may be important career enablements. Some internships may be arranged on a grace and favour basis, that is through links with parents or other social contacts. Those who can afford to take an unpaid internship recognize that the investment of time spent in an internship may deliver longer term career benefits. Such social links are less likely to be available to young BME people as well as white working-class young people, therefore they are least able to access social and cultural capital associated with the internship.

However, if you are not British, you may have further problems in getting an internship as the following interviewee discovered:

> I spoke to someone at BT and earlier the internships were open to everyone but now they have changed it and even to be able to apply for the summer internship you have to have the right to work in the UK permanently. Because I can understand the logic because they say that they use their summer intern programme as the feed to the graduate programme. (Sunita)

Young people who attend elite universities are also at an advantage in getting internships. Miranda, a working-class Oxbridge graduate, was aware of her chances and took advantage of them. Her internships were with top organizations and were paid:

> When I got to uni I did lots of internships, they were really well paid and there are loads of offers for ethnic minorities. I did one in the civil service, the fast-track one. One with

the Metropolitan Police … Places like Oxford, it opens so many doors. . We had Goldman Sachs for a sponsor, Civil service for a sponsor. You know we were the Holy Grail really, ethnic minorities as interns. They wanted us so bad. And we were like 'Hey, you want to throw money at me and give me like really good work experience. I am so there.' (Miranda)

Miranda's story reflects the interests of employers to build up a more diverse workforce but it also suggests that employers are targeting what they perceive as the brightest and the best, the 'holy grail' of ethnic minority young people. Nevertheless, Miranda provides good evidence of the forward-thinking approach to paid internships. The practice of paying interns would seem crucial to an organization seeking to be a fair employer.

Internships in the context of the professions have recently been highlighted as one of the closed doors faced by people from middle-income as well as low-income families in the Milburn report on fair access to the professions. (Milburn 2009). The Report states that 'It's not true that many young people do not have aspirations, it is that they are blocked' (2009: 6). The Report recommends an internship code which will provide a fair and transparent system for advertising and recruiting to internships (2009: 47). The Report is important in highlighting inequities based on social mobility and differential access to internships. Its insights are however limited as issues of gender and race equality were excluded from the analysis. The idea of the proposed internship code has potential value. Sadly, given the level of adherence to existing equality legislation, this is unlikely, particularly given the voluntary status of the proposed code.

The agency route

Agencies were a major route used to solve that impossible paradox: young people have difficulty getting a job because they have no experience, but they cannot get experience because they cannot get a job.

When I qualified, teachers were saying, you know, you should get a position soon and blablabla. And you know, they will say that but once you qualify they won't help you, they left you alone. There wasn't much advice, like you know, obviously look in papers … – but it took me a long time before someone said best to go for agency work … someone will find you [work] and then, you will be permanent. (Naz, childcare worker)

This view was echoed by another childcare worker:

If wasn't for the agency staff there, and that I had to turn up for the job out of the blue, I don't think I would have got it to be honest. Because recently I have been to interviews and I don't seem to get anywhere with them. They will send me a nice letter to say 'You did really well but …' (Selma)

Despite these acknowledged successes, it is also the case that some young black workers are sceptical and critical about the agency role. There was a view that the time they invested in attending the agency was not born out in the benefits gained. It was recognized that their CVs had improved, but they felt the time spent to achieve this was disproportionate. One young person noted that he had been on the agency books for two years, but still had no work, whereas he commented that others had joined more recently and soon were employed. The motives of the agency also came into question in relation to referrals from Job Centres, since it was known that they received payments for them. This no doubt filtered into the trust relations that these young people felt they had with the agency.

We are reminded of Article 6 of the EU Directive on Agencies which specifies that 'every effort must be made to improve temporary workers' training, both in the temporary agency and in the user undertaking'. We noted positive perceptions on the work of organizations but also scepticism by our young people. As Gray (2002) states, Article 6 holds considerable promise, but only if implemented effectively. We observed painstaking work by some agency advisers with young people to improve their chances in the labour market. Some of this work has been the result of the New Labour's New Deal initiatives. However, other work sinks or swims according to the changing priorities of the policy-makers and large corporations. One major problem is that there is little continuity in the funding and maintenance of schemes targeted at BME youth. This was a major concern expressed by those organizations explicitly set up to provide opportunities for young BME people.

Do young BME people think that they are discriminated against?

An important aspect of the selection process is whether a young black person's application is treated on the same terms as a young white person's application. Many of the young people we interviewed tended to underplay the possibilities of discrimination. This is entirely understandable given that no-one wants to believe that their opportunities are constrained before they start. Some reported that they had been warned by careers advisers that things could be harder for them because they were black, although they were careful to point out that this was not part of their current experience, whereas others were not so sure. Sadly, this doubt is confirmed by many of the statistics. For example, Berthoud (2000) found systematic disadvantages by ethnic group with young Caribbean men faring worst. Most perturbing is his finding that 'there is no hint that employment disadvantage observed among young Caribbean men is a temporary phenomenon which will disappear with the passage of time' (ibid.: 80). Similarly Caribbean, Pakistani and Bangladeshi women are the most disadvantaged in the labour market (Bradley and Healy 2008; EOC 2007).

Young people often express a 'matter-of-fact' approach to dealing with discrimination. There was a recognition that some occupations might be more difficult to get into than others. Parental influence may be important in this respect. Parents might advise on what they saw as a safer route seeking to protect their children from any adverse effects of possible discrimination:

> I think they (her parents) were a bit concerned about me doing law because they'd heard how competitive it was and I think being a black female they were a bit worried about, just even generally because it's quite difficult to get a university place and then from then on getting a job. So they were quite concerned. I think they did probably want me to do like something safer in their mind like medicine. (Elena)

Our focus group participants, most of whom came from more disadvantaged backgrounds, etched a more mixed picture. Some felt that things were not as bad as they were often portrayed and believed that people who worked hard would get on. The importance of education and self-improvement was stressed by most. This is a common belief of first-generation migrants, and clearly transferred through the generations. In many ways, these were the hard-workers; they believed that hard work and qualifications would see them through.

However, others believed that it was harder to get work if you were black and some had already experienced unpleasant examples of discrimination or racism, feeling that employers considered the differences in colour to be an indicator of difference in ability to do the work or to 'fit in'. This notion of 'fit' is potentially discriminatory and is expressed by a focus group member as 'they see you as something else', as an outsider or worse as a danger. The following two young men sum this up:

> They see an Asian guy or a black guy coming for an interview, they automatically think that the guy is on the street or anything like that. (Jake)

> Well, it's been difficult sometimes, you know, because most of the companies don't like if you are black because they think if you are black you are criminals or something. (Samuel)

The stereotypes around criminality are more often associated with young black men and stereotypes of terrorists with young Asian men and women. Different stereotypes may also be evident with young women as Miranda experienced.

> I said I wanted to be an editor and they said 'oh you are a bit bubbly for editorial.' You are thinking an editor, that's a person who interacts with all the different departments in the publishing house and with the author, you'd think bubbly was an alright trait... You don't want to get to the point where you are paranoid, but there is always this assumption that black people have a big personality. (Miranda)

It is evident from this and other studies that personality attributes may be perceived and evaluated differently and negatively according to ethnicity and gender (Bradley and Healy 2008; Bradley et al. 2007). Indeed negative evaluations by interviewers take different forms according to stereotypes based on ethnicity, as Miranda indicates, and this was also reported to us by young women who wear a hijab. Thus many young BME people enter the recruitment process expecting to be discriminated against. The impact of such a belief on their ability to shine at interview will of course be variable. Some with strong self-belief may take the view that 'they will show them'; others may find it difficult to demonstrate their full abilities in what they perceive to a negative context. As a result they are more likely to become discouraged.

Some young people expressed a strong suspicion that BME applicants may be screened out in the 'sifting' phase before interview. For example, after many rejections, Ali and his friend decided to test whether he was being discriminated against because of his name, by using identical applications and using an 'English' name:

> And then we tried this experiment, it's me and a friend from Birmingham. And we sent one with a different name on it, we put Lee Smith on the letter as opposed to my name and we got a response from that place and that was exactly a place that I had written to before from which I didn't get a response. And that in public relations, you would have thought that in public relations you wouldn't get anything like that but it does happen sometimes. (Ali)

Ali, of course, was replicating a long-standing social science research technique of matched letters (e.g. Esmail 2004; Noon 1993), which, like Ali's experiment, has persistently revealed bias against obviously non-white names.

Other young people expected that they would be discriminated against but were optimistic in their belief that the law would prevent this. They considered that employers must behave fairly to comply with the law. Their view was that it was easier to get in, than to get on. This is interesting in the context of studies that report that organizations play lip-service to the law (see Chapter 1). It is nevertheless important, since those who hold this view are more likely to consider taking organizations to task if they perceive that they have been victims of discriminatory behaviour. Raf and Jake had strong views based on their negative experiences:

> Then the true colours come out because obviously a company, every company going now, they got to stick to the equal opportunity policy, otherwise they get a kick up the bum. So the company is going to be out if they don't employ ethnic minorities. So they are only employing people because they got to stick to the policy. They all think it, only because the policy is in force, this is why the majority of Asian and ethnic and black people are managing to get into companies nowadays.

However, even the most optimistic were aware that BME people had difficulty in getting into certain types of jobs. They all observed that most managers were white, and from the experience of their parents they knew that jobs were ethnically segregated. Miranda had perceived how this may currently be displayed in recruitment situations: 'People who work in publicity, they have to be blonde and very posh. Because they are the outward-facing people.'

The importance of the intersection between class and ethnicity is evident in Miranda's comment. As a working-class black young woman at Oxbridge, she had experienced rejection by some of the other students, white and black, who she described as 'posh'. However, she also believed that her human capital together with her ethnicity might give her the edge in 'getting in' to organizations in the contemporary climate, where many large employers compete in their attempts to be a diversity friendly employer. It is outside the scope of this study, to consider how this edge might translate into 'getting on' for BME young people generally or whether this may simply be the means to enable a few to get on, who may by default be perceived as 'tokens'.

Notwithstanding their differing perceptions of the possible discrimination they would face, there was little evidence from the young people we interviewed that there was a 'victim' mentality. On the contrary there was a belief that hard work would enable them to overcome any potential discrimination. Indeed despite the recognition of a discriminatory labour market, the young people in this study tended to be very realistic in evaluating their situation and opportunities.

Responses to labour markets

The young people in our study have diverse experiences and backgrounds so it would be unwise to generalize in our conclusions. However, we are able to discern a number of overlapping patterns that emerge which enable us to construct five 'ideal types'. We are not suggesting these types are fixed; indeed, people's circumstances change over time and the young people themselves may influence or learn to influence these changes. We did find that when we presented these categories to mature and successful BME professionals they resonated with their own experience.

The strategist

The strategist was a determined individual who understood the importance of working hard, but knew that this might not be sufficient. We noted systematic strategies undertaken to ensure that they stood out from their peer group who might have the same qualifications but would not have the distinctive attributes that the strategist was able to demonstrate. Such attributes would be acquired by gaining information and filtering it; getting experience in the voluntary and paid sectors and understanding what they had achieved from this; ensuring that they demonstrated 'soft' but also basic literacy and numeracy skills. The strategist will have high levels of tenacity and be prepared to persist to achieve the ends they desire. They will plan carefully for the next phase of their career, but also have the flexibility and foresight to recognize opportunities when they present themselves. As we saw in Kirton's chapter, such strategies may take a distinctly gendered turn when work-life balances issues are incorporated.

The hard-worker

We have already mentioned that many young people held the belief that application, effort and determination were the key to success in the labour market. There is a degree of overlap between the hard-worker and the strategist. The former sees effort and qualifications as a passport to a better life. Their plans are about obtaining further qualifications to equip them for the kind of career that they want. Sometimes they may, as it were, collect qualifications without a very clear idea of where they will lead. They may not take the time to assess what are the 'extras' needed to pursue the desired career. Like the strategist, the hard-worker will be tenacious in achieving their goals. However, there is a danger that, by assuming their hard work will be noticed, if is unrewarded or unrecognized for a lengthy period of time they may move into the *discouraged* category. It may be that the hard-worker will aim for the professional and skilled areas of work, where skill is seen as overruling any personality attributes or 'soft skills'.

The opportunist

The opportunist may encompass elements of the other types but the dominant characteristic is the preparedness to take risks, to say yes to opportunities as they arise. In many ways the opportunist may have the most positive outlook and a self-belief that will encourage the unthinkable to be a possibility. The opportunist may, or may not, be a hard-worker or even a strategist but will be able to build social capital and when an opportunity arises will have the enthusiasm and commitment to exploit it.

The sceptic

We may all be become sceptics at some time in our lives. But it was noteworthy that those who were more highly educated appeared less sceptical, or as is more likely, did not allow scepticism to dominate their actions. It may be that they considered that their qualifications would act as a shield against potential discrimination. The sceptic, whether highly educated or not, will critically appraise an organizations' policies and recognize that the rhetoric and reality may not coincide. The sceptic may be particularly vulnerable if their levels of education are not high or if they are unemployed. The critical appraisal of an organization's motives may lead to an expectation of rejection or the propensity to challenge an organization's actions. Sceptics have a strong awareness of racism and discrimination, which they may blame for their failure to get what they want. Equally, scepticism may drive a strategic approach. The sceptics in our study came over as very bright even though they may not always have the qualifications to demonstrate their intelligence.

The discouraged

The discouraged young worker is likely to be crushed by circumstances. They may have under-performed at school, have had many set backs in the educational and job market and have very low expectations. At key periods in their lives they may have experienced family problems and break-up, bereavement or health problems. They may have been let down by teachers, employers or workmates. If they experience racism and discrimination it tends to confirm a belief that they are doomed to fail. Thus, discouraged workers may have low motivation and self-esteem and may find themselves in a downward spiral of exclusion from accessing the cultural and social capital to make their way in the labour market. Those who are discouraged may particularly benefit from key enablements, but it is they who may least be able to access such resources.

The above analytical ideal types are valuable in understanding the career motivations of all young people, men and women, but the transitions between types will result from the young people themselves and the gendered and racialized contexts they face. The types allow the unevenness of career development to be exposed and highlight the dialectical relationship between self and circumstance in career development. The ideal types recognize the heterogeneity among young people and it may be that these types come into play at different moments in the career trajectory; so that for BME young men and women, the discouragement effect resulting from discrimination may operate differently according to their ethnic origin and their gender and at critical moments. Thus while it is clear that ethnicity matters in their experiences, circumstances may vary, as does cultural and social capital, and it is this heterogeneity that warns against a persistent 'othering' of young BME people.

What is clear from this study is that young BME people are aware of their potential disadvantages, yet optimistic about the future. The positive influences on our young people entailed giving them skills and social and cultural resources to fulfil their potential and enable them to avoid becoming discouraged. We conclude by drawing on the words of an ACDiversity mentor we interviewed; his stark message to young people is:

> If you don't supersede your circumstances, your circumstance is going to get you. (Kwame Kwei-Amah, actor/playwright)

Acknowledgments

We are grateful to the European Social Fund who co-financed the project, to Roger McKenzie of the TUC with whom we formulated the original idea and the importance of researching the work experiences of young BME people. We are also grateful to Charlene Williams, the Research Fellow on the project, to Erin van der Maas who covered for Charlene Williams during her maternity leave and to the those who undertook additional interviews in London (Rebecca Lennard), in Bristol (Ranji Devadason and Nasar Meer) and Birmingham (Ciara Silke) and to Liz Kwast and Jenny Melville for their transcription work.

We are particularly grateful to the young people who took part in the research who gave their time to be interviewed, as well as the gatekeepers and critical actors in young BME people's lives. The real names of the young people have not been used.

Note

1. See http://www.acdiversity.org/ for an overview of ACDiversity's activities.

References

Battu, H. and P. J. Sloane (2004) 'Over-education and ethnic minorities in Britain', *The Manchester School*, 72(4): 535–59.

Berthoud, R. (2000) 'Ethnic employment penalties in Britain', *Journal of Ethnic and Migration Studies*, 26(3): 389–416.

Bradley, H. (2007) *Gender*. Cambridge: Polity.

Bradley, H. and J. Van Hoof (2005) *Young people in Europe*. Bristol: The Policy Press.

Bradley, H. and G. Healy (2008) *Ethnicity and gender at work*. London: Palgrave.

Bradley, H., G. Healy, C. Forson and P. Kaul (2007). Workplace Cultures and Ethnic Minority Women. Manchester, Equal Opportunities Commission.

Connor, H., C. Tyers, T. Modood, and J. Hillage (2004) 'Why the difference? A closer look at higher education minority ethnic students and graduates' research. Brief: RB552 DfES.

Cregan, C. (1999) *Young people in the workplace: job, union and mobility patterns*. London: Mansell.

Dale, A., N. Shaheen, V. Kalra and E. Fieldhouse (2002) 'The labour market prospects for Pakistani and Bangladeshi women', *Work, Employment and Society*, 16(1): 5–25.

EOC (2007) Moving on up? The way forward – Report of the EOC's investigation into Bangladeshi, Pakistani and black Caribbean women and work. Manchester, Equal Opportunities Commission.

ESRC (2009) http://www.esrcsocietytoday.ac.uk/ESRCInfoCentre/PO/releases/2009/september/recessionbritain.aspx, accessed 12 October 2009.

Esmail, A. (2004) 'The prejudices of good people', *British Medical Journal*, 328(7454): 1448–9.

The European Commission (2005) *European policies concerning youth*. EU: Brussels.

Furlong, A. and F. Cartmel (1997) *Young people and social change*. Milton Keynes: Open University Press.

Gray, A. (2002) 'Job seekers and gatekeepers: the role of the private employment agency in the placement of the unemployed', *Work, Employment and Society*, 16(4): 655–74.

Healy, G., H. Bradley and C. Williams (2006) Making career choices: the experiences of young black and minority ethnic people entering the labour market. London, Centre for Research in Equality and Diversity, Queen Mary, University of London.

Heath, A. and S. Y. Cheung (2006) *Ethnic penalties in the labour market: Employers and discrimination*. dwp.gov.uk. London: Department for Work and Pensions.

Jones, G. (2002) *The great divide*. York: Joseph Rowntree Foundation.

Kirton, G. (2009) 'Career plans and aspirations of recent black and minority ethnic business graduates', *Work Employment Society*, 23(1): 12–29.

Local Government Association (2009) http://www.lga.gov.uk/lga/core/page.do?pageId= 1623810, accessed 12 October 2009.

Loughlin, C. and J. Barling (2000) 'Young workers' work values, attitudes and behaviours', *Journal of Occupational and Organizational Psychology*, 74(4): 543–58.

Milburn, A. (2009) Unleashing aspirations – the final report of the panel on fair access to the professions. London: Cabinet Office.

Moss, P. and C. Tilly (2001) *Stories employers tell – race, skill and hiring in America.* New York, Russell Sage Foundation.

Newburn, T. and M. Shiner (2005) *Dealing with disaffection: young people, mentoring and social inclusion.* Cullompton: Willan Publishing.

Noon, M. (1993) 'Racial discrimination in speculative application: evidence from the UK's top 100 firms', *Human Resource Management Journal,* 3(4): 35–47.

Reay, D., J. Davies, M. David and Stephen J. Ball (2001) 'Choices of degree or degrees of choice? class, 'race' and the higher education choice process', *Sociology*, 35(4): 855–74.

Roberts, K. (1995) *Youth and employment in modern Britain.* Oxford: Oxford University Press.

Strategy Unit (2003) *Ethnic minorities and the labour market.* London: Cabinet Office.

Tinklin, T., L. Croxford, A. Ducklin and B. Frame (2005) 'Gender and attitudes to work and family roles: the views of young people at the millennium', *Gender and Education,* 17(2): 129–42.

Tysome, T. (2006) *The Higher,* 14 July.

Williams, C. and G. Healy (2005) 'Who attends diversity careers' fairs? A survey of ACDiversity Careers' Fair', Queen Mary, University of London.

Index

horizontal segregation *see* segregation
Horne, S. 30
household tasks 224–5, 228, 246, 252–3, 263, 267
Howard, P. 38, 48
Hoyano, L. 119
human agency 122–3
human capital 123, 124, 135, 217–18
  black women 151, 153–5, 159–60, 162, 163
  and race 207
  women 152, 217
  young BME 272, 283
human rights 3, 5, 40, 78
Human Rights Act 1998 (UK) 39, 81, 87
Hurd, H. 112
Hurricane Katrina, impact on black
    neighbourhoods 196
Hurst, C. 197
husbands
  careers prioritized 253, 263
  and household tasks 224–5
  job relocation 224
  sharing of domestic and family tasks 267
  supporting role of 164–5, 246
Huse, M. 183
hybridity 80
Hyman, R. 139, 140
Hyter, M. 18

identity
  formation of race/ethnic and gender 255–6
  interactional constitution of 255–6
  multiple 256, 266–7
  politics 4
  three levels of 256
Iganski, P. 112
immigration
  UK 80, 82–3, 84, 201–2, 205
  see also migrant workers
Immigration Act 1971 (UK) 202
Imperial College 131
incitement to hatred 111, 114
inclusion
  academic trends 19–22
  discourse gaining momentum 32–3
  as focus of corporate videos 28
  not an ever-present phenomenon 30
  strategies of 128
  use of term 11, 13, 20–2
income inequality
  global 143
  racial 199, 203–4, 206
income tax credits 95, 99, 104
incrementalism 177
India, casual workers 143

Indian Citizenship Act 1924 (US) 197
Indians
  self-employment 151
  traditional gender roles 253, 262
individual difference 10
industrial sector, and temporary work 142
inequality
  and national histories 195–6
  regimes 174, 175, 237, 241, 245–6, 248
  sustaining system of 1
Ingraham, C. 100
institutional racism 77–8, 82, 88, 116
institutional sociology 97, 103
institutional theory 98
integration 49
International Convention on the Elimination of
    All Forms of Racial Discrimination
    (1965) 79
International Labour Organization (ILO) 143
internships 278–80
interpretation services 37, 40, 44, 46
intersectionality 2, 4–10, 15
  age, gender and sexuality 243
  age and race/ethnicity 270–87
  challenges for legislation 7–8
  and class 33
  class and ethnicity 283–4
  gender, race/ethnicity and age 252–67
  gender, race/ethnicity and migration 151–67
  gender, sexuality and class 233–49
  and inequality regimes 236–8
  methodological analysis 8
  and oppression 5, 6
  and policy formation 9
  use of term 4
interviews
  preparation for 277
  and racism 203
  sifting of candidates 283
invisibilization 238, 241, 244, 248
invisible disability 110–11
Ipswich and Suffolk Council for Racial Equality
    (ISCRE) 25
Ireland
  immigration from 201
  linguistic diversity 37–42, 45–50
Irish language 37, 38, 40, 41, 42, 43, 45–6, 47, 48
Islam *see* Muslims
Italy, gender quotas 179
Ivancevich, J. 127

Jackson, S. 100
Jacob, Advocate General 63
Jacobs, J. 107, 112